THE CITIZEN KANE BOOK

THE

RAISING KANE

by Pauline Kael

With Illustrations

An Atlantic Monthly Press Book
Little, Brown and Company — Boston – Toronto

CITIZEN KANE BOOK

THE SHOOTING SCRIPT

by Herman J. Mankiewicz and Orson Welles

Now Published for the First Time and Illustrated
With Eighty-one Frames from the Film

and the Cutting Continuity of the Completed Film

FIRST PUBLISHED IN ENGLAND 1971 BY MARTIN SECKER & WARBURG LIMITED
14 CARLISLE STREET, SOHO SQUARE, LONDON W1V 6NN

FIRST EDITION
SBN: 436 23030 5

The notes on the shooting script were prepared by Gary Carey.

Designed by Barbara B. Pitnof.

PRINTED IN THE UNITED STATES OF AMERICA

Contents

Raising Kane

by Pauline Kael

C*itizen Kane* is perhaps the one American talking picture that seems as fresh now as the day it opened. It may seem even fresher. A great deal in the movie that was conventional and almost banal in 1941 is so far in the past as to have been forgotten and become new. The Pop characterizations look modern, and rather better than they did at the time. New audiences may enjoy Orson Welles' theatrical flamboyance even more than earlier generations did, because they're so unfamiliar with the traditions it came out of. When Welles was young — he was twenty-five when the film opened — he used to be accused of "excessive showmanship," but the same young audiences who now reject "theatre" respond innocently and wholeheartedly to the most unabashed tricks of theatre — and of early radio plays — in *Citizen Kane*. At some campus showings, they react so gullibly that when Kane makes a demagogic speech about "the underprivileged," stray students will applaud enthusiastically, and a shout of "Right on!" may be heard. Though the political ironies are not clear to young audiences, and though young audiences don't know much about the subject — William Randolph Hearst, the master jingo journalist, being to them a stock villain, like Joe McCarthy; that is, a villain without the contours of his particular villainy — they nevertheless respond to the effrontery, the audacity, and the risks. Hearst's career and his power provided a dangerous subject that stimulated and energized all those connected with the picture — they felt they were *doing* something instead of just working on one more cooked-up story that didn't relate to anything that mattered. And to the particular kinds of people who shaped this enterprise the dangers involved made the subject irresistible.

Citizen Kane, the film that, as Truffaut said, is "probably the one that has started the largest number of filmmakers on their careers," was not an ordinary assignment. It is one of the few films ever made inside a major studio in the United States *in freedom* — not merely in freedom from interference but in freedom from the routine methods of experienced directors. George J. Schaefer, who, with the help of Nelson Rockefeller, had become president of R.K.O. late in 1938, when it was struggling to avert bankruptcy, needed a miracle to save the company, and after the national uproar over Orson Welles' *The War of the Worlds* broadcast Rockefeller apparently thought that Welles — "the wonder boy" — might come up with one, and urged Schaefer to get him. But Welles, who was committed to the theatre and wasn't especially enthusiastic about making movies, rejected the first offers; he held out until Schaefer offered him complete control over his productions. Then Welles brought out to Hollywood from New York his own production unit — the Mercury Theatre company, a group of actors and associates he could count on — and, because he was inexperienced in movies and was smart and had freedom, he was able to find in Hollywood people who had been waiting all their lives to try out new ideas. So a miracle did come about, though it was not the kind of miracle R.K.O. needed.

Kane does something so well, and with such spirit, that the fullness and completeness of it continue to satisfy us. The formal elements themselves produce elation; we are kept aware of how marvellously worked out the ideas are. It would be high-toned to call this method of keeping the audience aware "Brechtian," and it would be wrong. It comes out of a different tradition — the same commercial-comedy tradition that Walter Kerr analyzed so beautifully in his review of the 1969 Broadway revival of *The Front Page,* the 1928 play by Ben Hecht and Charles MacArthur, when he said, "A play was held to be something of a machine in those days. . . . It was a machine for surprising and delighting the audience, regularly, logically, insanely, but accountably. A play was like a watch that laughed." The mechanics of movies are rarely as entertaining as they are in *Citizen Kane,* as cleverly designed to be the kind of fun that keeps one alert and conscious of the enjoyment of the artifices themselves.

Walter Kerr goes on to describe the second-act entrance prepared for Walter Burns, the scheming, ruthless managing editor of *The Front Page:*

He can't just come on and declare himself. . . . He's got to walk into a tough situation in order to be brutally nonchalant, which is

what we think is funny about him. The machinery has not only given him and the play the right punctuation, the change of pace that refreshes even as it moves on. It has also covered him, kept him from being obvious while exploiting the one most obvious thing about him. You might say that the machinery has covered itself, perfectly squared itself. We are delighted to have the man on, we are delighted to have him on at this time, we are aware that it is sleight-of-hand that has got him on, and we are as delighted by the sleight-of-hand as by the man.

Citizen Kane is made up of an astonishing number of such bits of technique, and of sequences built to make their points and get their laughs and hit climax just before a fast cut takes us to the next. It is practically a collection of blackout sketches, but blackout sketches arranged to comment on each other, and it was planned that way right in the shooting script.

It is difficult to explain what makes any great work great, and particularly difficult with movies, and maybe more so with *Citizen Kane* than with other great movies, because it isn't a work of special depth or a work of subtle beauty. It is a shallow work, a *shallow* masterpiece. Those who try to account for its stature as a film by claiming it to be profound are simply dodging the problem — or maybe they don't recognize that there is one. Like most of the films of the sound era that are called masterpieces, *Citizen Kane* has reached its audience gradually over the years rather than at the time of release. Yet, unlike the others, it is conceived and acted as entertainment in a popular style (unlike, say, *Rules of the Game* or *Rashomon* or *Man of Aran,* which one does not think of in crowd-pleasing terms). Apparently, the easiest thing for people to do when they recognize that something is a work of art is to trot out the proper schoolbook terms for works of art, and there are articles on *Citizen Kane* that call it a tragedy in fugal form and articles that explain that the hero of *Citizen Kane* is time — time being a proper sort of modern hero for an important picture. But to use the conventional schoolbook explanations for greatness, and pretend that it's profound, is to miss what makes it such an American triumph — that it manages to create something aesthetically exciting and durable out of the playfulness of American muckraking satire. *Kane* is closer to comedy than to tragedy, though so overwrought in style as to be almost a Gothic comedy. What might possibly be considered tragic in it has such a Daddy Warbucks quality that if it's tragic at all it's comic-strip tragic. The mystery in *Kane* is largely fake, and the Gothic-thriller atmosphere and the Rosebud gimmickry (though fun) are such obvious penny-dreadful popular theatrics that they're not so very different from the fake mysteries that Hearst's *American Weekly* used to whip up — the haunted castles and the curses fulfilled. *Citizen Kane* is a "popular" masterpiece — not in terms of actual popularity but in terms of its conceptions and the way it gets its laughs and makes its points. Possibly it was too complexly told to be one of the greatest commercial successes, but we can't really tell whether it might have become even a modest success, because it didn't get a fair chance.

2.

Orson Welles brought forth a miracle, but he couldn't get by with it. Though Hearst made some direct attempts to interfere with the film, it wasn't so much what he did that hurt the film commercially as what others feared he might do, to them and to the movie industry. They knew he

was contemplating action, so they did the picture in for him; it was as if they decided whom the king might want killed, and, eager to oblige, performed the murder without waiting to be asked. Before *Kane* opened, George J. Schaefer was summoned to New York by Nicholas Schenck, the chairman of the board of Loew's International, the M-G-M affiliate that controlled the distribution of M-G-M pictures. Schaefer had staked just about everything on Welles, and the picture looked like a winner, but now Schenck made Schaefer a cash offer from Louis B. Mayer, the head of production at M-G-M, of $842,000 if Schaefer would destroy the negative and all the prints. The picture had actually cost only $686,033; the offer handsomely included a fair amount for the post-production costs.

Mayer's motive may have been partly friendship and loyalty to Hearst, even though Hearst, who had formerly been associated with M-G-M, had, some years earlier, after a dispute with Irving Thalberg, taken his investment out of M-G-M and moved his star, Marion Davies, and his money to Warner Brothers. M-G-M had lost money on a string of costume clinkers starring Miss Davies (*Beverly of Graustark*, et al.), and had even lost money on some of her good pictures, but Mayer had got free publicity for M-G-M releases out of the connection with Hearst, and had also got what might be called deep personal satisfaction. In 1929, when Herbert Hoover invited the Mayers to the White House — they were the first "informal" guests after his inauguration — Hearst's *New York American* gave the visit a full column. Mayer enjoyed fraternizing with Hearst and his eminent guests; photographs show Mayer with Hearst and Lindbergh, Mayer with Hearst and Winston Churchill, Mayer at lunch with Bernard Shaw and Marion

Davies — but they never, of course, show Mayer with both Hearst and Miss Davies. Candid cameramen sometimes caught the two together, but Hearst, presumably out of respect for his wife, did not pose in groups that included Miss Davies. Despite the publicity showered on her in the Hearst papers, the forms were carefully observed. She quietly packed and left for her own house on the rare occasions when Mrs. Hearst, who lived in the East, was expected to be in residence at San Simeon. Kane's infatuation for the singer Susan Alexander in the movie was thus a public flaunting of matters that Hearst was careful and considerate about. Because of this, Mayer's longtime friendship for Hearst was probably a lesser factor than the fear that the Hearst press would reveal some sordid stories about the movie moguls and join in one of those recurrent crusades against movie immorality, like the one that had destroyed Fatty Arbuckle's career. The movie industry was frightened of reprisals. (The movie industry is always frightened, and is always proudest of films that celebrate courage.) As one of the trade papers phrased it in those nervous weeks when no one knew whether the picture would be released, "the industry could ill afford to be made the object of counterattack by the Hearst newspapers."

There were rumors that Hearst was mounting a general campaign; his legal staff had seen the script, and Louella Parsons, the Hearst movie columnist, who had attended a screening of the film flanked by lawyers, was agitated and had swung into action. The whole industry, it was feared, would take the rap for R.K.O.'s indiscretion, and, according to the trade press at the time (and Schaefer confirms this report), Mayer was not putting up the $842,000 all by himself. It was a joint offer from the top movie magnates, who were combining for common protection. The offer was presented to Schaefer on the ground that it was in the best interests of everybody concerned — which was considered to be the entire, threatened industry — for *Citizen Kane* to be destroyed. Rather astonishingly, Schaefer refused. He didn't confer with his board of directors, because, he says, he had good reason to think they would tell him to accept. He refused even though R.K.O., having few theatres of its own, was dependent on the other companies and he had been warned that the big theatre circuits — controlled by the men who wanted the picture destroyed — would refuse to show it.

Schaefer knew the spot he was in. The première had been tentatively set for February 14th at the Radio City Music Hall — usually the showcase for big R.K.O. pictures, because R.K.O. was partly owned by the Rockefellers and the Chase National Bank, who owned the Music Hall. The manager of the theatre had been enthusiastic about the picture. Then, suddenly, the Music Hall turned it down. Schaefer phoned Nelson Rockefeller to find out why, and, he says, "Rockefeller told me that Louella Parsons had warned him off it, that she had asked him, 'How would you like to have the *American Weekly* magazine section run a double-page spread on John D. Rockefeller?' " According to Schaefer, she had also called David Sarnoff, another large investor in R.K.O., and similarly threatened him. In mid-February, with a minor contract dispute serving as pretext, the Hearst papers blasted R.K.O. and Schaefer in front-page stories; it was an unmistakable public warning. Schaefer was stranded; he had to scrounge for theatres, and, amid the general fear that Hearst might sue and would almost certainly remove advertising for any houses that showed *Citizen Kane*, he couldn't get bookings. The solution was for R.K.O. to take the risks of any lawsuits, but when the company leased an independent theatre in Los Angeles and refurbished the Palace (then a vaudeville house), which R.K.O. owned, for the New York opening, and did the same for a theatre R.K.O. owned in Chicago, Schaefer had trouble launching an advertising campaign. (Schenck, not surprisingly, owned a piece of the biggest movie-advertising agency.) Even after the early rave reviews and the initial enthusiasm, Schaefer couldn't get bookings except in the theatres that R.K.O. itself owned and in a few small art houses that were willing to take the risk. Eventually, in order to get the picture into theatres, Schaefer threatened to sue Warners', Fox, Paramount, and Loew's on a charge of conspiracy. (There was reason to believe the company heads had promised Hearst they wouldn't show it in their theatres.) Warners' (perhaps afraid of exposure and the troubles with their stockholders that might result from a lawsuit) gave in and booked the picture, and the others followed, halfheartedly — in some cases, theatres paid for the picture but didn't play it.

By then, just about everybody in the industry was scared, or mad, or tired of the whole thing, and though the feared general reprisals against the industry did not take place, R.K.O. was getting bruised. The Hearst papers banned publicity on R.K.O. pictures and dropped an announced serialization of the novel *Kitty Foyle* which had been timed for the release of the R.K.O. film version. Some R.K.O. films didn't get reviewed and others got bad publicity. It was all petty harassment, of a kind that could be blamed on the overzealous Miss Parsons and other Hearst employees, but it was obviously sanctioned by Hearst, and it was steady enough to keep the industry uneasy.

By the time *Citizen Kane* got into Warners' theatres, the picture had acquired such an odd reputation that people seemed to distrust it, and it didn't do very well. It was subsequently withdrawn from circulation, perhaps because of the vicissitudes of R.K.O., and until the late fifties, when it was reissued and began to play in the art houses and to attract a new audience, it was seen only in pirated versions in 16 mm. Even after Mayer had succeeded in destroying the picture commercially, he went on planning vengeance on Schaefer for refusing his offer. Stockholders in R.K.O. began to hear that the company wasn't prospering because Schaefer was anti-Semitic and was therefore having trouble getting proper distribution for R.K.O. pictures. Schaefer says that Mayer wanted to get control of R.K.O. and that the rumor was created to drive down the price of the stock — that Mayer hoped to scare out Floyd Odlum, a major stockholder, and buy his shares. Instead, Odlum, who had opposed Nelson Rockefeller's choice of Schaefer to run the company, bought enough of Sarnoff's stock to have a controlling interest, and by mid-1942 Schaefer was finished at R.K.O. Two weeks after he left, Welles' unit was evicted from its offices on the lot and given a few hours to move out, and the R.K.O. employees who had worked with Welles were punished with degrading assignments on B pictures. Mayer's friendship with Hearst was not ruffled. A few years later, when Mayer left his wife of forty years, he rented Marion Davies' Beverly Hills mansion. Eventually, he was one of Hearst's honorary pallbearers. *Citizen Kane* didn't actually lose money, but in Hollywood bookkeeping it wasn't a big enough moneymaker to balance the scandal.

3.

Welles was recently quoted as saying, "Theatre is a collective experience; cinema is the work of one single person." This is an extraordinary remark from the man who brought his own Mercury Theatre players to Hollywood (fifteen of them appeared in *Citizen Kane*), and also the Mercury co-producer John Houseman, the Mercury composer Bernard Herrmann, and various assistants, such as Richard Wilson, William Alland, and Richard Barr. He not only brought his whole supportive group — his family, he called them then — but found people in Hollywood, such as the cinematographer Gregg Toland, to contribute their knowledge and gifts to *Citizen Kane*. Orson Welles has done some marvellous things in his later movies — some great things — and there is more depth in the somewhat botched *The Magnificent Ambersons*, of 1942 (which also used many of the Mercury players), than in *Citizen Kane*, but his principal career in the movies has been in adaptation, as it was earlier on the stage. He has never again worked on a subject with the immediacy and impact of *Kane*. His later films — even those he has so painfully struggled to finance out of his earnings as an actor — haven't been *conceived* in terms of daring modern subjects that excite us, as the very idea of *Kane* excited us. This particular kind of journalist's sense of what would be a scandal as well as a great subject, and the ability to write it, belonged not to Welles but to his now almost forgotten associate Herman J. Mankiewicz, who wrote the script, and who inadvertently destroyed the picture's chances. There is a theme that is submerged in much of *Citizen Kane* but that comes to the surface now and then, and it's the linking life story of Hearst and of Mankiewicz and of

Welles — the story of how brilliantly gifted men who seem to have everything it takes to do what they want to do are defeated. It's the story of how heroes become comedians and con artists.

The Hearst papers ignored Welles — Hearst may have considered this a fit punishment for an actor — though they attacked him indirectly with sneak attacks on those associated with him, and Hearst would frequently activate his secular arm, the American Legion, against him. But the Hearst papers worked Mankiewicz over in headlines; they persecuted him so long that he finally appealed to the American Civil Liberties Union for help. There was some primitive justice in this. Hearst had never met Welles, and, besides, Welles was a kid, a twenty-five-year-old prodigy (whose daughter Marion Davies' nephew was bringing up) — hardly the sort of person one held responsible. But Mankiewicz was a friend of both Marion Davies and Hearst, and had been a frequent guest at her beach house and at San Simeon. There, in the great baronial banquet hall, Hearst liked to seat Mankiewicz on his left, so that Mankiewicz, with all his worldliness and wit (the Central Park West Voltaire, Ben Hecht had called him a few years earlier), could entertain the guest of honor and Hearst wouldn't miss any of it. Mankiewicz betrayed their hospitality, even though he liked them both. They must have presented an irresistible target. And so Hearst, the yellow-press lord who had trained Mankiewicz's generation of reporters to betray *anyone* for a story, became at last the victim of his own style of journalism.

4.

In the first Academy Award ceremony, for 1927–28, Warner Brothers, which had just produced *The Jazz Singer*, was honored for

"Marking an Epoch in Motion Picture History." If the first decade of talkies — roughly, the thirties — has never been rivalled in wit and exuberance, this is very largely because there was already in Hollywood in the late silent period a nucleus of the best American writers, and they either lured their friends West or were joined by them. Unlike the novelists who were drawn to Hollywood later, most of the best Hollywood writers of the thirties had a shared background; they had been reporters and critics, and they knew each other from their early days on newspapers and magazines.

In his autobiography, Ben Hecht tells of being broke in New York — it was probably the winter of 1926 — and of getting a telegram from Herman Mankiewicz in Hollywood:

WILL YOU ACCEPT THREE HUNDRED PER WEEK TO WORK FOR PARAMOUNT PICTURES? ALL EXPENSES PAID. THE THREE HUNDRED IS PEANUTS. MILLIONS ARE TO BE GRABBED OUT HERE AND YOUR ONLY COMPETITION IS IDIOTS. DON'T LET THIS GET AROUND.

A newspaper photograph shows Mankiewicz greeting Hecht, "noted author, dramatist, and former newspaperman," upon his arrival. After Hecht had begun work at Paramount, he discovered that the studio chief, B. P. Schulberg — who at that time considered writers a waste of money — had been persuaded to hire him by a gambler's ploy: Mankiewicz had offered to tear up his own two-year contract if Hecht failed to write a successful movie. Hecht, that phenomenal fast hack who was to become one of the most prolific of all motion-picture writers (and one of the most frivolously cynical about the results), worked for a week and turned out the script that became Josef von Sternberg's great hit *Underworld*. That script brought Hecht the first Academy Award for an original story, and a few years later he initiated the practice of using Oscars as doorstops. The studio heads knew what they had in Hecht as soon as they read the script, and they showed their gratitude. Hecht has recorded:

I was given a ten-thousand-dollar check as a bonus for the week's work, a check which my sponsor Mankiewicz snatched out of my hand as I was bowing my thanks.
"You'll have it back in a week," Manky said. "I just want it for a few days to get me out of a little hole."
He gambled valiantly, tossing a coin in the air with Eddie Cantor and calling heads or tails for a thousand dollars. He lost constantly. He tried to get himself secretly insured behind his good wife Sara's back, planning to hock the policy and thus meet his obligation. This plan collapsed when the insurance-company doctor refused to accept him as a risk.
I finally solved the situation by taking Manky into the Front Office and informing the studio bosses of our joint dilemma. I asked that my talented friend be given a five-hundred-a-week raise. The studio could then deduct this raise from his salary. . . .
I left . . . with another full bonus check in my hand; and Manky, with his new raise, became the highest paid writer for Paramount Pictures, Inc.

The bait that brought the writers in was money, but those writers who, like Mankiewicz, helped set the traps had their own reason: conviviality. Mankiewicz's small joke "Don't let this get around" came from a man who lived for talk, a man who saw moviemaking as too crazy, too profitable, and too *easy* not to share with one's friends. By the early thirties, the writers who lived in Hollywood or commuted there included not only Mankiewicz and Hecht and Charles MacArthur but George S. Kaufman and Marc Connelly, and Nathanael West and his brother-in-law S. J. Perelman, and Preston Sturges, Dorothy Parker, Arthur Kober, Alice Duer Miller, John O'Hara, Donald Ogden Stewart, Samson Raphaelson (the *New York Times* reporter who wrote the play *The Jazz Singer*), Gene Fowler, and Nunnally Johnson, and such already famous playwrights as Philip Barry, S. N. Behrman, Maxwell Anderson, Robert E. Sherwood, and Sidney Howard. Scott Fitzgerald had already been there for his first stretch, in 1927, along with Edwin Justus Mayer, and by 1932 William Faulkner began coming and going, and from time to time Ring Lardner and Moss Hart would turn up. In earlier periods, American writers made a living on newspapers and magazines; in the forties and fifties, they went into the academies (or, once they got to college, never left). But in the late twenties and the thirties they went to Hollywood. And though, apparently, they one and all experienced it as prostitution of their talents — joyous prostitution in some cases — and though more than one fell in love with movies and thus suffered not only from personal frustration but from the corruption of the great, still new art, they nonetheless as a group were responsible for that sustained feat of careless magic we call "thirties comedy." *Citizen Kane* was, I think, its culmination.

5.

Herman J. Mankiewicz, born in New York City in 1897, was the first son of a professor of education, who then took a teaching position in Wilkes-Barre, where his second son, Joseph L. Mankiewicz, was born in 1909, and where the boys and a sister grew up. Herman Mankiewicz graduated from Columbia in 1916, and after a period as managing editor of the *American Jewish Chronicle* he became a flying cadet with the United States Army in 1917 and, in 1918, a private first class with the Fifth Marines, 2nd Division, A.E.F. In 1919 and 1920, he was the director of the American Red Cross News Service in Paris, and after returning to this country to marry a great beauty, Miss Sara Aaronson, of Baltimore, he took his bride overseas with him while he worked as a foreign correspondent in Berlin from 1920 to 1922, doing political reporting for George Seldes on the *Chicago Tribune*. During that time, he also sent pieces on drama and books to the *New York Times* and *Women's Wear*. Hired in Berlin by Isadora Duncan, he became her publicity man for her return to America. At home again, he took a job as a reporter for the *New York World*. He was a gifted, prodigious writer, who contributed to *Vanity Fair,* the *Saturday Evening Post,* and many other magazines, and, while still in his twenties, collaborated with Heywood Broun, Dorothy Parker, Robert E. Sherwood, and others on a revue (*Round the Town*), and collaborated with George S. Kaufman on a play (*The Good Fellow*) and with Marc Connelly on another play (*The Wild Man of Borneo*). From 1923 to 1926, he was at the *Times,* backing up George S. Kaufman in the drama department; while he was there, he also became the first regular theatre critic for *The New Yorker,* writing weekly from June, 1925, until January, 1926, when Walter Wanger offered him a motion-picture contract and he left for Hollywood. The first picture he wrote was the Lon Chaney success *The Road to Mandalay.* In all, he worked on over seventy movies. He went on living and working in Los Angeles until his death, in 1953. He left three children: Don, born in Berlin in 1922, who is a novelist (*Trial*) and a writer for the movies (co-scenarist of *I Want to Live!*) and television ("Marcus Welby, M.D."); Frank, born in New York in 1924, who became a lawyer, a journalist, a Peace Corps worker, and Robert Kennedy's press assistant, and is now a columnist and television commentator; and Johanna, born in Los Angeles in 1937, who is a journalist (on *Time*) and is married to Peter Davis, the writer-producer of "The Selling of the Pentagon."

Told this way, Herman Mankiewicz's career sounds exemplary, but these are just the bare bones of the truth. Even though it would be easy to document this official life of the apparently rising young man with photographs of Mankiewicz in his Berlin days dining with the Chancellor, Mankiewicz in his newspaperman days outside the *Chicago Tribune* with Jack Dempsey, and so on, it would be hard to explain his sudden, early aging and the thickening of his features and the transparently cynical look on his face in later photographs.

It was a lucky thing for Mankiewicz that he got the movie job when he did, because he would never have risen at the *Times*, and though he wrote regularly for *The New Yorker* (and remarked of those of the Algonquin group who didn't, "The part-time help of wits is no better than the full-time help of half-wits"), *The New Yorker*, despite his pleas for cash, was paying him partly in stock, which wasn't worth much at the time. Mankiewicz drank heavily, and the drinking newspaperman was in the style of the *World* but not in the style of the *Times*. In October, 1925, he was almost fired. The drama critic then was Brooks Atkinson, and the drama editor was George S. Kaufman, with Mankiewicz second in line and Sam Zolotow third. Mankiewicz was sent to cover the performance of Gladys Wallis, who was the wife of the utilities magnate Samuel Insull, as Lady Teazle in *School for Scandal*. Mrs. Insull, who had abandoned her theatrical career over a quar-

ter of a century before, was, according to biographers, bored with being a nobody when her husband was such a big somebody. She was fifty-six when she resumed her career, as Lady Teazle, who is meant to be about eighteen. The play had opened in Chicago, where, perhaps astutely, she performed for charity (St. Luke's Hospital), and the press had described her as brilliant. The night of the New York opening, Mankiewicz came back to the office drunk, started panning Mrs. Insull's performance, and then fell asleep over his typewriter. As Zolotow recalls it, "Kaufman began to read the review, and it was so venomous he was outraged. That was the only time I ever saw Kaufman lose his temper." The review wasn't printed. The *Times* suffered the humiliation of running this item on October 23, 1925:

A NEW SCHOOL FOR SCANDAL

The *School for Scandal*, with Mrs. Insull as Lady Teazle, was produced at the Little Theatre last night. It will be reviewed in tomorrow's *Times*.

Mankiewicz was in such bad shape that night that Kaufman told Zolotow to call Sara Mankiewicz and have her come get him and take him home. Mrs. Mankiewicz recalls that he still had his head down on his typewriter when she arrived, with a friend, to remove him. She says he took it for granted that he was fired, but nevertheless went to work promptly the next day. Zolotow recalls, "In the morning, Herman came down to the office and asked me to talk to Mr. Birchall, the assistant managing editor, on his behalf. Herman had brought a peace offering of a bottle of Scotch and I took it to Birchall. He had a red beard, and he tugged at it and he stabbed the air a few times with his index finger and said,

'Herman is a bad boy, a bad boy.' But he took the bottle and Herman kept his job until he got the movie offer."

The review — unsigned — that the *Times* printed on October 24, 1925, was a small masterpiece of tact:

As Lady Teazle, Mrs. Insull is as pretty as she is diminutive, with a clear smile and dainty gestures. There is a charming grace in her bearing that makes for excellent deportment. But this Lady Teazle seems much too innocent, too thoroughly the country lass that Joseph terms her, to lend credit to her part in the play.

Scattered through various books, and in the stories that are still told of him in Hollywood, are clues that begin to give one a picture of Herman Mankiewicz, a giant of a man who mongered his own talent, a man who got a head start in the race to "sell out" to Hollywood. The pay was fantastic. After a month in the movie business, Mankiewicz — though his Broadway shows had not been hits, and though this was in 1926, when movies were still silent — signed a year's contract giving him $400 a week and a bonus of $5,000 for each story that was accepted, with an option for a second year at $500 a week and $7,500 per accepted story, the company guaranteeing to accept at least four stories per year. In other words, his base pay was $40,800 his first year and $56,000 his second; actually, he wrote so many stories that he made much more. By the end of 1927, he was head of Paramount's scenario department, and in January, 1928, there was a newspaper item reporting that he was in New York "lining up a new set of newspaper feature writers and playwrights to bring to Hollywood," and that "most of the newer writers on Paramount's staff who contributed the most successful stories of the past year were se-

lected by 'Mank.' " One reason that Herman Mankiewicz is so little known today is, ironically, that he went to Hollywood so early, before he had gained a big enough reputation in the literary and theatrical worlds. Screenwriters don't make names for themselves; the most famous ones are the ones whose names were famous before they went to Hollywood, or who made names later in the theatre or from books, or who, like Preston Sturges, became directors.

Mankiewicz and other *New Yorker* writers in the twenties and the early thirties were very close to the world of the theatre; many of them were writing plays, writing about theatre people, reviewing plays. It's not surprising that within a few years the magazine's most celebrated contributors were in Hollywood writing movies. Of the ten friends of the editor Harold Ross who were in the original prospectus as advisory editors, six became screenwriters. When Mankiewicz gave up the drama critic's spot, in 1926, he was replaced by Charles Brackett, and when Brackett headed West, Robert Benchley filled it while commuting, and then followed. Dorothy Parker, the book reviewer Constant Reader, went West, too. Nunnally Johnson, who was to work on over a hundred movies, was a close friend of Harold Ross's and had volunteered to do the movie reviewing in 1926 but had been told that that job was for "old ladies and fairies." Others in the group didn't agree: Benchley had written on movies for the old *Life* as early as 1920, and John O'Hara later took time out from screenwriting to become the movie critic for *Newsweek* — where he was to review *Citizen Kane*. The whole group were interested in the theatre and the movies, and they were fast, witty writers, used to regarding their work not as deathless prose but as stories written to order for the market, used also to the newspaperman's pretense of putting a light value on what they did — the "Look, no hands" attitude. Thus, they were well prepared to become the scenarists and gag writers of the talkies.

6.

The comic muse of the most popular "daring" late silents was a carefree, wisecracking flapper. Beginning in 1926, Herman Mankiewicz worked on an astounding number of films in that spirit. In 1927 and 1928, he did the titles (the printed dialogue and explanations) for at least twenty-five films that starred Clara Bow, Bebe Daniels, Nancy Carroll, Esther Ralston, George Bancroft, Thomas Meighan, Jack Holt, Richard Dix, Wallace Beery, and other public favorites. He worked on the titles for Jules Furthman's script of *Abie's Irish Rose,* collaborated with Anita Loos on the wisecracks for *Gentlemen Prefer Blondes,* and did the immensely successful *The Barker* and *The Canary Murder Case,* with William Powell, Louise Brooks, James Hall, and Jean Arthur. By then, sound had come in, and in 1929 he did the script as well as the dialogue for *The Dummy,* with Ruth Chatterton and Fredric March (making his screen début), wrote William Wellman's *The Man I Love,* with Richard Arlen, Pat O'Brien, and Mary Brian, and worked for Josef von Sternberg and many other directors.

Other screenwriters made large contributions, too, but probably none larger than Mankiewicz's at the beginning of the sound era, and if he was at that time one of the highest-paid writers in the world, it was because he wrote the kind of movies that were disapproved of as "fast" and immoral. His heroes weren't soft-eyed and bucolic; he brought good-humored toughness to the movies, and energy and astringency. And the public responded, because it was eager

for modern American subjects. Even those of us who were children at the time loved the fast-moving modern-city stories. The commonplaceness — even tawdriness — of the imagery was such a relief from all that silent "poetry." The talkies were a great step down. It's hard to make clear to people who didn't live through the transition how sickly and unpleasant many of those "artistic" silent pictures were — how you wanted to scrape off all that mist and sentiment.

Almost from the time the motion-picture camera was invented, there had been experiments with sound and attempts at synchronization, and the public was more than ready for talking pictures. Many of the late silents, if one looks at them now, seem to be trying to talk to us, crying out for sound. Despite the legend of paralysis of the medium when sound first came in, there was a burst of inventiveness. In musicals, directors like René Clair and, over here, Ernst Lubitsch and, to a lesser degree, Rouben Mamoulian didn't use sound just for lip synchronization; they played with sound as they had played with images, and they tried to use sound without losing the movement of silents or the daring of silent editing. Some of the early talkies were static and inept; newly imported stage directors literally staged the action, as if the space were stage space, and the technicians had to learn to handle the microphones. But movies didn't suddenly become stagebound because of the microphone. Many of the silents had always been stagebound, for the sufficient reason that they had been adapted from plays — from the war-horses of the repertory, because they had proved their popularity, and from the latest Broadway hits, because the whole country wanted to see them. The silent adaptations were frequently deadly, not just because of construction based on the classical unities, with all those entrances and exits and that painful emptiness on the screen of plays worked out in terms of absolutely essential characters only, but because everything kept stopping for the explanatory titles and the dialogue titles.

Even in the movies adapted from novels or written directly for the screen, the action rarely went on for long; silents were choked with titles, which were perhaps, on the average, between ten and twenty times as frequent as the interruptions for TV commercials. The printed dialogue was often witty, and often it was essential to an understanding of the action, but it broke up the rhythm of performances and the visual flow, and the titles were generally held for the slowest readers, so that one lost the mood of the film while staring at the dialogue for the third scanning. (It seems to me, thinking back on it, that we were so eager for the movie to go on that we gulped the words down and then were always left with them for what, to our impatience, seemed an eternity, and that the better the movie, the more quickly we tried to absorb and leap past the printed words, and the more frustrating the delays became.) The plain fact that many silent movies were plays without the spoken dialogue, plays deprived of their very substance, was what made the theatre-going audience — and the Broadway crowd of writers — so contemptuous of them. Filmed plays without the actors' voices, and with the deadening delays for the heterogeneous audience to read the dialogue, were an abomination. Many of the journalists and playwrights and wits of the Algonquin Round Table had written perceptively about motion pictures (Alexander Woollcott, who managed to pan some of the greatest films, was an exception); they had, in general, been cynical only about the slop

and the silent filmed plays. But though they had been active in the theatre, there had been no real place for them in movies; now, with the introduction of sound, they could bring to the screen the impudence that had given Broadway its flavor in the twenties — and bring it there before the satirical references were out of date. Sound made it possible for them to liberate movies into a new kind of contemporaneity.

7.

There is an elaborate body of theory that treats film as "the nocturnal voyage into the unconscious," as Luis Buñuel called it, and for a director such as Buñuel "the cinema seems to have been invented to express the life of the subconscious." Some of the greatest work of D. W. Griffith and other masters of the silent film has a magical, fairy-tale appeal, and certainly Surrealists like Buñuel, and other experimental and avant-garde filmmakers as well, have drawn upon this dreamlike vein of film. But these artists were the exceptions; much of the dreamy appeal to the "subconscious" and to "universal" or "primitive" fantasies was an appeal to the most backward, not to say reactionary, elements of illiterate and semi-literate mass society. There was a steady load of calendar-art guck that patronized "the deserving poor" and idealized "purity" (i.e., virginity) and "morality" (i.e., virginity plus charity). And all that is only one kind of movie anyway. Most of the dream theory of film, which takes the audience for passive dreamers, doesn't apply to the way one responded to silent comedies — which, when they were good, kept the audience in a heightened state of consciousness. When we join in laughter, it's as if the lights were on in the theatre. And not just the Mack Sennett comedies and Keaton and Chaplin kept us fully awake but the spirited, bouncy comediennes, like Colleen Moore and Marion Davies, and the romantic comedy "teams," and the suave, "polished" villains, like William Powell. My favorite movies as a child were the Bebe Daniels comedies — I suppose they were the movie equivalent of the series books one reads at that age. During 1927 and 1928, Paramount brought a new one out every few months; Bebe, the athletic madcap, would fence like Douglas Fairbanks, or she would parody Valentino by kidnapping and taming a man, or she might be a daredevil newsreel camerawoman or a cub reporter.

I did not know until I started to look into the writing of *Citizen Kane* that the man who wrote *Kane* had worked on some of those pictures, too — that Mankiewicz had, in fact, written (alone or with others) about forty of the films I remember best from the twenties and thirties (as well as many I didn't see or don't remember). Mankiewicz didn't work on *every* kind of picture, though. He didn't do Westerns, and once, when a studio attempted to punish him for his customary misbehavior by assigning him to a Rin Tin Tin picture, he turned in a script that began with the craven Rin Tin Tin frightened by a mouse and reached its climax with a house on fire and the dog taking a baby *into* the flames. I had known about Mankiewicz's contribution to *Kane* and a few other films, but I hadn't realized how extensive his career was. I had known that he was the producer of *Million Dollar Legs* (with W. C. Fields and Jack Oakie and Lyda Roberti) and *Laughter* (with Fredric March and Nancy Carroll), but I hadn't known, for example, that he had produced two of the Marx Brothers films that I've always especially liked, the first two made in Hollywood and written directly for the screen — *Monkey Business* and *Horse Feathers* — and part of

Duck Soup as well. A few years ago, some college students asked me what films I would like to see again just for my own pleasure, and without a second's thought I replied *Duck Soup* and *Million Dollar Legs,* though at that time I had no idea there was any connection between them. Yet surely there is a comic spirit that links them — even the settings, Freedonia and Klopstokia, with Groucho as Prime Minister of one and Fields as President of the other — and now that I have looked into Herman Mankiewicz's career it's apparent that he was a key linking figure in just the kind of movies my friends and I loved best.

When the period of the great silent comedians, with their international audience, was over, a new style of American comedy developed. One couldn't really call a colloquial, skeptical comedy a "masterpiece," as one could sometimes call a silent comedy a masterpiece, especially if the talkie looked quite banal and was so topical it felt transient. But I think that many of us enjoyed these comedies more, even though we may not have felt very secure about the aesthetic grounds for our enjoyment. The talking comedies weren't as aesthetically pure as the silents, yet they felt liberating in a way that even great silents didn't. The elements to which we could respond were multiplied; now there were vocal nuances, new kinds of timing, and wonderful new tricks, like the infectious way Claudette Colbert used to break up while listening to someone. It's easy to see why Europeans, who couldn't follow the slang and the jokes and didn't understand the whole satirical frame of reference, should prefer our action films and Westerns. But it's a bad joke on our good jokes that film enthusiasts here often take their cues on the American movie past from Europe, and so they ignore the tradition of comic irreverence and become con-

Herman Mankiewicz on the set of Laughter, *with Diane Ellis and Nancy Carroll, and, at the piano, Fredric March.*

noisseurs of the "visuals" and "mises en scène" of action pictures, which are usually too silly even to be called reactionary. They're sub-reactionary — the antique melodramas of silent days with noise added — a mass art better suited, one might think, to Fascism, or even feudalism, than to democracy.

There is another reason the American talking comedies, despite their popularity, are so seldom valued highly by film aestheticians. The dream-art kind of film, which lends itself to beautiful visual imagery, is generally the creation of the "artist" director, while the astringent film is more

often directed by a competent, unpretentious craftsman who can be made to look very good by a good script and can be turned into a bum by a bad script. And this competent craftsman may be too worldly and too practical to do the "imaginative" bits that sometimes helped make the reputations of "artist" directors. Ben Hecht said he shuddered at the touches von Sternberg introduced into *Underworld:* "My head villain, Bull Weed, after robbing a bank, emerged with a suitcase full of money and paused in the crowded street to notice a blind beggar and give him a coin — before making his getaway." That's exactly the sort of thing that quantities of people react to emotionally as "deep" and as "art," and that many film enthusiasts treasure — the inflated sentimental with a mystical drip. The thirties, though they had their own load of sentimentality, were the hardest-headed period of American movies, and their plainness of style, with its absence of false "cultural" overtones, has never got its due aesthetically. Film students — and their teachers — often become interested in movies just because they are the kind of people who are emotionally affected by the blind-beggar bits, and they are indifferent by temperament to the emancipation of American movies in the thirties and the role that writers played in it.

I once jotted down the names of some movies that I didn't associate with any celebrated director but that had nevertheless stayed in my memory over the years, because something in them had especially delighted me — such rather obscure movies as *The Moon's Our Home* (Margaret Sullavan and Henry Fonda) and *He Married His Wife* (Nancy Kelly, Joel McCrea, and Mary Boland). When I looked them up, I discovered that Dorothy Parker's name was in the credits of *The Moon's Our Home* and John O'Hara's in the credits of *He Married His Wife*. Other writers worked on those films, too, and perhaps they were the ones who were responsible for what I responded to, but the recurrence of the names of that group of writers, not just on rather obscure remembered films but on almost *all* the films that are generally cited as proof of the vision and style of the most highly acclaimed directors of that period, suggests that the writers — and a particular group of them, at that — may for a brief period, a little more than a decade, have given American talkies their character.

8.

There is always a time lag in the way movies take over (and broaden and emasculate) material from the other arts — whether it is last season's stage success or the novels of the preceding decade or a style or an idea that has run its course in its original medium. (This does not apply to a man like Jean-Luc Godard, who is not a mass-medium movie director.) In most productions of the big studios, the time lag is enormous. In the thirties, after the great age of musical comedy and burlesque, Hollywood, except for Paramount, was just discovering huge operettas. After the Broadway days of Clifton Webb, Fred Astaire, the Marx Brothers, Fanny Brice, W. C. Fields, and all the rest, M-G-M gave us Nelson Eddy and Jeanette MacDonald, and Universal gave us Deanna Durbin. This is the history of movies. J. D. Salinger has finally come to the screen through his imitators, and Philip Roth's fifties romance arrived at the end of the sixties. It may be that for new ideas to be successful in movies, the way must be prepared by success in other media, and the audience must have grown tired of what it's been getting and be ready for something new. There are always a few people in Hollywood who are considered mad dreamers for trying to do in movies things that have already been done in the other arts. But once one of them breaks through and has a hit, he's called a genius and everybody starts copying him.

The new spirit of the talkies was the twenties moved West in the thirties. George S. Kaufman was writing the Marx Brothers stage shows when he and Mankiewicz worked together at the *Times;* a little later, Kaufman directed the first Broadway production of *The Front Page.* Kaufman's collaborators on Broadway plays in the twenties and the early thirties included Marc Connelly, Edna Ferber, Ring Lardner, Morrie Ryskind, and Moss Hart as well as Mankiewicz — the nucleus of the Algonquin-to-Hollywood group. Nunnally Johnson says that the two most brilliant men he has ever known were George S. Kaufman and Herman Mankiewicz, and that, on the whole, Mankiewicz was the more brilliant of the two. I think that what Mankiewicz did in movies was an offshoot of the gag comedy that Kaufman had initiated on Broadway; Mankiewicz spearheaded the movement of that whole Broadway style of wisecracking, fast-talking, cynical-sentimental entertainment onto the national scene. Kaufman's kind of impersonal, visionless comedy, with its single goal of getting the audience to laugh, led to the degeneration of the Broadway theatre, to its play doctors and gimmickry and scattershot jokes at defenseless targets, and so it would be easy to look down on the movie style that came out of it. But I don't think the results were the same when this type of comedy was transplanted to movies; the only bad long-range consequences were to the writers themselves.

Kaufman fathered a movement that is so unmistakably the bastard child of the arts as to seem fatherless; the gag comedy was perfectly suited to the commercial mass art of the movies, so that it appears to be an almost inevitable development. It suited the low common denominator of the movies even better than it suited the needs of the relatively selective theatre audience, and the basic irresponsibility of this kind of theatre combined with the screenwriters' lack of control over their own writing to produce what one might call the brothel period of American letters. It was a gold rush, and Mankiewicz and his friends had

exactly the skills to turn a trick. The journalists' style of working fast and easy and working to order and not caring too much how it was butchered was the best kind of apprenticeship for a Hollywood hack, and they had loved to gather, to joke and play games, to lead the histrionic forms of the glamorous literary life. Now they were gathered in cribs on each studio lot, working in teams side by side, meeting for lunch at the commissary and for dinner at Chassen's, which their old friend and editor Harold Ross had helped finance, and all over town for drinks. They adapted each other's out-of-date plays and novels, and rewrote each other's scripts. Even in their youth in New York, most of them had indulged in what for them proved a vice: they were "collaborators" — dependent on the fun and companionship of joint authorship, which usually means a shared shallowness. Now they collaborated all over the place and backward in time; they collaborated promiscuously, and within a few years were rewriting the remakes of their own or somebody else's rewrites. Mankiewicz adapted Kaufman and Ferber's *The Royal Family* and *Dinner at Eight,* turned Alice Duer Miller's *Come Out of the Kitchen* into *Honey,* and adapted George Kelly's *The Show-Off* and James Thurber's *My Life and Hard Times* and works by Laurence Stallings and other old friends while Ben Hecht or Preston Sturges or Arthur Kober was working over something of his. They escaped the cold, and they didn't suffer from the Depression. They were a colony — expatriates without leaving the country — and their individual contributions to the scripts that emerged after the various rewrites were almost impossible to assess, because their attitudes were so similar; they made the same kind of jokes, because they had been making them to each other for so long. In Hollywood, they sat around building on to each other's gags, covering up implausibilities and dull spots, throwing new wisecracks on top of jokes they had laughed at in New York. Screenwriting was an extension of what they used to do for fun, and now they got paid for it. They had liked to talk more than to write, and this weakness became their way of life. As far as the official literary culture was concerned, they dropped from sight. To quote a classic bit of dialogue from Budd Schulberg's *The Disenchanted:*

"Bane had two hits running on Broadway at the same time. Even Nathan liked 'em. Popular 'n satirical. Like Barry, only better. The critics kept waiting for him to write that great American play."
"What happened to him?"
"Hollywood."

Hollywood destroyed them, but they did wonders for the movies. In New York, they may have valued their own urbanity too highly; faced with the target Hollywood presented, they became cruder and tougher, less tidy, less stylistically elegant, and more iconoclastic, and in the eyes of Hollywood they were slaphappy cynics, they were "crazies." They were too talented and too sophisticated to put a high value on what they did, too amused at the spectacle of what they were doing and what they were part of to be respected the way a writer of "integrity," like Lillian Hellman, was later to be respected — or, still later, Arthur Miller. Though their style was often flippant and their attitude toward form casual to the point of contempt, they brought movies the subversive gift of sanity. They changed movies by raking the old moralistic muck with derision. Those sickly Graustarkian romances with beautiful, pure highborn girls and pathetic lame girls and

dashing princes in love with commoners, and all the Dumas and Sabatini and Blasco-Ibáñez, now had to compete with the freedom and wildness of American comedy. Once American films had their voice and the Algonquin group was turned loose on the scripts, the revolting worship of European aristocracy faded so fast that movie stars even stopped bringing home Georgian princes. In the silents, the heroes were often simpletons. In the talkies, the heroes were to be the men who weren't fooled, who were smart and learned their way around. The new heroes of the screen were created in the image of their authors: they were fast-talking newspaper reporters.

That Walter Burns whose entrance in *The Front Page* Kerr described was based on Walter Howey, who was the city editor of the *Chicago Tribune,* at $8,000 a year, until Hearst lured him away by an offer of $35,000 a year. Howey is generally considered the "greatest" of all Hearst editors — by those who mean one thing by it, and by those who mean the other. He edited Hearst's *New York Mirror* at a time when it *claimed* to be ten per cent news and ninety per cent entertainment. The epitome of Hearstian journalism, and a favorite of Hearst's until the end, he was one of the executors of Hearst's will. At one time or another, just about all the Hollywood writers had worked for Walter Howey and/or spent their drinking hours with friends who did. He was the legend: the classic model of the amoral, irresponsible, irrepressible newsman who cares about nothing but scoops and circulation. He had lost an eye (supposedly in actual fighting of circulation wars), and Ben Hecht is quoted as saying you could tell which was the glass eye because it was the warmer one. Hecht used him again in *Nothing Sacred,* as Fredric March's editor — "a cross between a Ferris wheel and a werewolf" — and he turns up under other names in other plays and movies. In a sense, all those newspaper plays and movies were already about Hearst's kind of corrupt, manic journalism.

The toughest-minded, the most satirical of the thirties pictures often featured newspaper settings, or, at least, reporters — especially the "screwball" comedies, which had some resemblances to later "black" comedy and current "freaky" comedy but had a very different spirit. A newspaper picture meant a contemporary picture in an American setting, usually a melodrama with crime and political corruption and suspense and comedy and romance. In 1931, a title like *Five Star Final* or *Scandal Sheet* signalled the public that the movie would be a tough modern talkie, not a tearjerker with sound. Just to touch a few bases, there was *The Front Page* itself, in 1931, with Pat O'Brien as the reporter and Adolphe Menjou as Walter Burns; Lee Tracy as the gossip columnist in *Blessed Event* and as the press agent in *Bombshell;* Clark Gable as the reporter in *It Happened One Night;* Paul Muni giving advice to the lovelorn in *Hi, Nellie;* Spencer Tracy as the editor in *Libeled Lady;* Stuart Erwin as the correspondent in *Viva Villa!;* Jean Harlow stealing the affections of a newspaperman from girl reporter Loretta Young in *Platinum Blonde;* Jean Arthur as the girl reporter in *Mr. Deeds Goes to Town;* a dozen pictures, at least, with George Bancroft as a Walter Howey–style bullying editor; all those half-forgotten pictures with reporter "teams" — Fredric March and Virginia Bruce, or Joel McCrea and Jean Arthur, or Loretta Young and Tyrone Power (*Love Is News*); Cary Grant as the editor and Joan Bennett as the reporter in *Wedding Present;* and then Cary Grant as Walter Burns in *His Girl Friday,* with Rosalind Russell as the re-porter; and then Cary Grant and James Stewart (who had been a foreign correspondent in *Next Time We Love*) both involved with a newsmagazine in *The Philadelphia Story,* in 1940. Which takes us right up to *Citizen Kane,* the biggest newspaper picture of them all — the picture that ends with the introduction of the cast and a reprise of the line "I think it would be fun to run a newspaper."

9.

After years of swapping stories about Howey and the other werewolves and the crooked, dirty press, Mankiewicz found himself on story-swapping terms with the power behind it all, Hearst himself. When he had been in Hollywood only a short time, he met Marion Davies and Hearst through his friendship with Charles Lederer, a writer, then in his early twenties, whom Ben Hecht had met and greatly admired in New York when Lederer was still in his teens. Lederer, a child prodigy, who had entered college at thirteen, got to know Mankiewicz, the MacArthurs, Moss Hart, Benchley, and their friends at about the same time or shortly after he met Hecht, and was immediately accepted into a group considerably older than he was. Lederer was Marion Davies' nephew — the son of her sister Reine, who had been in operetta and musical comedy. In Hollywood, Charles Lederer's life seems to have revolved around his aunt, whom he adored. (Many others adored her also, though *Citizen Kane* was to give the world a different — and false — impression.) She was childless, and Lederer was very close to her; he spent a great deal of his time at her various dwelling places, and took his friends to meet both her and Hearst. The world of letters being small and surprising, Charles Lederer was among those who worked on the adaptation of *The Front Page* to the screen in 1931 and again when it was remade as *His Girl Friday* in 1940, and, the world being even smaller than that, Lederer married Orson Welles' ex-wife, Virginia Nicholson Welles, in 1940, at San Simeon. (She married two prodigies in succession; the marriage to Welles had lasted five years and produced a daughter.)

Hearst was so fond of Lederer that on the evening of the nuptials he broke his rule of one cocktail to guests before dinner and no hard liquor thereafter. A guest who gulped the cocktail down was sometimes able to swindle another, but this is the only occasion that I can find recorded on which Hearst dropped the rule — a rule that Marion Davies customarily eased by slipping drinks to desperate guests before Hearst joined them but that nevertheless made it possible for Hearst to receive, and see at their best, some of the most talented alcoholics this country has ever produced. Not all writers are attracted to the rich and powerful, but it's a defining characteristic of journalists to be drawn to those who live at the center of power. Even compulsive drinkers like Mankiewicz and Dorothy Parker were so fascinated by the great ménage of Hearst and his consort — and the guest lists of the world-famous — that they managed to stay relatively sober for the evenings at Marion Davies' beach house (Colleen Moore described it as "the largest house on the beach — and I mean the beach from San Diego to the Canadian border") and the weekends at San Simeon.

If *Kane* has the same love-hate as *The Front Page,* the same joyous infatuation with the antics of the unprincipled press, it's because Mankiewicz, like Hecht and MacArthur, revelled in the complexities of corruption. And Hearst's life was a *specta-cle.* For short periods, this was intoxication enough. A man like Hearst seems to embody more history than other people do; in his company a writer may feel that he has been living in the past and on the outskirts and now he's living in the dangerous present, right where the decisions are really made.

Hearst represented a new type of power. He got his first newspaper in 1887, when he was twenty-four, by asking his father for it, and, in the next three decades, when, for the first time, great masses of people became literate, he added more and more papers, until, with his empire of thirty newspapers and fifteen magazines, he was the most powerful journalist and publisher in the world. He had brought the first comic strips to America in 1892, and his battling with Pulitzer a few years later over a cartoon character named the Yellow Kid revived the term "yellow journalism." Because there was no tradition of responsibility in this new kind of popular journalism, which was almost a branch of show business, Hearst knew no restraints; perhaps fortunately, he was unguided. Ultimately, he was as purposeless about his power as the craziest of the Roman emperors. His looting of the treasures of the world for his castle at San Simeon symbolized his imperial status. Being at his table was being at court, and the activities of the notables who were invited there were slavishly chronicled in the Hearst papers.

The new social eminence of the Mankiewiczes, who sometimes visited San Simeon for as long as ten days at a time, can be charted from Louella Parsons' columns. By the end of 1928, Louella was announcing Mankiewicz's writing assignments with a big bold headline at the top of the column, and was printing such items as:

Marion Davies and friends at a party in her honor in 1931. Standing left to right: Clarence Brown, Robert Z. Leonard, Jack Conway, Irving Thalberg, Adolphe Menjou, King Vidor, Samuel Goldwyn, George Fitzmaurice, Herman Mankiewicz, Dr. Harry Martin, John Gilbert, Lloyd Pantages. Seated: Mona Maris, Mrs. Robert Leonard, Mrs. Jack Conway, Eleanor Boardman (Mrs. King Vidor), Mrs. Samuel Goldwyn, Marion Davies, Louella Parsons, Mrs. George Fitzmaurice, Mrs. Herman Mankiewicz, Catherine Dale Owen, Aileen Pringle, Hedda Hopper.

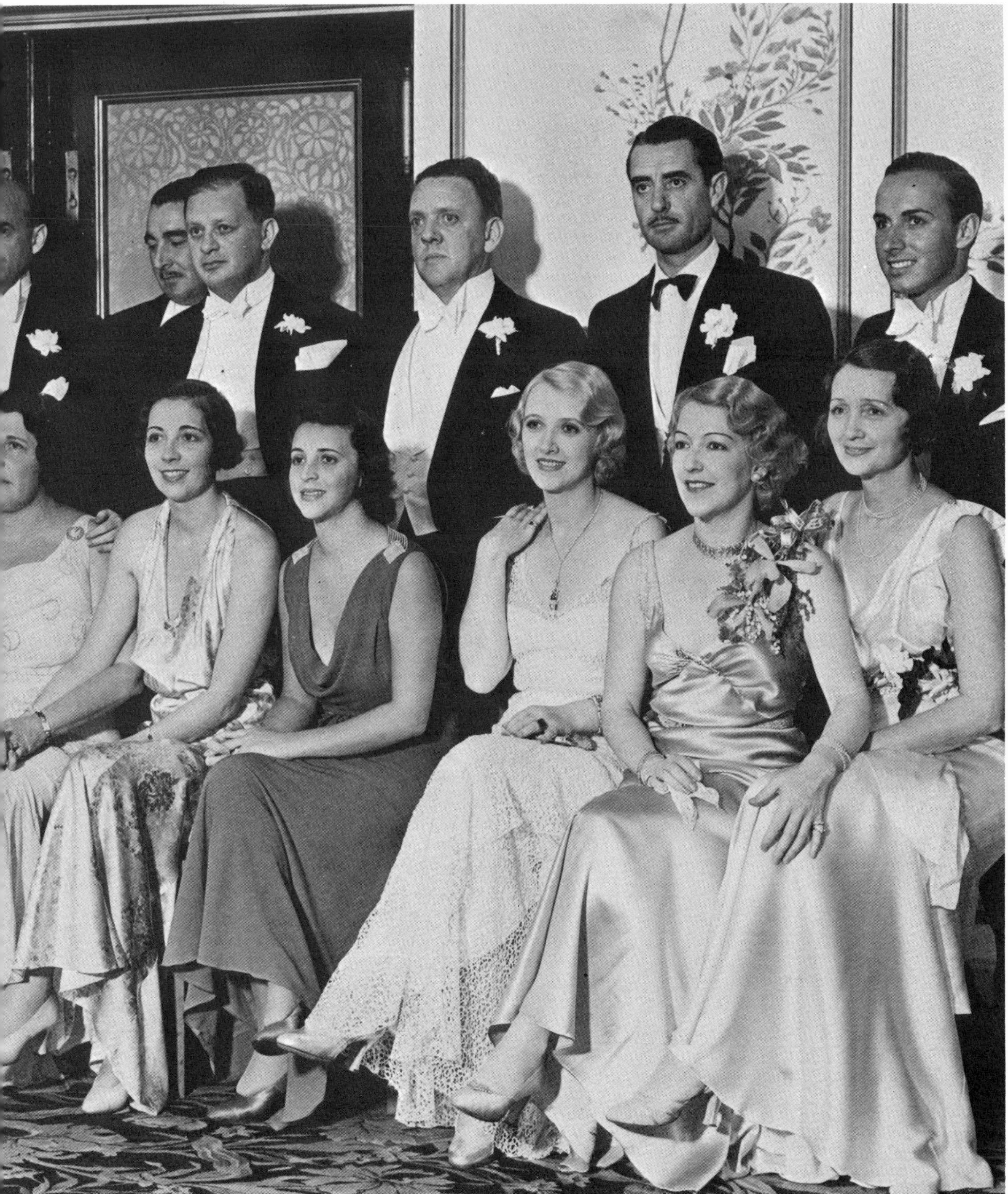

WILLIAM GRIMES

One of the few scenario writers in Hollywood who didn't have to unlearn much that he had learned is Herman Mankiewicz. Herman came to Paramount directly from the stage, and naturally he knows the technique just as well as if he hadn't written movies in the interval.

It was worth another item in the same column that Herman Mankiewicz had been observed "taking his son down Hollywood Boulevard to see the lighted Christmas trees." In 1931, the Mankiewiczes were so prominent that they were among those who gave Marion Davies a homecoming party at the Hotel Ambassador; the other hosts were Mr. and Mrs. Irving Thalberg, Mr. and Mrs. King Vidor, Mr. and Mrs. Samuel Goldwyn, John Gilbert, Lewis Milestone, Hedda Hopper, and so on. Hedda Hopper, who worked as a movie columnist for a rival newspaper chain but was a close friend of Marion Davies (to whom, it is said, she owed her job), was also an enthusiastic reporter of Mankiewicz's activities during the years when he and his ravishing Sara were part of the Hearst-Davies social set.

When writers begin to see the powerful men operating in terms of available alternatives, while they have been judging them in terms of ideals, they often develop "personal" admiration for the great bastards whom they have always condemned and still condemn. Hearst was to Mankiewicz, I suspect, what Welles was to be to him a little later — a dangerous new toy. And he needed new toys constantly to keep off the booze. Mankiewicz could control himself at San Simeon in the late twenties and the very early thirties, as, in those days, he could control himself when he was in charge of a movie. Producing the Marx Brothers comedies kept him busy and entertained for a while. With the title of "supervisor"

(a term for the actual working producer, as distinguished from the studio executive whose name might appear above or below the name of the movie), he worked on their pictures from the inception of the ideas through the months of writing and then the shooting. But he got bored easily, and when he started cutting up in the middle of preparing *Duck Soup,* in 1933, he was taken off the picture. When the Marx Brothers left Paramount and went to M-G-M, he joined them again, in the preparation of *A Night at the Opera,* in 1935, and the same thing happened; he was replaced as supervisor by his old boss George S. Kaufman.

His credits began to taper off after 1933, and in 1936 Mankiewicz didn't get a single credit. That year, he published an article called "On Approaching Forty," a brief satirical account of what had happened to him as a writer. It began:

Right before me, as I write, is a folder in which my wife keeps the blotters from Mr. Eschner, the insurance man, Don's first report card, the letter from the income tax people about the gambling loss at Tia Juana, the press photograph of me greeting Helen Kane (in behalf of the studio) at the Pasadena Station and my literary output. There are four separate pieces of this output and they are all excellent. I hope some friend will gather them into a little book after my death. There is plenty of ninety point Marathon in the world, and wide margins can't be hard to find.

He includes those tiny pieces in their entirety, and after one of them — the first three sentences of a short story — he comments:

I moved to Hollywood soon after I had made this notation and was kept so busy with one thing and another — getting the pool filled, playing the Cadillac and Buick salesmen against each other, only to compromise on a Cadillac and a Buick, after all, and locating the finance company's downtown office — that the first thing I knew, a story, a good deal like the one I had in mind, appeared in the *Saturday Evening Post,* and in *Collier's,* too.

This is the end of his article:

The fourth note looks rather naked now, all by itself on the desk. It says, simply: "Write piece for *New Yorker* on reaching thirty-fifth birthday. No central idea. Just flit from paragraph to paragraph."

People who complain that my work is slipshod would be a little surprised to find that I just am *not* always satisfied with the first thing I put down. I'm changing that thirty-fifth to fortieth right now.

"On Approaching Forty" didn't come out in *The New Yorker;* it appeared in the *Hollywood Reporter.*

Ambivalence was the most common "literary" emotion of the screenwriters of the thirties, as alienation was to become the most common "literary" emotion of the screenwriters of the sixties. The thirties writers were ambivalently nostalgic about their youth as reporters, journalists, critics, or playwrights, and they glorified the hard-drinking, cynical newspaperman. They were ambivalent about Hollywood, which they savaged and satirized whenever possible. Hollywood paid them so much more money than they had ever earned before, and the movies reached so many more people than they had ever reached before, that they were contemptuous of those who hadn't made it on their scale at the same time that they hated themselves for selling out. They had gone to Hollywood as a paid vacation from their playwriting or journalism, and screenwriting became their only

writing. The vacation became an extended drunken party, and while they were there in the debris of the long morning after, American letters passed them by. They were never to catch up; nor were American movies ever again to have in their midst a whole school of the richest talents of a generation.

We in the audience didn't have to wake up *afterward* to how good those films of the thirties were; in common with millions of people, I enjoyed them while they were coming out. They were immensely popular. But I did take them for granted. There was such a steady flow of bright comedy that it appeared to be a Hollywood staple, and it didn't occur to me that those films wouldn't go on being made. It didn't occur to me that it required a special gathering of people in a special atmosphere to produce that flow, and that when those people stopped enjoying themselves those pictures couldn't be made. And I guess it didn't occur to older, more experienced people, either, because for decades everybody went on asking why Hollywood wasn't turning out those good, entertaining comedies anymore.

By the end of the thirties, the jokes had soured. The comedies of the forties were heavy and pushy, straining for humor, and the comic impulse was misplaced or lost; they came out of a different atmosphere, a different *feeling.* The comic spirit of the thirties had been happily self-critical about America, the happiness born of the knowledge that in no other country were movies so free to be self-critical. It was the comedy of a country that didn't yet hate itself. Though it wasn't until the sixties that the self-hatred became overt in American life and American movies, it started to show, I think, in the phony, excessive, duplicit use of patriotism by the rich, guilty liberals of Hollywood in the war years.

10.

In the forties, a socially conscious film historian said to me, "You know, Paramount never made a good movie," and I brought up the names of some Paramount movies —*Easy Living* and *Trouble in Paradise* and lovely trifles like *Midnight* — and, of course, I couldn't make my point, because those movies weren't what was thought of in the forties as a good movie. I knew I wouldn't get anywhere at all if I tried to cite *Million Dollar Legs* or *Mississippi*, or pictures with the Marx Brothers or Mae West; I would be told they weren't even movies. Though Paramount made some elegant comedies in the "Continental" style, many of the best Paramount pictures were like revues — which was pretty much the style of the Broadway theatre they'd come out of, and was what I liked about them. They entertained you without trying to change your life, yet didn't congratulate you for being a slobbering bag of mush, either. But by the forties these were considered "escapist entertainment," and that was supposed to be *bad*. Many of the thirties comedies, especially the Paramount ones, weren't even "artistic" or "visual" movies — which is why they look so good on television now. They also sound good, because what that historian thought of as their irresponsibility is so much more modern than the sentimentalities of the war years. What was believed in was implicit in the styles of the heroes and heroines and in the comedy targets; the writers had an almost aristocratic disdain for putting beliefs into words. In the forties, the writers convinced themselves that they believed in everything, and they kept putting it all into so many bad words. It's no wonder the movies had no further use for a Groucho or a Mae West; one can imagine what either of them might have done to those words.

It's common to blame the McCarthyism of the fifties and the removal of blacklisted writers for the terrible, flat writing in American movies of recent years, but the writers might have recovered from McCarthyism (they might even have stood up to it) if they hadn't been destroyed as writers long before. The writing that had given American talkies their special flavor died in the war, killed not in battle but in the politics of Stalinist "anti-Fascism." For the writers, Hollywood was just one big crackup, and for most of them it took a political turn. The lost-in-Hollywood generation of writers, trying to clean themselves of guilt for their wasted years and their irresponsibility as *writers*, became political in the worst way — became a special breed of anti-Fascists. The talented writers, the major ones as well as the lightweight yet entertaining ones, went down the same drain as the clods — drawn into it, often, by bored wives, less successful brothers. They became naïvely, hysterically pro-Soviet; they ignored Stalin's actual policies, because they so badly needed to believe in something. They had been so smart, so gifted, and yet they hadn't been able to beat Hollywood's contempt for the writer. (Walter Wanger had put twenty-seven of them to work in groups in succession on the script of Vincent Sheean's *Personal History*.) They lived in the city where Irving Thalberg was enshrined; Thalberg, the saint of M-G-M, had rationalized Mayer's system of putting teams of writers to work simultaneously and in relays on the same project. It had been lunatic before, but Thalberg made it seem mature and responsible to fit writers into an assembly-line method that totally alienated them and took away their last shreds of pride. And most of the Algonquin group had been in Hollywood so long they weren't even famous anymore.

Talented people have rarely had the self-control to flourish in the Hollywood atmosphere of big money and conflicting pressures. The talented — especially those who weren't using their talents to full capacity — have become desperate, impatient, unreliable, self-destructive, and also destructive, and so there has always been some validity in the businessman's argument that he couldn't afford to take chances on "geniuses." Thalberg didn't play around with a man like Mankiewicz; after throwing him off *A Night at the Opera,* he didn't use him again.

The writers who had become accustomed to being assembly-line workers were ready to believe it when, in the forties, they were told that, like factory workers, they were "part of the team on the assembly line" and needed "that strengthening of the spirit which comes from identity with the labor of others." Like the producers, the Screen Writers Guild respected discipline and responsibility, but though the businessmen had never been able to organize people of talent — producers like Thalberg just kept discarding them — the union ideologues knew how. The talented rarely become bureaucrats, but the mediocre had put down roots in Hollywood — it doesn't take long in Los Angeles, the only great city that is purely modern, that hasn't even an architectural past in the nineteenth century. In the forties, the talented merged with the untalented and became almost indistinguishable from them, and the mediocre have been writing movies ever since. When the good writers tried to regain their self-respect by becoming political activists in the Stalinist style, it was calamitous to talent; the Algonquin group's own style was lost as their voice blended into the preachy, self-righteous chorus.

The comedy writers who had laughed at cant now learned to write it and were rehabilitated as useful citizens of the community of mediocrity. It was just what the newly political congratulated themselves on — their constructive, uplifting approach — that killed comedy. When they had written frivolously, knowing that they had no control over how their writing would be used, or buried, or rewritten, they may have failed their own gifts and the dreams of their youth, but the work they turned out had human dimensions; they were working at less than full capacity, but they were still honest entertainers. Their humor was the humor of those trapped by human weakness as well as by "the system," and this was basic comedy — like the jokes and camaraderie of Army men. But when they became political in that morally superior way of people who are doing something for themselves but pretending it's for others, their self-righteousness was insufferable. They may have told lies in the themes and plots of the thirties comedies, but they didn't take their own lies seriously, they didn't *believe* their own lies, the way they did in the forties. In the forties, the Screen Writers Guild and the Hollywood Writers Mobilization (for wartime morale-building) held conferences at which "responsible" writers brought the irresponsibles into line. The irresponsibles were told they were part of an army and must "dedicate their creative abilities to the winning of the war." And, in case they failed to understand the necessity for didactic, "positive" humor, there were panels and seminars that analyzed jokes and pointed out which ones might do harm. It was explained to the writers that "catch-as-catch-can," "no-holds-barred" comedy was a thing of the past. "A very funny line may make black-market dealings seem innocent and attractive," they were told, and "Respect for officers must be maintained at all times, in any scene, in any situation."

Show-business people are both giddy and

desperately, sincerely intense. When Stalinism was fashionable, movie people became Stalinists, the way they later became witches and warlocks. Apparently, many of the Hollywood Stalinists didn't realize they were taking any risks; they performed propaganda services for the various shifts in Russia's foreign policy and, as long as the needs of American and Russian policy coincided, this took the form of superpatriotism. When the war was over and the Cold War began, history left them stranded, and McCarthy moved in on them. The shame of McCarthyism was not only "the shame of America" but the shame of a bunch of newly rich people who were eager to advise the world on moral and political matters and who, faced with a test, informed on their friends — and, as Orson Welles put it, not even to save their lives but to save their swimming pools. One might think that whatever they had gained emotionally from their activity they would have lost when they informed on each other, but it doesn't seem to have always worked that way. They didn't change their ideas when they recanted before the House Un-American Activities Committee; they merely gave in and then were restored to themselves. And they often seem to regard it not as their weakness but as their martyrdom. Show-business-Stalinism is basically not political but psychological; it's a fashionable form of hysteria and guilt that is by now not so much pro-Soviet as just abusively anti-American. America is their image of Hell (once again, because of Vietnam, they're in a popular position), and they go on being "political" in the same way, holding the same faith, and for the same reasons, as in the late thirties and the forties. The restoration there is fairly general. In Hollywood recently, a man who used to be "involved" told me he wanted to become

more active again, and added, "But, you know, I'm scared. The people who are urging me to do more are the same ones who ratted on me last time."

Mankiewicz was too well informed politically to become a Communist Party-liner. Because he didn't support this line, he was — and only in part jokingly — considered a "reactionary" by the activists of the Screen Writers Guild. Yet he went on to write the movie they point to with pride in Hollywood, the movie they all seem to feel demonstrates what *can* be done and what movies should be doing, and it's their all-time favorite because they understand it — and correctly — as a leftist film. Its leftism is, however, the leftism of the twenties and early thirties, before the left became moralistic. There were other expressions of the tough spirit of the thirties that came after the thirties were over. There may be a little of it in the newspaper film of the fifties *Sweet Smell of Success,* but the ambivalence there is harsher, grimmer, more artistically "serious" than it was in the thirties; there's some in the happy mockery of Hollywood in *Singin' in the Rain,* which takes off from Kaufman and Hart's *Once in a Lifetime,* and in the films of Preston Sturges, who alone somehow managed to stay funny and tart. The only writer of this whole group who became a director with an individual style, Sturges kept American comedy alive singlehanded through the mawkish forties. Maybe he was able to because he was a cynic and so politically baroque that he wasn't torn by doubts and guilts. The political show in Hollywood in the forties was just one more crazy scene to him; he'd grown up rich and eccentric in Europe, the son of that expatriate lady (called Mary in *The Loves of Isadora*) who gave Isadora Duncan the fatal scarf.

But Mankiewicz climaxed an era in *Kane.*

He wrote a big movie that is untarnished by sentimentality, and it may be the only big biographical movie ever made in this country of which that can be said. *Kane* is unsanctimonious; it is without scenes of piety, masochism, or remorse, without "truths" — in that period when the screen-writers were becoming so politically "responsible" that they were using all the primitive devices to sell their messages, and movies once again became full of blind beggars, and omens of doom, and accidental death as punishment for moral and sexual infractions, and, of course, Maria Ouspenskaya seeing into people's hearts — the crone as guru.

11.

Orson Welles wasn't around when *Citizen Kane* was written, early in 1940. Mankiewicz, hobbling about on a broken leg in a huge cast, was packed off — away from temptation — to Mrs. Campbell's Guest Ranch, in Victorville, California, sixty-five miles from Los Angeles, to do the script. He had a nurse and a secretary to watch over him and John Houseman to keep him working, and they all lived there for about three months — in a combination dude ranch and rest home, where liquor was forbidden and unavailable — until the first draft of *Citizen Kane,* called simply and formidably *American,* was completed.

That insurance-company doctor who refused to accept Mankiewicz as a risk back in 1927 had no need to be prophetic. Ben Hecht once described a summer earlier in the twenties when he and his wife and Charles MacArthur were living in a borrowed house near Woodstock, New York, with no money, and Harpo, Groucho, Chico, and Zeppo Marx and their wives, sweethearts, and children came to stay, and then Herman Mankiewicz arrived, carrying two suitcases. "He had decided to spend his vacation from the *New York Times* drama section with us," Hecht wrote. "He had not been allowed to bring any money with him because of Sara's certainty that he would spend it on liquor, and thus impair the influence of country air and sunshine. . . . Herman's larger suitcase contained sixteen bottles of Scotch and nothing else." A few weeks later, Hecht and MacArthur went in to New York to try to sell a play they'd just written, and encountered Mankiewicz, who, having sent his wife and children out of town to escape the heat, was "occupying Prince Bibesco's grand suite in the Plaza Hotel while His Highness capered in Long Island."

Hecht went on, "We moved in with him, there being no rent to pay. We discovered, while helping Herman to undress the first night, that his torso was bound with yards of adhesive tape. He had slipped while trying to get out of the bathtub and lamed his back. When Herman was asleep, MacArthur and I rolled him on his stomach and with an indelible pencil wrote ardent and obscene love messages on his taping. We signed them Gladys and chuckled over the impending moment in Far Rockaway when Herman would undress before his keen-eyed Sara."

Not only was Mankiewicz alcoholic and maniacally accident-prone; he was a gambler, constantly in debt. There was a sequence in a thirties movie about a gambling newspaperman that was based on the way the other writers at Paramount used to line up with him when he got his check on Friday afternoon and walk with him to the bank so they could get back some of the money he'd borrowed from them during the week. His old friends say that he would bet from sheer boredom; when he ran out of big sporting events, he would bet on anything — on high-school football games or whether it would rain. He got to the point where he was bored with just betting; he wanted the stakes to be dangerously high. He once explained, "It's not fun gambling if I lose two thousand and just write a check for it. What's thrilling is to make out a check for fifteen thousand dollars knowing there's not a penny in the bank." James Thurber referred to him as an "incurable compulsive gambler." He described how Mankiewicz went to a psychiatrist to see if anything could be done about it. "I can't cure you of gambling," the analyst told him on his last visit, "but I can tell you why you do it."

By the late thirties, Mankiewicz had just about run out of studios to get fired from. Scott Fitzgerald described him in those years as "a ruined man." His friends would get him jobs and he would lose them — sometimes in spectacular ways that became part of Hollywood legend. Perhaps the best-known is his exit from Columbia Pictures. In his biography of Harry Cohn, who was then the head of the studio, Bob Thomas describes it this way:

The most famous incident in the Columbia dining room concerned an erratic genius named Herman J. Mankiewicz. . . . The free-wheeling world of journalism seemed better suited to his temperament than did Hollywood. He possessed two failings that were inimical to the autocratic studio domains: he drank, and he was scornful of his bosses.

These faculties tumbled him from the position of a major screenwriter, and he had difficulty finding jobs. His agent, Charles Feldman, proposed a post at Columbia. Cohn was interested, since he enjoyed hiring bargain talent discarded by the major studios. . . . Cohn agreed to employ him at $750 a week.

"I want to make good," said Mankiewicz when he reported to William Perlberg, then Columbia's executive producer.

"Fine," said the producer. . . . "But . . . don't go in the executive dining room. You know what will happen if you tangle with Cohn."

Mankiewicz concurred. . . . His work habits were exemplary, and he produced many pages a day. But . . . his office was on the third floor, near the door to the executive dining room. As Riskin, Swerling, and other fellow-writers emerged after lunch, he could hear them laughing over wisecracks and jokes that had been told inside. Mankiewicz himself was considered one of Hollywood's premier wits and raconteurs, and he rankled over his banishment.

One day Perlberg entered the dining room and was startled to find Mankiewicz sitting at the end of the table. The writer held a napkin to his mouth and promised, "I won't say a word."

When Cohn entered the room, he gave Mankiewicz a warm greeting, then assumed his monarchial position at the head of the table.

Cohn began the conversation: "Last night I saw the lousiest picture I've seen in years."

He mentioned the title, and one of the more courageous of his producers spoke up: "Why, I saw that picture at the Downtown Paramount, and the audience howled over it. Maybe you should have seen it with an audience."

"That doesn't make any difference," Cohn replied. "When I'm alone in a projection room, I have a foolproof device for judging whether a picture is good or bad. If my fanny squirms, it's bad. If my fanny doesn't squirm, it's good. It's as simple as that."

There was a momentary silence, which was filled by Mankiewicz at the end of the table: "Imagine — the whole world wired to Harry Cohn's ass!"

Mankiewicz's attitude toward himself and his work is summed up in one very short, very famous story. A friend who hadn't seen him for a while asked, "How's Sara?"

Mankiewicz, puzzled: "Who?"

"Sara. Your wife, Sara."

"Oh, you mean Poor Sara."

The only evidence of an instinct for self-preservation in the life of Herman Mankiewicz is his choice of keen-eyed Sara. He was in bad shape by 1939, but Mayer kept him on the payroll — some said so that top people at M-G-M could collect their gambling winnings from him. But Mayer also seems to have had some affection for him, and Sara had become a close friend of Mayer's daughter Irene. Mayer became concerned about Mankiewicz's gambling debts, and, assuming that Mankiewicz was also concerned about them, he concluded that if he got the debts straightened out, Mankiewicz would pull himself together. Mayer called him in and asked him how much money he needed to get financially clear. Mankiewicz came up with the figure of $30,000, and Mayer offered to advance him that sum on a new contract if he would swear a solemn vow never to gamble again. Mankiewicz went through an elaborate ritual of giving Mayer his sacred word, and walked out with the $30,000. The very next day, it is said, Mankiewicz was playing poker on the lot, and he had just raised the stakes to $10,000 when he looked up and saw Mayer standing there. Mankiewicz left the studio and didn't return. A few days after that — early in September of 1939 — Thomas Phipps, a nephew of Lady Astor's, who was also employed as a writer at M-G-M, was driving to New York to court a lady there, and, with nothing better to do, Mankiewicz decided to go along. As Mankiewicz described the trip some months later, in a guest column he wrote, filling in for Hedda Hopper on vacation, it was fairly giddy right from the start. Mankiewicz said that each song on the car radio sent Phipps swooning, because either he had heard it while he was with his lady or he had heard it while he was not with her. On the outskirts of Albuquerque, the car skidded and turned over. Mankiewicz's jocular account included as the climax "thirty-four weeks in a cast in bed and thirty-two weeks in a brace." Phipps had a broken collarbone; when it healed, he proceeded on his romantic way to New York. Mankiewicz had a compound fracture of the left leg, which, together with further injuries suffered while the fracture was healing, left him with a limp for the rest of his life.

During the long recuperation — very long, because on his first night out on the town after his cast was removed, he went on crutches to Chasen's, got drunk, slipped and broke more bones, and had to be put in another cast — Mankiewicz, bedridden and in exile from the studios, began to write the Mercury Theatre's "Campbell Playhouse" radio shows, with the actors often gathered around his bed for story conferences, and even rehearsals. Welles, having come to Hollywood in July to fulfill his contract with Schaefer, had been flying to and from New York for the series; in October he arranged to have the shows originate in Los Angeles, and in November he hired Mankiewicz to write five of them. Welles had met Mankiewicz sometime earlier in New York. This is John Houseman's recollection of those events, set down in a letter to Sara Mankiewicz after her husband's death:

I remember so well the day Orson came back to the theatre from 21, telling me he had met this amazingly civilized and charming man. I can just see them there at lunch together — magicians and highbinders at work on each other, vying with each other in wit and savoir-faire and mutual appreciation. Both came away enchanted and convinced that, between them, they were the two most dashing and gallantly intelligent gentlemen in the Western world. And they were not so far wrong! Soon after that I met Herman myself, but I didn't get to know him until . . . he lay in bed at Tower Road, his leg in a monstrous plaster cast . . . and we started to do those peculiar collaborative radio shows in the beginning of our long conspiracy of love and hate for Maestro, the Dog-Faced Boy. Then came *Kane* and Victorville and those enchanted months of inhabiting Mrs. Campbell's ranch with our retinue of nurse and secretary and our store of Mickey Finns!

Tower Road was where the Mankiewiczes lived and the Mercury group gathered. The Dog-Faced Boy is, of course, Orson Welles (Cocteau once described him as "a dog who has broken loose from his chain and gone to sleep on the flower bed"), and the Mickey Finns were a medical concoction that was supposed to make Mankiewicz hate alcohol. It failed. The secretary, Mrs. Rita Alexander (she lent her name to the character of Susan Alexander), recalls that during her first week, before Sara Mankiewicz had had a chance to give her a briefing, Mankiewicz persuaded her to take him in to the town of Victorville, where he could get a drink. She withstood his wiles after that. He really wasn't in condition to do much drinking; the broken bones included a hip break, and he was in such poor condition that even eating presented problems. Mrs. Alexander recalls spoon-feeding him bicarbonate of soda, and recalls his courtly, formal apologies for the belches that rocked the room.

12.

There are monsters, and there are also sacred monsters; both Welles and Mankiewicz deserve places in the sacred-monster category. Some writers on film — particularly in England — blithely say that Kane wasn't based on Hearst, using as evidence statements that Welles made to the press in early 1941, when he was trying to get the picture released. But those who think Louella Parsons got the *mistaken* idea that the picture was about Hearst don't understand what kind of man the young Welles was. Welles and Mankiewicz wanted to do something startling, something that would cap the invasion of the Martians — which had, after all, panicked only the boobs, and inadvertently at that, though Welles now makes it sound deliberate. This time, he and Mankiewicz *meant* to raise cain. The pun is surely theirs, and Hearst had walked right into it; he was so fond of a story called *Cain and Mabel,* which he'd bought and produced as a Cosmopolitan Picture back in 1924, that he remade it late in 1936, at Warners', starring Clark Gable and Marion Davies. It had been one of her last pictures before her retirement. Cain and Mabel — it was a perfect description of Hearst and Marion. In 1960, when Welles was interviewed on British television, he said, "Kane isn't really founded on Hearst in particular." I suppose he was feeling rather expansive at that moment, and it may have seemed to limit his importance if his Kane had been based on anyone "in particular." In the same interview, he said, "You asked me did Mr. Hearst try to stop it. *He* didn't. . . . He was like Kane in that he wouldn't have stooped to such a thing." This was rather droll, but Welles seemed to mean it. He didn't seem to know much about Hearst anymore; probably he'd forgotten. One may also fairly conclude that Welles, with that grandeur which he seems to have taken over from the theatre into his personal life, was elevating Hearst, lending Hearst some of his own magnitude. More characteristically, however, his grandeur is double-edged, as in this typical statement on Gregg Toland:

I had a great advantage not only in the real genius of my cameraman but in the fact that he, like all men who are masters of a craft, told me at the outset that there was nothing about camerawork that any intelligent being couldn't learn in half a day. And he was right.

Welles was thus telling us that he learned all there was to know about camerawork in half a day. What, one wonders, was the craft that Toland needed to master? Welles, like Hearst, and like most very big men, is capable of some very small gestures. And so was Mankiewicz, who brought his younger, more stable brother, Joe, out to Hollywood and helped him get started, but, as soon as Joe had some success, began behaving atrociously, referring to him as "my idiot brother."

Mankiewicz's ambivalence was generally on a higher level, however. There are many different kinds of senses of humor, and the one that sometimes comes through Mankiewicz anecdotes is the perverse soul of Kane himself. There is, for example, the story that Ezra Goodman tells in *The Fifty Year Decline and Fall of Hollywood.* Hollywood was not often elegant and correct, but the producer Arthur Hornblow, Jr., was known for the punctiliousness of his social functions. At a dinner party that he gave for Hollywood notables, Herman Mankiewicz drank too much and threw up on the table. "A deadly hush descended over the assembled guests. . . . Mankiewicz broke the silence himself: 'It's all right, Arthur; the white wine came up with the fish.'"

The man who in those circumstances could put his host down was a fit companion for Welles. They were big eaters, big talkers, big spenders, big talents; they were not men of what is ordinarily called "good character." They were out to get not only Hearst but each other. The only religious remark that has ever been attributed to Mankiewicz was recorded on the set of *Citizen Kane:* Welles walked by, and Mankiewicz muttered, "There, but for the grace of God, goes God."

13.

Herman Mankiewicz didn't — to be exact — write *Citizen Kane;* he dictated it. The screenwriters may have felt like whores and they may have been justified in that feeling, but they were certainly well-paid whores. In New York, they hadn't had secretaries, but the movie business was mass culture's great joke on talent. The affectation of "Look, no hands" became the literal truth. Mankiewicz dictated the script while the nurse watched over him and John Houseman stood by in attendance. This was a cut-rate job — Mankiewicz was getting $500 a week for his ghostly labors — but it was still in the royal tradition of screenwriting. Outside the movie business, there has probably never been a writer in the history of the world who got this kind of treatment. There was an urgency about it: Welles and most of the Mercury Theatre company were in Hollywood doing their weekly radio shows and waiting while this odd little group spent the spring of 1940 in Victorville preparing the script for Orson Welles' début in films.

Welles had come to Hollywood the previous July in a burst of publicity, but his first two film projects hadn't got under way. Within a few months of his arrival, he was being jeered at because nothing had happened. Although his contract with R.K.O. gave him freedom from interference, Schaefer and his legal staff had to approve the project and clear the shooting script and, of course, the budget. It had been agreed that his first project would be Conrad's *Heart of Darkness,* which he had already done as a radio drama. He was to play both Marlow and Kurtz, the two leading roles, and it was reported in the trade press that he was working on the script with John Houseman and Herbert Drake, who was the Mercury's press agent. In the latter part of 1939, Welles brought actors out from New York and shot long test sequences, but the budget looked too high to the poverty-stricken studio, and the production was repeatedly postponed. He decided to do something while he was waiting — something that he could start on right away, to get the Mercury actors on the R.K.O. payroll — and he hit on a spy thriller with a political theme: *The Smiler with the Knife*, from the novel by Nicholas Blake (C. Day Lewis). Welles adapted the book himself — "in seven days," according to the trade press — but this project was abandoned almost at once because of differences with Schaefer over casting. (Welles wanted to use Lucille Ball, then a contract player at R.K.O., in the lead, and Schaefer didn't think she could carry the picture. As the whole world knows, she wound up owning the studio, but Schaefer wasn't necessarily wrong; she never did carry a picture.) There was still hope for *Heart of Darkness* — and a lot of money had already been spent on it — but things seemed to be falling apart for the Mercury group. By the end of 1939, Welles was desperate for a subject that would be acceptable to R.K.O. The movie plans were up in the air, and there was dissension within the Mercury group about staying on in Hollywood with nothing definite in sight to work on. Some of the actors left to take jobs elsewhere, and some were beginning to get film roles — a development that upset Welles, because he wanted them to be "new faces" in his first film.

A policy meeting was arranged to discuss the failing fortunes of the group and to decide whether to keep them all in Los Angeles or send some of them back to New York. The more or less administrative heads of the Mercury Theatre met for dinner in an upper room at Chasen's. The group included Welles; Houseman, who had founded the Mercury Theatre with him; two all-purpose assistants, Richard Wilson and William Alland; the press agent, Drake; and several others. Houseman argued that the actors should return to New York, but nothing had been settled by the time the coffee and brandy arrived, and then Welles, in a sudden access of rage, shouted that Houseman wanted to desert him, that Houseman had always been against him, and he threw the coffee warmers — full of Sterno canned heat — at Houseman. He did not throw them very precisely, it seems; he threw them not so much with intent to hit as in Houseman's general direction. Dave Chasen, having been summoned by a waiter, opened the door, and, with the aplomb he had used back in the thirties in vaudeville, when he was the stooge of the comedian Joe Cook, he took one look — a curtain was on fire by then — and closed the door. The men in the room stamped out the fire, and Houseman went home and sent Welles a letter of resignation. The partnership was ended, and a week later Houseman left for New York.

Welles' tantrum and how it ended the partnership that had created the Mercury Theatre was the talk of the actors who gathered around Mankiewicz's bed, and it must have registered on Mankiewicz in a special way: it must have practically thrust on him the recognition of an emotional link between Welles and William Randolph Hearst, whose tantrums had been the stuff of legend among newspapermen for half a century, and whose occasional demonstrations of childishness were the gossip of guests at San Simeon. A week or two after the Chasen's dinner party, Mankiewicz proposed to Welles that they make a "prismatic" movie about the life of a man seen from several different points of view. Even before he went to work in Hollywood and met Hearst, when he was still at the *New York Times,* Mankiewicz was already caught up in the idea of a movie about Hearst. Marion Fisher, the Mankiewicz baby-sitter, whose family lived in the same Central Park West building, was learning to type in high school and Mankiewicz offered to "test her typing." He dictated a screenplay, organized in flashbacks. She recalls that he had barely started on the dictation, which went on for several weeks, when she remarked that it seemed to be about William Randolph Hearst, and he said, "You're a smart girl." Mankiewicz couldn't pay her but she and her parents saw about fifty shows on the theatre tickets he gave them, and it was a great year for Broadway — 1925. Although in the intervening years Mankiewicz had often talked to friends about what a movie Hearst's life would make, his first suggestions to Welles for the "prismatic" movie were Dillinger and, when Welles was cool to that, Aimee Semple McPherson. Only after Welles had rejected that, too, and after they had discussed the possibilities in the life of Dumas, did he propose Hearst. Mankiewicz must have been stalling and playing games to lead Welles on, because although he was interested in both Dillinger and Aimee Semple McPherson, and subsequently did prepare scripts on them, this movie had to be a starring vehicle for Welles, and what major role could Welles play in the life of either Dillinger or Aimee? From what Mankiewicz told friends at the time, when he sprang the name Hearst, Welles leaped at it.

Welles had grown up hearing stories about Hearst from Dr. Maurice Bernstein, who was his guardian after his parents died. Dr. Bernstein was a good friend of Ashton Stevens, who had originally been the drama critic on Hearst's flagship paper, the *San Francisco Examiner,* and had gone on to work for Hearst in Chicago. Welles himself was a Hearst-press "discovery"; it was Ashton Stevens, whom Dr. Bernstein got in touch with, who had publicized the nineteen-year-old Orson Welles when he produced *Hamlet* on a vacant second floor in Illinois. But Welles, being a knowledgeable young man, would have known a great deal about Hearst even without this personal connection, for Hearst was the unifying hatred of all liberals and leftists. Welles, with his sense of the dramatic, would have known at once what a sensational idea a movie about Hearst was. Aimee and Dillinger just didn't have the dimensions that Hearst had; Hearst was even right for Welles *physically.* Welles and Mankiewicz must have enjoyed thinking what a scandal a movie about him would make. Mankiewicz didn't need to have misgivings about repercussions, because the risks would all be Welles'. Schaefer had signed Welles up to a widely publicized four-way contract as producer, director, writer, and actor. It was understood that he would take the credit for the script, just as he did for the scripts of the radio plays. His R.K.O. contract stated that "the screenplay for each picture shall be written by Mr. Orson Welles," and Welles probably took this stipulation as no more than his due — a necessity of his station. He probably accepted the work that others did for him the way modern Presidents accept the work of speech-writers.

The title *American* suggests how Mankiewicz felt about the project. Several years before, in 1933, his friend and drinking companion Preston Sturges had written a big one, an original called *The Power and the Glory,* which, when it was produced, with Spencer Tracy and Colleen Moore in the leading roles, made Tracy a star. *The Power and the Glory* was about a ruthless railroad tycoon who fails in his personal life, and it was told in flashbacks and narration from his funeral. It was an impressive picture, and it was lauded in terms similar to those later used about *Kane.* "Its subject," William Troy wrote in the *Nation,* "is the great American Myth, and its theme is futility." The ballyhoo included putting a bronze tablet in the New York theatre where it opened to commemorate "the first motion picture in which narratage was used as a method of telling a dramatic story." (Hollywood, big on ballyhoo but short on real self-respect, failed to transfer the nitrate negative to safety stock, and modern prints of *The Power and the Glory* are tattered remnants.) Not only is the tycoon treated ambivalently by Sturges but in the boyhood sequence he is injured through his own arrogance, so that he acquires a jagged, lightninglike scar on his hand — the mark of Cain. The idea of the big-businessman as a Cain figure was basic to this genre, which had become popular in the Depression thirties, when many business giants of the twenties were revealed to be swindlers, or, at the very least, ruthless. In another 1933 film, *I Loved a Woman,* a tycoon's mistress sang at the Chicago Opera House. (It was where the tycoons' mistresses did sing in the twenties.) In 1937, Mankiewicz himself had done a trial run on the tycoon theme (with Edward Arnold as a lumber baron) in *John Meade's Woman.* To do Hearst, a much more dangerous man — the only tycoon who was also a demagogue — in a technique similar to Sturges's but from several different points of view would make a really big picture.

But there was a sizable hurdle: How could they get R.K.O. to approve this project? Welles and Mankiewicz went on talking about it for a couple of weeks, while Mankiewicz continued writing the weekly radio shows. When they decided to go ahead and try to slip it over on the studio somehow, Welles still had to find a way to get Mankiewicz to do the writing; the Mercury company couldn't be kept waiting in Los Angeles indefinitely while Mankiewicz wandered loose. Mankiewicz had had to be hauled off to sanatoriums to be dried out too many times for Welles to take chances, and the screenwriters who had worked with Mankiewicz at Metro told too many stories about his losing interest in the scripts he was assigned to and drinking so much during working hours that the other writers would load him into a studio car in mid-afternoon and have the driver haul him home, where Sara would unload him and put him to bed, and he would sleep it off before dinner and be ready for the night's drinking. He had just injured himself again, in his fall at Chasen's, and his bones were being reset, but soon he would be off on the town once more, despite cast or crutches, and there would be no way to hold him down to work. Welles hit on the scheme of packing Mankiewicz off to the country to recuperate. In early January, 1940, Welles flew to New York, and over lunch at "21" the young magician prevailed on Houseman to return to the Coast and do him and the Mercury one last service by running herd on Mankiewicz; only a month had passed since the fiery scene at Chasen's. (It was to be not the last but the next-to-last collaborative project of Welles and Houseman. A week after *American* was done and the troupe had left Victorville, Houseman and Welles were on bad terms again, but

Mankiewicz, who was said to have read every new book by publication date, even when he was in the worst possible shape, told them that they'd be crazy if they didn't buy a new book that was just coming out, and dramatize it. Houseman went to work on it, and as a result Richard Wright's *Native Son* was adapted for the stage and produced so quickly that Welles had it playing in New York by the time *Citizen Kane* opened.)

Both Houseman and Mankiewicz unquestionably had mixed feelings about Welles by the time they found themselves at the guest ranch. Houseman admits that right from the beginning, when Mankiewicz started on the script, they planned to have Welles re-enact his tantrum. It was set for the scene in which Susan leaves Kane (Welles' wife, Virginia, had brought suit for divorce during the month Welles had his tantrum), and Mankiewicz wrote it up rather floridly and with explicit directions, in a passage beginning, "Kane, in a truly terrible and absolutely silent rage . . ." When it was time to shoot the scene, the various members of the group who had been at Chasen's — or had heard about what happened there, and everybody *had* — encouraged Welles to do what he had done that night. Last year, William Alland, describing the making of the film in an interview printed in the magazine of the Directors Guild of America, said:

There was one scene which stands out above all others in my memory; that was the one in which Orson broke up the roomful of furniture in a rage. Orson never liked himself as an actor. He had the idea that he should have been feeling more, that he intellectualized too much and never achieved the emotion of losing himself in a part.

When he came to the furniture-breaking scene, he set up four cameras, because he obviously couldn't do the scene many times. He did the scene just twice, and each time he threw himself into the action with a fervor I had never seen in him. It was absolutely electric; you felt as if you were in the presence of a man coming apart.

Orson staggered out of the set with his hands bleeding and his face flushed. He almost swooned, yet he was exultant. "I really felt it," he exclaimed. "I really felt it!"

Strangely, that scene didn't have the same power when it appeared on the screen. It might have been how it was cut, or because there hadn't been close-in shots to depict his rage. The scene in the picture was only a mild reflection of what I had witnessed on that movie stage.

Writing that scene into the movie was a cruel trick on Welles, designed to make him squirm. He had been built up so much that he was by then the white hope (as it used to be called) of the theatre. In 1938, even George S. Kaufman and Moss Hart had taken him to be that; they had written one of their worst maudlin "serious" plays (and a flop) — *The Fabulous Invalid,* a cavalcade-of-the-American-theatre sort of play — and had modelled its hero on Welles. The hero — the leader of a new acting company — made a classic final curtain speech to his actors:

We haven't got very much money, but we've got youth and, I think, talent. They'll tell you the theatre is dying. I don't believe it. Anything that can bring us together like this, and hold us to this one ideal in spite of everything, isn't going to die. They'll tell you it isn't important, putting makeup on your face and playacting. I don't believe it. It's important to keep alive a thing that can lift men's spirits above the everyday reality of their lives. We mustn't let that die. Remember — you're going to be kicked around, and a lot of the time you're not going to have enough to eat, but you're going to get one thing in return. The chance to write, and act, say the things you want to say, and do the things you want to do. And I think that's enough.

For the people who did much of the work on Welles' projects, the temptation must have been strong to expose what they considered this savior's feet of clay.

The menagerie at Mrs. Campbell's being scarcely a secret, they had many visitors (Welles himself came to dinner once or twice), and several of these visitors, as well as Houseman and Mrs. Alexander, describe how Herman Mankiewicz turned out the script that became *Citizen Kane*. Mankiewicz couldn't go anywhere without help; he sat up, in the cast that covered one leg and went up to his middle, and played cribbage with Mrs. Alexander during the day, while telling her stories about Hearst and Marion Davies and San Simeon. Then, at night, from about eight-thirty to eleven-thirty or twelve, he dictated, and she would type it out so he could have it the next day. Mrs. Alexander recalls that during the first days on the job, when she was fascinated by the romantic significance of "Rosebud" and asked him how the story would turn out, he said, "My dear Mrs. Alexander, I don't know. I'm making it up as I go along." Welles was so deeply entangled in the radio shows and other activities and a romance with Dolores Del Rio at the time the script was being prepared that even when he came to dinner at Victorville, it was mainly a social visit; the secretary didn't meet him until after Mankiewicz had finished dictating the long first draft. Welles probably made suggestions in his early conversations with Mankiewicz, and since he received copies of the work weekly while it was in progress at Victorville, he may have given advice by phone or letter. Later, he almost certainly made suggestions for cuts that helped Mankiewicz hammer the script into tighter form, and he is known to have made

a few changes on the set. But Mrs. Alexander, who took the dictation from Mankiewicz, from the first paragraph to the last, and then, when the first draft was completed and they all went back to Los Angeles, did the secretarial work at Mankiewicz's house on the rewriting and the cuts, and who then handled the script at the studio until after the film was shot, says that Welles didn't write (or dictate) one line of the shooting script of *Citizen Kane*.

Toward the end of the period at the ranch, Mankiewicz began to realize that he'd made a very bad financial deal, and that the credit might be more important than he'd anticipated. After talks with Mrs. Alexander and the Mercury people who visited on weekends, he decided he was going to get screen credit, no matter what his bargain with Welles had been. Meanwhile, Houseman, who says that according to his original agreement to go off to the ranch he was supposed to get some kind of credit, discovered once again, and as so many others had, that it wasn't easy to get your name on anything Orson Welles was involved in. Houseman was apparently fed up with arguments, and he says he waived his claim when he saw how determined Welles was; he left for New York and got started on the preparations for *Native Son*. But Mankiewicz was an experienced Hollywood hand and veteran of credit brawls who kept all his drafts and materials, and a man who relished trouble. He had ample proof of his authorship, and he took his evidence to the Screen Writers Guild and raised so much hell that Welles·was forced to split the credit and take second place in the listing.

At the time the movie came out, Mankiewicz's contribution to the film was generally known. The screen credit was to Herman J. Mankiewicz and Orson Welles. The *Hollywood Reporter* simplified the credit to "Written by Herman Mankiewicz"; Burns Mantle, in his newspaper column, referred to Mankiewicz's having written it; and, of course, Ben Hecht explained to the readers of *PM,* "This movie was not written by Orson Welles. It is the work of Herman J. Mankiewicz." In that period, it was well known that if the producer of a film wanted a screenplay credit it was almost impossible to prevent him from getting it. So many producers took a writing credit as a *droit du seigneur* for a few consultations or suggestions that the Screen Writers Guild later instituted a rule calling for compulsory arbitration whenever a producer sought a credit. Under the present rules of the Guild, Welles' name would probably not have appeared. And so it was by an awful fluke of justice that when Academy Awards night came, and Welles should have got the awards he deserved as director and actor, the award he got (the only Academy Award he has ever got) was as co-author of the Best Original Screenplay.

14.

The Mercury group weren't surprised at Welles' taking a script credit; they'd had experience with this foible of his. Very early in his life as a prodigy, Welles seems to have fallen into the trap that has caught so many lesser men — believing his own publicity, believing that he really was the whole creative works, producer-director-writer-actor. Because he *could* do all these things, he imagined that he *did* do them. (A Profile of him that appeared in *The New Yorker* two years before *Citizen Kane* was made said that "outside the theatre . . . Welles is exactly twenty-three years old.") In the days before the Mercury Theatre's weekly radio shows got a sponsor, it was considered a good publicity technique to build up public identification with Welles' name, so he was credited with just about everything, and

was named on the air as the writer of the Mercury shows. Probably no one but Welles believed it. He had written some of the shows when the program first started, and had also worked on some with Houseman, but soon he had become much too busy even to collaborate; for a while Houseman wrote them, and then they were farmed out. By the time of the *War of the Worlds* broadcast, on Halloween, 1938, Welles wasn't doing any of the writing. He was so busy with his various other activities that he didn't always direct the rehearsals himself, either — William Alland or Richard Wilson or one of the other Mercury assistants did it. Welles might not come in until the last day, but somehow, all agree, he would pull the show together "with a magic touch." Yet when the Martian broadcast became accidentally famous, Welles seemed to forget that Howard Koch had written it. (In all the furor over the broadcast, with front-page stories everywhere, the name of the author of the radio play wasn't mentioned.) Koch had been writing the shows for some time. He lasted for six months, writing about twenty-five shows altogether — working six and a half days a week, and frantically, on each one, he says, with no more than half a day off to see his family. The weekly broadcasts were a "studio presentation" until after the *War of the Worlds* (Campbell's Soup picked them up then), and Koch, a young writer, who was to make his name with the film *The Letter* in 1940 and win an Academy Award for his share in the script of the 1942 *Casablanca,* was writing them for $75 apiece. Koch's understanding of the agreement was that Welles would get the writing credit on the air for publicity purposes but that Koch would have any later benefit, and the copyright was in Koch's name. (He says that it was, however, Welles' idea that he do the Martian show in the form of radio bulletins.) Some years later, when C.B.S. did a program about the broadcast and the panic it had caused, the network re-created parts of the original broadcast and paid Koch $300 for the use of his material. Welles sued C.B.S. for $375,000, claiming that he was the author and that the material had been used without his permission. He lost, of course, but he may still think he wrote it. (He frequently indicates as much in interviews and on television.)

"Foible" is the word that Welles' former associates tend to apply to his assertions of authorship. Welles could do so many different things in those days that it must have seemed almost accidental when he didn't do things he claimed to. Directors, in the theatre and in movies, are by function (and often by character, or, at least, disposition) cavalier toward other people's work, and Welles was so much more talented and magnetic than most directors — and so much younger, too — that people he robbed of credit went on working with him for years, as Koch went on writing more of the radio programs after Welles failed to mention him during the national publicity about the panic. Welles was dedicated to the company, and he was exciting to work with, so the company stuck together, working for love, and even a little bit more money (Koch was raised to $125 a show) when they got a sponsor and, also as a result of the *War of the Worlds* broadcast, the movie contract that took them to Hollywood.

If there was ever a young man who didn't need unearned credits, it was Orson Welles, yet though he was already too big, he must have felt he needed to dazzle the world. Welles was hated in Hollywood long before he'd made a movie; he was hated almost upon his arrival. From time to time, Hollywood used to work up considerable puerile resentment against "outsiders" who dared to make movies. The scope of Welles' reputation seems to have infuriated Hollywood; it was a cultural reproach from the East, and the Hollywood people tried to protect themselves by closing ranks and making Welles a butt of their humor. Gene Lockhart composed a stupid, nasty ditty called "Little Orson Annie," which was sung at Hollywood parties; the name stuck and was used by the columnists, though Hedda Hopper supported him and suggested that Hollywood reserve judgment, and Louella Parsons, on December 31st, selected him as "the most discussed personality to come to the films in 1939." Yet for Welles, with his beard (he was growing it for the Shakespearean production he intended to stage as soon as he could pick up his Hollywood loot), to be ensconced in the Mary Pickford–Buddy Rogers estate, right next door to Shirley Temple, was too much for Hollywood. Welles became the victim of practical jokers. One night when he was dining at Chasen's, an actor cut off his tie with a table knife. Not all the jokes were so Freudian, but they were mostly ugly. Welles had come with an unprecedented contract. Probably the old Hollywoodians not only expected him to fall on his face but hoped he would, so that their mediocrity and prosperity would be vindicated. But Welles was the braggart who makes good. And, despite their resentment, they *were* dazzled by *Citizen Kane*.

15.

The picture got a thunderous reception, even in the Hollywood press. In recent years, the rumor has spread that *Citizen Kane* opened to bad reviews — presumably on the theory that it was so far ahead of its time that it wasn't understood — and this is now recorded in many film histories. But it was very well understood by the press (who would understand a newspaper picture better?), and it got smashing reviews. It isn't, after all, a difficult picture. In some ways, it was probably better understood then than it is now, and, as far as I can determine, it was more highly praised by the American press than any other movie in history. The New York opening of *Citizen Kane,* which had been scheduled for February 14, 1941, finally took place on May 1st, and a week later it opened in Los Angeles. In January, Hedda Hopper had "doubted" whether the picture would ever be released, and some of the trade press had predicted that it wouldn't be. Possibly it wouldn't have been except for the screenings that Welles arranged and the publicity that he got.

The whole industry was already involved in the picture. Although technically Welles had the right of final cut, the editor, Robert Wise, was instructed by the studio, with Welles' consent, to take a print to New York in January. Wise ran it for the heads of all the major companies and their lawyers, and for six weeks he and his then assistant, Mark Robson, who was on the Coast, fussed over the movie, making tiny, nervous changes — mostly a word here or there — that the executives and lawyers hoped would render the picture less objectionable to Hearst. Meanwhile, Schaefer had engaged Time, Inc.'s legal specialist on invasion-of-privacy suits; the lawyer instructed Schaefer that if he made one small cut in the film, no one could win such a suit. The dangerous section was a bit of dialogue by Raymond, the butler, suggesting that the old man was senile. Schaefer says he had no difficulty persuading Welles to agree to the cut. However, at the beginning of March, Hearst sent for Walter Howey, and no one was sure what they might be poking into. "Nor are private lives to be overlooked," Hedda Hopper predicted; and her predictions were the same

as threats. Hearst's maneuvers were in the true Kane spirit: In January, Hedda Hopper had warned that "the refugee situation would be looked into," which meant that there would be pressure for a legal review of whether various imported stars and directors should be allowed to remain in the country, and the industry would be attacked for employing foreigners; that is, refugees from Hitler. Three days after the press previews, the Hearst newspapers, the American Legion, the Veterans of Foreign Wars, and other patriotic organizations went into action to rid radio of "subversives." The "subversives" they were after were William Saroyan, Maxwell Anderson, Marc Connelly, Robert E. Sherwood, Stephen Vincent Benét, Paul Green, Sherwood Anderson, and James Boyd, who were involved with Welles in a series of C.B.S. radio plays on the general theme of freedom, which, although it had been encouraged by the Justice Department, was now condemned as un-American and as tending to promote Communism. Before *Citizen Kane* was released, *PM* reported that Hearst photographers were following Welles "in G-man style," trying to get something on him, while *Variety* reported "persistent inquiries at the draft board as to why Welles hadn't been drafted." It was along about this time that Hearst himself saw the picture. Schaefer says, "Hearst personally sent to me at the studio and asked to see a print, and we let him have it. This was before it opened. There was no response, no comment. Orson knew this." Welles may have feared that Schaefer would buckle unless he squeezed him from the other side, or, as Schaefer claims, it may have been Welles' way of getting more publicity, but, for whatever reason, Welles began to issue threats: he gave R.K.O. the deadline of March 30th for releasing the picture or facing a lawsuit. On March 11th, Welles called a press conference to alert the press to the danger that the film might be suppressed, and gave out this statement:

I believe that the public is entitled to see *Citizen Kane*. For me to stand by while this picture was being suppressed would constitute a breach of faith with the public on my part as producer. I have at this moment sufficient financial backing to buy *Citizen Kane* from R.K.O. and to release it myself. Under my contract with R.K.O. I have the right to demand that the picture be released and to bring legal action to force its release. R.K.O. must release *Citizen Kane*. If it does not do so immediately, I have instructed my attorney to commence proceedings.

I have been advised that strong pressure is being brought to bear in certain quarters to cause the withdrawal of my picture *Citizen Kane* because of an alleged resemblance between incidents in the picture and incidents in the life of Mr. William Randolph Hearst.

Any such attempts at suppression would involve a serious interference with freedom of speech and with the integrity of the moving picture industry as the foremost medium of artistic expression in the country.

There is nothing in the facts to warrant the situation that has arisen. *Citizen Kane* was not intended to have nor has it any reference to Mr. Hearst or to any other living person. No statement to the contrary has ever been authorized by me. *Citizen Kane* is the story of a wholly fictitious character.

The script for *Citizen Kane* was scrutinized and approved by both R.K.O. Radio Pictures and the Hays office. No one in those organizations nor anyone associated with me in the production of the picture believed that it represented anything but psychological analysis of an imaginary individual. I regret exceedingly that anyone should interpret *Citizen Kane* to have a bearing upon any living person, or should impugn the artistic purposes of its producers.

Several of the magazines responded to his plea for the pressure of publicity by reviewing the picture before it opened, obviously with the intention of helping to get it released. A review in *Time* on March 17, 1941, began:

As in some grotesque fable, it appeared last week that Hollywood was about to turn upon and destroy its greatest creation.

It continued:

To most of the several hundred people who have seen the film at private showings, *Citizen Kane* is the most sensational product of the U.S. movie industry. It has found important new techniques in picture-making and story telling. . . . It is as psychiatrically sound as a fine novel. . . . It is a work of art created by grown people for grown people.

In *Newsweek*, also on March 17, 1941, John O'Hara began his review with

It is with exceeding regret that your faithful bystander reports that he has just seen a picture which he thinks must be the best picture he ever saw.

With no less regret he reports that he has just seen the best actor in the history of acting.

Name of picture: *Citizen Kane*.

Name of actor: Orson Welles.

Reason for regret: you, my dear, may never see the picture.

I saw *Citizen Kane* the other night. I am told that my name was crossed off a list of persons who were invited to look at the picture, my name being crossed off because some big shot remembered I had been a newspaperman. So, for the first time in my life, I indignantly denied I was a newspaperman. Nevertheless, I had to be snuck into the showing of *Citizen Kane* under a phony name. That's what's going on about this wonderful picture. Intrigue.

Why intrigue? Well, because. A few obsequious and/or bulbous middle-aged ladies think the picture ought not to be shown, owing to the fact that the picture is rumored to have something to do with a certain publisher, who, for the first time in his life, or maybe the second, shall be nameless. That the nameless publisher might be astute enough to realize that for the first time in his rowdy life he had been made a human being did not worry the loyal ladies. Sycophancy of that kind, like curtseying, is deliberate. The ladies merely wait for a chance to show they can still do it, even if it means cracking a femur. This time I think they may have cracked off more than they can chew. I hope.

Along the way, O'Hara said such things as

My intention is to make you want to see the picture; if possible, to make you wonder why you are not seeing what I think is as good a picture as was ever made. . . . And aside from what it does not lack, *Citizen Kane* has Orson Welles. It is traditional that if you are a great artist, no one gives a damn about you while you're still alive. Welles has had plenty of that. He got a tag put to his name through the Mars thing, just as Scott Fitzgerald, who wrote better than any man in our time, got a Jazz Age tag put to his name. I say, if you plan to have any grandchildren to see and to bore, see Orson Welles so that you can bore your grandchildren with some honesty. There never has been a better actor than Orson Welles. I just got finished saying there never has been a better actor than Orson Welles, and I don't want any of your lip.

Do yourself a favor. Go to your neighborhood exhibitor and ask him why he isn't showing *Citizen Kane*.

The same day — March 17, 1941 — *Life*, which was to run several more features on the movie in the following months, came out with four pages of pictures and a review:

Few movies have ever come from Hollywood with such powerful narrative, such original technique, such exciting photography. Director Welles and Cameraman Gregg Toland do brilliantly with a camera everything Hollywood has always said you couldn't do. They shoot into bright lights, they shoot into the dark and against low ceilings, till every scene comes with the impact of something never seen before. Even the sound track is new. And for narrative Welles has tapped a segment of life fearfully skirted by the U.S. cinema: the swift and brutal biography of a power-mad newspaper tycoon, a man of twisted greatness who buys or bullies his way into everything but friends' love and his nation's respect. To a film industry floundering in a rut, *Citizen Kane* offers enough new channels to explore for five years to come.

Hearst must have known he would be in for a bad time if the picture should be withheld; the Luce magazines — *Time* and *Life* — had always been eager to embarrass him, and certainly wouldn't let the subject drop. (The financial backing that Welles said he had to buy the picture was probably from Henry Luce.) One surmises that Hearst decided not to try to block its release — though the petty harassment of R.K.O. and others involved went on, like a reflex to a blow.

Here is a representative selection from the reviews:

Variety: A film possessing the sure dollar mark.

Times (Bosley Crowther): Suppression of this film would have been a crime. . . . *Citizen Kane* is far and away the most surprising and cinematically exciting motion picture to be seen here in many a moon. . . . It comes close to being the most sensational film ever made in Hollywood.

Herald Tribune (Howard Barnes): A young

man named Orson Welles has shaken the medium wide-awake with his magnificent film, *Citizen Kane*. His biography of an American dynast is not only a great picture; it is something of a revolutionary screen achievement. . . . From any standpoint *Citizen Kane* is truly a great motion picture.

Post (Archer Winsten): It goes without saying this is the picture that wins the majority of 1941's movie prizes in a walk, for it is inconceivable that another will come along to challenge it. . . . Orson Welles with this one film establishes himself as the most exciting director now working. . . . Technically the result marks a new epoch.

PM (Cecelia Ager): Before *Citizen Kane*, it's as if the motion picture was a slumbering monster, a mighty force stupidly sleeping, lying there sleek, torpid, complacent — awaiting a fierce young man to come kick it to life, to rouse it, shake it, awaken it to its potentialities, to show it what it's got. Seeing it, it's as if you never really saw a movie before: no movie has ever grabbed you, pummelled you, socked you on the button with the vitality, the accuracy, the impact, the professional aim, that this one does.

Esquire (Gilbert Seldes): Welles has shown Hollywood how to make movies. . . . He has made the movies young again, by filling them with life.

Cue (Jesse Zunser): It is an astounding experience to watch Orson Welles, 25-year-old Boy Genius of the Western World, in the process of creating on the screen one of the awesome products of his fertile imagination. You come away limp, much as if you had turned into Broadway and suddenly beheld Niagara Falls towering behind the Paramount Building, the Matterhorn looming over Bryant Park, and the Grand Canyon yawning down the middle of Times Square.

Hollywood Reporter: A great motion picture. . . . A few steps ahead of anything that has been made in pictures before.

Chicago Journal of Commerce (Claudia Cassidy): Anyone who has eyes in his head and

ears to hear with will enjoy *Citizen Kane* for the unleashed power of its stature on the screen.

Even Kate Cameron, in the *Daily News,* gave it four stars, and on Sunday, May 4th, Bosley Crowther (though he had some second thoughts of his own) wrote in the *Times,* "The returns are in from most of the local journalistic precincts and Orson Welles' *Citizen Kane* has been overwhelmingly selected as one of the great (if not the greatest) motion pictures of all time. . . ." The *Film Daily* said, "Welles can prepare his mantel for a couple of Oscars."

16.

Had it not been for the delays and the nervous atmosphere that made the picture *seem* unpopular and so *become* unpopular, it might have swept the Academy Awards. It had taken the New York Film Critics Award with ease, but early in 1942, when the 1941 Academy Awards were given, the picture had the aroma of box-office failure — an aroma that frightens off awards in Hollywood. The picture had been nominated in nine categories, and at the ceremony, each time the title or Orson Welles' name was read, there were hisses and loud boos. The prize for the Original Screenplay was perhaps partly a love gesture to Herman Mankiewicz, one of their own; the film community had closed ranks against Orson Welles.

While the picture was being shot, Welles, like a good showman, had done his best to preserve the element of surprise, and he had been smart about keeping a tight, closed set. He didn't want interference from anybody, and even though the R.K.O. executives had read the script, when one of them "dropped in" once to see what was going on, Welles coolly called a halt in the shooting, and the Mercury players went outside and played baseball until he left. There were visitors, of course. Invitations to attend the first official day of shooting were sent to the press, and Welles was simply careful about what he shot that day. And the crew didn't go out to play baseball when Louella Parsons visited the set a few weeks later; they were just very careful, so that even though she had heard rumors that the picture was about Hearst, everything looked so innocent and Welles denied the rumors so disarmingly that she went on giving him an enthusiastic press. (She later described his outfoxing her on this occasion as "one of the classic double crosses of Hollywood.") But Mankiewicz, with his "Don't let this get around," was practically incapable of keeping a secret. He was so proud of his script that he lent a copy to Charles Lederer. In some crazily naïve way, Mankiewicz seems to have imagined that Lederer would be pleased by how good it was. But Lederer, apparently, was deeply upset and took the script to his aunt and Hearst. It went from them to Hearst's lawyers (who marked various passages) before it was returned to Mankiewicz, and thus Hearst and his associates were alerted early to the content of the film. It was probably as a result of Mankiewicz's idiotic indiscretion that the various forces were set in motion that resulted in the cancellation of the première at the Radio City Music Hall, the commercial failure of *Citizen Kane,* and the subsequent failure of Orson Welles. This was how, even before the film was finished, Hearst's minions were in action, and how there was time for Mayer and his people to set about their attempt to suppress the film, and, having failed in that, to destroy it commercially.

In the aftermath of the pressures, and of the disappointing returns on the film, the members of the Academy could feel very courageous about the writing award. Mankiewicz had become a foolhardy hero in taking on Hearst; *Kane* was Mankiewicz's finest moment. They wanted him to have a prize; he deserved it and he needed it. Hollywood loves the luxury of show-business sentimentality, and Hollywood loves a comeback. The members of the Academy destroyed Orson Welles that night, but they probably felt good because their hearts had gone out to crazy, reckless Mank, their own resident loser-genius, the has-been who was washed up in the big studios, who was so far down he had been reduced to writing Welles' radio shows. At the beginning of the thirties, he had been earning $4,000 a week; at the end of the thirties, he was a ghost. What they couldn't know was that *Kane* was Welles' finest moment, too; the reason they couldn't know it was that their failure to back him that night was the turning point. Welles had made *Citizen Kane* at twenty-five, and he seemed to have the world before him. They'd had time to get used to Mank's self-destructiveness, and he'd been down on his luck so long he was easy to love; besides, they admired the pranks that had got him thrown out of one studio after another. Welles was self-destructive in a style they weren't yet accustomed to.

One may speculate that if the members of the Academy had supported Welles and voted *Citizen Kane* Best Picture of the Year, if they had backed the nation's press and their own honest judgment, the picture might have got into the big theatrical showcases despite the pressures against it. If they had, *Kane* might have made money, and things might have gone differently for Welles — and for American movies. The Academy had plenty of sentiment but not enough guts. And so Orson Welles peaked early. Later, as his situation changed and his fortunes sank and *Kane* became the golden opportunity of his youth, his one great chance of freedom to accomplish something, then, when he looked back, he may really have needed to believe what he was quoted as saying in France: "Le seul film que j'aie jamais écrit du premier au dernier mot et pu mener à bien est *Citizen Kane.*" The literal translation is "The only film that I ever wrote from first word to last and was able to bring to a successful issue is *Citizen Kane,*" but I think that what it means is "The picture came out well." What else can it mean when one considers the contributions of Mankiewicz and Toland and all the rest? Men cheated of their due are notoriously given to claiming more than their due. The Academy members had made their token gesture to *Citizen Kane* with the screenplay award. They failed what they believed in; they gave in to the scandal and to the business pressures. They couldn't yet know how much guilt they *should* feel: guilt that by their failure to support *Citizen Kane* at this crucial time — the last chance to make *Kane* a financial success — they had started the downward spiral of Orson Welles, who was to become perhaps the greatest loser in Hollywood history.

17.

Like D. W. Griffith, Orson Welles came into the movies in order to make money so that he could continue in the theatre, and, like Griffith, he discovered that movies were the medium in which he could do what he had barely dreamed of doing in the theatre. Soon — even before he started on *Citizen Kane* — Welles was desperate for money to make movies. It took guile to get *Kane* approved. Robert Wise, whom the head of the R.K.O. editing department had assigned to the picture because he was close to Welles' age, says, "Orson sneaked the project onto R.K.O. He told the studio that he was merely shooting tests." Sets were built, and shooting began on June 29, 1940; the "test shots" were fully produced. The Mercury actors and associates were there anyway, most of them under personal contract to Welles, as Mankiewicz was. But Dorothy Comingore, not a member of the Mercury Theatre but a Hollywood bit player (who, as Linda Winters, had worked in Westerns and with the Three Stooges and in Blondie and Charlie Chan pictures), says that she lived on unemployment checks of $18 a week while she "tested for one month" for the role of Susan Alexander. She adds, "All these tests were incorporated into the film; they were never retaken." After a month, with the studio buzzing about how brilliant the footage was, the movie was practically a *fait accompli,* and Welles was able to bulldoze Schaefer into approving the project. All the people who were already at work on *Citizen Kane* — the cameraman, the grips, the composer, the assistants, and the actors — met at Herman Mankiewicz's house for breakfast, and Welles announced that the picture had been approved and could formally begin. They officially started on July 30, 1940, and they finished "principal photography" eighty-two shooting days later, on October 23, 1940, even though Welles — almost as accident-prone as Mankiewicz — broke his ankle during the scene when he ran down the stairs from Susan's room while yelling that he'd get Boss Gettys.

Yet it took more than guile to function in the motion-picture business at that time. It helped to be mercenary, of course, but what really counted then was not to care *too* much about your work. After *Citizen*

Kane, the contract that gave Welles the right of final cut was cancelled, so he did not have control of *The Magnificent Ambersons,* and it was shortened and mangled. The industry was suspicious of him, and not just because of the scandal of *Kane,* and the general fear of Hearst, and *Kane's* unsatisfactory financial returns. Alva Johnston described the Hollywood attitude toward Welles in an article in the *Saturday Evening Post* in 1942, the year after *Kane* came out:

Big agents soon lost interest in the boy genius. They learned that he wasn't interested in money. Welles became known as a dangerous Red because, when his first picture project was shelved after the studio had wasted a good deal of money on it, he offered to make another picture for nothing.

Genius got a bad name on account of Welles. It was brought into complete disrepute by Saroyan. The gifted Armenian came to Hollywood with a small agent and insisted on working without a salary, leaving it to M-G-M to set a value on his services after his work was completed. He said, "I'll trust the studio." The $10,000,000-a-year agency business is wholly based on the motto "Don't trust the studio." Since the Welles and Saroyan affairs, it has been practically impossible to interest a big agent in an intellectual giant.

When you write straight reporting about the motion-picture business, you're writing satire. Motion-picture executives prefer to do business with men whose values they understand. It's very easy for these executives — businessmen running an art — to begin to fancy that they are creative artists themselves, because they are indeed very much like the "artists" who work for them, because the "artists" who work for them are, or have become, businessmen. Those who aren't businessmen are the Hollywood unreliables — the ones whom, it is always explained to you, the studios can't hire, because they're crazy. As soon as movies became Welles' passion, and he was willing to work on any terms, he was finished in the big studios — they didn't trust him. And so, somehow, Welles aged before he matured — and not just physically. He went from child prodigy to defeated old man, though today, at fifty-five, he is younger by a decade or two than most of the big American directors.

In later years, Welles, a brilliant talker, was to give many interviews, and as his power in the studios diminished, his role in past movies grew larger. Sometimes it seems that his only power is over the interviewers who believe him. He is a masterful subject. The new generation of film historians have their own version of "Look, no hands": they tape-record interviews. Young interviewers, particularly, don't bother to check the statements of their subjects — they seem to regard that as outside their province — and thus leave the impression that the self-aggrandizing stories they record are history. And so, as the years go on, if one trusts what appears in print, Welles wrote not only *Kane* but just about everything halfway good in any picture he ever acted in, and in interviews he's beginning to have directed anything good in them, too. Directors are now the most interviewed group of people since the stars in the forties, and they have told the same stories so many times that not only they believe them, whether they're true or false, but everybody is beginning to.

This worship of the director is cyclical — Welles or Fellini is probably adored no more than von Stroheim or von Sternberg or De Mille was in his heyday — but such worship generally doesn't help in sorting out what went into the making of good pictures and bad pictures. The directors try to please the interviewers by telling them the anecdotes that have got a good response before. The anecdotes are sometimes charming and superficial, like the famous one — now taken for motion-picture history — about how Howard Hawks supposedly discovered that *The Front Page* would be better if a girl played the reporter Hildy, and thus transformed the play into *His Girl Friday* in 1940. ("I was going to prove to somebody that *The Front Page* had the finest modern dialogue that had been written, and I asked a girl to read Hildy's part and I read the editor, and I stopped and I said, 'Hell, it's better between a girl and a man than between two men.'") Now, a charming story is not nothing. Still, this is nothing but a charming and superficial story. *His Girl Friday* turned out joyously, but if such an accident did cause Hawks to see how easy it was to alter the play, he still must have done it rather cynically, in order to make it conform to the box-office patterns then current. By the mid-thirties — after the surprise success of *It Happened One Night* — the new independent, wisecracking girl was very popular, especially in a whole cycle of newspaper pictures with rival girl and boy reporters. Newspaper pictures were now "romantic comedies," and, just as the movies about lady fliers were almost all based on Amelia Earhart, the criminal-mouthpiece movies on William Fallon, and the gossip-column movies on Walter Winchell, the movies about girl reporters were almost all based on the most highly publicized girl reporter — Hearst's Adela Rogers St. Johns. Everybody had already been stealing from and unofficially adapting *The Front Page* in the "wacky" romantic newspaper comedies, and one of these rewrites, *Wedding Present,* in 1936 (by Adela Rogers St. Johns' then son-in-law Paul Gallico), had tough

editor (Cary Grant) and smart girl reporter (Joan Bennett) with square fiancé (Conrad Nagel). This was the mold that *The Front Page* was then squeezed into to become *His Girl Friday,* with Cary Grant, Rosalind Russell, and Ralph Bellamy (already a favorite square from *The Awful Truth*) in the same roles, and Rosalind Russell was so obviously playing Adela Rogers St. Johns that she was dressed in an imitation of the St. Johns girl-reporter striped suit.

Some things that students now, seeing films out of the context of the cycles they were part of, may take to be brilliant inventions were fairly standard; in fact, the public at the time was so familiar with the conventions of the popular comedies that the clichés were frequently spoofed within the pictures. But today, because of the problems peculiar to writing the history of modern mass-art forms, and because of the jumbled circumstances in which movies survive, with knowledge of them acquired in haphazard fashion from television, and from screenings here and there, film enthusiasts find it simpler to explain movies in terms of the genius-artist-director, the schoolbook hero — the man who did it all. Those who admire *Citizen Kane,* which is constructed to present different perspectives on a man's life, seem naïvely willing to accept Welles' view of its making; namely, that it is his sole creation.

Howard Hawks must wonder what the admiration of the young is worth when he learns from them that he invented overlapping dialogue in *His Girl Friday,* since it means that they have never bothered to look at the text of the original Hecht and MacArthur play. Welles, too, has been said to have invented overlapping dialogue, and just about everything else in *Kane.* But unearned praise is insulting, and a burden; Welles sometimes says, "I drag my myth around with me." His true achievements are heavy enough to weigh him down. Welles is a great figure in motion-picture history: he directed what is almost universally acclaimed as the greatest American film of the sound era; he might have become the greatest all-around American director of that era; and in his inability to realize all his artistic potentialities he is the greatest symbolic figure in American film history since Griffith.

18.

In the past few years, I have heard two famous "artist" directors, after showings of their early films, explain how it happened that in the screen credits there was someone else listed for the script. It seems there was this poor guy on the lot who needed a credit desperately, and the company asked the director if he'd give the stumblebum a break; the incompetent turned in some material, but the director couldn't use any of it. Some listeners must swallow this, because in the latest incense-burning book on Josef von Sternberg the screen credits are simply ignored, and he, rather than Ben Hecht, is listed as the author of *Underworld*. Herman J. Mankiewicz has been similarly dropped from one film after another. The directors' generosity to those poor credit-hungry guys seems to have cutoff points in time (the directors' creative roles get bigger when the writers are dead) and in space (when the directors are interviewed abroad). Orson Welles, however, didn't need time or distance; he omitted any mention of his writer right from the start. (This custom is now being followed by many directors.) In later years, when he has been specifically asked by interviewers whether Mankiewicz wrote the scenario for *Citizen Kane,* he has had a set reply. "Everything concerning Rosebud belongs to him,"

he has said. Rosebud is what was most frequently criticized in the movie, and Gilbert Seldes, in one of the most solid and intelligent reviews of *Kane* (in *Esquire*), called it "a phony" and "the only bit of stale stuff in the picture." Welles himself has said, "The Rosebud gimmick is what I like least about the movie. It's a gimmick, really, and rather dollar-book Freud."

Welles may have been goaded into malice; he had probably never come up against a man so well equipped to deal with him as Mankiewicz. Welles, who used to tell stories about how when he was seventeen he became a *torero* in Seville and entered several *corridas* and was billed on the posters as "The American," may have got a few welts, starting with Mankiewicz's original title — *American*. When Welles read the script, he must certainly have recognized what he was caught in. There's no doubt that Welles — the fabulous Orson Welles — wasn't accustomed to sharing credit. However, his persistent lack of generosity toward Mankiewicz started at the time the movie came out, and it may have its basis in a very specific grievance. Mankiewicz may have outsmarted Welles on the credits more than once. Nunnally Johnson says that while *Citizen Kane* was being shot, Mankiewicz told him that he had received an offer of a ten-thousand-dollar bonus from Welles (through Welles' "chums") to hold to the original understanding and keep his name off the picture. Mankiewicz said that Welles had been brooding over the credits, that he could see how beautiful they would be: "Produced by Orson Welles. Directed by Orson Welles. Starring Orson Welles." It was perfect until he got to "Herman J. Mankiewicz" in the writing credit, which spoiled everything. Mankiewicz said he was tempted by Welles' offer. As usual, he needed money, and, besides, he was fearful of what would happen when the picture came out — he might be blackballed forever. William Randolph Hearst, like Stalin, was known to be fairly Byzantine in his punishments. At the same time, Mankiewicz knew that *Citizen Kane* was his best work, and he was proud of it. He told Johnson that he went to Ben Hecht with his dilemma, and that Hecht, as prompt with advice as with scripts, said, "Take the ten grand and double-cross the son of a bitch."

I asked Nunnally Johnson if he thought Mankiewicz's story was true, and Mankiewicz actually had got the offer and had taken Hecht's advice. Johnson replied, "I like to believe he did." It's not unlikely. Mankiewicz wrote the first draft in about three months and tightened and polished it into the final shooting script of *Citizen Kane* in a few more weeks, and he probably didn't get more than eight or nine thousand dollars for the whole job; according to the cost sheets for the movie, the screenplay cost was $34,195.24, which wasn't much, even for that day, and the figure probably includes the salary and expenses of John Houseman and the others at Victorville. Mankiewicz may easily have felt he deserved an extra ten thousand. "An Irish bum," Johnson calls him — and if that makes him sound lovable, the operative word is still "bum." If Mankiewicz made up the story he told Johnson — and he was probably capable of such juicy slander — this kind of invention may be a clue to why Welles tries to turn the credit into blame. And if Mankiewicz did get the offer, did take the money, and did double-cross Welles, this might equally well explain why Welles doesn't want Mankiewicz to get any honor.

But Welles needed Mankiewicz. Since sound came in, almost every time an actor has scored in a role and become a "star," it has been because the role provided a realistic base for contradictory elements. Welles has never been able to write this kind of vehicle for himself. *Kane* may be a study of egotism and a movie about money and love, but it isn't just another movie about a rich man who isn't loved; it's a scandalously unauthorized, muckraking biography of a man who was still alive and — though past his peak influence — still powerful, so it conveyed shock and danger, and it drew its strength from its reverberations in the life of the period. Mankiewicz brought to the film the force of journalism. The thirties had been full of movie biographies of tycoons and robber barons, and some, like *The Power and the Glory,* were complexly told, but even Preston Sturges, as if in awe of the material, had taken a solemn, almost lachrymose approach to the money-doesn't-bring-happiness theme. Mankiewicz did it better: the prismatic technique turned into a masterly juggling act. There's an almost palpable sense of enjoyment in the script itself; Mankiewicz was skillful at making his points through comedy, and frequently it's higher, blacker comedy than was customary in the thirties pictures. Welles is a different kind of writer — theatrical and Gothic, not journalistic, and not *organized.* His later thrillers are portentous without having anything to portend, sensational in a void, entertaining thrillers, often, but *mere* thrillers.

Lacking the realistic base and the beautifully engineered structure that Mankiewicz provided, Welles has never again been able to release that charming, wicked rapport with the audience that he brought to *Kane* both as actor and as director (or has been able to release it only in distorted form, in self-satire and self-humiliation). He has brought many qualities to film — and there was perhaps a new, mellowed vitality in his work in the flawed *Falstaff* of a few years ago — but he has brought no more great original characters. In his movies, he can create an atmosphere but not a base. And without that the spirit that makes Kane so likable a bastard is missing. Kane, that mass of living contradictions, was conceived by Mankiewicz, an atheist who was proud of his kosher home, a man who was ambivalent about *both* Hearst and Welles.

However, things that get printed often enough begin to seep into the general consciousness of the past, so there is a widespread impression that Welles wrote *Citizen Kane*. And even if one hadn't heard that he wrote it, and despite the presence in the film of so many elements and interests that are unrelated to Welles' other work (mundane activities and social content are not his forte), Kane and Welles are identified in our minds. This is not only a tribute to Welles as an actor but a backhanded tribute to Mankiewicz, who wrote the role for Welles the actor and wrote Welles the capricious, talented, domineering prodigy into the role, combining Welles' personality and character traits with Hearst's life in publishing and politics and acquisition.

If one asks how it is that Herman J. Mankiewicz, who wrote the film that many people think is the greatest film they've ever seen, is almost unknown, the answer must surely be not just that he died too soon but that he outsmarted himself. As a result of his wicked sense of humor in drawing upon Welles' character for Kane's, his own authorship was obscured. Sensing the unity of Kane and Welles, audiences assume that Kane is Welles' creation, that Welles is playing "the role he was born to play," while film scholars, seeing the material from Welles' life in the movie, interpret the film as Welles working out

autobiographical themes. It is a commonplace in theatre talk to say that Olivier *is* Archie Rice or Olivier *is* Macbeth without assuming that the actor has conceived the role, but in movies we don't see other actors in the same role (except in remakes, which are usually very different in style), and film is so vivid and the actor so large and so close that it is a common primitive response to assume that the actor invented his lines. In this case, the primitive response is combined with the circumstances that Welles' name had been heavily featured for years, that the role was a new creation, that the movie audience's image of Welles was set by this overpowering role, in which they saw him for the first time, and that not only was the role partly based on him but he began to live up to it. Herman Mankiewicz died, and his share faded from knowledge, but Welles carries on in a baronial style that always reminds us of Kane. Kane seems an emanation of Welles, and if Mankiewicz didn't take the ten thousand, he might just as well have, because he helped stamp Welles all over the film.

19.

James Agee, who didn't begin reviewing until later in 1941, wrote several years afterward that Welles had been "fatuously overrated as a 'genius,'" and that he himself, annoyed by all the talk, had for a while underrated him. At the time the film was released, the most perceptive movie critic in the United States was Otis Ferguson (an early volunteer and early casualty in the Second World War), on the *New Republic*. Ferguson saw more clearly than anybody else what was specifically good and bad in *Kane,* and though he was wrong, I think, in maintaining that unobtrusive technique is the only good technique, he did perceive that *Citizen Kane* challenged this concept.

One of the games that film students some-times play is to judge a director on whether you have the illusion that the people on the screen will go on doing what they're doing after the camera leaves them. Direc-tors are rated by how much time you think elapsed before the actors grabbed their coats or ordered a sandwich. The longer the time, the more of a film man the di-rector is said to be; when a director is stage-oriented, you can practically see the actors walking off the set. This game doesn't help in judging a film's content, but it's a fairly reliable test of a director's film tech-nique; one could call it a test of movie believability. However, it isn't applicable to *Citizen Kane.* You're perfectly well aware that the people won't go on doing what they're doing — that they have, indeed, completed their actions on the screen. *Kane* depends not on naturalistic believability but on our enjoyment of the very fact that those actions *are* completed, and that they all fit into place. This bravura is, I think, the picture's only true originality, and it wasn't an intentional challenge to the con-cept of unobtrusive technique but was (mainly) the result of Welles' discovery of — and his delight in — the fun of making movies.

The best American directors in the thir-ties had been developing an unpretentious American naturalism; modern subjects and the advent of sound had freed them from the heavy dead hand of Germanic stage lighting and design. And so Ferguson was dismayed to see this all come back, and it *was* depressing that the critics who had always fallen for the synthetic serious were bowing and scraping and calling the picture "deep" and "realistic." Probably so many people called it realistic because the social satire made contact with what they felt about Hearst and the country; when they used the term, they were referring to the content rather than the style. But it was the "retrogressive" style that upset Ferguson — because it was when Orson Welles, an "art-ist" director, joined the toughness and cynicism and the verbal skills of the thirties to that incomparable, faintly absurd, won-derfully overblown style of his that people said "art." Where Ferguson went wrong was in not recognizing one crucial element: that the unconcealed — even flaunted — pleasure that Welles took in all that clap-trap made it new.

And it has kept it new. Even a number of those who worked on *Kane,* such as Houseman and Dorothy Comingore, have observed that the film seems to improve with the years. At the time, I got more simple, frivolous pleasure from Preston Sturges's *The Lady Eve,* which had come out a few months earlier, and I found more excitement in John Huston's *The Maltese Falcon,* which came out a few months later. At the time (I was twenty-one), I enjoyed *Kane* for the performances and the wit, but I was very conscious of how shallow the iconoclasm was. I don't think I was wrong, exactly, but now the movie seems marvel-lous to me. It's an *exuberant* shallow icono-clasm, and that youthful zest for shock and for the Expressionist theatricality seems to transform the shallowness. Now the movie sums up and preserves a period, and the youthful iconoclasm is preserved in all its freshness — even the freshness of its callow-ness. Now that the political theme (in its specific form, that is) is part of the past, the naïveté and obviousness fade, and what re-mains is a great American archetype and a popular legend — and so it has a strength that makes the artificially created comic world of a movie like *The Lady Eve* disap-pear by comparison. *Citizen Kane* has such energy it drives the viewer along. Though

Mankiewicz provided the basic apparatus for it, that magical exuberance which fused the whole scandalous enterprise was Welles'. Works of art are enjoyed for different reasons in different periods; it may even be one of the defining characteristics of a lasting work of art that it yields up different qualities for admiration at different times. Welles' "magic," his extraordinary pleasure in playacting and illusion and in impressing an audience — what seems so charming about the movie now — was what seemed silly to me then. It was bouncy Pop Gothic in a period when the term "comic strip" applied to works of art was still a term of abuse. Now Welles' discovery of moviemaking — and the boyishness and excitement of that discovery — is preserved in *Kane* the way the snow scene is preserved in the glass ball.

Seeing the movie again recently, I liked the way it looked; now that the style no longer boded a return to the aestheticism of sets and the rigidly arranged figures of the German silents, I could enjoy it without misgivings. In the thirties, Jean Renoir had been using deep focus (that is, keeping the middle range and the background as clear as the foreground) in a naturalistic way. The light seemed (and often was) "natural." You looked at a scene, and the drama that you saw going on in it was just part of that scene, and so you had the sense of discovering it for yourself, of seeing drama in the midst of life. This was a tremendous relief from the usual studio lighting, which forced your attention to the dramatic action in the frame, blurred the rest, and rarely gave you a chance to feel that the action was part of anything larger or anything continuous. In Welles' far more extreme use of deep focus, and in his arrangement of the actors in the compositions, he swung back to the most co-

ercive use of artificial, theatrical lighting. He used light like a spotlight on the stage, darkening or blacking out the irrelevant. He used deep focus not for a naturalistic effect but for the startling dramatic effect of having crucial action going on in the background (as when Kane appears in a distant doorway). The difference between Renoir's style and Welles' style seems almost literally the difference between day and night. Welles didn't have (nor did he, at that time, need) the kind of freedom Renoir needed and couldn't get in Hollywood — the freedom to shoot outside the studio and to depart from the script and improvise. *Kane* is a studio-made film — much of it was shot in that large room at R.K.O. where, a few years earlier, Ginger Rogers and Fred Astaire had danced their big numbers. However, Welles had the freedom to try out new solutions to technical problems, and he made his theatrical technique work spectacularly. Probably it was the first time in American movies that Expressionism had ever worked for comic and satiric effects (except in bits of some of the early spoof horror films), and probably it would have been impossible to tell the *Kane* story another way without spending a fortune on crowds and set construction. Welles' method is a triumph of ingenuity in that the pinpoints of light in the darkness conceal the absence of detailed sets (a chair or two and a huge fireplace, and one thinks one is seeing a great room), and the almost treacherously brilliant use of sound conceals the absence of crowds. We see Susan at the *deserted* cabaret; we see her from the back on the opera-house stage and we imagine that she is facing an audience; we get a sense of crowds at the political rally without seeing them. It was Welles' experience both in the theatre and in radio that enabled him to produce a huge historical film on a shoe-string; he produced the *illusion* of a huge historical film.

But, seeing *Kane* now, I winced, as I did the first time, at the empty virtuosity of the shot near the beginning when Kane, dying, drops the glass ball and we see the nurse's entrance reflected in the glass. I noticed once again, though without being bothered by it this time, either, that there was no one in the room to hear the dying Kane say "Rosebud." I was much more disturbed by little picky defects, like the obtrusive shot up to the bridge before the reporter goes into the hospital. What is strange about reseeing a movie that one reacted to fairly intensely many years ago is that one may respond exactly the same way to so many details and *be aware* each time of having responded that way before. I was disappointed once again by the clumsily staged "cute" meeting of Kane and Susan, which seemed to belong to a routine comedy, and I thought the early scenes with Susan were weak not just because while listening to her dull, sentimental singing Welles is in a passive position and so can't animate the scenes but — and mainly — because the man of simple pleasures who would find a dumb girl deeply appealing does not tie in with the personality projected by Orson Welles. (And as Welles doesn't project any sexual interest in either Kane's first wife, Emily, or in Susan, his second wife, we don't know how to interpret Susan's claim that he just likes her voice.) Most of the newspaper-office scenes looked as clumsily staged as ever, and the first appearance of Bernstein, Kane's business manager, arriving with a load of furniture, was still confusing. (He seems to be a junk dealer — probably because an earlier scene in *American* introducing him was eliminated.) I disliked again the attempt to wring hu-

mor out of the sputtering confusion of Carter, the old Dickensian editor. It's a scene like the ones Mankiewicz helped prepare for the Marx Brothers, but what was probably intended to make fun of a stuffed shirt turned into making fun of a helpless old man trying to keep his dignity, which is mean and barbarous. I still thought Susan became too thin a conception, and more shrill and shrewish than necessary, and, as Emily, Ruth Warrick was all pursed lips — a stereotype of refinement. I was still uncomfortable during the visit to Jed Leland in the hospital; Leland's character throughout is dependent on Joseph Cotten's obvious charm, and the sentimental-old-codger bit in this sequence is really a disgrace. The sequence plays all too well at a low conventional level — pulling out easy stops. I still didn't see the function of the sequence about Kane's being broke and losing control of his empire, since nothing followed from it. (I subsequently discovered that things weren't going well on the set at one point, and Welles decided to go back to this scene, which had been in an earlier draft and had then been eliminated. What it coördinated with was, unfortunately, not restored.) This sequence also has the most grating bad line in the movie, when Kane says, "You know, Mr. Bernstein, if I hadn't been very rich, I might have been a really great man."

What's still surprising is how well a novice movie director handled so many of the standard thirties tricks and caricatures — the device of the alternative newspaper headlines, for example, and the stock explosive, hand-waving Italian opera coach (well played by Fortunio Bonanova). The engineering — the way the sequences are prepared for and commented on by preceding sequences, the way the five accounts tie together to tell the story — seems as ingenious as ever; though one is aware that the narrators are telling things they couldn't have witnessed, one accepts this as part of the convention. The cutting (which a reading of the script reveals to have been carried out almost exactly as it was planned) is elegantly precise, and some sequences have a good, sophomoric musical-comedy buoyancy.

What had changed for me — what I had once enjoyed but now found almost mysteriously *beautiful* — was Orson Welles' performance. An additional quality that old movies acquire is that people can be seen as they once were. It is a pleasure we can't get in theatre; we can only hear and read descriptions of past fabulous performances. But here in *Kane* is the young Welles, and he seems almost embarrassed to be exposed as so young. Perhaps he *was* embarrassed, and that's why he so often hid in extravagant roles and behind those old-man false faces. He seems unsure of himself as the young Kane, and there's something very engaging (and surprisingly *human*) about Welles unsure of himself; he's a big, overgrown, heavy boy, and rather sheepish, one suspects, at being seen as he is. Many years later, Welles remarked, "Like most performers, I naturally prefer a live audience to that lie-detector full of celluloid." Maybe his spoiled-baby face was just too nearly perfect for the role, and he knew it, and knew the hostile humor that lay behind Mankiewicz's putting so much of him in the role of Hearst the braggart self-publicist and making Kane so infantile. That statement of principles that Jed sends back to Kane and that Kane then tears up must surely refer to the principles behind the co-founding of the Mercury Theatre by Welles and Houseman. Lines like Susan's "You're not a professional magician, are you?" may have made Welles flinch. And

it wasn't just the writer who played games on him. There's the scene of Welles eating in the newspaper office, which was obviously caught by the camera crew, and which, to be "a good sport," he had to use. Welles is one of the most self-conscious of actors — it's part of his rapport with the audience — and this is what is so nakedly revealed in this role, in which he's playing a young man his own age and he's insecure (and with some reason) about what's coming through. Something of the young, unmasked man is revealed in these scenes — to be closed off forever after.

Welles picks up assurance and flair as Kane in his thirties, and he's also good when Kane is just a little older and jowly. I think there's no doubt that he's more sure of himself when he's playing this somewhat older Kane, and this is the Kane we remember best from the first viewing — the brash, confident Kane of the pre-election-disaster period. He's so fully — classically — American a showoff one almost regrets the change of title. But when I saw the movie again it was the younger Kane who stayed with me — as if I had been looking through a photograph album and had come upon a group of pictures of an old friend, long dead, as he had been when I first met him. I had almost forgotten Welles in his youth, and here he is, smiling, eager, looking forward to the magnificent career that everyone expected him to have.

20.

Just as Welles suggested the radio-bulletin approach to the H. G. Wells landing-of-the-Martians material to Howard Koch, he may very well have suggested the "March of Time" summary of Hearst's career in his early talks with Mankiewicz. Welles had worked as an actor for the "March of Time" radio program in 1934 and 1935, and he had worked steadily as a narrator and radio actor (his most famous role was the lead in the popular weekly mystery show "The Shadow") until he went to Hollywood. The "March of Time" is exactly the kind of idea the young Welles *would* have suggested. It's the sort of technique that was being used in the experimental theatre of the late thirties — when the Federal Theatre Project (in which Welles and Houseman had worked together) staged the documentary series "The Living Newspaper," and when members of the Group Theatre and other actors were performing anti-Fascist political cabaret. The imitation "March of Time" was not a new device, even in movies; it had already been used, though humorlessly, to convey the fact that a theme was current, part of "today's news," and to provide background information — as in *Confessions of a Nazi Spy,* of 1939. What was needed to transform that device and make it the basis for the memorable parody in *Citizen Kane* was not only Welles' experience and not only his "touch" but the great sense of mischief that he and Mankiewicz shared. The smug manner of the "March of Time" was already a joke to many people; when I was a student at Berkeley in the late thirties, there was always laughter in the theatres when the "March of Time" came on, with its racy neo-conservatism and its ritual pomposity — with that impersonal tone, as if God above were narrating. There was an element of unconscious self-parody in the important tone of the "March of Time," as in all the Luce enterprises, and, in his script, Mankiewicz pushed it further. He used consciously those elements which part of the public already found funny, bringing into a mass medium what was already a subject for satire among the knowledgeable.

Mankiewicz's "On Approaching Forty" had not appeared in *The New Yorker,* but a few weeks after it was printed, in 1936, Wolcott Gibbs, who was to take Mankiewicz's old chair as *The New Yorker*'s drama critic (and who was the first occupant of that chair not to emigrate to Hollywood), published the celebrated Profile "Time — Fortune — Life — Luce," which was written in mock Timese ("Backward ran sentences until reeled the mind," and so on, concluding with "Where it all will end, knows God!"), and this was probably not merely the spur to Mankiewicz but the competition. Mankiewicz's pastiche was fully worked out in the first long draft of the script, the processed prose and epigrams already honed to perfection ("For forty years appeared in Kane newsprint no public issue on which Kane papers took no stand. No public man whom Kane himself did not support or denounce — often support, then denounce"). And even on paper — without Welles' realization of the plan — the section is good enough to invite the comparison that I suspect Mankiewicz sought with the Gibbs parody. (Mankiewicz's widow keeps the Oscar statuette for *Citizen Kane* on the mantel, along with the latest *Who's Who in America* with the marker set at her sons' listings, and on the shelf next to the mantel are the bound volumes of *The New Yorker* in which her husband's reviews appeared.)

Part of the fun of the "March of Time" parody for the audiences back in 1941 was that, of course, we kept *recognizing* things about Hearst in it, and its daring meant great suspense about what was to follow in the picture. But Mankiewicz tried to do more with this parody than is completely evident either in the final script or in the film itself. He tried to use the "March of Time" as a historical framing device to close one era and open the next, with Hearstian journalism giving way to the new

Luce empire. In the movie, it seems a structural gimmick — though a very cleverly *used* gimmick, which is enjoyable in itself. In Mankiewicz's original conception, in the long first-draft *American,* which ran three hundred and twenty-five pages, that device is more clearly integral to the theme. In Mankiewicz's conception, the Hearst-Kane empire is doomed: Kane's own death is being "sent" to the world by the filmed "March of Time" (called "News on the March" in the movie), which means the end of the newspaper business as Hearst knew it. The funny thing is that Mankiewicz, in commenting on Hearst's lack of vision, overestimated Luce's vision. After Luce took news coverage from newspapers into newsmagazines, he moved into photo-journalism and then into news documentaries, but he didn't follow through on what he had started, and he failed to get into television production. Now, after *his* death, the Luce organization is trying to get back into film activities.

In Mankiewicz's original conception, the historical line of succession was laid out as in a chronicle play. Hearst supplanted the old-style quiet upper-class journalism with his penny-dreadful treatment of crime and sex and disasters, his attacks on the rich, his phony lawsuits against the big corporations that he called "predators," his screaming patriotism, his faked photographs, and his exploitation of superstition, plus puzzles, comics, contests, sheet music, and medical quackery. His youthful dedication to the cause of the common people declined into the cheap chauvinism that infected everything and helped to turn the readers into a political mob. The irony built into the structure was that his own demise should be treated in the new, lofty style of Luce.

And it was in terms of this framework that the elements of admiration in the ambivalent portrait of Kane made sense. Hearst represented a colorful kind of journalism that was already going out. Mankiewicz was summing up the era of *The Front Page* at the end of it, and was treating it right at its source in the American system that made it possible for a rich boy to inherit the power to control public opinion as his own personal plaything. *American* (and, to a lesser degree, *Citizen Kane*) was a there-were-giants-in-those-days valedictory to the old-style big scoundrels. The word had been used straight by Mrs. Fremont Older in 1936 when she published the authorized biography, *William Randolph Hearst, American.* "American" was Hearst's shibboleth; his Sunday magazine section was the *American Weekly,* and he had been changing his newspaper titles to include the word "American" whenever possible ever since Senator Henry Cabot Lodge accused him of being un-American in those days after the McKinley assassination when Hearst was hanged in effigy. Hearst's attacks on McKinley as "the most despised and hated creature in the hemisphere" had culminated in an editorial that said "Killing must be done" shortly before it was. When the storm died down, Hearst became super-American. For Mankiewicz, Hearst's Americanism was the refuge of a scoundrel, though by no means his last refuge; *that,* in the first draft, was clearly blackmail. What the title was meant to signify was indicated by Kane in the "News on the March" segment when he said, "I am, have been, and will be only one thing — an American." That was pure flag-waving Pop before we had a name for it: "American" as it was used by the American Legion and the Daughters of the American Revolution. In addition, Mankiewicz may have wanted to score off his movie friends who since the middle thirties — the period of the Popular

Front — had also been draping themselves in the flag. In that period, the Communist left had become insistent about its Americanism, in its rather embarrassing effort to tout American democracy, which it had called "imperialism" until the U.S.S.R. sought the United States as an ally against Hitler. In the later title, "Citizen" is similarly ironic; Hearst, the offspring of an economic baron, and himself a press lord and the master of San Simeon, was a "citizen" the way Louis XIV at Versailles was a citizen. And joining the word to "Kane" (Cain) made its own point.

Both the parodistic use of Timese and the facelessness of Luce's company men served a historical purpose in the first script. But *American* was much too long and inclusive and loose, and much too ambitious, and Mankiewicz rapidly cut it down (copies of these gradually shorter drafts were saved) until it reached the hundred and fifty-six pages of the final shooting script — which still made for a then unusually long picture, of a hundred and nineteen minutes. In the trimming, dialogue that was crucial to the original dramatic conception of the Hearst-Luce succession was cut. (In terms of the final conception, though, it's perfectly clear why.) This deleted exchange between Thompson, the investigating reporter for the Rawlston (Luce) organization, and Raymond, Kane's butler, makes the point about the line of succession from Hearst to Luce all too explicitly:

THOMPSON

Well, if you get around to your memoirs — don't forget, Mr. Rawlston wants to be sure of getting first chance. We pay awful well for long excerpts.

RAYMOND

Maybe he'd like to buy the excerpts of what Mr. Kane said about him.

THOMPSON
Huh?

RAYMOND

He thought Rawlston would break his neck sooner or later. He gave that weekly magazine of yours three years.

THOMPSON

(*Smugly*) He made a bit of a mistake.

RAYMOND

He made a lot of mistakes.

Welles, who did such memorable casting in the rest of the movie, used a number of his own faceless executive assistants in the vapid roles of the Luce men. They are the performers in *Citizen Kane* that nobody remembers, and they didn't go on to become actors. William Alland, whose voice was fine as the voice of "News on the March" but who was a vacuum as Thompson, the reporter, became a producer and investment broker; another of Welles' assistants, Richard Wilson, who also played a reporter, is now a director (*Three in the Attic*); still another, Richard Barr, is the well-known New York theatrical producer. Among the "News on the March" men, there were some bit players who did have potential faces (Alan Ladd was one of them), but they weren't presented as personalities. Nevertheless, in a movie as verbally explicit as *Citizen Kane* the faceless idea doesn't really come across. You probably don't get the intention behind it in *Kane* unless you start thinking about the unusual feebleness of the scenes with the "News on the March" people and about the fact that though Thompson is a principal in the movie in terms of how much he appears, there isn't a shred of characterization in his lines or in his performance; he is such a shadowy presence that you may even have a hard time remembering whether you ever saw his face, though this movie introduced to the screen a large group of performers who made strong, astonishingly distinct impressions, sometimes in very brief roles. Perhaps the acting and the group movement of the faceless men needed to be more stylized, the dialogue more satirical; as it was done, it's just dull rather than purposefully blank. Welles probably thought it didn't matter how bad these actors were, because they should be colorless anyway; after R.K.O. gave him the go-ahead on the project, he didn't reshoot the test scene he had made of the projection-room sequence. But the movie misses on the attitudes *behind* Luce's new journalism. It's true that for the practitioners of Timese impersonality becomes their personal style and reporters become bureaucrats, but there's also a particular aura of programmed self-importance and of awareness of power — the ambitiousness of colorless people.

Among the minor absurdities of the script is that the "News on the March" men never think of sending a cameraman along with the inquiring reporter, though Gable had just played a newsreel cameraman in *Too Hot to Handle,* in 1938, and though in *The Philadelphia Story,* which had opened on Broadway in 1939, and which Mankiewicz's brother Joe produced for the screen in 1940, while *Kane* was being shot, the magazine team, also obviously from Luce, includes a photographer. There's something rather pathetic — almost as if *Kane* were a Grade B movie that didn't have a big enough budget for a few extra players — about that one lonely sleuthing reporter travelling around the country while a big organization delays the release of an important newsreel documentary on the head

of a rival news chain. Maybe Mankiewicz, despite his attempt to place Hearst historically through the "March of Time" framework, still thought in terms of the older journalism and of all the gimmicky movies about detective-reporters. And Mankiewicz was by temperament a reckless, colorful newspaperman. That deleted material about the Luce organization's wanting Raymond's memoirs, with Raymond's teaser "He made a lot of mistakes," is part of an elaborate series of scandalous subplots, closely paralleling scandals in Hearst's life, that were cut out in the final script. In the movie, Susan says to Thompson, "Look, if you're smart, you'll get in touch with Raymond. He's the butler. You'll learn a lot from him. He knows where all the bodies are buried." It's an odd, cryptic speech. In the first draft, Raymond *literally* knew where the bodies were buried: Mankiewicz had dished up a nasty version of the scandal sometimes referred to as the Strange Death of Thomas Ince. Even with this kind of material cut down to the barest allusions, Mankiewicz, in *Citizen Kane,* treated the material of Hearst's life in Hearstian yellow-journalism style.

21.

Welles is right, of course, about Rosebud — it *is* dollar-book Freud. But it is such a primitive kind of Freudianism that, like some of the movie derivations from Freud later in the forties — in *The Seventh Veil,* for instance — it hardly seems Freudian at all now. Looking for "the secret" of a famous man's last words is about as phony as the blind-beggar-for-luck bit, yet it does "work" for some people; they go for the idea that Rosebud represents lost maternal bliss and somehow symbolizes Kane's loss of the power to love or be loved. The one significant change from Hearst's life —

Kane's separation from his parents — seems to be used to explain Kane, though there is an explicit disavowal of any such intention toward the end. Someone says to Thompson, "If you could have found out what Rosebud meant, I bet that would've explained everything." Thompson replies, "No, I don't think so. No. Mr. Kane was a man who got everything he wanted, and then lost it. Maybe Rosebud was something he couldn't get or something he lost. Anyway, it wouldn't have explained anything. I don't think any word can explain a man's life. No. I guess Rosebud is just a piece in a jigsaw puzzle, a missing piece."

Nevertheless, the structure of the picture — searching for the solution to a mystery — and the exaggerated style make it appear that Rosebud *is* the key to Kane's life, and the public responds to what is presented dramatically, not to the reservations of the moviemakers. Rosebud has become part of popular culture, and people remember it who have forgotten just about everything else in *Citizen Kane;* the jokes started a week before the movie opened, with a child's sled marked "Rosebud" dragged on-stage in the first act of *Native Son,* and a couple of years ago, in *Peanuts,* Snoopy walked in the snow pulling a sled and Charlie Brown said, "Rosebud?" The Rosebud of Rosebud is as banal as Rosebud itself. It seems that as a child Herman Mankiewicz had had a sled, which may or may not have carried the label "Rosebud" (his family doesn't remember); he wasn't dramatically parted from the sled, but he once had a bicycle that was stolen, and he mourned that all his life. He simply put the emotion of the one onto the other.

Though Rosebud was in the long first draft, it didn't carry the same weight there, because the newspaper business itself undermined Kane's idealism. In that draft, Kane,

like Hearst, in order to reach the masses he thought he wanted to serve and protect, built circulation by turning the newspapers into pulp magazines, and, in order to stay in business and expand, squeezed non-advertisers. The long script went as far as to show that, in the process of becoming one of the mighty, Kane-Hearst, like Louis B. Mayer and so many other tycoons, developed close ties to the underworld. Mankiewicz was trying to give a comprehensive view of the contradictions that emerge when an idealist attempts to succeed in business and politics. Fragments of this are left, but their meaning is no longer clear. For example, the point of the sequence of Kane's buying up the staff of the *Chronicle,* the paper that was outselling his *Inquirer* by featuring crime and sex, was that the *Chronicle*'s staff would change him by deflecting him from an idealistic course (and Jed tries to point this out to Bernstein), but as it appears in the film it almost seems that in buying the *Chronicle*'s staff Kane is corrupting *them.*

It is just a fragment, too, that Kane's first wife, Emily, is the niece of the President of the United States. Hearst's only wife, Millicent, the daughter of a vaudeville hoofer, was a teen-age member of a group called The Merry Maidens when he met her. Emily was probably made the niece of the President in order to link Kane with the rich and to make a breach in the marriage when Kane was held responsible for the assassination of the President (as Hearst was accused of having incited the death of President McKinley).

In the condensation, the whole direction was, for commercial reasons, away from the newspaper business that dominated the early script, and, for obvious reasons, away from factual resemblances to Hearst's life. This was generally accomplished by making things funny. For example, Hearst had actually been cheated out of the office of mayor of New York by fraud at the polls, and this incident was included in *American.* In *Citizen Kane* it became, instead, a joke: when Kane loses the election for governor, the Kane papers automatically claim "FRAUD AT POLLS." This version is, of course, a quick way of dramatizing the spirit of yellow journalism, and it's useful and comic, but the tendency of this change, as of many others, was, whether deliberately or unconsciously, to make things easier for the audience by playing down material on how wealth and the power it buys can also buy the love of the voters. Hearst (the son of a senator whose money had got him into the Senate) did buy his way into public office; as a young man, he was twice elected to Congress, and he had tried to get the Democratic nomination for President just before he decided to run for mayor of New York. The movie flatters the audience by saying that Kane couldn't buy the people's love — that he "was never granted elective office by the voters of his country."

Actually, it wasn't the voters but crooked politicians who defeated Hearst. When the Tammany boss Charles F. Murphy refused to help Hearst get the Democratic nomination for mayor, he ran as an independent, campaigning against the corrupt Tammany "boodlers," and he printed a cartoon of Murphy in prison stripes. Kane gives Boss Jim Gettys this treatment. Murphy was so deeply wounded by the cartoon that he arranged for Hearst's ballots to be stolen, and, it is said, even managed to rig the recount. That reckless cartoon was the turning point in Hearst's political career. The movie gives Gettys a different revenge; namely, exposing Kane's "love nest" — which was something that also happened to Hearst, but on another occasion, long after he had aban-

doned his political ambitions, when his *Los Angeles Examiner* was attacking the *Los Angeles Times,* and the *Times* used his own tactics against him by bringing up his "double life" and his "love nest" with Marion Davies. The movie ultimately plays the same game. *Citizen Kane* becomes a movie about the private life of a public figure — the scandals and tidbits and splashy sensations that the Hearst press always preferred to issues. The assumption of the movie was much like that of the yellow press: that the mass audience wasn't interested in issues, that all it wanted was to get "behind the scenes" and find out the dirt.

22.

As the newspaper business and the political maneuvering were pared away, the personal material took on the weight and the shape of the solution to a mystery. Even so, if the movie had been directed in a more matter-of-fact, naturalistic style, Thompson's explanation that Rosebud was just a piece in a jigsaw puzzle would have seemed quite sensible. Instead, Welles' heavily theatrical style overemphasized the psychological explanation to such a point that when we finally glimpse the name on the sled we in the audience are made to feel that we're in on a big secret — a revelation that the world missed out on. However, Rosebud is so cleverly worked into the structure that, like the entrance that Hecht and MacArthur prepared for Walter Burns, it is enjoyable as beautiful tomfoolery even while we are conscious of it as "commercial" mechanics. I think what makes Welles' directorial style so satisfying in this movie is that we are constantly aware of the mechanics — that the pleasure *Kane* gives doesn't come from illusion but comes from our enjoyment of the dexterity of the illusionists and the working of the machinery. *Kane,* too, is a clock that laughs. *Citizen Kane* is a film made by a very young man of enormous spirit; he took the Mankiewicz material and he played with it, he turned it into a magic show. It is Welles' distinctive quality as a movie director — I think it is his genius — that he never hides his cleverness, that he makes it possible for us not only to enjoy what he does but to share his enjoyment in doing it. Welles' showmanship is right there on the surface, just as it was when, as a stage director, he set *Julius Caesar* among the Nazis, and set *Macbeth* in Haiti with a black cast and, during the banquet scene, blasted the audience with a recording of the "Blue Danube Waltz" — an effect that Kubrick was to echo (perhaps unknowingly?) in *2001*. There is something childlike — and great, too — about his pleasure in the magic of theatre and movies. No other director in the history of movies has been so open in his delight, so eager to share with us the game of pretending, and Welles' silly pretense of having done everything himself is just another part of the game.

Welles' magic as a director (at this time) was that he could put his finger right on the dramatic fun of each scene. Mankiewicz had built the scenes to end at ironic, dramatic high points, and Welles probably had a more innocently brazen sense of melodramatic timing than any other movie director. Welles also had a special magic beyond this: he could give *élan* to scenes that were confused in intention, so that the movie seems to go from dramatic highlight to highlight without lagging in between. There doesn't appear to be any waste material in *Kane,* because he charges right through the weak spots as if they were bright, and he almost convinces you (or *does* convince you) that they're shining

jewels. Perhaps these different kinds of magic can be suggested by two examples. There's the famous sequence in which Kane's first marriage is summarized by a series of breakfasts, with overlapping dialogue. The method was not new, and it's used here on a standard marriage joke, but the joke is a basic good joke, and the method is honestly used to sum up as speedily as possible the banality of what goes wrong with the marriage. This sequence is adroit, and Welles brings out the fun in the material, but there's no *special* Wellesian magic in it — except, perhaps, in his own acting. But in the cutting from the sequence of Kane's first meeting with Susan (where the writing supplies almost no clue to why he's drawn to this particular twerp of a girl beyond his finding her relaxing) to the political rally, Welles' special talent comes into play. Welles directs the individual scenes with such flourish and such *enjoyment of flourish* that the audience reacts as if the leap into the rally were clever and funny and logical, too, although the connection between the scenes isn't established until later, when Boss Jim Gettys uses Susan to wreck Kane's political career. As a director, Welles is so ebullient that we go along with the way he wants us to feel; we're happy to let him "put it over on us." Given the subject of Hearst and the witty script, the effect is of complicity, of a shared knowingness between Welles and the audience about what the movie is about. Kane's big smile at the rally seals the pact between him and us. Until Kane's later years, Welles, in the role, has an almost total empathy with the audience. It's the same kind of empathy we're likely to feel for smart kids who grin at us when they're showing off in the school play. It's a beautiful kind of emotional nakedness — ingenuously exposing the sheer love of playacting

— that most actors lose long before they become "professional." If an older actor — even a very good one — had played the role, faking youth for the young Kane the way Edward Arnold, say, sometimes faked it, I think the picture might have been routine. Some people used to say that Welles might be a great director but he was a bad actor, and his performances wrecked his pictures. I think just the opposite — that his directing style is such an emanation of his adolescent love of theatre that his films lack a vital unifying element when he's not in them or when he plays only a small part in them. He needs to be at the center. *The Magificent Ambersons* is a work of feeling and imagination and of obvious effort — and the milieu is much closer to Welles' own background than the milieu of *Kane* is — but Welles isn't in it, and it's too bland. It feels empty, uninhabited. Without Orson Welles' physical presence — the pudgy, big prodigy, who incarnates egotism — *Citizen Kane* might (as Otis Ferguson suggested) have disintegrated into vignettes. We feel that he's making it all happen. Like the actor-managers of the old theatre, he's the man onstage running the show, pulling it all together.

23.

Mankiewicz's script, though nominally an "original" — and in the best sense original — was in large part an adaptation of the material (much of it published) of Hearst's life. Hearst's life was so full of knavery and perversity that Mankiewicz simply sorted out the plums. Mankiewicz had been a reporter on the *New York World,* the Pulitzer paper, where Hearst himself had worked for a time before he persuaded his father to give him the *San Francisco Examiner.* When Hearst got the *Examiner,* he changed it in imitation of the *World,* and then expanded to New York, where he bought a paper and started raiding and decimating the *World*'s staff. One of his favorite tactics was to hire away men he didn't actually want at double or treble what Pulitzer was paying them, then fire them, leaving them stranded (a tactic memorialized in *The Front Page* when Walter Burns hires and fires the poetic reporter Bensinger). Kane's business practices are so closely patterned on Hearst's that in reading about Hearst one seems to be reading the script. Descriptions — like the one in the *Atlantic Monthly* in 1931 — of how Hearst cynically bought away the whole of Pulitzer's Sunday staff might be descriptions of Kane's maneuver. In 1935, *Fortune* described Hearst's warehouse in the Bronx in terms that might have been the specifications for the warehouse in the film, and by 1938 even the *Reader's Digest* was reprinting, from the *Saturday Evening Post,* a description of Hearst's empire in phrases that might be part of the script:

All his life Mr. Hearst bought, bought, bought — whatever touched his fancy. He purchased newspapers, Egyptian mummies, a California mountain range, herds of Tibetan yaks. He picked up a Spanish abbey, had it knocked down, crated, shipped to New York, and never has seen it since.

To his shares in the Homestake, largest gold producer in the United States, his Peruvian copper mines, his 900,000 acre Mexican cattle ranch, and his other inherited properties, he added 28 daily newspapers, 14 magazines here and in England, eight radio stations, wire services, a Hollywood producing unit, a newsreel, a castle in Wales, and one of the world's largest collections of objects d'art, gathered at a toll of $40,000,000.

Kane's dialogue is often almost Hearst verbatim; in the margin of the script that

Mankiewicz lent to Charles Lederer one of Hearst's lawyers annotated Kane's speech beginning, "Young man, there'll be no war. I have talked with the responsible leaders," with the words "This happens to be the gist of an authentic interview with WRH — occasion, his last trip from Europe." Some of the dialogue was legendary long before the movie was made. When Hearst was spending a fortune in his circulation war with Pulitzer, someone told his mother that Willie was losing money at the rate of a million dollars a year, and she equably replied, "Is he? Then he will only last about thirty years." This is no more than slightly transposed in the film, though it's really milked:

THATCHER

Tell me, honestly, my boy, don't you think it's rather unwise to continue this philanthropic enterprise . . . this "Inquirer" that is costing you a million dollars a year?

KANE

You're right, Mr. Thatcher. I did lose a million dollars last year. I expect to lose a million dollars this year. I expect to lose a million dollars next year. You know, Mr. Thatcher, at the rate of a million dollars a year . . . I'll have to close this place in sixty years.

(To audiences in 1941, Thatcher, appearing at the congressional-committee hearing, was obviously J. P. Morgan the younger, and the Thatcher Library was, of course, the Pierpont Morgan Library.)

Mankiewicz could hardly improve on the most famous of all Hearst stories, so he merely touched it up a trifle. According to many accounts, Hearst, trying to foment war with Spain, had sent Richard Harding Davis to Havana to write about the Spanish atrocities and Frederic Remington to

sketch them. Remington grew restless there and sent Hearst a telegram:

EVERYTHING IS QUIET. THERE IS NO TROUBLE HERE. THERE WILL BE NO WAR. I WISH TO RETURN. — REMINGTON.

Hearst replied,

PLEASE REMAIN. YOU FURNISH THE PICTURES AND I'LL FURNISH THE WAR. — W. R. HEARST.

In the movie, Bernstein reads Kane a telegram from a reporter named Wheeler:

GIRLS DELIGHTFUL IN CUBA, STOP. COULD SEND YOU PROSE POEMS ABOUT SCENERY BUT DON'T FEEL RIGHT SPENDING YOUR MONEY, STOP. THERE IS NO WAR IN CUBA. SIGNED WHEELER.

And Bernstein asks, "Any answer?"
Kane replies:

DEAR WHEELER, YOU PROVIDE THE PROSE POEMS, I'LL PROVIDE THE WAR.

These stories were so well known at the time of the movie's release that in the picture spread on the movie in *Life* (with captions in the very style that Mankiewicz had parodied in his "News on the March") the magazine — unconsciously, no doubt — returned to the Hearst original, and flubbed even that:

Kane buys a newspaper in New York and sets out to be a great social reformer. But even at 25 he is unscrupulous and wangles the U.S. into war by fake news dispatches. To a cartoonist in Cuba he wires: "You get the pictures and I'll make the war."

One passage of dialogue that is bad because it sounds slanted to make an ideological point is almost a straight steal (and that's probably why Mankiewicz didn't realize how fraudulent it would sound), and was especially familiar because John Dos Passos had quoted it in *U.S.A.,* in his section on Hearst, "Poor Little Rich Boy." (That title might be the theme of the movie.) Dos Passos quotes Hearst's answer to fellow-millionaires who thought he was a traitor to his class:

You know I believe in property, and you know where I stand on personal fortunes, but isn't it better that I should represent in this country the dissatisfied than have somebody else do it who might not have the same real property relations that I may have?

Hearst apparently did say it, but even though it's made more conversational in the movie, it's unconvincing — it sounds like left-wing paranoia.

KANE

I'll let you in on another little secret, Mr. Thatcher. I think I'm the man to do it. You see, I have money and property. If I don't look after the interests of the under-privileged maybe somebody else will . . . maybe somebody without any money or property.

Despite the fake childhood events, Kane's life story follows Hearst's much more closely than most movie biographies follow acknowledged and named subjects. Kane is burned in effigy, as Hearst was, and there is even a reference to Kane's expulsion from Harvard; one of the best-known stories in America was how young Willie Hearst had been expelled from Harvard after sending each of his instructors a chamber pot with the recipient's name handsomely lettered on the inside bottom. Even many of the subsidiary characters are replicas of Hearst's associates. For example, Bernstein (given the name of Welles' old guardian) is ob-

viously Solomon S. Carvalho, the business manager of Pulitzer's *World,* whom Hearst hired away, and who became the watchdog of the *Journal*'s exchequer and Hearst's devoted business manager. There was no special significance in the use of Mankiewicz's secretary's last name for Susan Alexander, or in naming Jed Leland for Leland Hayward (Mankiewicz's agent, whose wife, Margaret Sullavan, spent a weekend visiting at Victorville), just as there was no significance in the fact that the actor Whitford Kane had been part of the nucleus of the Mercury Theatre, but the use of the name Bernstein for Kane's devoted, uncritical friend had some significance in relation not only to Welles but to Hearst, and it was Mankiewicz's way of giving Hearst points (he did it in the breakfast scene when Emily is snobbish about Bernstein) because, whatever else Hearst was, he was not a snob or an anti-Semite. (For one thing, Marion's brother-in-law — Charles Lederer's father — was Jewish.) No doubt Mankiewicz also meant to give Kane points when he had him finish Jed's negative review of Susan's singing in the same negative spirit — which was more than George S. Kaufman had done for Mankiewicz's review back at the *New York Times.* This episode is perversely entertaining but not convincing. *Kane* used so much of Hearst's already legendary life that for liberals it was like a new kind of folk art; we knew all this about Hearst from books and magazines but gasped when we saw it on the big movie screen, and so defiantly — almost contemptuously — undisguised.

The departure from Hearst's life represented by Susan Alexander's opera career, which is a composite of the loves and scandals of several Chicago tycoons, didn't weaken the attack on Hearst — it strengthened it. Attaching the other scandals to him made him seem the epitome of the powerful and spoiled, and thus stand for them all. Opera — which used to be called "grand opera" — was a ritual target of American comedy. It was an easier target for the public to respond to than Hearst's own folly — motion pictures — because the public already connected opera with wealth and temperament, tycoons in opera hats and women in jewels, imported prima donnas, and all the affectations of "culture." It was a world the movie public didn't share, and it was already absurd in American movies — the way valets and effete English butlers and the high-toned Americans putting on airs who kept them were absurd. George S. Kaufman and Morrie Ryskind had worked opera over in two of the Marx Brothers pictures; Mankiewicz had been taken off *A Night at the Opera,* but what he and Welles — with the assistance of Bernard Herrmann — did to opera in *Citizen Kane* was in almost exactly the same style, and as funny.

Mankiewicz was working overseas for the *Chicago Tribune* when Harold McCormick and his wife, Edith Rockefeller McCormick, were divorced, in 1921. The McCormicks had been the leading patrons of opera in Chicago; they had made up the Chicago Opera Company's deficits, which were awe-inspiring during the time the company was under the management of Mary Garden (she chose to be called the "directa"), rising to a million dollars one great, lavish season. After the divorce, McCormick married Ganna Walska, the preëminent temperamental mediocre soprano of her day. Mankiewicz combined this scandal with a far more widely publicized event that occurred a few years later, replacing Hearst and Cosmopolitan Pictures with Samuel Insull and his building of the Chicago Civic Opera House. Insull didn't build the opera house for his wife (dainty little Gladys Wal-

lis didn't sing), but there was a story to it, and it was the biggest opera story of the decade. After the McCormick-Rockefeller divorce, their joint largesse to opera ended, and the deficits were a big problem. Insull, "the Czar of Commonwealth Edison," who also loved opera (and dallied with divas), wanted to put it on a self-supporting business basis. He concluded that if an opera house should be built in a skyscraper, the rental of the upper regions would eventually cover the opera's deficits. The building was started in 1928; it had forty-five stories, with the opera company occupying the first six, and with Insull's office-lair on top. The structure was known as "Insull's throne," and it cost twenty million dollars. The opening of the new opera house was scheduled for November 4, 1929; six days before, on October 29th, the stock market crashed. The opening took place during the panic, with plainclothesmen and eight detective-bureau squads guarding the bejewelled patrons against robbers, rioters, and the mobsters who more or less ran the city. (The former Mrs. McCormick attended, wearing, according to one newspaper report, "her gorgeous diamond necklace, almost an inch wide and reaching practically to her waist"; Mrs. Insull wore pearls and "a wide diamond bracelet.") Mankiewicz must have placed the episode of the opera house in Chicago in order to give it roots — to make it connect with what the public already knew about Chicago and robber barons and opera. (Chicago was big on opera; it was there that the infant Orson Welles played Madame Butterfly's love child.) Insull's opera house never really had a chance to prove or disprove his financial theories. Mary Garden quit after one year there, calling it "that long black hole," and in 1932, when Insull's mammoth interlocking directorate of power plants collapsed and he fled to Greece, the opera house was closed. Insull was extradited, and in the mid-thirties he stood trial for fraud and embezzlement; he died two years before *Citizen Kane* was written.

The fretful banality of Susan Alexander is clearly derived from Mankiewicz's hated old adversary Mrs. Insull — notorious for her "discordant twitter" and her petty dissatisfaction with everything. The Insulls had been called the least popular couple who had ever lived in Chicago, and there was ample evidence that they hadn't even liked each other. Opera and the Insulls provided cover for Mankiewicz and Welles. George J. Schaefer, who is quite open about this, says that when he couldn't get an opening for *Kane,* because the theatres were frightened off by the stories in the Hearst press about injunctions and lawsuits, he went to see Hearst's lawyers in Los Angeles and took the position that Kane could be Insull. No one was expected to be fooled; it was simply a legal maneuver.

There was also an actual (and malicious) scrap of Hearst's past in the opera idea in the first draft. As Mankiewicz planned it, Susan was to make her début in Massenet's *Thaïs.* As a very young man, Hearst had been briefly engaged to the San Francisco singer Sybil Sanderson. In order to break the engagement, Miss Sanderson's parents had sent her to study in Paris, where she became well known in opera and as the "constant companion" of Massenet, who wrote *Thaïs* for her. But to use *Thaïs* would have cost a fee, so Bernard Herrmann wrote choice excerpts of a fake French-Oriental opera — *Salammbô.* (Dorothy Comingore did her own singing in the movie except for the opera-house sequence; that was dubbed by a professional singer who deliberately sang badly.) The Kane amalgam may also contain a dab or two from the lives of other magnates, such as Frank Munsey and Pulitzer, and more than a dab from the life of Jules Brulatour, who got his start in business by selling Eastman Kodak film. Hope Hampton, his blond protégée and later his wife, had a career even more ridiculous than Susan Alexander's. After she failed as a movie actress, Brulatour financed her career at the Chicago Opera Company at the end of the twenties, and then, using his power to extend credit to movie companies for film stock, he pushed the near-bankrupt Universal to star her in a 1937 disaster, in which she sang eight songs.

The only other major addition to Hearst's actual history comes near the beginning of the movie. The latter days of Susan Alexander as a tawdry-looking drunken singer at El Rancho in Atlantic City, where she is billed as "Susan Alexander Kane" — which tells us at once that she is so poor an entertainer that she must resort to this cheap attempt to exploit her connection with Kane — may have been lifted from the frayed end of Evelyn Nesbit's life. After her divorce from Harry K. Thaw — the rich socialite who murdered Stanford White on her account — she drifted down to appearing in honky-tonks, and was periodically denounced in the press for "capitalizing her shame."

24.

Dorothy Comingore says, "When I read for Orson, Herman was in the room, with a broken leg and a crutch, and Orson turned to him and said, 'What do you think?' And Herman said, 'Yes, she looks precisely like the image of a kitten we've been looking for.'"

The handling of Susan Alexander is a classic of duplicity. By diversifying the material and combining several careers, Mankiewicz could protect himself. He could claim that Susan wasn't meant to be Marion Davies — that she was nothing at all like Marion, whom he called a darling and a minx. He could point out that Marion wasn't a singer and that Hearst had never built an opera house for her — and it was true, she wasn't and he hadn't, but she was an actress and he did run Cosmopolitan Pictures for her. Right at the beginning of the movie, Kane was said to be the greatest newspaper tycoon of this or any other generation, so he was obviously Hearst; Xanadu was transparently San Simeon; and Susan's fake stardom and the role she played in Kane's life spelled Marion Davies to practically everybody in the Western world. And even though Mankiewicz *liked* Marion Davies, he was the same Mankiewicz who couldn't resist the disastrous "Imagine — the whole world wired to Harry Cohn's ass!" He skewered her with certain identifying details that were just too good to resist, such as her love of jigsaw puzzles. They were a feature of San Simeon; the puzzles, which sometimes took two weeks to complete, were set out on tables in the salon, and the guests would work at them before lunch. And when Kane destroys Susan's room in a rage after she leaves him, he turns up a hidden bottle of booze, which was a vicious touch, coming from Mankiewicz, who had often been the beneficiary of Marion's secret cache. He provided bits that had a special *frisson* for those in the know.

One can sometimes hurt one's enemies, but that's nothing compared to what one can do to one's friends. Marion Davies, living in the style of the royal courtesans with a man who couldn't marry her without messes and scandal (his wife, Millicent, had become a Catholic, and she had also given him five sons), was an easy target. Hearst and Louella Parsons had set her up for it, and she became the victim of *Citizen Kane*.

In her best roles, Marion Davies was a spunky, funny, beautiful girl, and that's apparently what she *was* and why Hearst adored her. But, in his adoration, he insisted that the Hearst press overpublicize her and overpraise her constantly, and the public in general got wise. A typical Davies film would open with the theatre ventilating system pouring attar of roses at the audience, or the theatre would be specially redecorated, sometimes featuring posters that famous popular artists had done of her in the costumes of the picture. Charity functions of which she was the queen would be splashed all over the society pages, and the movie would be reviewed under eight-column headlines. In the news section, Mayor Hylan of New York would be saying, "*When Knighthood Was in Flower* is unquestionably the greatest picture I have ever seen. . . . No person can afford to miss this great screen masterpiece," or "*Little Old New York* is unquestionably the greatest screen epic I have ever looked upon, and Marion Davies is the most versatile screen star ever cast in any part. The wide range of her stellar acting is something to marvel at. . . . Every man, woman and child in New York City ought to see this splendid picture. . . . I must pay my tribute to the geniuses in all lines who created such a masterpiece."

When the toadying and praise were already sickening, Hearst fell for one of the dumbest smart con tricks of all time: A young movie reviewer named Louella O. Parsons, working for the *New York Telegraph* for $110 a week, wrote a column saying that although Marion Davies' movies were properly publicized, the star herself wasn't publicized *enough*. Hearst fell for it and hired Parsons at $250 a week, and she began her profitable lifework of praising (and destroying) Marion Davies. Some of

Davies' costume spectacles weren't bad — and she was generally charming in them — but the pictures didn't have to be bad for all the corrupt drumbeaters to turn the public's stomach. Other actresses were pushed to stardom and were accepted. (The flapper heroine Colleen Moore was Walter Howey's niece, and she was started on her career when she was fifteen. D. W. Griffith owed Howey a favor for getting *The Birth of a Nation* and *Intolerance* past the Chicago censors, and her movie contract was the payoff. She says that many of the Griffith stars were "payoffs.") Marion Davies had more talent than most of the reigning queens, but Hearst and Louella were too ostentatious, and they never let up. There was a steady march of headlines ("Marion Davies' Greatest Film Opens Tonight"); there were too many charity balls. The public can swallow just so much: her seventy-five-thousand-dollar fourteen-room mobile "bungalow" on the M-G-M lot, O.K.; the special carpet for alighting, no. Her pictures had to be forced on exhibitors, and Hearst spent so much on them that even when they did well, the cost frequently couldn't be recovered. One of his biographers reports a friend's saying to Hearst, "There's money in the movies," and Hearst's replying, "Yes. Mine."

Marion Davies was born in 1897, and, as a teen-ager, went right from the convent to the musical-comedy stage, where she put in two years as a dancer before Ziegfeld "glorified" her in the "Ziegfeld Follies of 1916." That was where William Randolph Hearst, already in his mid-fifties, spotted her. It is said, and may even be true, that he attended the "Follies" every night for eight weeks, buying two tickets — one for himself and the other for his hat — just "to gaze upon her." It is almost certainly true that from then "to the day of his death,"

as Adela Rogers St. Johns put it, "he wanted to know every minute where she was." Marion Davies entered movies in 1917, with *Runaway Romany,* which she also wrote, and then she began that really strange, unparalleled movie career. She had starred in about fifty pictures by the time she retired, in 1937 — all under Hearst's aegis, and under his close personal supervision. (Leading men were afraid to kiss her; Hearst was always watching.) The pictures were all expensively produced, and most of them were financial failures. Marion Davies was a mimic and a parodist and a very original sort of comedienne, but though Hearst liked her to make him laugh at home, he wanted her to be a romantic maiden in the movies, and — what was irreconcilable with her talent — dignified. Like Susan, she was tutored, and he spent incredible sums on movies that would be the perfect setting for her. He appears to have been sincerely infatuated with her in old-fashioned, sentimental, ladylike roles; he loved to see her in ruffles on garden swings. But actresses didn't become public favorites in roles like those, and even if they could get by with them sometimes, they needed startling changes of pace to stay in public favor, and Hearst wouldn't let Marion Davies do anything "sordid."

To judge by what those who worked with her have said, she was thoroughly unpretentious, and was depressed by Hearst's taste in roles for her. She finally broke out of the costume cycle in the late twenties and did some funny pictures: *The Red Mill* (which Fatty Arbuckle, whom Hearst the moralizer had helped ruin, directed, under his new, satirical pseudonym, Will B. Goodrich), *The Fair Coed,* my childhood favorite *The Patsy,* and others. But even when she played in a slapstick parody of Gloria Swanson's career (*Show People,* in 1928), Hearst wouldn't let her do a custard-pie sequence, despite her own pleas and those of the director, King Vidor, and the writer, Laurence Stallings. (King Vidor has described the conference that Louis B. Mayer called so that Vidor could make his case to Hearst for the plot necessity of the pie. "Presently, the great man rose and in a high-pitched voice said, 'King's right. But I'm right, too — because I'm not going to let Marion be hit in the face with a pie.'") She wanted to play Sadie Thompson in *Rain,* but he wouldn't hear of it, and the role went to Gloria Swanson (and made her a star all over again). When Marion Davies should have been playing hard-boiled, good-hearted blondes, Hearst's idea of a role for her was Elizabeth Barrett Browning in *The Barretts of Wimpole Street,* and when Thalberg reserved that one for *his* lady, Norma Shearer, Hearst, in 1934, indignantly left M-G-M and took his money and his "Cosmopolitan Pictures" label over to Warner Brothers. (The editors of his newspapers were instructed never again to mention Norma Shearer in print.) It was a long blighted career for an actress who might very well have become a big star on her own, and she finally recognized that with Hearst's help it was hopeless. By the time *Citizen Kane* came out, she had been in retirement for four years, but the sickening publicity had gone grinding on relentlessly, and, among the audiences at *Kane,* probably even those who remembered her as the charming, giddy comedienne of the late twenties no longer trusted their memories.

Mankiewicz, catering to the public, gave it the empty, stupid, no-talent blonde it wanted — the "confidential" backstairs view of the great gracious lady featured in the Hearst press. It was, though perhaps partly inadvertently, a much worse betrayal than if he'd made Susan more like Davies, because movie audiences assumed that Davies was a pathetic whiner like Susan Alexander, and Marion Davies was nailed to the cross of harmless stupidity and nothingness, which in high places is the worst joke of all.

25.

Right from the start of movies, it was a convention that the rich were vulgarly acquisitive but were lonely and miserable and incapable of giving or receiving love. As a mass medium, movies have always soothed and consoled the public with the theme that the rich can buy everything except what counts — love. (The convention remains, having absorbed the *Dolce Vita* variation that the rich use each other sexually because they are incapable of love.) It was consistent with this popular view of the emptiness of the lives of the rich to make Susan Alexander a cartoon character; the movie reduces Hearst's love affair to an infatuation for a silly, ordinary nothing of a girl, as if everything in his life were synthetic, his passion vacuous, and the object of it a cipher. What happened in Hearst's life was far more interesting: he took a beautiful, warm-hearted girl and made her the best-known kept woman in America and the butt of an infinity of dirty jokes, and he did it out of love and the blindness of love.

Citizen Kane, however, employs the simplification, so convenient to melodrama, that there is a unity between a man's private life and his public one. This simplification has enabled ambitious bad writers to make reputations as thinkers, and in the movies of the forties it was given a superficial plausibility by popular Freudianism. Hideous character defects traceable to childhood traumas explained just about anything the authors disapproved of. Mankiewicz certainly knew better, but as a screenwriter he dealt in ideas that had popular appeal. Hearst was a notorious anti-union, pro-Nazi Red-baiter, so Kane must have a miserable, deformed childhood. He must be *wrecked* in infancy. It was a movie convention going back to silents that when you did a bio or a thesis picture you started with the principal characters as children and showed them to be miniature versions of their later characters. This convention almost invariably pleased audiences, because it also demonstrated the magic of movies — the kids so extraordinarily resembled the adult actors they would turn into. And it wasn't just makeup — they really did, having been searched out for that resemblance. (This is *possible* in theatre, but it's rarely feasible.) That rather old-fashioned view of the predestination of character from childhood needed only a small injection of popular Freudianism to pass for new, and if you tucked in a trauma, you took care of the motivation for the later events. Since nothing very bad had happened to Hearst, Mankiewicz drew upon Little Orson Annie. He *orphaned* Kane, and used that to explain Hearst's career. (And, as Welles directed it, there's more real emotion and pain in the childhood separation sequence than in all the rest of the movie.)

Thus Kane was emotionally stunted. Offering personal emptiness as the explanation of Hearst's career really doesn't do much but feed the complacency of those liberals who are eager to believe that conservatives are "sick" (which is also how conservatives tend to see liberals). Liberals were willing to see this hollow-man explanation of Hearst as something much deeper than a cliché of popular melodrama, though the film's explaining his attempts to win public office and his empire-building and his art collecting by the childhood loss of maternal love is as unilluminating as the conservative conceit that Marx was a revolutionary because he hated his father. The point of the film becomes the cliché irony that although Hearst has everything materially, he has nothing humanly.

Quite by chance, I saw William Randolph Hearst once, when I was about nineteen. It was Father's Day, which sometimes falls on my birthday, and my escort bumped me into him on the dance floor. I can't remember whether it was at the Palace Hotel in San Francisco or at the St. Francis, and I can't remember the year, though it was probably 1938. But I remember Hearst in almost terrifying detail, with the kind of memory I generally have only for movies. He was dinner-dancing, just like us, except that his table was a large one. He was seated with Marion Davies and his sons with their wives or dates; obviously, it was a kind of family celebration. I had read the then current *Hearst, Lord of San Simeon* and Ferdinand Lundberg's *Imperial Hearst,* and probably almost everything else that was available about him, and I remember thinking, as I watched him, of Charles A. Beard's preface to the Lundberg book — that deliberately cruel premature "Farewell to William Randolph Hearst," with its tone of "He will depart loved by few and respected by none whose respect is worthy of respect. . . . None will be proud to do honor to his memory," and so on. You don't expect to bump into a man on the dance floor after you've been reading that sort of thing about him. It was like stumbling onto Caligula, and Hearst looked like a Roman emperor mixing with the commoners on a night out. He was a huge man — six feet four or five — and he was old and heavy, and he moved slowly about the dance floor with *her*. He seemed like some prehistoric monster gliding among the couples, quietly majestic, towering over everyone; he had little, odd eyes, like a whale's, and they looked pulled down, sinking into his cheeks. Maybe I had just never seen anybody so massive and dignified and old *dancing,* and maybe it was that plus who he was, but I've never seen anyone else who seemed to incarnate power and solemnity as he did; he was frightening and he was impressive, almost as if he were wearing ceremonial robes of office. When he danced with Marion Davies, he was indifferent to everything else. They looked isolated and entranced together; this slow, huge dinosaur clung to the frowzy-looking aging blonde in what seemed to be a ritual performance. Joined together, they were as alone as the young dancing couple in the sky with diamonds in *Yellow Submarine.* Maybe they *were* that couple a few decades later, for they had an extraordinary romance — one that lasted thirty-two years — and they certainly had the diamonds (or *had* had them). He seemed unbelievably old to me that night, when he was probably about seventy-five; they were still together when he died, in 1951, at the age of eighty-eight.

The private pattern that was devised as a correlative (and possible explanation) of Hearst's public role was false. Hearst didn't have any (recorded) early traumas, Marion Davies did have talent, and they were an extraordinarily devoted pair; far from leaving him, when he faced bankruptcy she gave him her money and jewels and real estate, and even borrowed money to enable him to keep his newspapers. He was well loved, and *still* he was a dangerous demagogue. And, despite what Charles A. Beard said and what Dos Passos said, and despite the way Mankiewicz presented him in *Citizen Kane,* and all the rest, Hearst and his consort were hardly lonely, with all those writers around, and movie stars and directors, and Shaw, and Winston Churchill, and week-

end parties with Marion Davies spiking teetotaller Calvin Coolidge's fruit punch (though only with liquor that came from fruit). Even Mrs. Luce came; the pictures of Hearst on the walls at Time-Life might show him as an octopus, but who could resist an invitation? Nor did Hearst lose his attraction or his friends after he lost his *big* money. After San Simeon was stripped of its silver treasures, which were sold at auction in the thirties, the regal-party weekends were finished, but he still entertained, if less lavishly, at his smaller houses. Dos Passos played the same game as *Citizen Kane* when he wrote of Hearst "amid the relaxing adulations of screenstars, admen, screenwriters, publicitymen, columnists, millionaire editors" — suggesting that Hearst was surrounded by third-raters and sycophantic hirelings. But the lists and the photographs of Hearst's guests tell another story. He had the one great, dazzling court of the first half of the twentieth century, and the statesmen and kings, the queens and duchesses at his table were as authentic as the writers and wits and great movie stars and directors. When one considers who even those screenwriters were, it's not surprising that Hearst wanted their company. Harold Ross must have wondered what drew his old friends there, for he came, too, escorted by Robert Benchley.

It is both a limitation and *in the nature of the appeal* of popular art that it constructs false, easy patterns. Like the blind-beggar-for-luck, *Kane* has a primitive appeal that is implicit in the conception. It tells the audience that fate or destiny or God or childhood trauma has already taken revenge on the wicked — that if the rich man had a good time he has suffered remorse, or, better still, that he hasn't really enjoyed himself at all. Before Mankiewicz began writing the script, he talked about what a great love story it would be — but who would buy tickets for a movie about a rich, powerful tycoon who also found true love? In popular art, riches and power destroy people, and so the secret of Kane is that he longs for the simple pleasures of his childhood before wealth tore him away from his mother — he longs for what is available to the mass audience.

26.

Even when Hearst's speeches, or facsimiles of them, were used in *Kane,* their character was transformed. If one looks at his actual remarks on property and then at Mankiewicz's adaptation of them, one can see how. Hearst's remarks are tight and slightly oblique, and it takes one an instant to realize what he's saying. Mankiewicz makes them easier to grasp (and rather florid) but kills some of their almost sinister double edge by making them consciously flip. He turns them into a joke. And when Mankiewicz didn't make the speeches flip, Welles' delivery did. When you hear Kane dictate the telegram to Cuba, you don't really think for a minute that it's *acted* on. And so the movie becomes a comic strip about Hearst, without much resonance, and certainly without much tragic resonance. Hearst, who compared himself to an elephant, *looked* like a great man. I don't think he actually was great in any sense, but he was *extraordinary,* and his power and wealth, plus his enormous size, made him a phenomenally commanding presence. Mankiewicz, like Dos Passos, may have believed that Hearst fell from greatness, or (as I suspect) Mankiewicz may have liked the facile dramatic possibilities of that approach. But he couldn't carry it out. He couldn't write the character as a tragic fallen hero, because he couldn't resist making him funny. Man-

kiewicz had been hacking out popular comedies and melodramas for too long to write drama; one does not *dictate* tragedy to a stenotypist. He automatically, because of his own temperament and his writing habits, turned out a bitchy satirical melodrama. Inside the three hundred and twenty-five pages of his long, ambitious first draft was the crowd-pleasing material waiting to be carved out. When one reads the long version, it's obvious what must go; if I had been doing the cutting I might have cut just about the same material. *And yet* that fat to be cut away is everything that tends to make it a political and historical drama, and what is left is the private scandals of a poor little rich boy. The scandals in the long draft — some of it, set in Italy during Kane's youth, startlingly like material that came to the screen twenty years later in *La Dolce Vita* — served a purpose beyond crowd pleasing: to show what a powerful man could cover up and get away with. Yet this, of course, went out, for reasons similar to the ones that kept Kane, unlike Hearst, from winning elected office — to reassure the public that the rich *don't* get away with it.

Welles now has a lumbering grace and a gliding, whalelike motion not unlike Hearst's, but when he played the role he became stiff and crusty as the older Kane, and something went blank in the aging process — not just because the makeup was erratic and waxy (especially in the bald-headed scenes, such as the one in the picnic tent) but because the character lost his connection with business and politics and became a fancy theatrical notion, an Expressionist puppet. Also, there are times when the magic of movies fails. The camera comes so close that it can reveal too much: Kane as an old man was an actor trying to look old, and Welles had as yet only a schoolboy's perception of how age weighs one down. On a popular level, however, his limitations worked to his advantage; they tied in with the myth of the soulless rich.

The conceptions are basically *kitsch;* basically, *Kane* is popular melodrama — Freud plus scandal, a comic strip about Hearst. Yet, partly because of the resonance of what was left of the historical context, partly because of the juiciness of Welles' young talent and of the varied gifts and personalities others brought to the film, partly because of the daring of the attack on the most powerful and dangerous press lord known to that time, the picture has great richness and flair; it's *kitsch* redeemed. I would argue that this is what is remarkable about movies — that shallow conceptions in one area can be offset by elements playing against them or altering them or affecting the texture. If a movie is good, there is a general tendency to believe that everything in it was conceived and worked out according to a beautiful master plan, or that it is the result of the creative imagination of the director, but in movies things rarely happen that way — even more rarely than they do in opera or the theatre. There are so many variables; imagine how different the whole feeling of *Kane* would be if the film had been shot in a naturalistic style, or even if it had been made at M-G-M instead of at R.K.O. Extraordinary movies are the result of the "right" people's getting together on the "right" project at the "right" time — in their lives and in history. I don't mean to suggest that a good movie is just a mess that happens to work (although there have been such cases) — only that a good movie is not always the result of a single artistic intelligence. It can be the result of a fortunate collaboration, of cross-fertilizing accidents. And I would argue that what redeems movies in general, what makes them so much easier to take than other arts, is that many talents in interaction in a work can produce something more enjoyable than one talent that is not of the highest. Because of the collaborative nature of most movies, masterpieces are rare, and even masterpieces may, like *Kane,* be full of flaws, but the interaction frequently results in special pleasures and surprises.

27.

The director should be in control not because he is the sole creative intelligence but because only if he is in control can he liberate and utilize the talents of his coworkers, who languish (as directors do) in studio-factory productions. The best interpretation to put on it when a director says that a movie is totally his is not that he did it all himself but that he wasn't interfered with, that he made the choices and the ultimate decisions, that the whole thing isn't an unhappy compromise for which no one is responsible; not that he was the sole creator but almost the reverse — that he was free to use all the best ideas offered him.

Welles had a vitalizing, spellbinding talent; he was the man who brought out the best in others and knew how to use it. What keeps *Citizen Kane* alive is that Welles wasn't prevented (as so many directors are) from trying things out. He was young and *open,* and, as the members of that crew tell it — and they remember it very well, because it was the only time it ever happened for many of them — they could always talk to him and make suggestions, as long as they didn't make the suggestions publicly. Most big-studio movies were made in such a restrictive way that the crews were hostile and bored and the atmosphere was oppressive. The worst aspect of the factory system was that almost everyone worked beneath his capacity. Working on *Kane,* in an atmosphere of freedom, the designers and technicians came forth with ideas they'd been bottling up for years; they were all in on the creative process. Welles was so eager to try out new ideas that even the tough, hardened studio craftsmen were caught up by his spirit, just as his co-workers in the theatre and in radio had been. *Citizen Kane* is not a great work that suddenly burst out of a young prodigy's head. There are such works in the arts (though few, if any, in movies), but this is not one of them. It is a superb example of collaboration; everyone connected with it seems to have had the time of his life because he was able to contribute something.

Welles had just the right background for the sound era. He used sound not just as an inexpensive method of creating the illusion of halls and crowds but to create an American environment. He knew how to convey the way people feel about each other by the way they sound; he knew how they sounded in different rooms, in different situations. The directors who had been most imaginative in the use of sound in the early talkies were not Americans, and when they worked in America, as Ernst Lubitsch did, they didn't have the ear for American life that Welles had. And the good American movie directors in that period (men like Howard Hawks and John Ford and William Wellman) didn't have the background in theatre or — that key element — the background in radio. Hawks handled the dialogue expertly in *His Girl Friday,* but the other sounds are not much more imaginative than those in a first-rate stage production. When Welles came to Hollywood, at the age of twenty-four, his previous movie experience had not been on a professional level, but he already knew more about the dramatic possibilities of sound

than most veteran directors, and the sound engineers responded to his inventiveness by giving him extraordinary new effects. At every point along the way, the studio craftsmen tried something out. Nearly all the thirty-five members of the R.K.O. special-effects department worked on *Kane;* roughly eighty per cent of the film was not merely printed but reprinted, in order to add trick effects and blend in painted sets and bits of stock footage. The view up from Susan singing on the opera stage to the stagehands high above on the catwalk, as one of them puts two fingers to his nose — which looks like a tilt (or vertical pan) — is actually made up of three shots, the middle one a miniature. When the camera seems to pass through a rooftop skylight into the El Rancho night club where Susan works, the sign, the rooftop, and the skylight are miniatures, with a flash of lightning to conceal the cut to the full-scale interior. The craftsmen were so ingenious about giving Welles the effects he wanted that even now audiences aren't aware of how cheaply made *Citizen Kane* was.

In the case of the cinematographer, Gregg Toland, the contribution goes far beyond suggestions and technical solutions. I think he not only provided much of the visual style of *Citizen Kane* but was responsible for affecting the conception, and even for introducing a few elements that are not in the script. It's always a little risky to assign credit for ideas in movies; somebody is bound to turn up a film that used whatever it is — a detail, a device, a technique — earlier. The most one can hope for, generally, is to catch on to a few late links in the chain. It was clear that *Kane* had visual links to James Wong Howe's cinematography in *Transatlantic* (Howe, coincidentally, had also shot *The Power and the Glory*), but I had always been puzzled by the fact that *Kane* seemed to draw not only on the Expressionist theatrical style of Welles' stage productions but on the German Expressionist and Gothic movies of the silent period. In *Kane,* as in the German silents, depth was used like stage depth, and attention was frequently moved from one figure to another within a fixed frame by essentially the same techniques as on the stage — by the actors' moving into light or by a shift of the light to other actors (rather than by the fluid camera of a Renoir, which follows the actors, or the fragmentation and quick cutting of the early Russians). There were frames in *Kane* that seemed so close to the exaggerations in German films like *Pandora's Box* and *The Last Laugh* and *Secrets of a Soul* that I wondered what Welles was talking about when he said he had prepared for *Kane* by running John Ford's *Stagecoach* forty times. Even allowing for the hyperbole of the forty times, why should Orson Welles have studied *Stagecoach* and come up with a film that looked more like *The Cabinet of Dr. Caligari?* I wondered if there might be a link between Gregg Toland and the German tradition, though most of Toland's other films didn't suggest much German influence. When I looked up his credits as a cameraman, the name *Mad Love* rang a bell; I closed my eyes and visualized it, and there was the Gothic atmosphere, and the huge, dark rooms with lighted figures, and Peter Lorre, bald, with a spoiled-baby face, looking astoundingly like a miniature Orson Welles.

Mad Love, made in Hollywood in 1935, was a dismal, static horror movie — an American version of a German film directed by the same man who had directed *The Cabinet of Dr. Caligari.* The American remake, remarkable only for its photography, was directed by Karl Freund, who had been head cinematographer at Ufa, in Germany. He had worked with such great directors as Fritz Lang and F. W. Murnau and G. W. Pabst, and, by his technical innovations, had helped create their styles; he had shot many of the German silent classics (*The Last Laugh, Variety, Metropolis, Tartuffe*). I recently looked at a print of *Mad Love,* and the resemblances to *Citizen Kane* are even greater than my memories of it suggested. Not only is the large room with the fireplace at Xanadu similar to Lorre's domain as a mad doctor, with similar lighting and similar placement of figures, but Kane's appearance and makeup in some sequences might be a facsimile of Lorre's. Lorre, who had come out of the German theatre and German films, played in a stylized manner that is visually imitated in *Kane.* And, amusingly, that screeching white cockatoo, which isn't in the script of *Kane* but appeared out of nowhere in the movie to provide an extra "touch," is a regular member of Lorre's household.

Gregg Toland was the "hottest" photographer in Hollywood at the time he called Welles and asked to work with him; in March he had won the Academy Award for *Wuthering Heights,* and his other recent credits included *The Grapes of Wrath* and the film in which he had experimented with deep focus, *The Long Voyage Home.* He brought along his own four-man camera crew, who had recently celebrated their fifteenth year of working together. This picture was made with love; the year before his death, in 1948, Toland said that he had wanted to work with Welles because he was miserable and felt like a whore when he was on run-of-the-mill assignments, and that "photographing *Citizen Kane* was the most exciting professional adventure of my career." I surmise that part of the adventure

Top: Peter Lorre and the cockatoo, from Mad Love.
Bottom: Peter Lorre facing the fireplace, from Mad Love.

was his finding a way to use and develop what the great Karl Freund had taught him.

Like the German cinematographers in the silent period, Toland took a more active role than the usual Hollywood cinematographer. For some years, whenever it was possible, he had been supervising the set construction of his films, so that he could plan the lighting. He probably responded to Welles' penchant for tales of terror and his desire for a portentous, mythic look, and since Welles didn't have enough financing for full-scale sets and was more than willing to try the unconventional, Toland suggested many of the Expressionist solutions. When a director is new to films, he is, of course, extremely dependent on his cameraman, and he is particularly so if he is also the star of the film, and is thus in front of the camera. Toland was a disciplined man, and those who worked on the set say he was a steadying influence on Welles; it is generally agreed that the two planned and discussed every shot together. With Welles, Toland was free to make suggestions that went beyond lighting techniques. Seeing Welles' facial resemblance to the tiny Lorre — even to the bulging eyes and the dimpled, sad expression — Toland probably suggested the makeup and the doll-like, jerky use of the body for Kane in his rage and as a lonely old man, and, having enjoyed the flamboyant photographic effect of the cockatoo in *Mad Love,* suggested that, too. When Toland provided Welles with the silent-picture setups that had been moribund under Karl Freund's direction, Welles used them in a childlike spirit that made them playful and witty. There's nothing static or Germanic in Welles' *direction,* and he had such unifying energy that just a couple of years ago an eminent movie critic cited the cockatoo in *Citizen Kane* as "an unforced metaphor arising naturally out of the action."

It's the Gothic atmosphere, partly derived from Toland's work on *Mad Love,* that inflates *Citizen Kane* and puts it in a different tradition from the newspaper comedies and the big bios of the thirties. *Citizen Kane* is, in some ways, a freak of art. Toland, although he used deep focus again later, reverted to a more conventional look for the films following *Kane,* directed by men who rejected technique "for its own sake," but he had passed on Freund's techniques to Welles. The dark, Gothic horror style, with looming figures, and with vast interiors that suggested castles rather than houses, formed the basis for much of Welles' later visual style. It suited Welles; it was the visual equivalent of The Shadow's voice — a gigantic echo chamber. Welles, too big for ordinary roles, too overpowering for normal characters, is stylized by nature — is by nature an Expressionist actor.

28.

Two years after the release of *Citizen Kane,* when Herman Mankiewicz had become respectable — his career had taken a leap after *Kane,* and he had had several major credits later in 1941 and had just won another Academy nomination, for his work on *Pride of the Yankees* — he stumbled right into Hearst's waiting arms. He managed to have an accident that involved so many of the elements of his life that it sounds like a made-up surreal joke. Though some of his other calamities are lost in an alcoholic fog — people remember only the bandages and Mankiewicz's stories about how he got them, and maybe even he didn't always know the facts — this one is all too well documented.

Driving home after a few drinks at Romanoff's, he was only a block and a half from his house when he hit a tiny car right at the gates of the Marion Davies residence. And it wasn't just any little car he hit; it was one driven by Lee Gershwin — Ira Gershwin's wife, Lenore, a woman Mankiewicz had known for years. He had adapted the Gershwins' musical *Girl Crazy* to the screen in 1932, and he had known the Gershwins before that, in the twenties, in New York; they were part of the same group. It was a gruesomely comic accident: Hearst was living on the grounds of the Marion Davies estate at the time, in that bungalow that Marion had used at M-G-M and then at Warners, and he was conferring with the publisher of his *New York Journal-American* when he heard the crash. Hearst sent the publisher down to investigate, and as soon as the man reported who was involved, Hearst went into action. Lee Gershwin had had two passengers — her secretary, who wasn't hurt, and her laundress, whom she was taking home, and who just got a bump. Mrs. Gershwin herself wasn't badly hurt, though she had a head injury that required some stitches. It was a minor accident, but Mankiewicz was taken to the police station, and he apparently behaved noisily and badly there. When he got home, a few hours later, his wife, Sara, sobered him up, and, having ascertained that Lee Gershwin had been treated at the hospital and had already been discharged, she sent him over to the Gershwins' with a couple of dozen roses. Marc Connelly, who was at the Gershwins' that night, says that when Mankiewicz arrived the house was full of reporters, and Ira Gershwin was serving them drinks and trying to keep things affable. Mankiewicz went upstairs to see Lee, who was lying in bed with her head bandaged. Amiable madman that he was, he noticed a painting on the bedroom wall, and his first remark was that he had a picture by the same artist. He apparently didn't have any idea that he was in serious trouble.

Hearst's persistent vindictiveness was one of his least attractive traits. Mankiewicz was charged with a felony, and the minor accident became a major front-page story in the Hearst papers across the country for four successive days, with headlines more appropriate to a declaration of war. It became the excuse for another Hearst campaign against the orgies and dissolute lives of the movie colony, and Hearst dragged it on for months. By then, the Hearst press was on its way to becoming the crank press, and Hearst had so many enemies that Mankiewicz had many friends. When Mankiewicz appealed to the American Civil Liberties Union, there had already been stories in *Time, Newsweek, Variety,* and elsewhere pointing out that the persecution in the Hearst papers was a reprisal for his having written the script of *Citizen Kane.* Mankiewicz, however, had to stand trial on a felony charge. And although he got through the mess of the trial all right, the hounding by the Hearst papers took its toll, and his reputation was permanently damaged.

In a letter to Harold Ross after the trial, Mankiewicz asked to write a Profile of Hearst that Ross was considering. "Honestly," he wrote, "I know more about Hearst than any other man alive. (There are a couple of deaders before their time who knew more, I think.) I studied his career like a scholar before I wrote *Citizen Kane.*" And then, in a paragraph that suggests his admiration, despite everything, for both Hearst and Welles, he wrote, "Shortly after I had been dragged from the obscurity of the police blotter and — a middle-aged, flat-footed, stylish-stout scenario writer — been promoted by the International News Service into Cary Grant, who, with a tank, had just drunkenly ploughed into a baby carriage occupied by the Dionne quintuplets, the Duchess of Kent, Mrs. Franklin

D. Roosevelt (the President's wife), and the favorite niece of the Pope, with retouched art combining the more unflattering features of Goering and Dillinger, I happened to be discussing Our Hero with Orson. With the fair-mindedness that I have always recognized as my outstanding trait, I said to Orson that, despite this and that, Mr. Hearst was, in many ways, a great man. He was, and is, said Orson, a horse's ass, no more nor less, who has been wrong, without exception, on everything he's ever touched. For instance, for fifty years, said Orson, Hearst did nothing but scream about the Yellow Peril, and then he gave up his seat and hopped off two months before Pearl Harbor."

29.

In 1947, Ferdinand Lundberg sued Orson Welles, Herman J. Mankiewicz, and R.K.O. Radio Pictures, Inc., for two hundred and fifty thousand dollars for copyright infringement, charging that *Citizen Kane* had plagiarized his book *Imperial Hearst*. On the face of it, the suit looked ridiculous. No doubt (as Houseman admits) Mankiewicz had drawn upon everything available about Hearst, in addition to his own knowledge, and no doubt the Lundberg book, which brought a great deal of Hearst material together and printed some things that had not been printed before, was especially useful, but John Dos Passos might have sued on similar grounds, since material that was in *U.S.A.* was also in the movie, and so might dozens of magazine writers. Hearst himself might have sued, on the basis that he hadn't been credited with the dialogue. The defense would obviously be that the material was in the public domain, and the suit looked like the usual nuisance-value suit that Hollywood is plagued by — especially since Lundberg offered to settle for a flat

payment of $18,000. But R.K.O. had become one of Howard Hughes' toys in the late forties, and a crew of expensive lawyers was hired. When the suit came to trial, in 1950, Welles was out of the country; he had given his testimony earlier, in the form of a deposition taken before the American vice-consul at Casablanca, Morocco. This deposition is a curious document, full of pontification and evasion and some bluffing so outrageous that one wonders whether the legal stenographer was able to keep a straight face. *Citizen Kane* had already begun to take over and change the public image of Hearst; Hearst and Kane had become inseparable, as Welles and Kane were, but Welles possibly didn't really know in detail — or, more likely, simply didn't remember — how close the movie was to Hearst's life. He seemed more concerned with continuing the old pretense that the movie was not about Hearst than with refuting Lundberg's charge of plagiarism, and his attempts to explain specific incidents in the movie as if their relationship to Hearst were a mere coincidence are fairly funny. He stated that "I have done no research into the life of William Randolph Hearst at any time," and that "in writing the screenplay of *Citizen Kane* I drew entirely upon my own observations of life," and then was helpless to explain how there were so many episodes from Hearst's life in the movie. When he was cornered with specific details, such as the picture of Jim Gettys in prison clothes, he gave up and said, "The dialogue for the scene in question was written in its first and second draftings exclusively by my colleague Mr. Mankiewicz. I worked on the third draft." When he was read a long list of events in the film that parallel Hearst's life as it is recorded in *Imperial Hearst,* he tried to use the Insull cover story and came up with the surprising information that the film dealt "quite as fully with the world of grand opera as with the world of newspaper publishing."

Mankiewicz, in a preparatory statement, freely admitted that many of the incidents and details came from Hearst's life but said that he knew them from personal acquaintance and from a lifetime of reading. He was called to testify at the trial, and John Houseman was called as a witness to Mankiewicz's labor on the script. Mankiewicz was indignant that anyone could suggest that a man of his knowledge would need to crib, and he paraded his credentials. It was pointed out that John Gunther had said Mankiewicz made better sense than all the politicians and diplomats put together, and that he was widely known to have a passionate interest in contemporary history, particularly as it related to power, and to have an enormous library. And, of course, he had known Hearst in the years of his full imperial glory, and his friends knew of his absorption in everything to do with Hearst. According to Houseman, he and Mankiewicz thought they were both brilliant in court; they treated the whole suit as an insult, and enjoyed themselves so much while testifying that they spent the time between appearances on the stand congratulating each other. Mankiewicz, in a final gesture of contempt for the charge, brought an inventory of his library and tossed it to the R.K.O. lawyers to demonstrate the width and depth of his culture. It was an inventory that Sara had prepared some years before, when (during a stretch of hard times) they had rented out their house on Tower Road; no one had bothered to look at the inventory — not even the R.K.O. attorneys before they put it into evidence. But Lundberg's lawyers did; they turned to "L," and there, neatly listed under

"Lundberg," were three copies of *Imperial Hearst.* During Mankiewicz's long recuperation, his friends had sent him many books, and since his friends knew of his admiration for many sides of the man he called "the outstanding whirling pagoda of our times," he had been showered with copies of this particular book. The inventory apparently made quite an impression in court, and the tide turned. The jury had been cordial to Mankiewicz's explanation of how it was that he knew details that were in the Lundberg book and were unpublished elsewhere, but now the width and depth of his culture became suspect. After thirty days, the trial resulted in a hung jury, and rather than go through another trial, R.K.O. settled for $15,000 — and also paid an estimated couple of hundred thousand dollars in lawyers' fees and court costs.

Mankiewicz went on writing scripts, but his work in the middle and late forties is not in the same spirit as *Kane.* It's rather embarrassing to look at his later credits, because they are yea-saying movies — decrepit "family pictures" like *The Enchanted Cottage.* The booze and the accidents finally added up, and he declined into the forties sentimental slop. He tried to rise above it. He wrote the script he had proposed earlier on Aimee Semple McPherson, and he started the one on Dillinger, but he had squandered his health as well as his talents. I have read the McPherson script; it is called *Woman of the Rock,* and it's a tired, persevering-to-the-end, burned-out script. He uses a bit of newspaper atmosphere, and Jed again, this time as a reporter, and relies on a flashback structure from Aimee's death to her childhood; there are "modern" touches — a semi-lesbian lady who manages the evangelist, for instance — and the script comes to life whenever he introduces sophisticated characters, but he can't write simple people, and even the central character is out of his best range. The one device that is interesting is the heroine's love of bright scarves, starting in childhood with one her father gives her and ending with one that strangles her when it catches on a car wheel, but this is stolen from Isadora Duncan's death, and to give the death of one world-famous lady to another is depressingly poverty-stricken. Mankiewicz's character hadn't changed. He had written friends that he bore the scars of his mistake with Charlie Lederer, but just as he had lent the script of *Kane* to Lederer, Marion Davies' nephew, he proudly showed *Woman of the Rock* to Aimee Semple McPherson's daughter, Roberta Semple, and that ended the project. His behavior probably wasn't deliberately self-destructive as much as it was a form of innocence inside the worldly, cynical man — I visualize him as so *pleased* with what he was doing that he wanted to share his delight with others. I haven't read the unfinished Dillinger; the title, *As the Twig Is Bent,* tells too hoary much.

In his drama column in *The New Yorker* in 1925, Mankiewicz parodied those who thought the Marx Brothers had invented all their own material in *The Cocoanuts* and who failed to recognize George S. Kaufman's contribution. It has been Mankiewicz's fate to be totally ignored in the books on the Marx Brothers movies; though his name is large in the original ads, and though Groucho Marx and Harry Ruby and S. J. Perelman all confirm the fact that he functioned as the producer of *Monkey Business* and *Horse Feathers,* the last reference I can find to this in print is in *Who's Who in America* for 1953, the year of his death. Many of the thirties movies he wrote are popular on television and at college showings, but when they have been discussed in film books his name has never, to

my knowledge, appeared. He is never mentioned in connection with *Duck Soup,* though Groucho confirms the fact that he worked on it. He is now all but ignored even in many accounts of *Citizen Kane.* By the fifties, his brother Joe — with *A Letter to Three Wives* and *All About Eve* — had become the famous wit in Hollywood, and there wasn't room for two Mankiewiczes in movie history; Herman became a parenthesis in the listings for Joe.

30.

Welles has offered his semi-defiant apologia for his own notoriously self-destructive conduct in the form of the old fable that he tells as Arkadin in *Confidential Report,* of 1955 — an "original screenplay" that, from internal evidence, he may very well have written. A scorpion wants to get across a lake and asks a frog to carry him on his back. The frog obliges, but midway the scorpion stings him. As they both sink, the frog asks the scorpion why he did it, pointing out that now he, too, will die, and the scorpion answers, "I know, but I can't help it; it's my character." The fable is inserted conspicuously, as a personal statement, almost as if it were a confession, and it's a bad story for a man to use as a parable of his life, since it's a disclaimer of responsibility. It's as if Welles believed in predestination and were saying that he was helpless. Yet Welles' characterization of himself seems rather odd. Whom, after all, has he fatally stung? He was the catalyst for the only moments of triumph that most of his associates ever achieved.

Every time someone in the theatre or in movies breaks through and does something good, people expect the moon of him and hold it against him personally when he doesn't deliver it. That windy speech Kaufman and Hart gave their hero in *The Fabu-*

lous Invalid indicates the enormous burden of people's hopes that Welles carried. He has a long history of disappointing people. In the *Saturday Evening Post* of January 20, 1940, Alva Johnston and Fred Smith wrote:

Orson was an old war horse in the infant prodigy line by the time he was ten. He had already seen eight years' service as a child genius. . . . Some of the oldest acquaintances of Welles have been disappointed in his career. They see the twenty-four-year-old boy of today as a mere shadow of the two-year-old man they used to know.

A decade after *Citizen Kane,* the gibes were no longer so good-natured; the terms "wonder boy" and "boy genius" were thrown in Welles' face. When Welles was only thirty-six, the normally gracious Walter Kerr referred to him as "an international joke, and possibly the youngest living has-been." Welles had the special problems of fame without commercial success. Because of the moderate financial returns on *Kane,* he lost the freedom to control his own productions; after *Kane,* he never had complete control of a movie in America. And he lost the collaborative partnerships that he needed. For whatever reasons, neither Mankiewicz nor Houseman nor Toland ever worked on another Welles movie. He had been advertised as a one-man show; it was not altogether his own fault when he became one. He was alone, trying to be "Orson Welles," though "Orson Welles" had stood for the activities of a group. But he needed the family to hold him together on a project and to take over for him when his energies became scattered. With them, he was a prodigy of accomplishments; without them, he flew apart, became disorderly. Welles lost his magic touch, and as his films began to be diffuse he acquired the reputation of being an intellectual, difficult-to-understand artist. When he appears on television to recite from Shakespeare or the Bible, he is introduced as if he were the epitome of the highbrow; it's television's more polite way of cutting off his necktie.

The Mercury players had scored their separate successes in *Kane,* and they went on to conventional careers; they had hoped to revolutionize theatre and films, and they became part of the industry. Turn on the TV and there they are, dispersed, each in old movies or his new series or his reruns. Away from Welles and each other, they were neither revolutionaries nor great originals, and so Welles became a scapegoat — the man who "let everyone down." He has lived all his life in a cloud of failure because he hasn't lived up to what was unrealistically expected of him. No one has ever been able to do what was expected of Welles — to create a new radical theatre and to make one movie masterpiece after another — but Welles' "figurehead" publicity had snowballed to the point where all his actual and considerable achievements looked puny compared to what his destiny was supposed to be. In a less confused world, his glory would be greater than his guilt.

The Shooting Script

Dated July 16, 1940

by Herman J. Mankiewicz
and Orson Welles

Introductory Note

The difference between a shooting script and a cutting continuity is that of before and after. The shooting script is written before the film is shot — it is the basis for the film; the cutting continuity is a stenographic record made from the finished film. Cutting continuities tend to be impersonal and rather boring to read, and if one examines only the cutting continuity, it is difficult to perceive the writers' contribution. Shooting scripts are much more readable, since they usually indicate the moods and intentions.

There is almost no way to judge the script of a film that has been made with the same objectivity that one judges the script of a film yet to be made. And it is particularly difficult to judge the script of a movie as famous as *Citizen Kane*. Inevitably while reading it one fills in with the actors' faces, the look of the shots — the whole feeling of the completed film; even if one hasn't seen the movie, many aspects of *Kane* would be familiar from stills reproduced over the years, and these images affect one's responses to the written material. But whether our knowledge of the movie informs this script and makes it vivid, or whether (as I think) it really has great verve on its own, it certainly violates the old theory that movie scripts make poor reading.

It was customary for scripts to include bargaining material — that is, scenes or bits of business and lines of dialogue that the moviemakers didn't expect to get Production Code approval for, but that they included for trading purposes — so they could get by with a few items they really wanted. Thus, the final, 156-page shooting script, dated July 16, 1940, which is published here, has a bordello scene that was eliminated. This letter, from the Production Code office, then headed by Joseph I. Breen, to R.K.O., states the objection to this scene, and a few other objections.

Mr. Joseph J. Nolan,   *July 15, 1940*
R.K.O.-Radio Pictures, Inc.,
780 North Gower Street,
Hollywood, California.

Dear Mr. Nolan:

We have read the second revised final script, dated July 9th, 1940, for your proposed production, titled *Citizen Kane,* and we are pleased to advise you that the material, except as noted hereinafter, is acceptable under the provisions of the Production Code and suggests no danger from the standpoint of political censorship.

There is one important detail in the story at hand which is quite definitely in violation of the Production Code and, consequently, cannot be approved. This is the locale, set down for scene 64, which is, inescapably, a brothel. Please have in mind that there is a specific regulation in the Production Code which prohibits the exhibition of brothels.

In all the circumstances, we suggest that the locale in this scene be changed and that there be nothing about the playing of the scene which would suggest that the place is a brothel.

Going through the script, page by page, we respectfully direct your attention to the following details:

Scenes 17, *et seq.:* Here, and elsewhere, it will be necessary that you hold to an *absolute minimum* all scenes of drinking and drunkenness, wherever these occur. Have in mind that such scenes are acceptable only when they are necessary "for characterization or proper plot motivation."

Page 83: There should be nothing about this scene which indicates that Georgie is a "madam," or that the girls brought into the party are prostitutes. This flavor should be very carefully guarded against.

Page 119: Please eliminate the word "Lord" from Kane's speech, ". . . the Lord only knows . . ."

Page 152: The action of the assistant "patting the statue on the fanny," should be eliminated.

You understand, of course, that our final judgment will be based upon our review of the finished picture.

Cordially yours,
Joseph I. Breen

The inclusion of the bordello scene in the script submitted to the Breen office wasn't just a schoolboy prank; for an experienced screenwriter to have turned in an innocent script would have been almost like finking. Today, these games are still played with the Rating Board, and now as then, the joke is that often the most flagrant material put in for swapping purposes sometimes gets by, while relatively innocuous material is considered objectionable.

P.K.

Prologue

Fade In

1 Ext. Xanadu — Faint Dawn — 1940 (Miniature)

Window, very small in the distance, illuminated. All around this an almost totally black screen. Now, as the camera moves slowly towards this window, which is almost a postage stamp in the frame, other forms appear; barbed wire, cyclone fencing, and now, looming up against an early morning sky, enormous iron grillwork. Camera travels up what is now shown to be a gateway of gigantic proportions and holds on the top of it — a huge initial "K" showing darker and darker against the dawn sky. Through this and beyond we see the fairy-tale mountaintop of Xanadu, the great castle a silhouette at its summit, the little window a distant accent in the darkness.

Dissolve

(A series of setups, each closer to the great window, all telling something of:)

2 The Literally Incredible Domain of Charles Foster Kane

Its right flank resting for nearly forty miles on the Gulf Coast, it truly extends in all directions farther than the eye can see. Designed by nature to be almost completely bare and flat — it was, as will develop, practically all marshland when Kane acquired and changed its face — it is now pleasantly uneven, with its fair share of rolling hills and one very good-sized mountain, all manmade. Almost all the land is improved, either through cultivation for farming purposes or through careful landscaping in the shape of parks and lakes. The castle itself, an enormous pile, compounded of several genuine castles, of European origin, of varying architecture — dominates the scene, from the very peak of the mountain.

Dissolve

3 Golf Links (Miniature)

Past which we move. The greens are straggly and overgrown, the fairways wild with tropical weeds, the links unused and not seriously tended for a long time.

Dissolve Out

Dissolve In

4 What Was Once a Good-Sized Zoo (Miniature)

Of the Hagenbeck type. All that now remains, with one exception, are the individual plots, surrounded by moats, on which the animals are kept, free and yet safe from each other and the landscape at large. (Signs on several of the plots indicate that here there were once tigers, lions, giraffes.)

Dissolve

5 The Monkey Terrace (Miniature)

In the f.g., a great obscene ape is outlined against the dawn murk. He is scratching himself slowly, thoughtfully, looking out across the estates of Charles Foster Kane, to the distant light glowing in the castle on the hill.

Dissolve

6 The Alligator Pit (Miniature)

The idiot pile of sleepy dragons. Reflected in the muddy water — the lighted window.

7 The Lagoon (Miniature)

The boat landing sags. An old newspaper floats on the surface of the water — a copy of the New York "Inquirer." As it moves across the frame, it discloses again the reflection of the window in the castle, closer than before.

8 The Great Swimming Pool (Miniature)

It is empty. A newspaper blows across the cracked floor of the tank.

Dissolve

9 The Cottages (Miniature)

In the shadows, literally the shadows, of the castle. As we move by, we see that their doors and windows are boarded up and locked, with heavy bars as further protection and sealing.

Dissolve Out

Dissolve In

10 A Drawbridge (Miniature)

Over a wide moat, now stagnant and choked with weeds. We move across it and through a huge solid gateway into a formal garden, perhaps thirty yards wide and one hundred yards deep, which extends right up to the very wall of the castle. The landscaping surrounding it has been sloppy and casual for a long time, but this particular garden has been kept up in perfect shape. As the camera makes its way through it, towards the lighted window of the castle, there are revealed rare and exotic blooms of all kinds. The dominating note is one of almost exaggerated tropical lushness, hanging limp and despairing — Moss, moss, moss. Angkor Wat, the night the last king died.

Dissolve

11 The Window (Miniature)

Camera moves in until the frame of the window fills the frame of the screen. Suddenly the light within goes out. This stops the action of the camera and cuts the music which has been accompanying the sequence. In the glass panes of the window we see reflected the ripe, dreary landscape of Mr. Kane's estate behind and the dawn sky.

Dissolve

12 Int. Kane's Bedroom — Faint Dawn — 1940

A very long shot of Kane's enormous bed, silhouetted against the enormous window.

Dissolve

13 Int. Kane's Bedroom — Faint Dawn — 1940

A snow scene. An incredible one. Big impossible flakes of snow, a too picturesque farmhouse and a snowman. The jingling of sleigh bells in the musical score now makes an ironic reference to Indian temple bells — the music freezes —

Rosebud!

The camera pulls back, showing the whole scene to be contained
in one of those glass balls which are sold in novelty stores all over
the world. A hand — Kane's hand, which has been holding the
ball, relaxes. The ball falls out of his hand and bounds down two
carpeted steps leading to the bed, the camera following. The ball
falls off the last step onto the marble floor where it breaks, the
fragments glittering in the first ray of the morning sun. This ray
cuts an angular pattern across the floor, suddenly crossed with a
thousand bars of light as the blinds are pulled across the window.

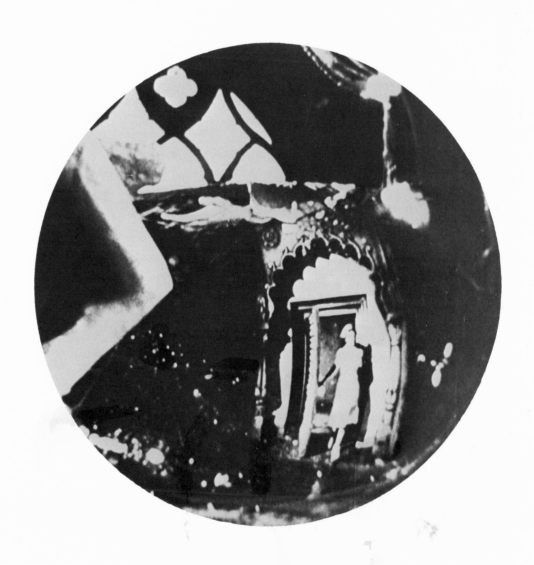

14 The Foot of Kane's Bed

The camera very close. Outlined against the shuttered window, we can see a form — the form of a nurse, as she pulls the sheet up over his head. The camera follows this action up the length of the bed and arrives at the face after the sheet has covered it.

Fade Out

Fade In

15 Int. of a Motion Picture Projection Room

On the screen as the camera moves in are the words:

MAIN TITLE

Stirring brassy music is heard on the sound track (which, of course, sounds more like a sound track than ours).

The screen in the projection rooms fills our screen as the second title appears:

CREDITS

(NOTE: Here follows a typical news digest short, one of the regular monthly or bimonthly features based on public events or personalities. These are distinguished from ordinary newsreels and short subjects in that they have a fully developed editorial or story line. Some of the more obvious characteristics of the "March of Time," for example, as well as other documentary shorts, will be combined to give an authentic impression of this now familiar type of short subject. As is the accepted procedure in these short subjects, a narrator is used as well as explanatory titles.)

Fade Out

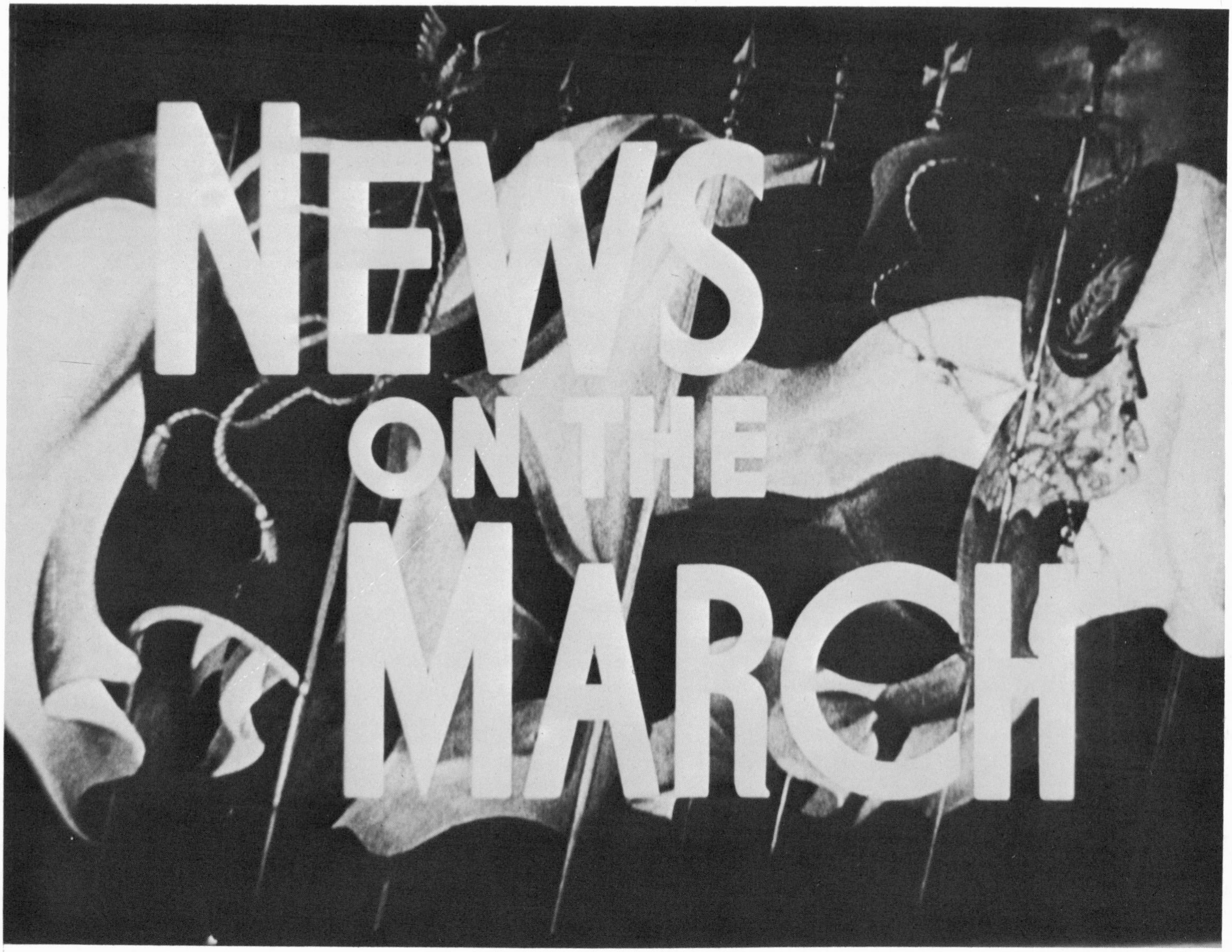
NEWS
ON THE
MARCH

NARRATOR

Legendary was the Xanadu where Kubla Khan decreed his stately pleasure dome (With quotes in his voice):

"Where twice five miles of fertile ground With walls and towers were girdled round."

(Dropping the quotes) Today, almost as legendary is Florida's Xanadu — world's largest private pleasure ground. Here, on the deserts of the Gulf Coast, a private mountain was commissioned, successfully built for its landlord. . . . Here for Xanadu's landlord will be held 1940's biggest, strangest funeral; here this week is laid to rest a potent figure of our century — America's Kubla Khan — Charles Foster Kane.

U.S.A.
Xanadu's Landlord
CHARLES FOSTER KANE

OPENING SHOT of great desolate expanse of Florida coastline. (Day — 1940)

Dissolve

TITLE:

TO FORTY-FOUR MILLION U.S. NEWS-BUYERS, MORE NEWSWORTHY THAN THE NAMES IN HIS OWN HEADLINES WAS KANE HIMSELF, GREATEST NEWSPAPER TYCOON OF THIS OR ANY OTHER GENERATION

SHOT of a huge, screen-filling picture of Kane.

PULL BACK to show that it is a picture on the front page of the "Inquirer," surrounded by the reversed rules of mourning, with masthead and headlines. (1940)

Dissolve

In journalism's history other names are honored more than Charles Foster Kane's, more justly revered. Among publishers, second only to James Gordon Bennett the First: his dashing expatriate son; England's Northcliffe and Beaverbrook; Chicago's Patterson and McCormick; Denver's Bonfils and Sommes; New York's late great Joseph Pulitzer; America's emperor of the news syndicate, another editorialist and landlord, the still mighty and once mightier Hearst. Great names all of them — but none of these so loved — hated — feared, so often spoken — as Charles Foster Kane.

A GREAT NUMBER of headlines, set in different types and different styles, obviously from different papers, all announcing Kane's death, all appearing over photographs of Kane himself. (Perhaps a fifth of the headlines are in foreign languages.) An important item in connection with the headlines is that many of them — positively not all — reveal passionately conflicting opinions about Kane. Thus, they contain variously the words, "patriot," "Democrat," "pacifist," "warmonger," "traitor," "idealist," "American," etc.

TITLE:

1895 TO 1940
ALL OF THESE YEARS HE COVERED,
MANY OF THESE YEARS HE WAS.

— The San Francisco earthquake. First with the news were the Kane Papers. First with relief of the sufferers, first with the news of their relief of the sufferers.

NEWSREEL SHOTS of San Francisco during and after the fire, followed by shots of special trains with large streamers: "Kane Relief Organization." Over these shots superimpose the date — 1906.

— Kane Papers scoop the world on the Armistice — publish, eight hours before competitors, complete details of the Armistice terms granted the Germans by Marshall Foch from his railroad car in the Forest of Compiègne.

ARTIST'S PAINTING of Foch's railroad car and peace negotiators, if actual newsreel shot unavailable. Over this shot superimpose the date — 1918.

SHOTS with the date — 1898 — (to be supplied).

SHOTS with the date — 1910 — (to be supplied).

SHOTS with the date — 1922 — (to be supplied).

NARRATOR

For forty years appeared in Kane newsprint no public issue on which Kane Papers took no stand.

HEADLINES, cartoons, contemporary newsreels or stills of the following:

1. Woman suffrage. (The celebrated newsreel shot of about 1914.)
2. Prohibition. (Breaking up of a speakeasy and such.)
3. T. V. A.
4. Labor riots.

No public man whom Kane himself did not support or denounce — often support, then denounce.

BRIEF CLIPS of old newsreel shots of William Jennings Bryan, Theodore Roosevelt, Stalin, Walter P. Thatcher, Al Smith, McKinley, Landon, Franklin D. Roosevelt and such. (Also recent newsreels of the elderly Kane with such Nazis as Hitler, Goering and England's Chamberlain and Churchill.)

NARRATOR

Its humble beginnings a dying daily —

SHOT of a ramshackle building with old-fashioned presses showing through plate-glass windows and the name "Inquirer" in old-fashioned gold letters. (1892)

Dissolve

Kane's empire, in its glory, held dominion over thirty-seven newspapers, thirteen magazines, a radio network. An empire upon an empire. The first of grocery stores, paper mills, apartment buildings, factories, forests, ocean liners —

THE MAGNIFICENT INQUIRER BUILDING of today.

A MAP OF THE U.S.A., *1891–1911,* covering the entire screen, which an animated diagram shows the Kane publications spreading from city to city. Starting from New York, miniature newsboys speed madly to Chicago, Detroit, St. Louis, Los Angeles, San Francisco, Washington, Atlanta, El Paso, etc., screaming, "Wuxtry, Kane Papers, Wuxtry."

An empire through which for fifty years flowed, in an unending stream, the wealth of the earth's third richest gold mine. . . .

SHOT of a large mine going full blast, chimneys belching smoke, trains moving in and out, etc. A large sign reads "Colorado Lode Mining Co." (1940) Sign reading: "Little Salem, Colo., 25 Miles."

Dissolve

AN OLD STILL SHOT of Little Salem as it was seventy years ago. (Identified by copperplate caption beneath the still.) (1870)

Famed in American legend is the origin of the Kane fortune. . . . How, to boarding-house-keeper Mary Kane, by a defaulting boarder, in 1868, was left the supposedly worthless deed to an abandoned mine shaft: the Colorado Lode.

SHOT of early tintype stills of Thomas Foster Kane and his wife Mary on their wedding day. A similar picture of Mary Kane some four or five years later with her little boy, Charles Foster Kane.

SHOT of Capitol in Washington, D.C.

Fifty-seven years later, before a congressional investigation, Walter P. Thatcher, grand old man of Wall Street, for years chief target of Kane Papers' attacks on "trusts," recalls a journey he made as a youth. . . .

SHOT of congressional investigating committee. (Reproduction of existing J. P. Morgan newsreel.) This runs silent under narration. Walter P. Thatcher is on the stand. He is flanked by his son, Walter P. Thatcher, Jr., and other partners. He is being questioned by some Merry-Andrew congressmen. At this moment a baby alligator has just been placed in his lap, causing considerable confusion and embarrassment.

NEWSREEL CLOSEUP of Thatcher, the sound
track of which now fades in.

THATCHER

. . . because of that trivial incident . . .

INVESTIGATOR

It is a fact, however, is it not, that in
1870 you did go to Colorado?

THATCHER

I did.

INVESTIGATOR

In connection with the Kane affairs?

THATCHER

Yes. My firm had been appointed trustee by Mrs. Kane for the fortune, which
she had recently acquired. It was her
wish that I should take charge of this
boy, Charles Foster Kane.

INVESTIGATOR

Is it not a fact that on that occasion
the boy personally attacked you after
striking you in the stomach with a sled?

Loud laughter and confusion

THATCHER

Mr. Chairman, I will read to this committee a prepared statement I have
brought with me — and I will then
refuse to answer any further questions.
Mr. Johnson, please!

*A young assistant hands him a sheet of
paper from a briefcase.*

THATCHER

(*Reading it*) "With full awareness of

the meaning of my words and the responsibility of what I am about to say, it is my considered belief that Mr. Charles Foster Kane, in every essence of his social beliefs and by the dangerous manner in which he has persistently attacked the American traditions of private property, initiative and opportunity for advancement, is — in fact — nothing more or less than a Communist."

NARRATOR

That same month in Union Square —

NEWSREEL OF UNION SQUARE MEETING, section of crowd carrying banners urging boycott of Kane Papers. A speaker is on the platform above the crowd.

SPEAKER

(*Fading in on sound track*) . . . till the words "Charles Foster Kane" are a menace to every workingman in this land. He is today what he has always been and always will be — *a Fascist!*

And yet another opinion — Kane's own.

SILENT NEWSREEL on a windy platform, flag-draped, in front of the magnificent Inquirer Building. On platform, in full ceremonial dress, is Charles Foster Kane. He orates silently.

TITLE:

"I AM, HAVE BEEN, AND WILL BE ONLY ONE THING — AN AMERICAN."
                    CHARLES FOSTER KANE

Same locale, Kane shaking hands out of frame.

DECK OF BOAT — Authentic newsreel interview on arrival in New York Harbor. Kane is posing for photographers (in his early seventies).

REPORTER

This is a microphone, Mr. Kane.

KANE

I know it's a microphone. You people still able to afford microphones with all that new income tax?

An embarrassed smile from the radio interviewer

REPORTER

The transatlantic broadcast says you're bringing back ten million dollars worth of art objects. Is that correct?

KANE

Don't believe everything you hear on the radio. Read the "Inquirer"!

REPORTER

How'd you find business conditions abroad, Mr. Kane?

KANE

How did I find business conditions, Mr. Bones? With great difficulty! (*Laughs heartily*)

REPORTER

Glad to be back, Mr. Kane?

KANE

I'm always glad to get back, young man. I'm an American. (*Sharply*) Anything else? Come, young man — when I was a reporter we asked them faster than that.

What do you think of the chances for a war in Europe?

KANE

Young man, there'll be no war. I have talked with all the responsible leaders of the Great Powers, and I can assure you that England, France, Germany and Italy are too intelligent to embark upon a project that must mean the end of civilization as we now know it. There will be no war!

Dissolve

TITLE:

FEW PRIVATE LIVES WERE
MORE PUBLIC

PERIOD STILL of Emily Norton. (1900)

Dissolve

NARRATOR

Twice married — twice divorced — first to a President's niece, Emily Norton — who left him in 1916 — died 1918 in a motor accident with their son.

RECONSTRUCTION of very old silent newsreel of wedding party on the back lawn of the White House. Many notables, including Kane, Emily, Thatcher Sr., Thatcher Jr., and recognizably Bernstein, Leland, et al., among the guests. Also seen in this group are period newspaper photographers and newsreel cameramen. (1900)

PERIOD STILL of Susan Alexander.

Dissolve

Two weeks after his divorce from Emily
Norton, Kane married Susan Alexander,
singer, at the town hall in Trenton, New
Jersey.

RECONSTRUCTED SILENT NEWSREEL. Kane, Susan and Bernstein emerging from side doorway of town hall into a ring of press photographers, reporters, etc. Kane looks startled,
recoils for an instant, then charges down
upon the photographers, laying about him
with his stick, smashing whatever he can
hit. (1917)

NARRATOR

For Wife Two, onetime opera-singing Su-san Alexander, Kane built Chicago's Mu-nicipal Opera House. Cost: Three million dollars.

STILL of architect's sketch with typically glorified "rendering" of the Chicago Municipal Opera House. (1919)

Dissolve

Conceived for Susan Alexander Kane, half finished before she divorced him, the still unfinished Xanadu. Cost: No man can say.

A GLAMOROUS SHOT of the almost finished Xanadu, a magnificent fairy-tale estate built on a mountain. (1927–1929)

SHOTS of its preparation. (1920–1929)

SHOTS of truck after truck, train after train, flashing by with tremendous noise.

SHOTS of vast dredges, steam shovels.

SHOT of ship standing offshore unloading into lighters.

In quick succession SHOTS follow each other, some reconstructed, some in miniature, some real shots (maybe from the dam projects) of building, digging, pouring concrete, etc.

One hundred thousand trees, twenty thou-sand tons of marble, are the ingredients of Xanadu's mountain.

MORE SHOTS as before, only this time we see (in miniature) a large mountain — at different periods in its development — rising out of the sands.

NARRATOR

Xanadu's livestock: the fowl of the air, the fish of the sea, the beast of the field and jungle — two of each; the biggest private zoo since Noah.

SHOTS of elephants, apes, zebras, etc., being herded, unloaded, shipped, etc. in various ways.

Contents of Xanadu's palace: paintings, pictures, statues, and more statues, the very stones of many another palace, shipped to Florida from every corner of the earth. Enough for ten museums — The loot of the world.

SHOTS of packing cases being unloaded from ships, from trains, from trucks, with various kinds of lettering on them (Italian, Arabian, Chinese, etc.) but all consigned to Charles Foster Kane, Xanadu, Florida.

A RECONSTRUCTED STILL of Xanadu — the main terrace. A group of persons in clothes of the period of 1929. In their midst, clearly recognizable, are Kane and Susan.

TITLE:

FROM XANADU, FOR THE PAST TWENTY-FIVE YEARS, ALL KANE ENTERPRISES HAVE BEEN DIRECTED, MANY OF THE NATION'S DESTINIES SHAPED.

Kane urged his country's entry into one war —

SHOTS of various authentically worded headlines of American papers since 1895.

— Opposed participation in another —

Spanish-American War SHOTS. (1898)

A GRAVEYARD in France of the world war and hundreds of crosses. (1919)

— Swung the election to one American President at least — so furiously attacked another as to be blamed for his death — called his assassin — burned in effigy.

OLD NEWSREELS of a political campaign.

NIGHT SHOT of crowd burning Charles Foster Kane in effigy. The dummy bears a grotesque, comic resemblance to Kane. It is tossed into the flames, which burn up . . . and then down. . . . (1916)

Fade Out

TITLE:

IN POLITICS — ALWAYS A BRIDESMAID, NEVER A BRIDE

Kane, molder of mass opinion though he was, in all his life was never granted elective office by the voters of his country. Few U.S. news publishers have been. Few, like one-time Congressman Hearst, have ever run for any office — most know better — conclude with other political observers that no man's press has power enough for himself. But Kane Papers were once strong indeed, and once the prize seemed almost his. In 1916, as independent candidate for governor, the best elements of the state behind him — the White House seemingly the next easy step in a lightning political career —

NEWSREEL SHOTS of great crowds streaming into a building — Madison Square Garden — then

SHOTS inside the vast auditorium, at one end of which is a huge picture of Kane. (1916)

SHOT OF BOX containing the first Mrs. Kane and young Charles Foster Kane aged nine and a half. They are acknowledging the cheers of the crowd. (Silent shot) (1916)

NEWSREEL SHOT of dignitaries on platform, with Kane alongside of speaker's table, beaming, hand upraised to silence the crowd. (Silent shot) (1916)

NEWSREEL SHOT — close-up of Kane delivering speech. (1916)

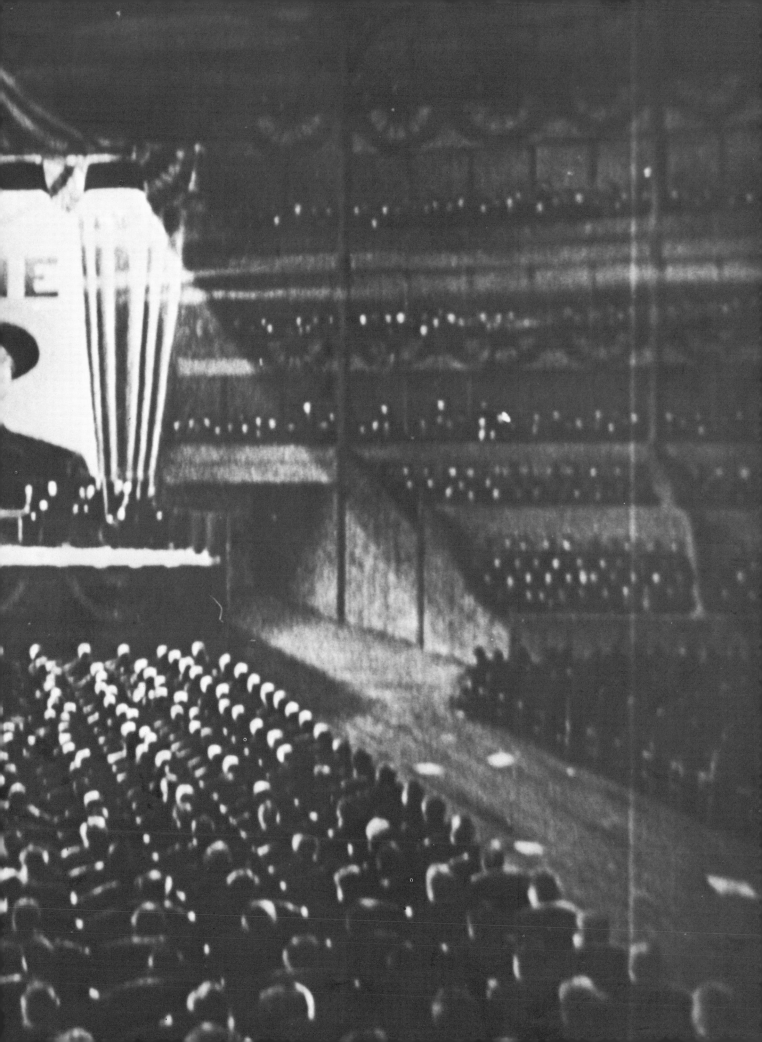

NARRATOR

Then, suddenly — less than one week before election — defeat! Shameful, ignominious — Defeat that set back for twenty years the cause of reform in the U.S., forever canceled political chances for Charles Foster Kane.

THE FRONT PAGE of a contemporary paper — a screaming headline — twin photos of Kane and Susan. (1916) Headline reads:

CANDIDATE KANE CAUGHT
IN LOVE NEST WITH "SINGER"

Then in the third year of the Great Depression . . . as to all publishers it sometimes must — to Bennett, to Munsey and Hearst it did — a paper closes! For Kane, in four short years: collapse. Eleven Kane Papers, four Kane magazines merged, more sold, scrapped —

PRINTED TITLE about depression.

ONCE MORE REPEAT THE MAP OF THE U.S.A., *1932–1939.* Suddenly the cartoon goes into reverse, the empire begins to shrink, illustrating the narrator's words.

THE DOOR OF A NEWSPAPER OFFICE with the sign: "Closed."

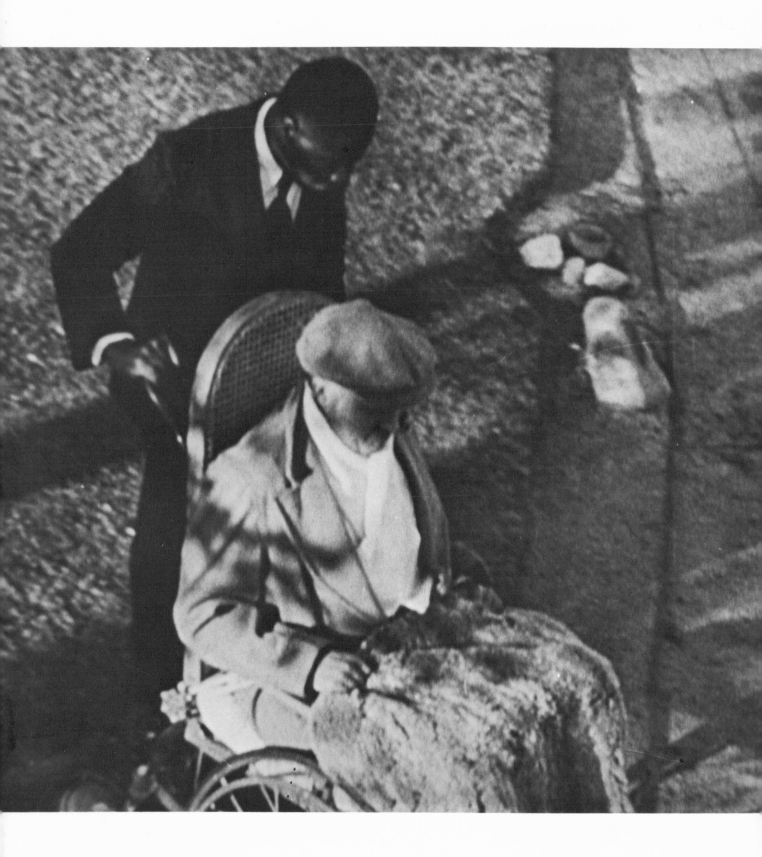

NARRATOR

Then four long years more — alone in his never finished, already decaying, pleasure palace, aloof, seldom visited, never photographed, Charles Foster Kane continued to direct his failing empire . . . vainly attempted to sway, as he once did, the destinies of a nation that had ceased to listen to him . . . ceased to trust him. . . .

SHOTS OF XANADU. (1940)

SERIES OF SHOTS, entirely modern, but rather jumpy and obviously bootlegged, showing Kane in a bath chair, swathed in steamer rugs, being perambulated through his rose garden, a desolate figure in the sunshine. (1935)

Then, last week, as it must to all men, death came to Charles Foster Kane.

EXT. THE NEW INQUIRER BUILDING, NEW YORK — NIGHT (1940) (Painting and Double Printing)
A moving electric sign, similar to the one on the Times Building — spells out the words:

CHARLES FOSTER KANE — DEAD

INSERT: DOOR with the sign PROJECTION ROOM on it.

16 Int. Projection Room — Day — 1940

(A fairly large one, with a long throw to the screen.) It is dark. Present are the editors of a news digest short, and of the Rawlston magazines. Rawlston himself is also present. During this scene, nobody's face is really seen. Sections of their bodies are picked out by a table light, a silhouette is thrown on the screen, and their faces and bodies are themselves thrown into silhouette against the brilliant slanting rays of light from the projection booth.

THOMPSON

That's it.

He rises, lighting a cigarette, and sits on corner of table. There is movement of men shifting in seats and lighting cigarettes

FIRST MAN

(*Into phone*) Stand by. I'll tell you if we want to run it again. (*Hangs up*)

THOMPSON

Well? — How about it, Mr. Rawlston?

RAWLSTON

(*Has risen*) How do you like it, boys?

A short silence

SECOND MAN

Well . . . er . . .

THIRD MAN

Seventy years of a man's life . . .

FOURTH MAN

That's a lot to try to get into a newsreel . . .

Thompson turns on the table lamp

RAWLSTON

(*As he walks to Thompson*) It's a good short, Thompson, but

what it needs is an angle — All that picture tells us is that
Charles Foster Kane is dead. I know that — I read the papers —

Laughter greets this

RAWLSTON (*Cont'd*)

What do you think, boys?

THIRD MAN

I agree.

FIRST MAN

You're right, Mr. Rawlston — it needs an angle.

RAWLSTON

You see, Thompson, it isn't enough to show what a man did —
You've got to tell us who he was —

THOMPSON

Umhum —

SECOND MAN

It needs that angle, Thompson.

RAWLSTON

Certainly! (*Getting an idea*) Wait a minute!

All lean forward, interested

RAWLSTON (*Cont'd*)

What were Kane's last words? Do you remember, boys?

THIRD MAN

Kane's last words —

SECOND MAN

Death speech —

RAWLSTON

What were the last words Kane said on earth? Maybe he told us
all about himself on his deathbed.

THOMPSON

Yes, and maybe he didn't. Maybe —

RAWLSTON

(*Riding over him*) All we saw on that screen was a big American
— (*Walks toward the screen*)

THIRD MAN

One of the biggest.

RAWLSTON

But how is he different from Ford? Or Hearst, for that matter?
Or Rockefeller — or John Doe?

There is a murmur of accord

RAWLSTON (*Cont'd*)

(*Walks toward Thompson*) I tell you, Thompson — a man's
dying words —

SECOND MAN

What were they?

THOMPSON

(*To Second Man*) You don't read the papers.

Laughter

RAWLSTON

When Mr. Charles Foster Kane died he said just one word —

THOMPSON

Rosebud!

FIRST MAN

Is that what he said? Just Rosebud?

Almost together

SECOND MAN

Umhum — Rosebud —

FOURTH MAN

Tough guy, huh? (*Derisively*) Dies calling for Rosebud!

Laughter

RAWLSTON

(*Riding over them*) Yes, Rosebud! — Just that one word! — But who was she —

SECOND MAN

Or what was it?

Tittering

RAWLSTON

Here's a man who might have been President. He's been loved and hated and talked about as much as any man in our time — but when he comes to die, he's got something on his mind called Rosebud. What does that mean?

THIRD MAN

A race horse he bet on once, probably —

FOURTH MAN

Yeh — that didn't come in —

RAWLSTON

All right — (*Strides toward Third and Fourth Men*) But what was the race?

There is a short silence

RAWLSTON (*Cont'd*)

Thompson!

THOMPSON

Yes, Mr. Rawlston.

RAWLSTON

Hold the picture up a week — two weeks if you have to —

THOMPSON

(*Feebly*) Don't you think, right after his death, if we release it now — it might be better than —

RAWLSTON

(*Decisively; cutting in on above speech*) Find out about Rosebud! — Go after everybody that knew him — that manager of his — (*Snaps fingers*) — Bernstein — his second wife — she's still living —

THOMPSON

Susan Alexander Kane —

SECOND MAN

She's running a nightclub in Atlantic City —

RAWLSTON

(*Crosses to Thompson*) See 'em all — all the people who worked for him — who loved him — who hated his guts — (*Pause*) I don't mean go through the city directory, of course.

The Third Man gives a hearty "yes-man" laugh. Others titter

THOMPSON

(*Rising*) I'll get to it right away, Mr. Rawlston.

RAWLSTON

(*Pats his arm*) Good! Rosebud dead or alive! It'll probably turn out to be a very simple thing.

Fade Out

(NOTE: Now begins the story proper — the search by Thompson for the facts about Kane — his researches — his interviews with the people who knew Kane.)

Fade In

17 *Ext. Cheap Cabaret — "El Rancho" — Atlantic City — Rain — Night — 1940 (Miniature)*

The first image to register is a sign:

"EL RANCHO"
Floor Show
Susan Alexander Kane
Twice Nightly

These words, spelled out in neon, glow out of the darkness. Then there is lightning which reveals a squalid rooftop on which the sign stands. Camera moves close to the skylight. We see through the skylight down into the cabaret. Directly below at a table sits the lone figure of a woman, drinking by herself.

Dissolve

18 Int. *"El Rancho" Cabaret — Night — 1940*

The lone figure at the table is Susan. She is fifty, trying to look much younger, cheaply blonded, in a cheap, enormously generous evening dress. The shadows of Thompson and the Captain

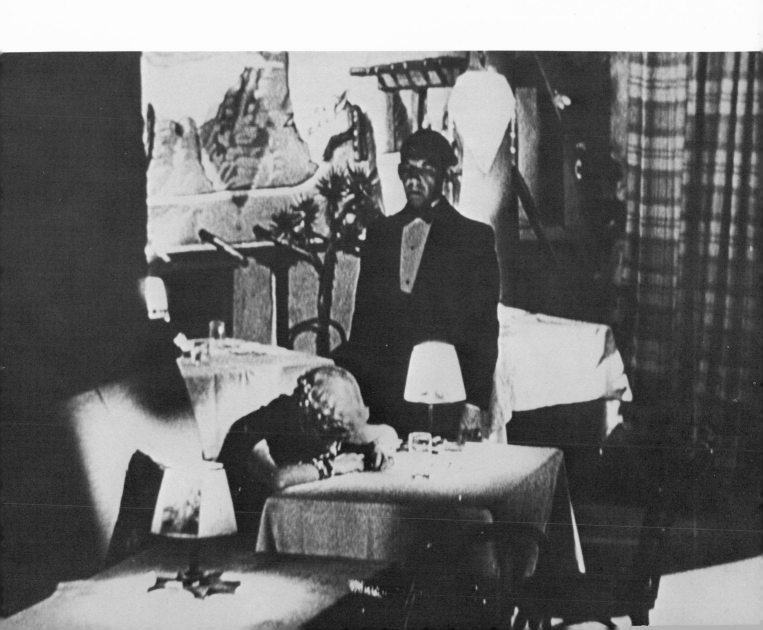

are seen moving toward the table from direction of doorway. The Captain appears, crosses to Susan, and stands behind her. Thompson moves into the picture in close f.g., his back to camera.

CAPTAIN

(*To Susan*) Miss Alexander — this is Mr. Thompson, Miss Alexander.

SUSAN

(*Without looking up*) I want another drink, John.

Low thunder from outside

CAPTAIN

Right away. Will you have something, Mr. Thompson?

THOMPSON

(*Starting to sit down*) I'll have a highball.

SUSAN

(*Looks at Thompson*) Who told you you could sit down here?

THOMPSON

I thought maybe we could have a drink together.

SUSAN

Think again!

There is an awkward pause

SUSAN (*Cont'd*)

Why don't you people let me alone? I'm minding my own business. You mind yours.

THOMPSON

If you'd just let me talk to you for a little while, Miss Alexander. All I want to ask you —

SUSAN

Get out of here! (*Almost hysterical*) Get out!

THOMPSON

(*Rising*) I'm sorry.

SUSAN

Get out.

THOMPSON

Maybe some other time —

SUSAN

Get out.

Thompson looks up at the Captain. The Captain indicates the door with a slight jerk of his head, then walks away from the table toward a waiter who is leaning against the wall in front of the door. Thompson follows

CAPTAIN

Gino — get her another highball. (*To Thompson as he passes them*) She's just not talking to anybody, Mr. Thompson.

THOMPSON

Okay

Walks to phone booth

WAITER

Another double?

CAPTAIN

Yeh —

During above Thompson has dropped coin into phone slot and dialed long distance operator (112). The waiter exits for the drink

THOMPSON

(*Into phone*) Hello — I want New York City — Courtland 7-9970. . . .

The Captain steps closer to the phone booth

THOMPSON (*Cont'd*)

This is Atlantic City 4–6827 — All right — (*Puts coins into slot; turns to Captain*) Hey — do you think she ought to have another drink?

CAPTAIN

Yeh. She'll snap out of it. Why, until he died, she'd just as soon talk about Mr. Kane as about anybody. Sooner —

THOMPSON

(*Into phone*) Hello — this is Thompson. Let me talk to the Chief, will you? (*Closes booth door*) Hello, Mr. Rawlston. She won't talk —

During above, waiter enters and sets highball in front of Susan. She drinks thirstily

RAWLSTON'S VOICE

Who — ?

THOMPSON

The second Mrs. Kane — about Rosebud or anything else! I'm calling from Atlantic City.

RAWLSTON'S VOICE

Make her talk!

THOMPSON

All right — I'm going over to Philadelphia in the morning — to the Thatcher Library, to take a look at that diary of his — they're expecting me. Then I've got an appointment in New York with Kane's general manager — what's his name — Bernstein. Then I'll come back here.

RAWLSTON'S VOICE

See everybody.

THOMPSON

Yes, I'll see everybody — that's still alive. Good-bye, Mr. Rawlston. (*Hangs up; opens door*) Hey — er —

CAPTAIN

John —

THOMPSON

John — you just might be able to help me. When she used to talk about Kane — did she ever happen to say anything — about Rosebud?

CAPTAIN

(*Looks over at Susan*) Rosebud?

Thompson slips him a bill

CAPTAIN (*Cont'd*)

(*Pocketing it*) Oh, thank you, Mr. Thompson. Thanks. As a matter of fact, just the other day, when all that stuff was in the papers — I asked her — she never heard of Rosebud.

Fade Out

Fade

19 Int. Thatcher Memorial Library — Day — 1940

A noble interpretation of Mr. Thatcher himself, executed in expensive marble, his stone eyes fixed on the camera.

We move down off of this, showing the pedestal on which the words "Walter Parks Thatcher" are engraved. Immediately below the inscription we encounter, in a medium shot, Bertha Anderson, an elderly, mannish spinster, seated behind her desk. Thompson, his hat in his hand, is standing before her.

BERTHA

(*Into a phone*) Yes. I'll take him in now. (*Hangs up and looks at Thompson*) The directors of the Thatcher Memorial Library have asked me to remind you again of the condition under which you may inspect certain portions of Mr. Thatcher's unpublished memoirs. Under no circumstances are direct quotations from his manuscript to be used by you.

THOMPSON

That's all right.

BERTHA

You may come with me.

She rises and starts towards a distant door. Thompson follows

Dissolve

*20 Int. The Vault Room — Thatcher Memorial Library — Day
— 1940*

A room with all the warmth and charm of Napoleon's tomb. As
we dissolve in, the door opens in and we see past Thompson's
shoulders the length of the room. The floor is marble. There is
a gigantic, mahogany table in the center of everything. Beyond
this is a safe from which a guard, with a revolver holster at his
hip, is extracting the journal of Walter P. Thatcher. He brings
it to Bertha.

BERTHA

(*To the guard*) Pages eighty-three to one hundred and forty-two,
Jennings.

GUARD

Yes, Miss Anderson.

BERTHA

(*To Thompson*) You will confine yourself, it is our understanding, to the chapter dealing with Mr. Kane.

THOMPSON

That's all I'm interested in.

BERTHA

You will be required to leave this room at four-thirty promptly.
*She leaves. Thompson starts to light a cigarette. The guard
shakes his head. With a sigh, Thompson bends over to read the
manuscript. Camera moves down over his shoulder onto page of
manuscript*

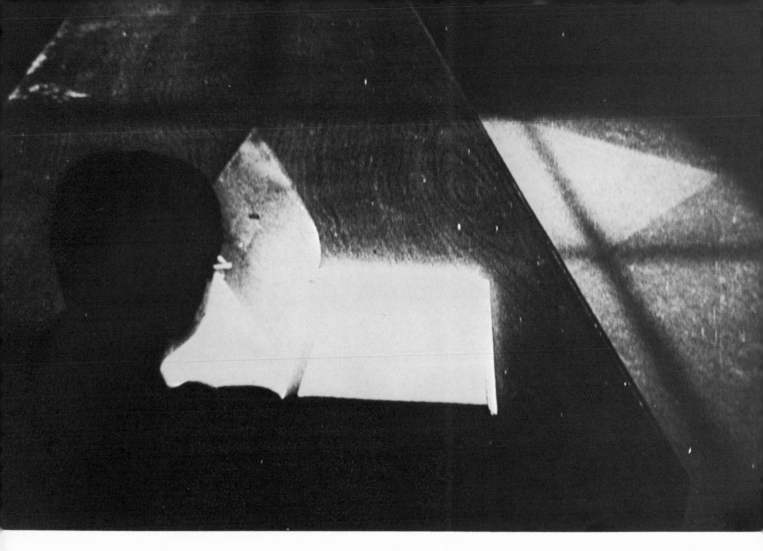

INSERT: MANUSCRIPT, neatly and precisely written:

CHARLES FOSTER KANE

When these lines appear in print, fifty years after my death, I am confident that the whole world will agree with my opinion of Charles Foster Kane, assuming that he is not then completely forgotten, which I regard as extremely likely. A good deal of nonsense has appeared about my first meeting with Kane, when he was six years old. . . . The facts are simple. In the winter of 1870 . . .

Dissolve

21 Ext. Mrs. Kane's Boardinghouse — Day — 1870

The white of a great field of snow. In the same position as the last word in above insert, appears the tiny figure of Charles Foster Kane, aged five. He throws a snowball at the camera. It sails toward us and out of scene.

22 *Reverse Angle — on the house, featuring a large sign reading:*

MRS. KANE'S BOARDINGHOUSE
HIGH CLASS MEALS AND LODGING
INQUIRE WITHIN

Charles Kane's snowball hits the sign.

23 *Int. Parlor — Mrs. Kane's Boardinghouse — Day — 1870*

Camera is angling through the window, but the window frame is not cut into scene. We see only the field of snow again. Charles is manufacturing another snowball. Now —

Camera pulls back, the frame of the window appearing, and we are inside the parlor of the boardinghouse. Mrs. Kane, aged about twenty-eight, is looking out towards her son.

MRS. KANE

(*Calling out*) Be careful, Charles!

THATCHER'S VOICE

Mrs. Kane —

MRS. KANE

(*Calling out the window*) Pull your muffler around your neck, Charles —

But Charles runs away. Mrs. Kane turns into camera and we see her face — a strong face, worn and kind

THATCHER'S VOICE

I think we'll have to tell him now —

Camera now pulls back further, showing Thatcher standing before a table on which is his stovepipe hat and documents. He is twenty-six and a very stuffy young man

MRS. KANE

I'll sign those papers now, Mr. Thatcher.

KANE SR.

You people seem to forget that I'm the boy's father.

At the sound of Kane Sr.'s voice, both have turned to him and camera pulls back still further, taking him in

MRS. KANE

It's going to be done exactly the way I've told Mr. Thatcher —

KANE SR.

If I want to, I can go to court. A father has the right to — A boarder that beats his bill and leaves worthless stock behind — that property is just as much my property as anybody's if it turns out to be valuable. I knew Fred Graves and if he'd had any idea this was going to happen — he'd have made out those certificates in both our names —

THATCHER

However, they were made out in Mrs. Kane's name.

KANE

He owed the money for the board to both of us. Besides, I don't
hold with signing my boy away to any bank as guardeen just because —

MRS. KANE

(*Quietly*) I want you to stop all this nonsense, Jim.

THATCHER

The bank's decision in all matters concerning his education, his places of residence and similar subjects are to be final.

KANE SR.

The idea of a bank being the guardeen . . .

Mrs. Kane has met his eye. Her triumph over him finds expression in his failure to finish his sentence

MRS. KANE

(*Even more quietly*) I want you to stop all this nonsense, Jim.

THATCHER

We will assume full management of the Colorado Lode — of which you, Mrs. Kane, I repeat, are the sole owner.

Kane Sr. opens his mouth once or twice, as if to say something, but chokes down his opinion

MRS. KANE

Where do I sign, Mr. Thatcher?

THATCHER

Right here, Mrs. Kane.

KANE SR.

(*Sulkily*) Don't say I didn't warn you — Mary, I'm asking you for the last time — anyone'd think I hadn't been a good husband and a —

Mrs. Kane looks at him slowly. He stops his speech

THATCHER

The sum of fifty thousand dollars a year is to be paid to yourself and Mr. Kane as long as you both live, and thereafter the survivor —

Mrs. Kane signs

KANE SR.

Well, let's hope it's all for the best.

MRS. KANE

It is — Go on, Mr. Thatcher —

Mrs. Kane, listening to Thatcher, of course, has had her other ear bent in the direction of the boy's voice. Kane Sr. walks over to close the window

24 *Ext. Mrs. Kane's Boardinghouse — Day — 1870*

Kane Jr., seen from the window. He is advancing on the snowman, snowballs in his hands. He drops to one knee.

KANE

If the rebels want a fight boys, let's give it to 'em! The terms are unconditional surrender. Up and at 'em! The Union forever!

25 *Int. Parlor — Mrs. Kane's Boardinghouse — Day — 1870*

Kane Sr. closes the window.

THATCHER

Everything else — the principal as well as all monies earned —
is to be administered by the bank in trust for your son, Charles
Foster Kane, until his twenty-fifth birthday, at which time he is
to come into complete possession.

Mrs. Kane rises and goes to the window, opening it

MRS. KANE

Go on, Mr. Thatcher.

26 *Ext. Mrs. Kane's Boardinghouse — Day — 1870*

Kane Jr. seen from the window.

KANE

You can't lick Andy Jackson! Old Hickory, that's me!

*He fires his snowball, well wide of the mark and falls flat on his
stomach, starting to crawl carefully toward the snowman*

THATCHER'S VOICE

It's nearly five, Mrs. Kane — don't you think I'd better meet
the boy —

27 *Int. Parlor — Mrs. Kane's Boardinghouse — Day — 1870*

Mrs. Kane at the window. Thatcher is now standing at her side.

MRS. KANE

I've got his trunk all packed — (*She chokes a little*) I've had it
packed for a couple of weeks —

She can't say any more. She starts for the hall door

THATCHER

I've arranged for a tutor to meet us in Chicago. I'd have brought
him along with me, but you were so anxious to keep everything
secret —

He stops. Mrs. Kane is already well into the hall. He looks at

Kane Sr., tightens his lips, and follows Mrs. Kane. Kane follows him

28 *Ext. Mrs. Kane's Boardinghouse — Day — 1870*

Kane, in the snow-covered field. He holds the sled in his hand. The Kane house, in the b.g., is a dilapidated, shabby, two-story frame building, with a wooden outhouse. Kane looks up as he sees the procession, Mrs. Kane at its head, coming toward him.

KANE

H'ya, Mom. (*Gesturing at the snowman*) See, Mom? I took the pipe out of his mouth. If it keeps on snowin', maybe I'll make some teeth and —

MRS. KANE

You better come inside, son. You and I have got to get you all ready for — for —

THATCHER

Charles, my name is Mr. Thatcher —

MRS. KANE

This is Mr. Thatcher, Charles.

THATCHER

How do you do, Charles.

KANE SR.

He comes from the East —

KANE

Hello. Hello, Pop.

KANE SR.

Hello, Charlie!

MRS. KANE

Mr. Thatcher is going to take you on a trip with him tonight, Charles. You'll be leaving on Number Ten.

KANE SR.

That's the train with all the lights.

KANE

You goin', Mom?

THATCHER

Your mother won't be going right away, Charles —

KANE

Where'm I going?

KANE SR.

You're going to see Chicago and New York — and Washington, maybe . . . isn't he, Mr. Thatcher?

THATCHER

(*Heartily*) He certainly is. I wish I were a little boy and going to make a trip like that for the first time.

KANE

Why aren't you comin' with us, Mom?

MRS. KANE

We have to stay here, Charles.

KANE SR.

You're going to live with Mr. Thatcher from now on, Charlie! You're going to be rich. Your Ma figures — that is — er — she and I have decided that this isn't the place for you to grow up in. You'll probably be the richest man in America someday and you ought to —

MRS. KANE

You won't be lonely, Charles . . .

THATCHER

We're going to have a lot of good times together, Charles . . . really we are.

Kane stares at him

THATCHER (*Cont'd*)

Come on, Charles. Let's shake hands. (*Kane continues to look at him*) Now, now! I'm not as frightening as all that! Let's shake, what do you say?

He reaches out for Charles's hand. Without a word, Charles hits him in the stomach with the sled. Thatcher stumbles back a few feet, gasping

THATCHER (*Cont'd*)

(*With a sickly grin*) You almost hurt me, Charles. Sleds aren't to hit people with. Sleds are to — to sleigh on. When we get to New York, Charles, we'll get you a sled that will —

He's near enough to try to put a hand on Kane's shoulder. As he does, Kane kicks him in the ankle

MRS. KANE

Charles!

He throws himself on her, his arms around her. Slowly Mrs. Kane puts her arms around him

KANE

(*Frightened*) Mom! Mom!

MRS. KANE

It's all right, Charles, it's all right.

KANE SR.

Sorry, Mr. Thatcher! What that kid needs is a good thrashing!

MRS. KANE

That's what you think, is it, Jim?

KANE SR.

Yes.

MRS. KANE

(*Looks at Mr. Kane; slowly*) That's why he's going to be brought up where you can't get at him.

Dissolve

INSERT: (NIGHT — 1870) (STOCK OR MINIATURE) OLD-FASHIONED RAILROAD WHEELS underneath a sleeper, spinning along the track.

Dissolve

29 Int. Train — Old-Fashioned Drawing Room — Night — 1870

Thatcher, with a look of mingled exasperation, annoyance, sympathy and inability to handle the situation, is standing alongside a berth, looking at Kane. Kane, his face in the pillow, is crying with heartbreaking sobs.

KANE

Mom! Mom!

Dissolve

INSERT: THE THATCHER MANUSCRIPT, which fills the screen. It reads:

. . . nothing but a lucky scoundrel, spoiled, unscrupulous, irresponsible. He acquired his first newspaper through a caprice. His whole attitude as a publisher . . .

Dissolve Out

Dissolve In

30 Int. Kane's Office — "Inquirer" — Day — 1898

Close-up on printed headline, which reads:

GALLEONS OF SPAIN OFF JERSEY COAST

Camera pulls back to reveal Thatcher, holding the "Inquirer" with its headline, standing in front of Kane's desk. Kane is seated behind the desk.

THATCHER

Is this really your idea of how to run a newspaper?

KANE

I don't know how to run a newspaper, Mr. Thatcher. I just try everything I can think of.

THATCHER

(*Reading the headline*) Galleons of Spain off Jersey coast. You know you haven't the slightest proof that this — this armada is off the Jersey coast.

KANE

Can you prove that it isn't?

Bernstein rushes in, a cable in his hand. He stops when he sees Thatcher

KANE (*Cont'd*)

(*Genially*) Mr. Bernstein, Mr. Thatcher.

BERNSTEIN

How are you, Mr. Thatcher?

Thatcher gives him the briefest of nods

BERNSTEIN (*Cont'd*)

We just had a wire from Cuba, Mr. Kane.

He stops, embarrassed

KANE

That's all right. We have no secrets from our readers. Mr.
Thatcher is one of our most devoted readers, Mr. Bernstein. He

knows what's wrong with every copy of the "Inquirer" since I took charge. Read the cable.

BERNSTEIN

(*Reading*) Food marvelous in Cuba — girls delightful stop could send you prose poems about scenery but don't feel right spending your money stop there's no war in Cuba signed Wheeler. Any answer?

KANE

Yes. Dear Wheeler — (*Pauses a moment*) — you provide the prose poems — I'll provide the war.

BERNSTEIN

That's fine, Mr. Kane.

Thatcher, bursting with indignation, sits down

KANE

I kinda like it myself. Send it right away.

BERNSTEIN

Right away.

Bernstein leaves. After a moment of indecision, Thatcher decides to make one last try

THATCHER

Charles, I came to see you about this — campaign of yours . . . er . . . the "Inquirer's" campaign — against the Metropolitan Transfer Company.

KANE

Good. You got some material we can use against them?

THATCHER

You're still a college boy, aren't you, Charles?

KANE

Oh, no, I was expelled from college — several colleges. Don't you remember?

Thatcher glares at him

KANE *(Cont'd)*

I remember. I think that's when I first lost my belief that you were omnipotent, Mr. Thatcher — when you told me that the dean's decision at Harvard, despite all your efforts was irrevocable — *(He thinks, and looks at Thatcher inquiringly)* — irrevocable —

Thatcher stares at him angrily, tight-lipped

KANE *(Cont'd)*

I can't tell you how often I've learned the correct pronunciation of that word, but I always forget.

THATCHER

(Not interested, coming out with it) I think I should remind you, Charles, of a fact you seem to have forgotten. You are yourself one of the company's largest individual stockholders.

KANE

The trouble is, Mr. Thatcher, you don't realize you're talking to two people. As Charles Foster Kane, who has eighty-two thousand, six hundred and thirty-one shares of Metropolitan Transfer — you see, I do have a rough idea of my holdings — I sympathize with you. Charles Foster Kane is a dangerous scoundrel, his paper should be run out of town and a committee should be formed to boycott him. You may, if you can form such a committee, put me down for a contribution of one thousand dollars.

THATCHER

(Angrily) Charles, my time is too valuable for me —

KANE

On the other hand — *(His manner becomes serious)* I am the publisher of the "Inquirer." As such, it is my duty — I'll let you in on a little secret, it is also my pleasure — to see to it that the decent, hardworking people of this city are not robbed blind by a group of money-mad pirates because, God help them, they have no one to look after their interests!

Thatcher has risen. He now puts on his hat and walks away

KANE *(Cont'd)*

— I'll let you in on another little secret, Mr. Thatcher.

Thatcher stops. Kane walks up to him

KANE (*Cont'd*)

I think I'm the man to do it. You see I have money and property. If I don't defend the interests of the underprivileged, somebody else will — maybe somebody *without* any money or any property — and that would be too bad.

THATCHER

(*Puts on his hat*) I happened to see your consolidated statement this morning, Charles. Don't you think it's rather unwise to continue this philanthropic enterprise — this "Inquirer" — that's costing you one million dollars a year?

KANE

You're right. We did lose a million dollars last year. We expect to lose a million next year, too. You know, Mr. Thatcher — at the rate of a million a year — we'll have to close this place — in sixty years.

Dissolve

31 Int. The Vault Room — Thatcher Memorial Library — Day

THE MANUSCRIPT:

The ordinary decencies of human life were, I repeat, unknown to him. His incredible vulgarity, his utter disregard . . .

Before the audience has had a chance to read this, Thompson, with a gesture of annoyance, has closed the manuscript. He turns to confront Miss Anderson, who has come to shoo him out

MISS ANDERSON

You have enjoyed a very rare privilege, young man. Did you find what you were looking for?

THOMPSON

No. Tell me something, Miss Anderson. You're not Rosebud, are you?

MISS ANDERSON

What?

THOMPSON

I didn't think you were. Well, thanks for the use of the hall.

He puts his hat on his head and starts out, lighting a cigarette as he goes. Miss Anderson, scandalized, watches him

Dissolve

32 Int. Bernstein's Office — Inquirer Skyscraper — Day — 1940

Close-up of a still of Kane, aged about sixty-five. Camera pulls back, showing it is a framed photograph on the wall. Under it sits Bernstein, back of his desk. Bernstein, always an undersized Jew, now seems even smaller than in his youth. He is bald as an egg, spry, with remarkably intense eyes. As camera continues to travel back, the back of Thompson's head and his shoulders come into the picture.

BERNSTEIN

(*Wryly*) Who's a busy man? Me? I'm chairman of the board. I got nothing but time. . . . What do you want to know?

THOMPSON

Well, we thought maybe — (*Slowly*) if we could find out what he meant by his last words — as he was dying —

BERNSTEIN

That Rosebud, huh? (*Thinks*) Maybe some girl? There were a lot of them back in the early days and —

THOMPSON

(*Amused*) It's hardly likely, Mr. Bernstein, that Mr. Kane could have met some girl casually and then, fifty years later, on his deathbed —

BERNSTEIN

You're pretty young, Mr. — (*Remembers the name*) — Mr. Thompson. A fellow will remember things you wouldn't think

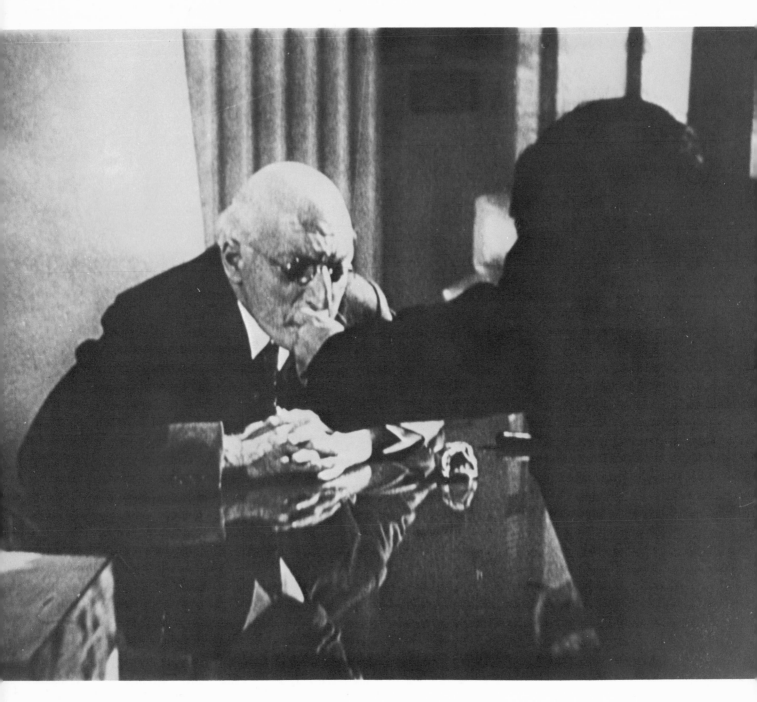

he'd remember. You take me. One day, back in 1896, I was crossing over to Jersey on a ferry and as we pulled out there was another ferry pulling in — (*Slowly*) — and on it there was a girl waiting to get off. A white dress she had on — and she was carrying a white parasol — and I only saw her for one second and she didn't see me at all — but I'll bet a month hasn't gone by since that I haven't thought of that girl. (*Triumphantly*) See what I mean? (*Smiles*)

THOMPSON

Yes. (*A near sigh*) But about Rosebud. I wonder —

BERNSTEIN

Who else you been to see?

THOMPSON

Well, I went down to Atlantic City —

BERNSTEIN

Susie? I called her myself the day after he died. I thought maybe somebody ought to — (*Sadly*) She couldn't even come to the phone.

THOMPSON

(*Ruefully*) She wasn't exactly in a condition to talk to me either. I'm going down to see her again in a couple of days. (*Pauses*) About Rosebud, Mr. Bernstein —

BERNSTEIN

If I had any idea who it was, believe me, I'd tell you.

THOMPSON

If you'd kind of just talk, Mr. Bernstein — about anything connected with Mr. Kane that you can remember — After all, you were with him from the beginning.

BERNSTEIN

From *before* the beginning, young fellow — (*Not too maudlinly*) And now it's after the end. (*After a pause*) Have you tried to see anybody else except Susie?

THOMPSON

I haven't *seen* anybody else, but I've been through that stuff of Walter Thatcher's. That journal of his —

BERNSTEIN

Thatcher! That man was the biggest darned fool I ever met.

THOMPSON

He made an awful lot of money.

BERNSTEIN

It's no trick to make a lot of money, if all you want is to make a
lot of money. You take Mr. Kane — it wasn't money he wanted.
Mr. Thatcher never did figure him out. Sometimes, even, I
couldn't — (*Suddenly*) You know who you ought to talk to? Mr.
Jed Leland. That is, if — he was Mr. Kane's closest friend, you
know. They went to school together.

THOMPSON

Harvard, wasn't it?

BERNSTEIN

Harvard — Yale — Cornell — Princeton — Switzerland. Mr. Leland — he never had a nickel — one of those old families where
the father is worth ten million, then one day he shoots himself
and it turns out there's nothing but debts. (*Reflectively*) He was
with Mr. Kane and me the first day Mr. Kane took over the
"Inquirer."

Dissolve

33 *Ext. The Old Inquirer Building — Day — 1890*

(The same shot as in news digest but this is the real thing, not a
still.) A hansom cab comes into the scene. In it are Kane and
Leland. They are both dressed like New York dandies. It is a
warm summer day. Kane jumps from the cab, as Leland follows
more slowly.

KANE

(*Pointing with his stick*) Take a look at it, Jed. It's going to look
a lot different one of these days.

*He is boisterously radiant. Jed agrees with a thoughtful smile.
As they start across the sidewalk toward the building, which they
then enter, a delivery wagon draws up and takes the place va-
cated by the cab. In its open back, almost buried by a bed, bed-*

*ding, trunks, framed pictures, etc., is Bernstein, who climbs out
with difficulty*

BERNSTEIN

(*To the driver*) Come on! I'll give you a hand with this stuff.

DRIVER

There ain't no bedrooms in this joint. That's a newspaper
building.

BERNSTEIN

You're getting paid, mister, for opinions — or for hauling?

Dissolve

34 *Int. City Room — Inquirer Building — Day — 1890*

The front half of the second floor constitutes one large city
room. Despite the brilliant sunshine outside, very little of it
is actually getting into the room because the windows are small
and narrow. There are about a dozen tables and desks, of the
old-fashioned type, not flat, available for reporters. Two tables,
on a raised platform at the end of the room, obviously serve the
city room executives. To the left of the platform is an open door
which leads into the sanctum.

As Kane and Leland enter the room an elderly, stout gent on the
raised platform strikes a bell and the other eight occupants of
the room — all men — rise and face the new arrivals. Carter, the
elderly gent, in formal clothes, rises and starts toward them.

CARTER

Welcome, Mr. Kane, to the "Inquirer." I am Herbert Carter.

KANE

Thank you, Mr. Carter. This is Mr. Leland.

CARTER

(*Bowing*) How do you do, Mr. Leland?

KANE

Mr. Leland is your new dramatic critic, Mr. Carter. I hope I
haven't made a mistake, Jedediah. It is dramatic critic you want
to be, isn't it? (*Pointing to the reporters*) Are they standing for
me?

CARTER

I thought it would be a nice gesture — the new publisher —

KANE

(*Grinning*) Ask them to sit down.

CARTER

You may resume your work, gentlemen. (*To Kane*) I didn't
know your plans and so I was unable to make any preparations.

KANE

I don't know my plans myself. As a matter of fact, I haven't got any. Except to get out a newspaper.

There is a terrific crash at the doorway. They all turn to see Bernstein sprawled at the entrance. A roll of bedding, a suitcase and two framed pictures were too much for him

KANE *(Cont'd)*

Oh, Mr. Bernstein! If you would come here a moment please, Mr. Bernstein?

Bernstein rises and comes over

KANE *(Cont'd)*

Mr. Carter, this is Mr. Bernstein. Mr. Bernstein is my general manager.

CARTER

(Frigidly) How do you do, Mr. Bernstein?

KANE

You've got a private office here, haven't you?

The delivery-wagon driver has now appeared in the entrance with parts of the bedstead and other furniture

CARTER

My little sanctum is at your disposal. But I don't think I understand —

KANE

I'm going to live right here. *(Reflectively)* As long as I have to.

CARTER

But a morning newspaper, Mr. Kane — After all, we're practically closed for twelve hours a day — except for the business offices —

KANE

That's one of the things, I think must be changed, Mr. Carter.
The news goes on for twenty-four hours a day.

Dissolve

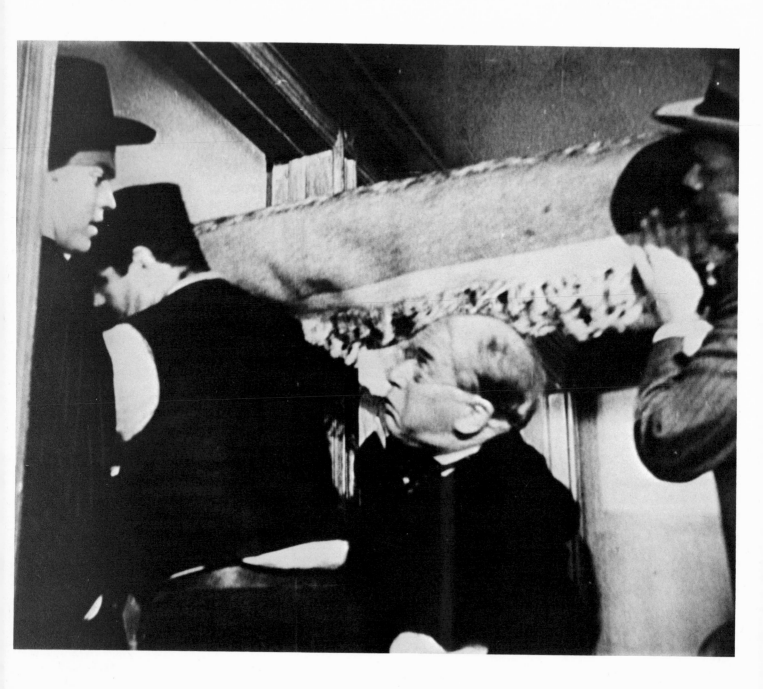

35 *Int. Kane's Office — Late Day — 1890*

Kane, in his shirt-sleeves, at a rolltop desk, is working feverishly on copy and eating a very sizable meal at the same time. Carter, still formally coated, is seated alongside him. Leland, seated in a corner, is looking on, detached, amused. On a corner of the desk, Bernstein is writing down figures.

KANE

I'm not criticizing, Mr. Carter, but here's what I mean. There's a front-page story in the "Chronicle" (*Points to it*) and a picture — of a woman in Brooklyn who is missing. Probably murdered. A Mrs. Harry Silverstone. Why didn't the "Inquirer" have that this morning?

CARTER

(*Stiffly*) Because we're running a newspaper, Mr. Kane, not a scandal sheet.

Kane has finished eating. He pushes away his plates

KANE

I'm still hungry, Jed.

LELAND

We'll go over to Rector's later and get something decent.

KANE

(*Pointing to the "Chronicle"*) The "Chronicle" has a two-column headline, Mr. Carter. Why haven't we?

CARTER

The news wasn't big enough.

KANE

If the headline is big enough, it *makes* the news big enough. The murder of this Mrs. Harry Silverstone —

CARTER

There's no proof that the woman was murdered — or even that she's dead.

KANE

(*Smiling a bit*) The "Chronicle" doesn't say she's murdered, Mr. Carter. It says she's missing; the neighbors are getting suspicious.

CARTER

It's not our function to report the gossip of housewives. If we were interested in that kind of thing, Mr. Kane, we could fill the paper twice over daily —

KANE

(*Gently*) That's the kind of thing we *are* going to be interested in from now on, Mr. Carter. I wish you'd send your best man up to see Mr. Silverstone. Have him tell Mr. Silverstone if he doesn't produce his wife at once, the "Inquirer" will have him arrested. (*Gets an idea*) Have him tell Mr. Silverstone he's a detective from the Central Office. If Mr. Silverstone asks to see his badge, your man is to get indignant and call Mr. Silverstone an anarchist. Loudly, so that the neighbors can hear.

CARTER

Really, Mr. Kane, I can't see that the function of a respectable newspaper —

KANE

Mr. Carter, you've been most understanding. Good day.
Carter leaves the room, closing the door behind him

LELAND

Poor Mr. Carter!

KANE

What makes these fellows think that a newspaper is something rigid, something inflexible, that people are supposed to pay two cents for —

BERNSTEIN

Three cents.

KANE

(*Calmly*) Two cents.
Bernstein lifts his head and looks at Kane

BERNSTEIN

(*Tapping on the paper*) This is all figured at three cents a copy.

KANE

Refigure it, Mr. Bernstein, at two cents. Ready for dinner, Jed?

BERNSTEIN

Mr. Leland, if Mr. Kane he should decide at dinner to cut the price to one cent, or maybe even he should make up his mind to give the paper away with a half-pound of tea —

LELAND

You people work too fast for me! Talk about new brooms!

BERNSTEIN

Who said anything about brooms?

KANE

It's a saying, Mr. Bernstein. A new broom sweeps clean.

BERNSTEIN

Oh!

Dissolve

36 *Int. Primitive Composing and Pressroom — New York "Inquirer" — Night — 1890*

The ground floor with the windows on the street. It is almost midnight. Grouped around a large table, on which are several locked forms of type, are Kane and Leland in elegant evening clothes, Bernstein, unchanged from the afternoon, Carter and Smathers, the composing room foreman, nervous and harassed.

KANE

Mr. Carter, front pages don't look like this any more. Have you seen the "Chronicle"?

CARTER

The "Inquirer" is not in competition with a rag like the "Chronicle."

BERNSTEIN

We should be publishing such a rag. The "Inquirer" — I wouldn't wrap up the liver for the cat in the "Inquirer" —

CARTER

Mr. Kane, I must ask you to see to it that this — this person learns to control his tongue. I don't think he's ever been in a newspaper office before.

KANE

You're right. Mr. Bernstein is in the wholesale jewelry business.

BERNSTEIN

Was in the wholesale jewelry business.

KANE

His talents seemed to be what I was looking for.

CARTER

(*Sputtering; he's really sore*) I warn you, Mr. Kane, it would go against my grain to desert you when you need me so badly — but I would feel obliged to ask that my resignation be accepted.

KANE

It *is* accepted, Mr. Carter, with assurances of my deepest regret.

CARTER

But Mr. Kane, I meant —

KANE

(*Turning to Smathers; quietly*) Let's do these pages over again.

SMATHERS

(*As though Kane were talking Greek*) We can't remake them, Mr. Kane.

KANE

Remake? Is that the right word?

SMATHERS

We go to press in five minutes.

KANE

(*Quietly*) Well, let's remake these pages, Mr. Smathers.

SMATHERS

We go to press in five minutes, Mr. Kane.

KANE

We'll have to publish half an hour late, that's all.

SMATHERS

You don't understand, Mr. Kane. We go to press in five minutes. We can't remake them, Mr. Kane.

Kane reaches out and shoves the forms onto the floor, where they scatter into hundreds of bits

KANE

You can remake them now, can't you, Mr. Smathers? After the type's been reset and the pages remade according to the way I told you before, Mr. Smathers, kindly have proofs pulled — is that right, Jed — proofs pulled? — and bring them to me. Then, if I can't find any way to improve them again — I suppose we'll have to go to press.

He starts out of the room, followed by Leland

BERNSTEIN

In case you don't understand, Mr. Smathers — he's a new broom.

Dissolve Out

Dissolve In

37 Ext. New York Street — Very Early Dawn — 1890

The picture is mainly occupied by the Inquirer Building, identified by sign. Over this newsboys are heard selling the "Chronicle." As the dissolve completes itself, camera moves toward the one lighted window — the window of Kane's office.

Dissolve

38 Int. Kane's Office — Very Early Dawn — 1890

The newsboys are still heard from the street below. Kane, in his shirt-sleeves, stands at the open window looking out. On the bed is seated Bernstein. Leland is in a chair.

NEWSBOYS' VOICES

"Chronicle"! — "Chronicle"! — H'ya — the "Chronicle"! — Get ya' "Chronicle"!

Kane closes the window and turns to the others

LELAND

We'll be on the street soon, Charlie — another ten minutes.

BERNSTEIN

It's three hours and fifty minutes late — but we did it —

Leland rises from the chair, stretching painfully

KANE

Tired?

LELAND

It's been a tough day.

KANE

A wasted day.

BERNSTEIN

Wasted?

LELAND

Charlie?

BERNSTEIN

You just made the paper over four times tonight, Mr. Kane — that's all —

KANE

I've changed the front page a little, Mr. Bernstein. That's not enough — There's something I've got to get into this paper besides pictures and print — I've got to make the New York "Inquirer" as important to New York as the gas in that light.

LELAND

What're you going to do, Charlie?

KANE

My Declaration of Principles — don't smile, Jed — (*Getting the idea*) Take dictation, Mr. Bernstein —

BERNSTEIN

I can't write shorthand, Mr. Kane —

KANE

I'll write it myself.

Kane grabs a piece of rough paper and a grease crayon. Sitting down on the bed next to Bernstein, he starts to write

BERNSTEIN

(*Looking over his shoulder*) You don't wanta make any promises, Mr. Kane, you don't wanta keep.

KANE

(*As he writes*) These'll be kept. (*Stops and reads what he has written*) I'll provide the people of this city with a daily paper that will tell all the news honestly. (*Starts to write again; reading as he writes*) I will also provide them —

LELAND

That's the second sentence you've started with "I" —

KANE

(*Looking up*) People are going to know who's responsible. And they're going to get the news — the true news — quickly and simply and entertainingly. (*With real conviction*) And no special interests will be allowed to interfere with the truth of that news. (*Writes again; reading as he writes*) I will also provide them with a fighting and tireless champion of their rights as citizens and human beings — Signed — Charles Foster Kane.

LELAND

Charlie —

Kane looks up

LELAND (*Cont'd*)

Can I have that?

KANE

I'm going to print it — (*Calls*) Mike!

MIKE

Yes, Mr. Kane.

KANE

Here's an editorial. I want to run it in a box on the front page.

MIKE

(*Very wearily*) Today's front page, Mr. Kane?

KANE

That's right. We'll have to remake again — better go down and
let them know.

MIKE

All right, Mr. Kane.

He starts away

LELAND

Just a minute, Mike.

Mike turns

LELAND *(Cont'd)*

When you're done with that, I'd like to have it back.

Mike registers that this, in his opinion, is another screwball and leaves. Kane looks at Leland

LELAND *(Cont'd)*

— I'd just like to keep that particular piece of paper myself. I've got a hunch it might turn out to be one of the important papers — of our time. (*A little ashamed of his ardor*) A document — like the Declaration of Independence — and the Constitution — and my first report card at school.

Kane smiles back at him, but they are both serious. The voices of the newsboys fill the air

VOICES OF NEWSBOYS

"Chronicle"! — H'ya, the "Chronicle"! Get ya' "Chronicle"! — the "Chronicle"!

Dissolve Out

Dissolve In

39 Ext. "Inquirer" Window on Street Level — Day — 1890

Close-up — front page of the "Inquirer" shows big boxed editorial with heading:

MY PRINCIPLES — A DECLARATION
By Charles Foster Kane

Camera continues pulling back and shows newspaper to be on the top of a pile of newspapers. As we draw further back, we see four piles — then six piles — until we see finally a big field of piles of "Inquirers." Hands come into the frame and start picking up the piles.

Camera pans to glass window on the street level of the "Inquirer." Painted on the glass are the words NEW YORK
DAILY INQUIRER — CIRCULATION 26,000 — this very
prominent. Through the glass we can see Kane, Leland and
Bernstein, leaning on the little velvet-draped rail at the back of
the window, peering out through the glass to the street, where
"Inquirer" newsboys are seen to be moving. During this, camera

tightens on window until CIRCULATION 26,000 fills frame. Then —

Dissolve

40 Ext. "Chronicle" Window — On Street Level — Day — 1890

Close-up of sign which reads: CIRCULATION 495,000

Camera pulls back to show this is a similar window on the street level of the Chronicle Building. The words NEW YORK DAILY CHRONICLE are prominently painted above this and through the glass we can see a framed photograph of some nine men. A sign over this reads: EDITORIAL AND EXECUTIVE STAFF OF THE NEW YORK CHRONICLE. A sign beneath it reads: GREATEST NEWSPAPER STAFF IN THE WORLD. Then camera continues pulling back to show Kane, Leland and Bernstein standing in front of the window, looking in. They look very tired and cold.

KANE

I know you're tired, gentlemen, but I brought you here for a reason. I think this little pilgrimage will do us good.

LELAND

(*Wearily*) The "Chronicle" is a good newspaper.

KANE

It's a good idea for a newspaper. Notice the circulation?

BERNSTEIN

(*Sullenly*) Four hundred ninety-five thousand.

KANE

Well, as the rooster said to his hens when they looked at the ostrich eggs — I am not criticizing, ladies — I am merely trying to show you what is being done in the same line by your competitors.

BERNSTEIN

Ah, Mr. Kane — with them fellows on the "Chronicle" — (*Indicates photograph*) it's no trick to get circulation.

KANE

You're right, Mr. Bernstein.

BERNSTEIN

(*Sighs*) You know how long it took the "Chronicle" to get that staff together? Twenty years.

KANE

I know.

Kane smiling, lights a cigarette, looking into the window. Camera moves in to hold on the photograph of the nine men

Dissolve

41 Int. City Room — The "Inquirer" — Night — 1898

The same nine men, arrayed as in the photograph but with Kane in the center of the first row.

Camera pulls back, revealing that they are being photographed

in a corner of the room. It is 1:30 at night. Desks, etc., have been pushed against the wall. Running down the center of the room is a long banquet table.

PHOTOGRAPHER

That's all. Thank you.

The photographic subjects rise

KANE

(*A sudden thought*) Make up an extra copy and mail it to the "Chronicle."

Kane makes his way to the head of the table

KANE (*Cont'd*)

Gentlemen of the "Inquirer"! Eight years ago — eight long, very busy years ago — I stood in front of the "Chronicle" window and looked at a picture of the nine greatest newspapermen in the world. I felt like a kid in front of a candy shop. Tonight I got my candy. Welcome, gentlemen, to the "Inquirer." It will make you happy to learn that our circulation this morning was the greatest in New York — six hundred and eighty-four thousand.

BERNSTEIN

Six hundred eighty-four thousand one hundred and thirty-two.

General applause

KANE

All of you — new and old — you're all getting the best salaries in town. Not one of you has been hired because of his loyalty. It's your talent I'm interested in — I like talent. Talent has made the "Inquirer" the kind of paper I want — the best newspaper in the world.

Applause

KANE (*Cont'd*)

Having thus welcomed you, perhaps you'll forgive my rudeness in taking leave of you. I'm going abroad next week for a vacation.

Murmurs

KANE (*Cont'd*)

I have promised my doctor for some time that I would leave when I could. I now realize that I can. This decision is in every way the best compliment that I could pay you.

Gratified murmurs

KANE (*Cont'd*)

I have promised Mr. Bernstein, and I herewith repeat that promise publicly, for the next three months to forget all about the new feature sections — the Sunday supplement — and not to try to think up any ideas for comic sections — and not to —

BERNSTEIN

(*Interrupting*) Say, Mr. Kane, so long as you're promising — there's a lot of statues in Europe you ain't bought yet —

KANE

(*Interrupting*) You can't blame me, Mr. Bernstein. They've been making statues for two thousand years, and I've only been buying for five.

BERNSTEIN

Nine Venuses already we got, twenty-six Virgins — two whole warehouses full of stuff — promise me, Mr. Kane.

KANE

I promise you, Mr. Bernstein.

BERNSTEIN

Thank you.

KANE

Oh, Mr. Bernstein —

BERNSTEIN

Yes?

KANE

You don't expect me to keep *any* of my promises, do you, Mr. Bernstein?

Terrific laughter

KANE *(Cont'd)*

Do you, Mr. Leland?

LELAND

Certainly not.

Laughter and applause

KANE

And now, gentlemen, your complete attention, please!

Kane puts his two fingers in his mouth and whistles. This is a signal. A band strikes up and enters in advance of a regiment of

very magnificent maidens. As some of the girls are detached from the line and made into partners for individual dancing —

BERNSTEIN

Isn't it wonderful? Such a party!

LELAND

Yes.

BERNSTEIN

(*To Leland*) What's the matter?

LELAND

— Bernstein, these men who are now with the "Inquirer" — who were with the "Chronicle" until yesterday — weren't they just as devoted to the "Chronicle" kind of paper as they are now to — our kind of paper?

BERNSTEIN

Sure. They're like anybody else. They got work to do. They do it. (*Proudly*) Only they happen to be the best men in the business.

LELAND

(*After a minute*) Do we stand for the same things the "Chronicle" stands for, Bernstein?

BERNSTEIN

(*Indignantly*) Certainly not. What of it? Mr. Kane he'll have them changed to his kind of newspapermen in a week.

LELAND

There's always a chance, of course, that they'll change Mr. Kane — without his knowing it.

KANE

(*Lightly*) Well, gentlemen, are we going to declare war on Spain?

LELAND

The "Inquirer" already has.

KANE

You long-faced, overdressed anarchist.

LELAND

I am not overdressed.

KANE

You are, too. Look at that necktie, Mr. Bernstein.
Bernstein embarrassed, beams from one to the other

LELAND

Charlie, I wish —

KANE

Are you trying to be serious?

LELAND

(*Holding the look for a minute and recognizing there isn't a chance*) No. (*Out of the corner of his mouth — almost as an afterthought*) Only I'm not going to Cuba.

KANE

(*To Bernstein*) He drives me crazy. Mr. Bernstein, we get two hundred applications a day from newspapermen all over the country who want to go to Cuba — don't we, Mr. Bernstein?

Bernstein is unable to answer

LELAND

Bernstein, don't you like my necktie?

KANE

(*Ignoring him*) I offer him his own byline — (*Pompously*) By Jed Leland — The "Inquirer's" Special Correspondent at the Front — I guarantee him — (*Turns to Leland*) Richard Harding Davis is doing all right. They just named a cigar after him.

LELAND

It's hardly what you'd call a cigar.

KANE

A man of very high standards, Mr. Bernstein.

LELAND

And it's hardly what you'd call a war either.

KANE

It's the best I can do. (*Looking up*) Hello, Georgie.

Georgie, a very handsome madam has walked into the picture. She leans over and speaks quietly in his ear

GEORGIE

Hello, Charlo.

LELAND

You're doing very well.

GEORGIE

Is everything the way you want it, dear?

KANE

(*Looking around*) If everybody's having fun, that's the way I want it.

GEORGIE

I've got some other little girls coming over —

LELAND

(*Interrupting*) If you want to know what you're doing — you're dragging your country into a war. Do you know what a war is, Charlie?

KANE

I've told you about Jed, Georgie. He needs to relax.

LELAND

There's a condition in Cuba that needs to be remedied maybe — but between that and a war.

KANE

You know Georgie, Jed, don't you?

GEORGIE

Glad to meet you, Jed.

KANE

Jed, how would the "Inquirer" look with no news about this nonexistent war with Pulitzer and Hearst devoting twenty columns a day to it.

LELAND

They only do it because you do.

KANE

And I only do it because they do it — and they only do it — it's a vicious circle, isn't it? (*Rises*) I'm going over to Georgie's, Jed — You know Georgie, don't you, Mr. Bernstein?

Bernstein shakes hands with Georgie

KANE

Georgie knows a young lady whom I'm sure you'd adore, Jed — Wouldn't he, Georgie?

LELAND

The first paper that had the courage to tell the actual truth about Cuba —

KANE

Why only the other evening I said to myself, if Jedediah were only here to adore this young lady — this — (*Snaps his fingers*) What's her name again?

Dissolve Out

Dissolve In

42 Int. Georgie's Place — Night — 1898

Georgie is introducing a young lady to Leland. On sound track we hear piano music.

GEORGIE

(*Right on the cue from preceding scene*) Ethel — this gentleman has been very anxious to meet you — Mr. Leland, this is Ethel.

ETHEL

Hello, Mr. Leland.

Camera pans to include Kane, seated at piano, with Bernstein and girls gathered around him

ONE OF THE GIRLS

Charlie! Play the song about you.

ANOTHER GIRL

Is there a song about Charlie?

KANE

You buy a bag of peanuts in this town and you get a song written about you.

Kane has broken into "Oh, Mr. Kane!" and he and the girls start to sing. Ethel leads the unhappy Leland over to the group. Kane, seeing Leland and taking his eye, motions to the professor who has been standing next to him to take over. The professor does so. The singing continues. Kane rises and crosses to Leland

KANE *(Cont'd)*

Say, Jed — you don't have to go to Cuba if you don't want to. You don't have to be a war correspondent if you don't want to. I'd want to be a war correspondent. *(Silence)* I've got an idea.

LELAND

Pay close attention, Bernstein. The hand is quicker than the eye.

KANE

I mean I've got a job for you.

LELAND

(Suspiciously) What is it?

KANE

The "Inquirer" is probably too one-sided about this Cuban thing — me being a warmonger and all. How's about your writing a piece every day — while I'm away — saying exactly what you think — *(Ruefully)* Just the way you say it to me, unless I see you coming.

LELAND

Do you mean that?

Kane nods

LELAND *(Cont'd)*

No editing of my copy?

KANE

(*No one will ever be able to know what he means*) No-o.

Leland keeps looking at him with loving perplexity, knowing he will never solve the riddle of this face

KANE (*Cont'd*)

We'll talk some more about it at dinner tomorrow night. We've only got about ten more nights before I go to Europe. Richard Carl's opening in *The Spring Chicken*. I'll get the girls. You get the tickets. A drama critic gets them free.

LELAND

Charlie —

KANE

It's the best I can do.

LELAND

(*Still smiling*) It doesn't make any difference about me, but one of these days you're going to find out that all this charm of yours won't be enough —

KANE

You're wrong. It does make a difference about you — Come to think of it, Mr. Bernstein, I don't blame Mr. Leland for not wanting to be a war correspondent. It isn't much of a war. Besides, they tell me there isn't a decent restaurant on the whole island.

Dissolve

43 *Int. Kane's Office — Day — 1898*

The shot begins on a close-up of a label. The words "From C. F. Kane, Paris, France," fill the screen. This registers as camera pulls back to show remainder of label in larger letters, which read: "To Charles Foster Kane, New York — HOLD FOR ARRIVAL." Camera continues pulling back, showing the entire sanctum piled to the ceiling with packing boxes, crated statues and art objects. One-third of the statues have been uncrated. Leland is in his shirt-sleeves; clearly he has been opening boxes, with claw hammer in one hand. Bernstein has come to the door.

BERNSTEIN

I got here a cable from Mr. Kane — Mr. Leland, why didn't you go to Europe with him? He wanted you to.

LELAND

I wanted him to have fun — and with me along —

This stops Bernstein. Bernstein looks at him

LELAND (*Cont'd*)

Bernstein, I wish you'd let me ask you a few questions — and answer me truthfully.

BERNSTEIN

Don't I always? Most of the time?

LELAND

Bernstein, am I a stuffed shirt? Am I a horse-faced hypocrite? Am I a New England schoolmarm?

BERNSTEIN

Yes.

Leland is surprised

BERNSTEIN (*Cont'd*)

If you thought I'd answer you different from what Mr. Kane tells you — well, I wouldn't.

Pause as Bernstein looks around the room

BERNSTEIN (*Cont'd*)

Mr. Leland, it's good he promised not to send back any statues.

LELAND

I don't think you understand, Bernstein. This is one of the rarest Venuses in existence.

BERNSTEIN

(*Studying the statue carefully*) Not so rare like you think, Mr. Leland. (*Handing cable to Leland*) Here's the cable from Mr. Kane.

Leland takes it, reads it, smiles

BERNSTEIN (*Cont'd*)

(*As Leland reads cable*) He wants to buy the world's biggest diamond.

LELAND

I didn't know Charles was collecting diamonds.

BERNSTEIN

He ain't. He's collecting somebody that's collecting diamonds. Anyway — (*Taking his eye*) he ain't only collecting statues.

Dissolve

44 Int. City Room — Day — 1898

Dissolve to elaborate loving cup on which is engraved:

WELCOME HOME, MR. KANE — *From 730 employees of the New York "Inquirer."*

As camera pulls back, it reveals that this cup is on a little table at the far end of the "Inquirer" city room. Next to the table stands Bernstein, rubbing his hands, Hillman and a few other executives. Throughout the entire city room, there is a feeling of cleanliness and anticipation.

COPY BOY

(*At stairway*) Here he comes!

Bernstein and Hillman start toward the door. All the others rise. Just as Bernstein gets to the door, it bursts open and Kane, an envelope in his hand, storms in

KANE

Hello, Mr. Bernstein!

Kane continues at the same rate of speed with which he entered, Bernstein following behind him, at the head of a train which includes Hillman and others. The race stops a couple of steps beyond the society editor's desk by Kane, who moves back to the desk, making something of a traffic jam. (A plaque on the desk which reads "Society Editor" is what caught Kane's eye)

KANE (*Cont'd*)

Excuse me, I've been away so long, I don't know your routine. Miss —

BERNSTEIN

(*Proudly*) Miss Townsend, Mr. Charles Foster Kane!

KANE

Miss Townsend, I'd — (*He's pretty embarrassed by his audience*) I — have a little social announcement here. (*He puts it on the desk*) I wish you wouldn't treat this any differently than you would — you would — any other — anything else.

He looks around at the others with some embarrassment. At that moment, Hillman hands Bernstein the cup

BERNSTEIN

(*Holding the cup*) Mr. Kane, on behalf of all the employees of the "Inquirer" —

KANE

(*Interrupting*) Mr. Bernstein, I can't tell you how much I appreciate — (*He takes the cup and starts to take a few steps — realizes that he is being a little boorish — turns around and hands the cup back to Bernstein*) Look, Mr. Bernstein — everybody — I'm sorry — I — I can't take it now.

Murmurs

KANE (*Cont'd*)

I'm busy. I mean — please — give it to me tomorrow.

He starts to run out. There is surprised confusion among the rest

BERNSTEIN

Say, he's in an awful hurry!

SAME COPY BOY

(*At window*) Hey, everybody! Lookee out here!

The whole staff rushes to the window

45 *Ext. Street in Front of Inquirer Building — Day — 1898*

Angle down from window — shot of Emily sitting in a barouche.

46 *Ext. Window of "Inquirer" City Room — Day — 1898*

Up shot of faces in the window, reacting and grinning.

47 *Int. City Room — Day — 1898*

Miss Townsend stands frozen at her desk. She is reading and re-reading with trembling hands the piece of flimsy which Kane gave her.

TOWNSEND

Mr. Bernstein!

Mr. Bernstein, at window, turns around

BERNSTEIN

Yes, Miss Townsend.

TOWNSEND

This — this announcement — (*She reads shakily*) Mr. and Mrs. Thomas Monroe Norton announce the engagement of their daughter, Emily Monroe Norton, to Mr. Charles Foster Kane.

Bernstein reacts

TOWNSEND (*Cont'd*)

Emily Monroe Norton — she's the niece of the President of the United States.

Bernstein nods his head proudly and turns back to look out the window

48 *Ext. Street in Front of Inquirer Building — Day — 1898*

Down shot of Kane, crossing the curb to the barouche. He looks up in this shot, sees the people in the window, waves gaily, steps into the barouche. Emily looks at him smilingly. He kisses her full on the lips before he sits down. She acts a bit taken aback because of the public nature of the scene, but she isn't really annoyed.

Dissolve

49 *Int. City Room — "Inquirer" — Day — 1898*

Bernstein and group at window.

BERNSTEIN

A girl like that, believe me, she's lucky! President's niece, huh!
Say, before he's through, she'll be a President's wife!

Dissolve

INSERT: FRONT PAGE "INQUIRER" (1898–1900)

Large picture of the young couple — Kane and Emily — occupying four columns — very happy.

INSERT: NEWSPAPER — KANE'S MARRIAGE TO EMILY WITH STILL
OF GROUP ON WHITE HOUSE LAWN (1900)

(Same setup as early newsreel in news digest.)

Dissolve

50 *Int. Bernstein's Office — "Inquirer" — Day — 1940*

Bernstein and Thompson. As the dissolve comes, Bernstein's
voice is heard.

BERNSTEIN

The way things turned out, I don't need to tell you — Miss
Emily Norton was no rosebud!

THOMPSON

It didn't end very well, did it?

BERNSTEIN

It ended — Then there was Susie — That ended too. (*Shrugs, a
pause*) I guess he didn't make her very happy — You know, I
was thinking — that Rosebud you're trying to find out about —

THOMPSON

Yes —

BERNSTEIN

Maybe that was something he lost. Mr. Kane was a man that

lost — almost everything he had. You ought to talk to Mr. Leland. Of course, he and Mr. Kane didn't exactly see eye to eye. You take the Spanish-American War. I guess Mr. Leland was right. That was Mr. Kane's war. We didn't really have anything to fight about — (*Chuckles*) But do you think if it hadn't been for that war of Mr. Kane's, we'd have the Panama Canal? I wish I knew where Mr. Leland was — (*Slowly*) Maybe even he's — a lot of the time now they don't tell me those things — maybe even he's dead.

THOMPSON

In case you'd like to know, Mr. Bernstein, he's at the Huntington Memorial Hospital on 180th Street.

BERNSTEIN

You don't say! Why I had no idea —

THOMPSON

Nothing particular the matter with him, they tell me. Just —

BERNSTEIN

Just old age. (*Smiles sadly*) It's the only disease, Mr. Thompson, you don't look forward to being cured of.

Dissolve Out

Dissolve In

51 Ext. Hospital Roof — Day — 1940

Close shot — Thompson. He is tilted back in a chair, leaning against a chimney. Leland's voice is heard for a few moments before Leland is seen.

LELAND'S VOICE

When you get to my age, young man, you don't miss anything. Unless maybe it's a good drink of bourbon. Even that doesn't make much difference, if you remember there hasn't been any good bourbon in this country for twenty years.

Camera has pulled back, revealing that Leland, wrapped in a blanket, is in a wheelchair, talking to Thompson. They are on the flat roof of a hospital

THOMPSON

Mr. Leland, you were —

LELAND

You don't happen to have a cigar, do you? I've got a young physician who thinks I'm going to stop smoking. . . . I changed the subject, didn't I? Dear, dear! What a disagreeable old man I've become. You want to know what I think of Charlie Kane? — Well — I suppose he had some private sort of greatness. But he kept it to himself. (*Grinning*) He never . . . gave himself away . . . He never gave anything away. He just . . . left you a tip. He had a generous mind. I don't suppose anybody ever had so many opinions. That was because he had the power to express them, and Charlie lived on power and the excitement of using it — But he didn't believe in anything except Charlie Kane. He never had a conviction except Charlie Kane in his life. I guess he died without one — That must have been pretty unpleasant. Of course, a lot of us check out with no special conviction about death. But we do know what we're leaving . . . we believe in something. (*Looks sharply at Thompson*) You're absolutely sure you haven't got a cigar?

THOMPSON

Sorry, Mr. Leland.

LELAND

Never mind — Bernstein told you about the first days at the office, didn't he? — Well, Charlie was a bad newspaperman even then. He entertained his readers but he never told them the truth.

THOMPSON

Maybe you could remember something that —

LELAND

I can remember everything. That's my curse, young man. It's the greatest curse that's ever been inflicted on the human race. Memory . . . I was his oldest friend. (*Slowly*) As far as I was concerned, he behaved like a swine. Not that Charlie ever was brutal. He just did brutal things. Maybe I wasn't his friend. If

I wasn't, he never had one. Maybe I was what nowadays you call a stooge.

THOMPSON

Mr. Leland, what do you know about Rosebud?

LELAND

Rosebud? Oh! His dying words — Rosebud — Yeh. I saw that in the "Inquirer." Well, I've never believed anything I saw in the "Inquirer." Anything else?

Thompson is taken aback

LELAND (*Cont'd*)

I'll tell you about Emily. I used to go to dancing school with her. I was very graceful. Oh! — we were talking about the first Mrs. Kane —

THOMPSON

What was she like?

LELAND

She was like all the other girls I knew in dancing school. They were nice girls. Emily was a little nicer. She did her best — Charlie did his best — well, after the first couple of months they never saw much of each other except at breakfast. It was a marriage just like any other marriage.

Dissolve

(NOTE: The following scenes cover a period of nine years — are played in the same set with only changes in lighting, special effects outside the window, and wardrobe.)

52 Int. Kane's Home — Breakfast Room — Day — 1901

Kane, in white tie and tails, and Emily formally attired. Kane is pouring a glass of milk for Emily out of a milk bottle. As he finishes, he leans over and playfully nips the back of her neck.

EMILY

(*Flustered*) Charles! (*She's loving it*) Go sit down where you belong.

KANE

(*On the way to his own place*) You're beautiful.

EMILY

I can't be. I've never been to six parties in one night before. I've never been up this late.

KANE

It's just a matter of habit.

EMILY

What do you suppose the servants will think?

KANE

They'll think we enjoyed ourselves. Didn't we?

EMILY

(*She gives him a purring smile. Then —*) Dearest — I don't see why you have to go straight off to the newspaper.

KANE

You never should have married a newspaperman. They're worse than sailors. I absolutely love you.

They look at each other

EMILY

Charles, even newspapermen have to sleep.

KANE

(*Still looking at her*) I'll call up Bernstein and tell him to put off my appointments till noon — What time is it?

EMILY

I don't know — it's late.

KANE

It's early.

Dissolve Out

Dissolve In

53 *Int. Kane's Home — Breakfast Room — Day — 1902*

Kane and Emily — different clothes — different food.

EMILY

Do you know how long you kept me waiting while you went to the office last night for ten minutes? Really, Charles, we were dinner guests at the Boardman's — we weren't invited for the weekend.

KANE

You're the nicest girl I ever married.

EMILY

Charles, if I didn't trust you — What do you do on a newspaper in the middle of the night?

KANE

My dear, your only corespondent is the "Inquirer."

Dissolve

54 *Int. Kane Home — Breakfast Room — 1904*

Kane and Emily — change of costume and food. Emily is dressed for the street.

EMILY

(*Kidding on the level*) Sometimes I think I'd prefer a rival of flesh and blood.

KANE

Ah, Emily — I don't spend that much time —

EMILY

It isn't just time — it's what you print — attacking the President —

KANE

You mean Uncle John.

EMILY

I mean the President of the United States.

KANE

He's still Uncle John, and he's still a well-meaning fathead —

EMILY

(*Interrupting*) Charles —

KANE

(*Continuing on top of her*) — who's letting a pack of high-pressure crooks run his administration. This whole oil scandal —

EMILY

He happens to be the President, Charles — not you.

KANE

That's a mistake that will be corrected one of these days.

Dissolve

55 *Int. Kane's Home — Breakfast Room — 1905*

Kane and Emily — change of costume and food.

EMILY

Charles, when people make a point of not having the "Inquirer" in their homes — Margaret English says that the reading room at the Assembly already has more than forty names that have agreed to cancel the paper —

KANE

That's wonderful. Mr. Bernstein will be delighted. You see, Emily, when your friends cancel the paper, that just takes another name off our deadbeat list. You know, don't you, it's practically a point of honor among the rich not to pay the newsdealer.

Dissolve Out

Dissolve In

56 Int. Kane's Home — Breakfast Room — 1906

Kane and Emily — change of costume and food.

EMILY

Your Mr. Bernstein sent Junior the most incredible atrocity yesterday. I simply can't have it in the nursery.

KANE

Mr. Bernstein is apt to pay a visit to the nursery now and then.

EMILY

Does he have to?

KANE

(*Shortly*) Yes.

Dissolve

57 *Int. Kane's Home — Breakfast Room — 1908*

Kane and Emily — change of costume and food.

EMILY

Really, Charles — people have a right to expect —

KANE

What I care to give them.

Dissolve

58 *Int. Kane's Home — Breakfast Room — 1909*

Kane and Emily — change of costume and food. They are both silent, reading newspapers. Kane is reading his "Inquirer." Emily is reading a copy of the "Chronicle."

Dissolve Out

Dissolve In

59 *Ext. Hospital Roof — Day — 1940*

Leland and Thompson.

THOMPSON

Wasn't he ever in love with her?

LELAND

He married for love — (*A little laugh*) That's why he did everything. That's why he went into politics. It seems we weren't enough. He wanted all the voters to love him, too. All he really wanted out of life was love — That's Charlie's story — how he lost it. You see, he just didn't have any to give. He loved Charlie Kane, of course, very dearly — and his mother, I guess he always loved her.

THOMPSON

How about his second wife?

LELAND

Susan Alexander? (*He chuckles*) You know what Charlie called her? — The day after he'd met her he told me about her — he said she was a cross-section of the American public — I guess he couldn't help it — she must have had something for him. (*With a smile*) That first night, according to Charlie — all she had was a toothache.

Dissolve Out

Dissolve In

60 *Ext. Corner Drugstore and Street on the West Side of New York — Night — 1915*

Susan, aged twenty-two, neatly but cheaply dressed, is leaving the drugstore. (It's about eight o'clock at night.) With a large, man-sized handkerchief pressed to her cheek, she is in considerable pain. A carriage crosses in front of the camera — passes — Susan continues down the street — Camera following her — encounters Kane — very indignant, standing near the edge of the sidewalk, covered with mud. She looks at him and smiles. He glares at her. She starts on down the street; turns, looks at him again, and starts to laugh.

KANE

(*Glowering*) It's not funny.

SUSAN

I'm sorry, mister — but you *do* look awful funny.

Suddenly the pain returns and she claps her hand to her jaw

SUSAN (*Cont'd*)

Ow!

KANE

What's the matter with you?

SUSAN

Toothache.

KANE

Hmm!

He has been rubbing his clothes with his handkerchief

SUSAN

You've got some on your face. (*Starts to laugh again*)

KANE

What's funny now?

SUSAN

You are. (*The pain returns*) Oh!

KANE

Ah ha!

SUSAN

If you want to come in and wash your face — I can get you some hot water to get that dirt off your trousers —

KANE

Thanks.

Susan starts, with Kane following her

Dissolve

61 *Int. Susan's Room — Night — 1915*

Susan comes into the room, carrying a basin, with towels over her arm. Kane is waiting for her. She doesn't close the door.

SUSAN

(*By way of explanation*) My landlady prefers me to keep this door open when I have a gentleman caller. She's a very decent woman. (*Making a face*) Ow!

Kane rushes to take the basin from her, putting it on the chiffonier. To do this, he has to shove the photograph to one side with the basin. Susan grabs the photograph as it is about to fall over

SUSAN (*Cont'd*)

Hey, you should be more careful. That's my Ma and Pa.

KANE

I'm sorry. They live here too?

SUSAN

No. They've passed on.

Again she puts her hand to her jaw

KANE

You poor kid, you are in pain, aren't you?

Susan can't stand it any more and sits down in a chair, bent over, whimpering a bit

KANE (*Cont'd*)

Look at me.

She looks at him

KANE (*Cont'd*)

Why don't you laugh? I'm just as funny in here as I was on the street.

SUSAN

I know, but you don't like me to laugh at you.

KANE

I don't like your tooth to hurt, either.

SUSAN

I can't help it.

KANE

Come on, laugh at me.

SUSAN

I can't — what are you doing?

KANE

I'm wiggling both my ears at the same time. (*He does so*) It took me two solid years at the finest boys' school in the world to learn that trick. The fellow who taught me is now president of Venezuela. (*He wiggles his ears again*)

Susan starts to smile

KANE (*Cont'd*)

That's it.

Susan smiles very broadly — then starts to laugh

Dissolve

62 *Int. Susan's Room — Night — 1915*

Close-up of a duck, camera pulls back, showing it to be a shadow-graph on the wall, made by Kane, who is now in his shirt-sleeves.

SUSAN

(*Hesitatingly*) A chicken?

KANE

No. But you're close.

SUSAN

A rooster?

KANE

You're getting further away all the time. It's a duck.

SUSAN

A duck. You're not a professional magician, are you?

KANE

No. I've told you. My name is Kane — Charles Foster Kane.

SUSAN

I know. Charles Foster Kane. Gee — I'm pretty ignorant, I guess you caught on to that —

KANE

You really don't know who I am?

SUSAN

No. That is, I bet it turns out I've heard your name a million times, only you know how it is —

KANE

But you like me, don't you? Even though you don't know who I am?

SUSAN

You've been wonderful! I can't tell you how glad I am you're here, I don't know many people and — (*She stops*)

KANE

And I know too many people. Obviously, we're both lonely. (*He smiles*) Would you like to know where I was going tonight — when you ran into me and ruined my Sunday clothes?

SUSAN

I didn't run into you and I bet they're not your Sunday clothes. You've probably got a lot of clothes.

KANE

I was only joking! (*Pauses*) I was on my way to the Western Manhattan Warehouse — in search of my youth.

Susan is bewildered

KANE (*Cont'd*)

You see, my mother died too — a long time ago. Her things were put into storage out West because I had no place to put them then. I still haven't. But now I've sent for them just the same. And tonight I'd planned to make a sort of sentimental journey — and now —

Kane doesn't finish. He looks at Susan. Silence

KANE (*Cont'd*)

Who am I? Well, let's see. Charles Foster Kane was born in New Salem, Colorado in eighteen six — (*He stops on the word "sixty" — obviously a little embarrassed*) I run a couple of newspapers. How about you?

SUSAN

Me?

KANE

How old did you say you were?

SUSAN

(*Very bright*) I didn't say.

KANE

I didn't think you did. If you had, I wouldn't have asked you
again, because I'd have remembered. How old?

SUSAN

Pretty old. I'll be twenty-two in August.

KANE

That's a ripe old age — What do you do?

SUSAN

I work at Seligman's.

KANE

Is that what you want to do?

SUSAN

I wanted to be a singer. I mean, I didn't. Mother did for me.

KANE

What happened to the singing?

SUSAN

Mother always thought — she used to talk about grand opera
for me. Imagine! — Anyway, my voice isn't that kind. It's just
— you know what mothers are like.

KANE

Yes.

SUSAN

As a matter of fact, I do sing a little.

KANE

Would you sing for me?

SUSAN

Oh, you wouldn't want to hear me sing.

KANE

Yes, I would. That's why I asked.

SUSAN

Well, I —

KANE

Don't tell me your toothache is bothering you again?

SUSAN

Oh, no, that's all gone.

KANE

Then you haven't any alibi at all. Please sing.

Susan, with a tiny ladylike hesitancy, goes to the piano and sings a polite song. Sweetly, nicely, she sings with a small, untrained voice. Kane listens. He is relaxed, at ease with the world

Dissolve Out

Dissolve In

INSERT: "INQUIRER" HEADLINE. (1916)

BOSS ROGERS PICKS DEMOCRATIC NOMINEE

Dissolve

INSERT: "INQUIRER" HEADLINE. (1916)

BOSS ROGERS PICKS REPUBLICAN NOMINEE

Dissolve

INSERT: FOUR COLUMN CARTOON ON BACK PAGE OF "INQUIRER." (1916)

This shows Boss Rogers, labeled as such, in convict stripes, dangling little marionette figures — labeled Democratic Candidate and Republican Candidate — from each hand. As camera pans to remaining four columns it reveals box. This is headed:

Put this man in jail, people of New York.

It is signed, in bold type, "Charles Foster Kane." The text between headline and signature, little of which need be read, tells of the boss-ridden situation.

Dissolve Out

Dissolve In

63 Int. Madison Square Garden — Night — 1916

The evening of the final great rally. Emily and Junior are to be
seen in the front of a box. Emily is tired and wears a forced
smile on her face. Junior, now aged nine and a half, is eager,
bright-eyed and excited. Kane is just finishing his speech.

KANE

It is no secret that I entered upon this campaign with no thought
that I could be elected governor of this state! It is no secret that
my only purpose was to bring as wide publicity as I could to the
domination of this state — of its every resource — of its every
income — of literally the lives and deaths of its citizens by Boss
Edward G. Rogers! It is now no secret that every straw vote,
every independent poll, shows that I will be elected. And I repeat
to you — my first official act as governor will be to appoint a
special district attorney to arrange for the indictment, prosecution and conviction of Boss Edward G. Rogers!

Terrific screaming and cheering from the audience

Dissolve

64 Int. Madison Square Garden — Night — 1916

The speakers' platform. Numerous officials and civic leaders are
crowding around Kane. Cameramen take flash photographs.

FIRST CIVIC LEADER

Great speech, Mr. Kane.

SECOND LEADER

(*Pompous*) One of the most notable public utterances ever made
by a candidate in this state —

KANE

Thank you, gentlemen. Thank you.

*He looks up and notices that the box in which Emily and Junior
were sitting is now empty. He starts toward rear of the platform,
through the press of people. Hillman approaches him*

HILLMAN

A wonderful speech, Mr. Kane.

Kane pats him on the shoulder as he walks along

HILLMAN *(Cont'd)*

If the election were held *today,* you'd be elected by a hundred thousand votes — on an Independent ticket there's never been anything like it!

Kane is very pleased. He continues with Hillman slowly through the crowd — a band playing off

KANE

It does seem too good to be true.

HILLMAN

Rogers isn't even pretending. He isn't just scared any more. He's

sick. Frank Norris told me last night he hasn't known Rogers to be that worried in twenty-five years.

KANE

I think it's beginning to dawn on Mr. Rogers that I mean what I say. With Mr. Rogers out of the way, Hillman, I think we may really begin to hope for a good government in this state. (*Stopping*)

A WELL-WISHER

Great speech, Mr. Kane!

ANOTHER WELL-WISHER

Wonderful, Mr. Kane!

Ad libs from other well-wishers

Dissolve Out

Dissolve In

*65 Ext. One of the Exits — Madison Square Garden — Night
— 1916*

Emily and Junior are standing, waiting for Kane.

JUNIOR

Is Pop governor yet, Mom?

*Kane appears with Hillman and several other men. He rushes
toward Emily and Junior. The men politely greet Emily*

KANE

Hello, Butch! Did you like your old man's speech?

JUNIOR

I was in a box, Father. I could hear every word.

KANE

I saw you! Good night, gentlemen.

*There are good-nights. Kane's car is at the curb and he starts to
walk toward it with Junior and Emily*

EMILY

I'm sending Junior home in the car, Charles — with Oliver —

KANE

But I'd arranged to go home with you myself.

EMILY

There's a call I want you to make with me, Charles.

KANE

It can wait.

EMILY

No, it can't. (*Kisses Junior*) Good night, darling.

JUNIOR

Good night, Mom.

KANE

(*As car drives off*) What's this all about, Emily? I've had a very
tiring day and —

EMILY

It may not be about anything at all. (*Starting to a cab at curb*) I intend to find out.

KANE

I insist on being told exactly what you have in mind.

EMILY

I'm going to — (*She looks at a slip of paper*) 185 West 74th Street.

Kane's reaction indicates that the address definitely means something to him

EMILY (*Cont'd*)

If you wish, you can come with me . . .

KANE

(*Nods*) I'll come with you.

He opens the door and she enters the cab. He follows her

Dissolve

66 *Int. Cab — Night — 1916*

Kane and Emily. He looks at her in search of some kind of enlightenment. Her face is set and impassive.

Dissolve Out

Dissolve In

67 *Ext. Susan's Apartment House Door — Night — 1916*

Kane and Emily, in front of an apartment door. Emily is pressing the bell.

KANE

I had no idea you had this flair for melodrama, Emily.

Emily does not answer. The door is opened by a maid, who recognizes Kane

THE MAID

Come in, Mr. Kane, come in.

She stands to one side for Kane and Emily to enter. This they start to do. Beyond them we see into the room

68 *Int. Susan's Apartment — Night — 1916*

As Kane and Emily enter, Susan rises from a chair. The other person in the room — a big, heavyset man, a little past middle age — stays where he is, leaning back in his chair, regarding Kane intently.

SUSAN

It wasn't my fault, Charlie. He made me send your wife a note.

He said I'd — oh, he's been saying the most terrible things, I didn't know what to do . . . I — (*She stops*)

ROGERS

Good evening, Mr. Kane. (*He rises*) I don't suppose anybody would introduce us. Mrs. Kane, I'm Edward Rogers.

EMILY

How do you do?

ROGERS

I made Miss — Miss Alexander send you the note. She was a little unwilling at first — (*Smiles grimly*) but she did it.

SUSAN

I can't tell you the things he said, Charlie. You haven't got any idea —

KANE

(*Turning on Rogers*) Rogers, I don't think I *will* postpone doing something about you until I'm elected. (*Starts toward him*) To start with, I think I'll break your neck.

ROGERS

(*Not giving way an inch*) Maybe you can do it and maybe you can't, Mr. Kane.

EMILY

Charles! (*He stops to look at her*) Your — your breaking this man's neck — (*She is clearly disgusted*) would scarcely explain this note — (*Glancing at the note*) Serious consequences for Mr. Kane — (*Slowly*) for myself, and for my son. What does this note mean, Miss —

SUSAN

(*Stiffly*) I'm Susan Alexander. (*Pauses*) I know what you think, Mrs. Kane, but —

EMILY

(*Ignoring this*) What does this note mean, Miss Alexander?

SUSAN

It's like this, Mrs. Kane. I happened to be studying singing — I always wanted to be an opera singer — and Mr. Kane happened — I mean, he's been helping me —

EMILY

What does this note mean, Miss Alexander?

ROGERS

She doesn't know, Mrs. Kane. She just sent it — because I made her see it wouldn't be smart for her not to send it.

KANE

In case you don't know, Emily, this — this gentleman — is —

ROGERS

I'm not a gentleman, Mrs. Kane, and your husband is just trying to be funny, calling me one. I don't even know what a gentleman is. You see, my idea of a gentleman, Mrs. Kane — well, if I owned a newspaper and if I didn't like the way somebody else was doing things — some politician, say — I'd fight them with everything I had. Only I wouldn't show him in a convict suit with stripes — so his children could see the picture in the paper. Or his mother.

EMILY

Oh!!

KANE

You're a cheap, crooked grafter — and your concern for your children and your mother —

ROGERS

Anything you say, Mr. Kane. Only we're talking now about what *you* are. That's what that note is about, Mrs. Kane. I'm going to lay all my cards on the table. I'm fighting for my life. Not just my political life. My life. If your husband is elected governor —

KANE

I'm *going* to be elected governor. And the first thing I'm going to do —

EMILY

Let him finish, Charles.

ROGERS

I'm protecting myself every way I know how, Mrs. Kane. This last week, I finally found out how I can stop your husband from being elected. If the people of this state learn what I found out this week, he wouldn't have a chance to — he couldn't be elected dog catcher.

KANE

You can't blackmail me, Rogers. You can't —

SUSAN

(*Excitedly*) Charlie, he said, unless you withdrew your name —

ROGERS

That's the chance I'm willing to give you, Mr. Kane. More of a chance than you'd give me. Unless you make up your mind by tomorrow that you're so sick that you've got to go away for a year or two — Monday morning every paper in this state — except yours — will carry the story I'm going to give them.

EMILY

What story, Mr. Rogers?

ROGERS

The story about him and Miss Alexander, Mrs. Kane.

Emily looks at Kane

SUSAN

There *is* no story. It's all lies. Mr. Kane is just —

ROGERS

(*To Susan*) Shut up! (*To Kane*) We've got evidence that would stand up in any court of law. You want me to give you the evidence, Mr. Kane?

KANE

You do anything you want to do.

ROGERS

Mrs. Kane, I'm not asking *you* to believe me. I'd like to show you —

EMILY

I believe you, Mr. Rogers.

ROGERS

I'd rather Mr. Kane withdrew without having to get the story published. Not that I care about him. But I'd be better off that way — and so would you, Mrs. Kane.

SUSAN

What about me? (*To Kane*) He said my name'd be dragged through the mud. He said everywhere I'd go from now on —

EMILY

There seems to me to be only one decision you can make, Charles. I'd say that it has been made for you.

KANE

Have you gone completely mad, Emily? You don't think I'm going to let this blackmailer intimidate me, do you?

EMILY

I don't see what else you can do, Charles. If he's right — and the papers publish this story he has —

KANE

Oh, they'll publish it all right. I'm not afraid of the story. You can't tell me that the voters of this state —

EMILY

I'm not interested in the voters of this state right now. I am interested in — well, Junior, for one thing.

SUSAN

Charlie! If they publish this story —

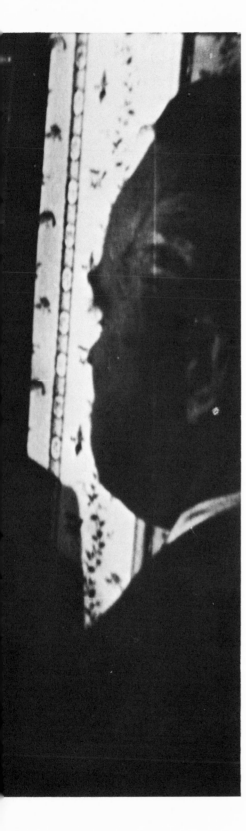

EMILY

They won't. Good night, Mr. Rogers. There's nothing more to be said. Are you coming, Charles?

KANE

No.

She looks at him. He starts to work himself into a rage

KANE (*Cont'd*)

There's only one person in the world to decide what I'm going to do — and that's me. And if you think — if any of you think —

EMILY

You decided what you were going to do, Charles — some time ago. Come on, Charles.

KANE

Go on! Get out! I can fight this all alone! Get out!

ROGERS

You're making a bigger fool of yourself than I thought you would, Mr. Kane. You're licked. Why don't you —

KANE

(*Turning on him*) Get out! I've got nothing to talk to you about. If you want to see me, have the warden write me a letter.

Rogers nods, with a look that says "So you say"

SUSAN

(*Starting to cry*) Charlie, you're just excited. You don't realize —

KANE

I know exactly what I'm doing. (*He is screaming*) Get out!

EMILY

(*Quietly*) Charles, if you don't listen to reason, it may be too late —

KANE

Too late for what? Too late for you and this — this public thief to take the love of the people of this state away from me? Well, you won't do it, I tell you. You won't do it!

SUSAN

Charlie, there are other things to think of. (*A sly look comes into her eyes*) Your son — you don't want him to read in the papers —

EMILY

It *is* too late now, Charles.

KANE

(*Rushes to the door and opens it*) Get out, both of you!

SUSAN

(*Rushes to him*) Charlie, please don't —

KANE

What are you waiting here for? Why don't you go?

EMILY

Good night, Charles.

She walks out. Rogers stops directly in front of Kane

ROGERS

You're the greatest fool I've ever known, Kane. If it was anybody else, I'd say what's going to happen to you would be a lesson to you. Only you're going to need more than one lesson. And you're going to get more than one lesson.

KANE

Don't worry about me. I'm Charles Foster Kane. I'm no cheap, crooked politician, trying to save himself from the consequences of his crimes —

69 Int. Apt. House Hallway — Night — 1916

Camera angling toward Kane from other end of the hall. Rogers and Emily are already down the hall, moving toward f.g. Kane in apartment doorway b.g.

KANE

(*Screams louder*) I'm going to send you to Sing Sing, Rogers. Sing Sing!

Kane is trembling with rage as he shakes his fist at Rogers's back. Susan, quieter now, has snuggled into the hollow of his shoulder as they stand in the doorway

Dissolve

INSERT: The "Chronicle" front page with photograph (as in the news digest) revealing Kane's relations with Susan. Headline reads:

CANDIDATE KANE FOUND IN
LOVE NEST WITH "SINGER"

Dissolve

70 Int. Composing Room — "Inquirer" — Night — 1916

Camera angles down on enormous headline in type with proof on top. In back of this headline lies complete front page, except for headline. Headline reads:

KANE GOVERNOR

Camera tilts up showing Bernstein, actually crying, standing with composing room foreman, Jenkins.

BERNSTEIN

(*To foreman*) With a million majority already against him, and the church counties still to be heard from — I'm afraid we got no choice. This one.

Camera pans to where he is pointing; shows enormous headline, the proof of which in small type reads:

KANE DEFEATED

and in large type screams:

FRAUD AT POLLS!

Dissolve Out

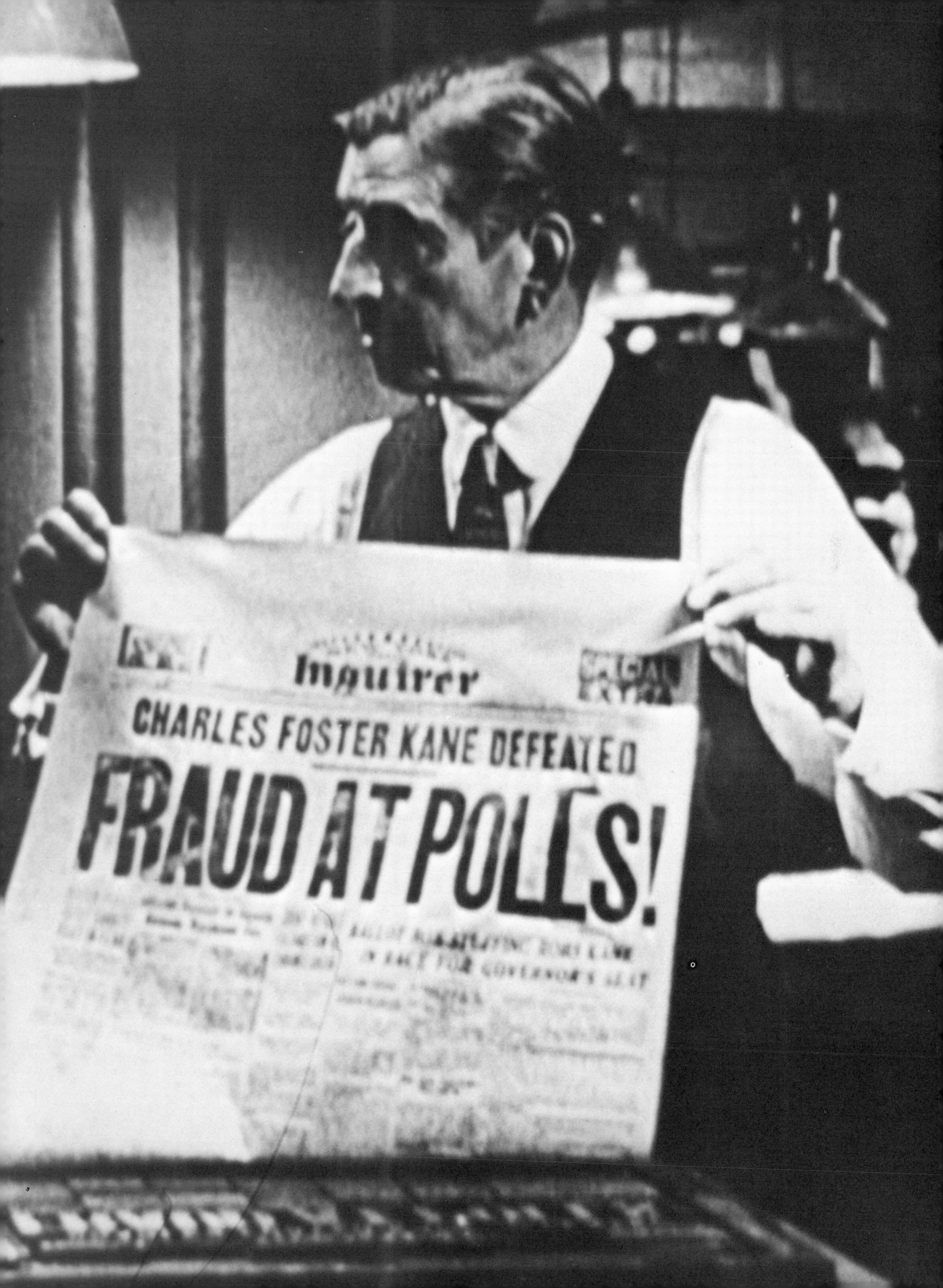
Inquirer
CHARLES FOSTER KANE DEFEATED
FRAUD AT POLLS!

Dissolve In

71 Int. Kane's Office — "Inquirer" — Night — 1916

Kane looks up from his desk as there is a knock on the door.

KANE

Come in.

Leland enters

KANE

(*Surprised*) I thought I heard somebody knock.

LELAND

(*A bit drunk*) I knocked. (*He looks at him defiantly*)

KANE

(*Trying to laugh it off*) Oh! An official visit of state, eh? (*Waves his hand*) Sit down, Jedediah.

LELAND

(*Sitting down angrily*) I'm drunk.

KANE

Good! It's high time —

LELAND

You don't have to be amusing.

KANE

All right. Tell you what I'll do. I'll get drunk, too.

LELAND

(*Thinks this over*) No. That wouldn't help. Besides, you never get drunk. (*Pauses*) I want to talk to you — about — about — (*He can't get it out*)

KANE

(*Looks at him sharply a moment*) If you've got yourself drunk to talk to me about Susan Alexander — I'm not interested.

LELAND

She's not important. What's much more important — (*He keeps glaring at Kane*)

KANE

(*As if genuinely surprised*) Oh! (*He gets up*) I frankly didn't think I'd have to listen to that lecture from you. (*Pauses*) I've betrayed the sacred cause of reform, is that it? I've set back the sacred cause of reform in this state twenty years. Don't tell me, Jed, *you* —

Despite his load, Leland manages to achieve a dignity about the silent contempt with which he looks at Kane

KANE

(*An outburst*) What makes the sacred cause of reform so sacred? Why does the sacred cause of reform have to be exempt from all the other facts of life? Why do the laws of this state have to be executed by a man on a white charger?

Leland lets the storm ride over his head

KANE (*Cont'd*)

(*Calming down*) But, if that's the way they want it — they've made their choice. The people of this state obviously prefer Mr. Rogers to me. (*His lips tighten*) So be it.

LELAND

You talk about the people as though they belong to you. As long as I can remember you've talked about giving the people their rights as though you could make them a present of liberty — in reward for services rendered. You remember the workingman? You used to write an awful lot about the workingman. Well, he's turning into something called organized labor, and you're not going to like that a bit when you find out it means that he thinks he's entitled to something as his right and not your gift. (*He pauses*) And listen, Charles. When your precious underprivileged really do get together — that's going to add up to something bigger — than your privilege — and then I don't know what you'll do. Sail away to a desert island, probably, and lord it over the monkeys.

KANE

Don't worry about it too much, Jed. There's sure to be a few of them there to tell me where I'm wrong.

LELAND

You may not always be that lucky. (*Pauses*) Charlie, why can't you get to look at things less personally? Everything doesn't have to be between you and — the personal note doesn't always —

KANE

(*Violently*) The personal note is all there is to it. It's all there ever is to it. It's all there ever is to anything! Stupidity in our government — crookedness — even just complacency and self-satisfaction and an unwillingness to believe that anything done by a certain class of people can be wrong — you can't fight those things impersonally. They're not impersonal crimes against the people. They're being done by actual persons — with actual names and positions and — the right of the American people to their own country is not an academic issue, Jed, that you debate — and then the judges retire to return a verdict — and the winners give a dinner for the losers.

LELAND

You almost convince me, almost. The truth is, Charlie, you just don't care about anything except you. You just want to convince people that you love them so much that they should love you back. Only you want love on your own terms. It's something to be played your way — according to your rules. And if anything goes wrong and you're hurt — then the game stops, and you've got to be soothed and nursed, no matter what else is happening — and no matter who else is hurt!

They look at each other

KANE

(*Trying to kid him into a better humor*) Hey, Jedediah!

Leland is not to be seduced

LELAND

Charlie, I wish you'd let me work on the Chicago paper — you said yourself you were looking for someone to do dramatic criticism there —

KANE

You're more valuable here.

There is silence

LELAND

Well, Charlie, then I'm afraid there's nothing I can do but to ask
you to accept —

KANE

(*Harshly*) All right. You can go to Chicago.

LELAND

Thank you.

*There is an awkward pause. Kane opens a drawer of his desk and
takes out a bottle and two glasses*

KANE

I guess I'd better *try* to get drunk, anyway.

Kane hands Jed a glass, which he makes no move to take

KANE (*Cont'd*)

But I warn you, Jedediah, you're not going to like it in Chicago.
The wind comes howling in off the lake, and the Lord only
knows if they've ever heard of lobster Newburg.

LELAND

Will a week from Saturday be all right?

KANE

(*Wearily*) Anytime you say.

LELAND

Thank you.

Kane looks at him intently and lifts the glass

KANE

A toast, Jedediah — to love on *my* terms. Those are the only
terms anybody knows — his own.

Dissolve

72 *Ext. Town Hall in Trenton (as in News Digest) — Day —*
    1917

Kane (as in news digest) is just emerging with Susan. He smashes
one camera and before he begins on a second, a cop removes a
newsreel cameraman. He smashes a second camera, and is just
about to start on a third.

PHOTOGRAPHER

Mr. Kane! Mr. Kane! It's the "Inquirer"!

*Kane sees the "Inquirer" painted on the side of the camera and
stops*

REPORTER

(*Quickly*) How about a statement, Mr. Kane?

ANOTHER REPORTER

On the level, Mr. Kane, are you through with politics?

KANE

I would say vice versa, young man. (*Smiles*) We're going to be a
great opera star.

REPORTER

Are you going to sing at the Metropolitan, Mrs. Kane?

KANE

We certainly are.

SUSAN

Charlie said if I didn't, he'd build me an opera house.

KANE

That won't be necessary.

Dissolve

INSERT: FRONT PAGE CHICAGO "INQUIRER," with photograph pro-
claiming that Susan Alexander opens at new Chicago Opera
House in *Thaïs* (as in news digest). (1919)

On sound track during above we hear the big expectant murmur of an opening night audience and the noodling of the orchestra.

Dissolve

73 Int. Chicago Opera House — Night — Set for Thaïs — 1919

The camera is just inside the curtain, angling upstage. We see
the set for *Thaïs* — and in the center of all this, in an elaborate
costume, looking very small and very lost, is Susan. She is almost
hysterical with fright. Applause is heard, and the orchestra starts
thunderously. The curtain starts to rise — the camera with it.
Susan squints and starts to sing. Camera continues on up with
the curtain the full height of the proscenium arch and then on
up into the gridiron. Susan's voice still heard but faintly. Two
typical stagehands fill the frame, looking down on the stage below. They look at each other. One of them puts his hand to his
nose.

Dissolve

74 Int. City Room — Chicago "Inquirer" — Night — 1919

It is late. The room is almost empty. Nobody is at work at the
desks. Bernstein is waiting anxiously with a little group of
Kane's hirelings, most of them in evening dress with overcoats
and hats. Everybody is tense and expectant.

CITY EDITOR

(*Turns to a young hireling; quietly*) What about Jed Leland?
Has he got in his copy?

HIRELING

Not yet.

BERNSTEIN

Go in and ask him to hurry.

CITY EDITOR

Well, why don't you, Mr. Bernstein? You know Mr. Leland.

BERNSTEIN

(*Slowly*) I might make him nervous. Mr. Leland, he's writing it
from the dramatic angle?

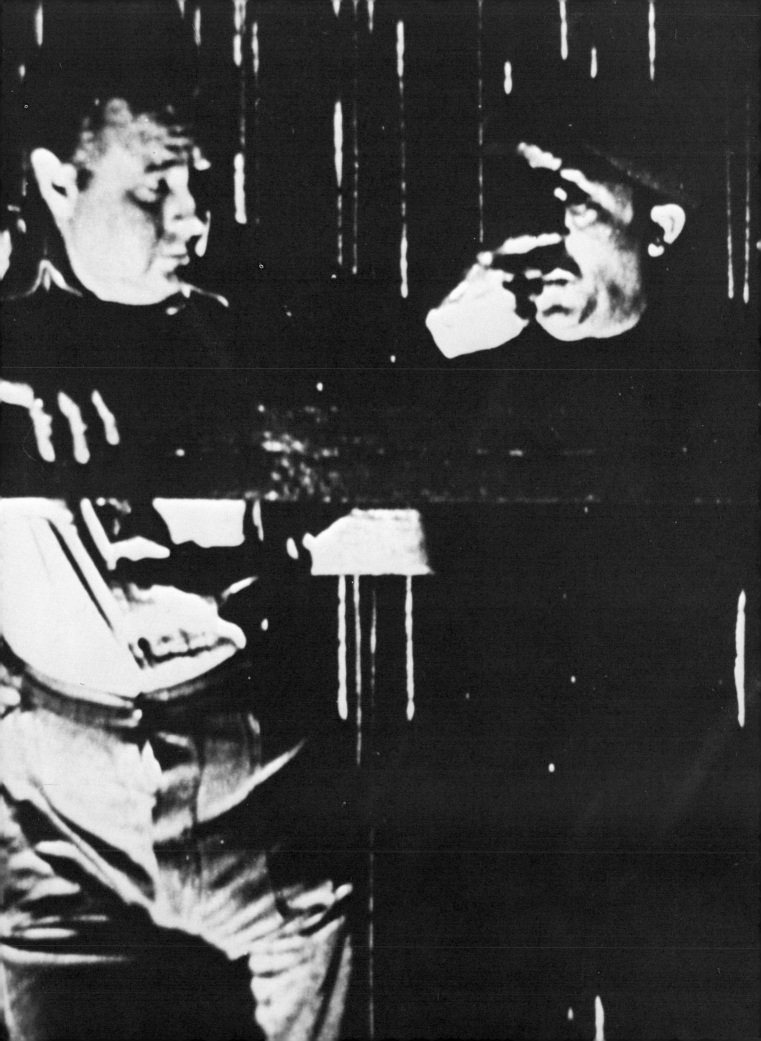

CITY EDITOR

Yes. I thought it was a good idea. We've covered it from the news end, of course.

BERNSTEIN

And the social. How about the music notice? You got that in?

CITY EDITOR

Oh, yes, it's already made up. Our Mr. Mervin wrote a swell review.

BERNSTEIN

Enthusiastic?

CITY EDITOR

Yes, very! (*Quietly*) Naturally.

BERNSTEIN

Well, well — isn't that nice?

KANE'S VOICE

Mr. Bernstein —

Bernstein turns

74A *Med. Long Shot of Kane*

He is in white tie, wearing his overcoat and carrying a folded opera hat.

BERNSTEIN

Hello, Mr. Kane.

The hirelings rush, with Bernstein, to Kane's side. Widespread, half-suppressed sensation

CITY EDITOR

Mr. Kane, this *is* a surprise!

KANE

We've got a nice plant here.

Everybody falls silent. There isn't anything to say

CITY EDITOR

Everything has been done exactly to your instructions, Mr. Kane. We've got two spreads of pictures and —

KANE

The music notice on the first page?

CITY EDITOR

Yes, Mr. Kane. (*Hesitatingly*) There's still one notice to come. The dramatic.

KANE

That's Leland, isn't it?

CITY EDITOR

Yes, Mr. Kane.

KANE

Has he said when he'll finish?

CITY EDITOR

We haven't heard from him.

KANE

He used to work fast — didn't he, Mr. Bernstein?

BERNSTEIN

He sure did, Mr. Kane.

KANE

Where is he?

ANOTHER HIRELING

Right in there, Mr. Kane.

The hireling indicates the closed glass door of a little office at the other end of the city room. Kane takes it in

BERNSTEIN

(*Helpless but very concerned*) Mr. Kane —

KANE

That's all right, Mr. Bernstein.

Kane crosses the length of the long city room to the glass door indicated before by the hireling. The city editor looks at Bernstein. Kane opens the door and goes into the office, closing the door behind him

BERNSTEIN

Mr. Leland and Mr. Kane — they haven't spoken together for four years —

CITY EDITOR

You don't suppose —

BERNSTEIN

There's nothing to suppose. (*A long pause; finally . . .*) Excuse me. (*Starts toward the door*)

Dissolve Out

Dissolve In

75 *Int. Leland's Office — Chicago "Inquirer" — Night — 1919*

Bernstein comes in. An empty bottle is standing on Leland's desk. He has fallen asleep over his typewriter, his face on the keys. A sheet of paper is in the machine. A paragraph has been typed. Kane is standing at the other side of the desk looking down at him. This is the first time we see murder in Kane's face. Bernstein looks at Kane, then crosses to Leland. He shakes him.

BERNSTEIN

(*Straightens, looks at Kane; a pause*) He ain't been drinking before, Mr. Kane. Never. We would have heard.

KANE

(*Finally, after a pause*) What does it say there?

Bernstein stares at him

KANE (*Cont'd*)

What's he written?

Bernstein leans over near-sightedly, painfully reading the paragraph written on the page

BERNSTEIN

(*Reading*) "Miss Susan Alexander, a pretty but hopelessly incompetent amateur — (*Waits for a minute to catch his breath; doesn't like it*) last night opened the new Chicago Opera House in a performance of — of —" (*Looks up miserably*) I still can't pronounce that name, Mr. Kane.

Kane doesn't answer. Bernstein looks at Kane for a moment, then looks back, tortured

BERNSTEIN (*Cont'd*)

(*Reading again*) "Her singing, happily, is no concern of this department. Of her acting, it is absolutely impossible to —" (*Continues to stare at the page*)

KANE

(*After a short silence*) Go on!

BERNSTEIN

(*Without looking up*) That's all there is.

Kane snatches the paper from the roller and reads it for himself. Slowly a queer look comes into his face. Then he speaks, very quietly

KANE

Of her acting, it is absolutely impossible to say anything except that it represents in the opinion of this reviewer a new low — (*Then sharply*) Have you got that, Mr. Bernstein? In the opinion of this reviewer —

BERNSTEIN

(*Miserably*) I didn't see that.

KANE

It isn't there, Mr. Bernstein. I'm dictating it.

BERNSTEIN

But Mr. Kane, I can't — I mean — I —

KANE

Get me a typewriter. I'll finish the notice.

Bernstein retreats from the room

Dissolve Out

Dissolve In

76 *Int. Leland's Office — Chicago "Inquirer" — Night — 1919*

Long shot — of Kane in his shirt-sleeves, illuminated by a desk light, typing furiously. As the camera starts to pull even further away from this . . .

Dissolve

77 *Int. Leland's Office — Chicago "Inquirer" — Night — 1919*

Leland, sprawled across his typewriter. He stirs and looks up drunkenly, his eyes encountering Bernstein, who stands beside him.

BERNSTEIN

Hello, Mr. Leland.

LELAND

Hello, Bernstein. Where is it — where's my notice — I've got to finish it!

BERNSTEIN

(*Quietly*) Mr. Kane is finishing it.

LELAND

Kane? — Charlie —? (*Painfully rises*) Where is he?

During all this, the sound of a busy typewriter has been heard. Leland's eyes follow the sound. Slowly he registers Kane out in the city room

78 *Int. City Room — Chicago "Inquirer" — Night — 1919*

Kane, in white tie and shirt-sleeves, is typing away at a machine, his face, seen by the desk light before him, set in a strange half-smile. Leland stands in the door of his office, staring across at him.

LELAND

I suppose he's fixing it up — I knew I'd never get that through.

BERNSTEIN

(*Moving to his side*) Mr. Kane is finishing your piece the way you started it.

Leland turns incredulously to Bernstein

BERNSTEIN (*Cont'd*)

He's writing a bad notice like you wanted it to be — (*Then with a kind of quiet passion, rather than triumph*) I guess that'll show you.

Leland picks his way across to Kane's side. Kane goes on typing, without looking up

KANE

(*After pause*) Hello, Jedediah.

LELAND

Hello, Charlie — I didn't know we were speaking.

Kane stops typing, but doesn't turn

KANE

Sure, we're speaking, Jed — You're fired.

He starts typing again, the expression on his face doesn't change

Dissolve

79 *Ext. Hospital Roof — Day — 1940*

Thompson and Leland. It is getting late. The roof is now deserted.

THOMPSON

Everybody knows that story, Mr. Leland, but — why did he do it? How could he write a notice like that when —

LELAND

You just don't know Charlie. He thought that by finishing that piece he could show me he was an honest man. He was always trying to prove something. That whole thing about Susie being an opera singer — that was trying to prove something. Do you know what the headline was the day before the election? Candidate Kane found in love nest with quote singer unquote. He was going to take the quotes off the singer. (*Pauses*) Hey, nurse! Five years ago he wrote from that place of his down South — (*As if trying to think*) you know. Shangri-La? El Dorado? (*Pauses*) Sloppy Joe's? What's the name of that place? . . . All right. Xanadu. I knew what it was all the time. You caught on, didn't you?

THOMPSON

Yes.

LELAND

I guess maybe I'm not as hard to see through as I think. Anyway,

I never even answered his letter. Maybe I should have. He must have been pretty lonely down there in that coliseum those last years. He hadn't finished it when she left him — he never finished it — he never finished anything, except my notice. Of course, he built the joint for her.

THOMPSON

That must have been love.

LELAND

I don't know. He was disappointed in the world. So he built one of his own — an absolute monarchy — It was something bigger than an opera house anyway — (*Calls*) Nurse! (*Lowers his voice*) Say, I'll tell you one thing you can do for me, young fellow.

THOMPSON

Sure.

LELAND

On your way out, stop at a cigar store, will you, and send me up a couple of cigars?

THOMPSON

Sure, Mr. Leland. I'll be glad to.

LELAND

Hey, nurse!

A nurse has already appeared and stands behind him

NURSE

Yes, Mr. Leland.

LELAND

I'm ready to go in now. You know when I was a young man, there was an impression around that nurses were pretty. It was no truer then than it is now.

NURSE

Here let me take your arm, Mr. Leland.

LELAND

(*Testily*) All right, all right. You won't forget, will you, about the cigars? And tell them to wrap them up to look like toothpaste, or something, or they'll stop them at the desk. That young doctor I was telling you about, he's got an idea he wants to keep me alive.

Fade Out

Fade In

80 Ext. "El Rancho" Cabaret in Atlantic City — Early Dawn — 1940

Neon sign on the roof:

"EL RANCHO"
Floor Show
Susan Alexander Kane
Twice Nightly

Camera as before, moves through the lights of the sign and down on the skylight, through which is seen Susan at her regular table, Thompson seated across from her. Very faintly during this, idle piano music playing.

Dissolve

81 Int. "El Rancho" Cabaret — Early Dawn — 1940

Susan and Thompson are facing each other. The place is almost deserted. Susan is sober. On the other side of the room somebody is playing a piano.

THOMPSON

I'd rather you just talked. Anything that comes into your mind — about yourself and Mr. Kane.

SUSAN

You wouldn't want to hear a lot of what comes into my mind about myself and Mr. Charlie Kane. (*She tosses down a drink*) You know — maybe I shouldn't ever have sung for Charlie that first time. Hah! — I did a lot of singing after that. To start with, I sang for teachers at a hundred bucks an hour. The teachers got that, I didn't.

THOMPSON

What did you get?

SUSAN

What do you mean?

Thompson doesn't answer

SUSAN *(Cont'd)*

I didn't get a thing. Just the music lessons. That's all there was to it.

THOMPSON

He married you, didn't he?

SUSAN

He never said anything about marriage until it all came out in the papers about us — and he lost the election and that Norton woman divorced him. What are you smiling about? I tell you he was really interested in my voice. *(Sharply)* What do you think he built that opera house for? I didn't want it. I didn't want to sing. It was his idea — everything was his idea — except my leaving him.

Dissolve

82 Int. Living Room — Kane's Home in New York — Day — 1917–1918

Susan is singing. Matisti, her voice teacher, is playing the piano. Kane is seated nearby. Matisti stops.

MATISTI

Impossible! Impossible!

KANE

It is not your job to give Mrs. Kane your opinion of her talents. You're supposed to train her voice. Nothing more.

MATISTI

(Sweating) But, it is impossible. I will be the laughing stock of the musical world! People will say —

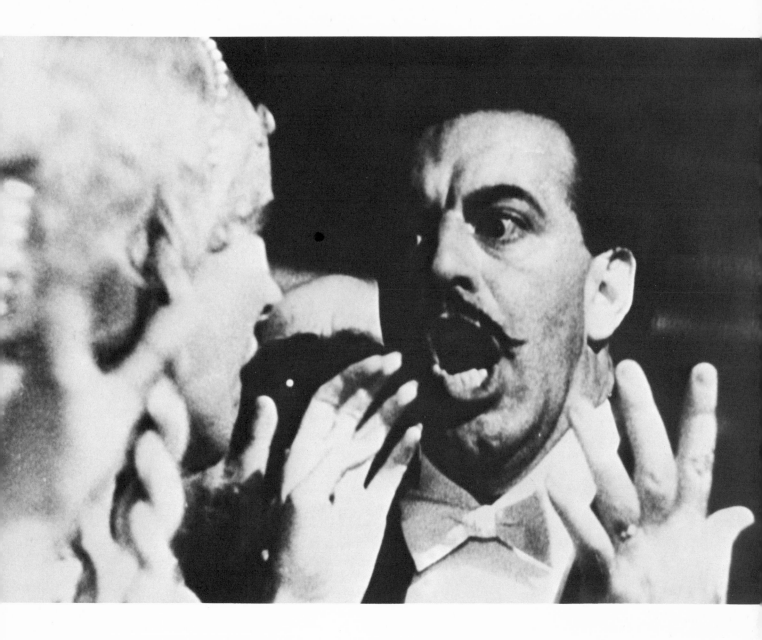

KANE

If you're interested in what people will say, Signor Matisti, I may
be able to enlighten you a bit. The newspapers, for instance. I'm
an authority on what the papers will say, Signor Matisti, because
I own eight of them between here and San Francisco. . . . It's
all right, dear. Signor Matisti is going to listen to reason. Aren't
you, maestro?

247

MATISTI

Mr. Kane, how can I persuade you —

KANE

You can't.

There is a silence. Matisti rises

KANE *(Cont'd)*

I knew you'd see it my way.

Dissolve

83 *Int. Chicago Opera House — Night — 1919*

It is the same opening night — it is the same moment as before — except that the camera is now upstage angling toward the audience. The curtain is down. We see the same tableau as before. As the dissolve commences, there is the sound of applause and now, as the dissolve completes itself, the orchestra begins — the stage is cleared — Susan is left alone. The curtain rises. Susan starts to sing. Beyond her, we see the prompter's box, containing the anxious face of the prompter. Beyond that, an apprehensive conductor.

84 Close-up

Kane's face — he is seated in the audience — listening.

A sudden but perfectly correct lull in the music reveals a voice
from the audience — a few words from a sentence.

THE VOICE

— really pathetic.

Music crashes in and drowns out the rest of the sentence, but
hundreds of people around the voice have heard it (as well as
Kane) and there are titters which grow in volume.

85 *Close-up*

Susan's face — singing.

86 *Close-up*

Kane's face — listening.
There is the ghastly sound of three thousand people applauding as little as possible. Kane still looks. Then, near the camera, there is the sound of about a dozen people applauding very, very loudly. Camera moves back, revealing Bernstein and Hillman and other Kane stooges, seated around him, beating their palms together.

87 The Stage from Kane's Angle

The curtain is down — Still the polite applause, dying fast. Nobody comes out for a bow.

88 Close-up

Kane — breathing heavily. Suddenly he starts to applaud furiously.

89 The Stage from the Audience Again

Susan appears for her bow. She can hardly walk. There is a little polite crescendo of applause, but it is sickly.

90 Close-up

Kane — still applauding very, very hard, his eyes on Susan.

91 The Stage Again

Susan, finishing her bow, goes out through the curtains. The light on the curtain goes out and the houselights go up.

92 Close-up

Kane — still applauding very, very hard.

Dissolve Out

Dissolve In

93 Int. Hotel Room — Chicago — Day — 1919

Kane — Susan in a negligee. The floor is littered with newspapers.

SUSAN

Stop telling me he's your friend. (*She points at the paper*) A friend don't write that kind of an article. Anyway, not the kind of friends I know. Of course, I'm not high-class like you and I didn't go to any swell schools —

KANE

That's enough, Susan.

A look at him convinces Susan that he really means it's enough. There's a knock at the door

SUSAN

(*Screeching*) Come in!

A copy boy enters

COPY BOY

Mr. Leland said I was to come right up — He was very anxious —

KANE

(*Interrupting*) Thanks, son.

He shoves the kid out. He opens the envelope as Susan returns to the attack

SUSAN

The idea of him trying to spoil my debut!

Kane has taken a folded piece of paper out of the envelope and is holding it — looking into the envelope

KANE

He won't spoil anything else, Susan.

SUSAN

And you — you ought to have your head examined! Sending him a letter he's fired with a twenty-five thousand dollar check! What kind of firing do you call that? You did send him a twenty-five thousand dollar check, *didn't* you?

KANE

(*Slowly tipping over the envelope as pieces of torn papers fall to the floor*) Yes, I sent him a twenty-five thousand dollar check.

Kane now unfolds the piece of paper and looks at it

INSERT: Kane's original grease pencil copy of his Declaration of Principles.

SUSAN'S VOICE

What's that?

KANE'S VOICE

An antique.

BACK TO SCENE:

SUSAN

You're awful funny, aren't you? Well, I can tell you one thing you're not going to keep on being funny about — my singing. I'm through. I never wanted to —

KANE

(*Without looking up*) You are continuing your singing, Susan. (*He starts tearing the paper*) I'm not going to have myself made ridiculous.

SUSAN

You don't propose to have *yourself* made ridiculous? What about me? I'm the one that has to do the singing. I'm the one that gets the razzberries. Why can't you just —

KANE

(*Looking up — still tearing the paper*) My reasons satisfy me, Susan. You seem to be unable to understand them. I will not tell them to you again. (*He has started to walk menacingly toward her, tearing the paper as he walks*) You are to continue with your singing.

His eyes are relentlessly upon her. She sees something that frightens her. She nods slowly; indicating surrender

Dissolve

INSERT: FRONT PAGE of the San Francisco "Inquirer" (1919) containing a large portrait of Susan as Thaïs. It is announced that Susan will open an independent season in San Francisco in *Thaïs*. The picture remains constant but the names of the papers change from New York to St. Louis, to Los Angeles to Cleveland, to Denver to Philadelphia — all "Inquirers."

During all this, on the sound track, Susan's voice is heard singing her aria very faintly.

Dissolve

94 Int. Susan's Bedroom — Kane's N.Y. Home — Late Night — 1920

Camera angles across the bed and Susan's form towards the door, from the other side of which comes loud knocking and Kane's voice calling Susan's name. Then:

KANE'S VOICE

Joseph!

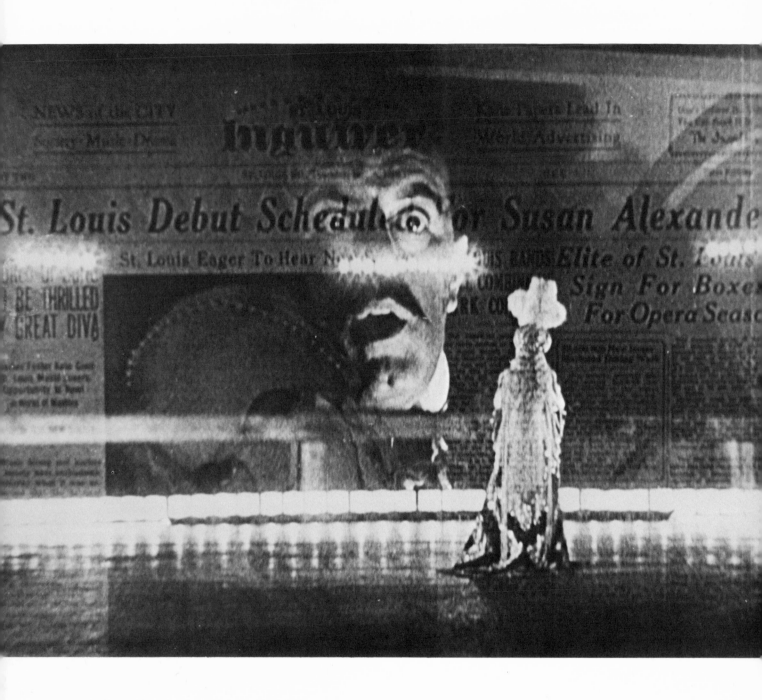

JOSEPH'S VOICE

Yes, sir.

KANE'S VOICE

Do you have the keys to Mrs. Kane's bedroom?

JOSEPH'S VOICE

No, Mr. Kane. They must be on the inside.

KANE'S VOICE

We'll have to break down the door.

JOSEPH'S VOICE

Yes, sir.

The door crashes open. Light floods the room, revealing Susan, fully dressed, stretched out on the bed. She is breathing, but heavily. Kane rushes to her, kneels at the bed, and feels her forehead. Joseph has followed him in

KANE

Get Dr. Corey.

Joseph rushes out

Dissolve

95 *Int. Susan's Bedroom — Kane's N.Y. Home — Late Night — 1920*

A little later. All the lights are lit. At start of scene, Dr. Corey removes his doctor's bag from in front of camera lens, revealing Susan, in a nightgown, is in bed. She is breathing heavily. A nurse is bending over the bed, straightening the sheets.

DR. COREY'S VOICE

She'll be perfectly all right in a day or two, Mr. Kane.

The nurse walks away from the bed toward b.g. We now see Kane, who was hidden by the nurse's body, seated beyond the bed. He is holding an empty medicine bottle. Dr. Corey walks to him

KANE

I can't imagine how Mrs. Kane came to make such a foolish mistake. (*Susan turns her head away from Kane*) The sedative Dr. Wagner gave her is in a somewhat larger bottle. — I suppose the strain of preparing for the new opera has excited and confused her. (*Looks sharply up at Dr. Corey*)

Yes, yes — I'm sure that's it.

Dr. Corey turns and walks toward the nurse

KANE

There are no objections to my staying here with her, are there?

DR. COREY

No — not at all. But I'd like the nurse to be here, too. Good night, Mr. Kane.

Dr. Corey hurries out the door

Dissolve

96 *Int. Susan's Bedroom — Kane's N.Y. Home — Very Early Dawn — 1920*

The lights are out. Camera pans from nurse, who is seated stiffly in a chair, toward Kane, seated beside the bed staring at Susan, to Susan who is asleep.

Dissolve

97 *Int. Susan's Bedroom — Kane's N.Y. Home — Day — 1920*

Sunlight is streaming into the room. A hurdy-gurdy is heard. Kane is still seated beside the bed, looking at Susan, who is asleep. After a moment Susan gasps and opens her eyes. She looks toward the window, Kane leans toward her. She looks up at him, then away.

SUSAN

(*Painfully*) Charlie — I couldn't make you see how I felt — I just couldn't go through with the singing again — You don't know what it's like to feel that people — that a whole audience doesn't want you.

KANE

(*Angrily*) That's when you've got to fight them!

She looks up at him silently with pathetic eyes

KANE (*Cont'd*)

(*After a moment; gently*) All right. You won't have to fight them any more — It's their loss.

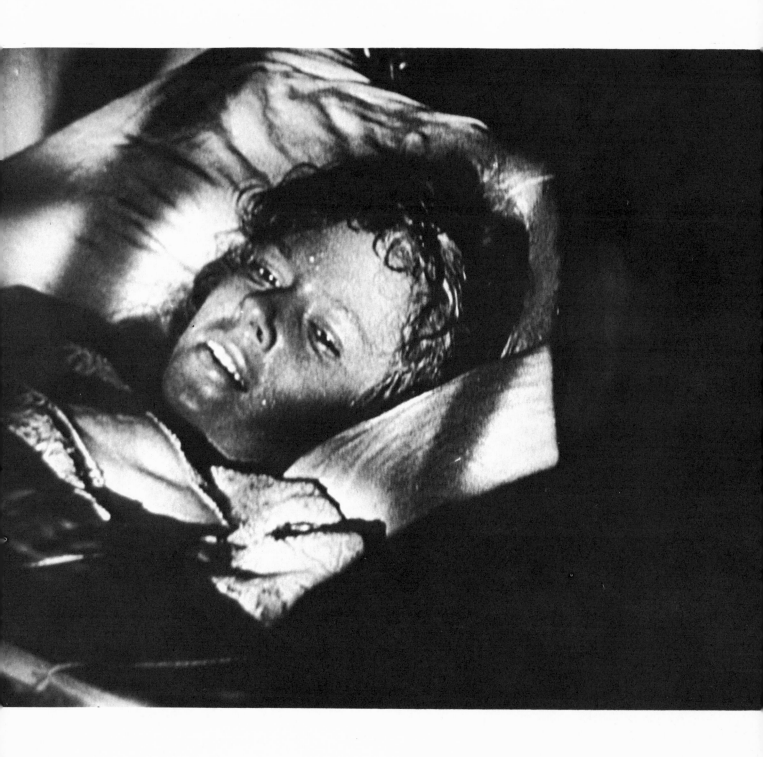

She continues to look at him, but now gratefully

Dissolve

98 Ext. Establishing Shot of Xanadu — Half Built — 1925

Dissolve

99 Int. Great Hall — Xanadu — 1929

Close-up of an enormous jigsaw puzzle. A hand is putting in the
last piece. Camera moves back to reveal jigsaw puzzle spread out
on the floor.

Susan is on the floor before her jigsaw puzzle. Kane is in an easy
chair. Candelabra illuminates the scene.

SUSAN

What time is it?

There is no answer

SUSAN (*Cont'd*)

Charlie! I said, what time is it?

KANE

(*Looks up — consults his watch*) Eleven-thirty.

SUSAN

I mean in New York. (*No answer*) I said what time is it in New York!

KANE

Eleven-thirty.

SUSAN

At night?

KANE

Umhmm. The bulldog's just gone to press.

SUSAN

(*Sarcastically*) Hurray for the bulldog! (*Sighs*) Eleven-thirty! The shows're just getting out. People are going to nightclubs and restaurants. Of course, we're different because we live in a palace.

KANE

You always said you wanted to live in a palace.

SUSAN

A person could go nuts in this dump.

Kane doesn't answer

SUSAN (*Cont'd*)

Nobody to talk to — nobody to have any fun with.

KANE

Susan —

SUSAN

Forty-nine thousand acres of nothing but scenery and — statues. I'm lonesome.

KANE

I thought you were tired of house guests. Till yesterday morning, we've had no less than fifty of your friends at any one time. As a matter of fact, Susan, if you'll look carefully in the west wing, you'll probably find a dozen vacationists still in residence.

SUSAN

You make a joke out of everything! Charlie, I want to go back to New York. I'm tired of being a hostess. I wanta have fun. Please, Charlie, please!

KANE

Our home is here, Susan. I don't care to visit New York.

Dissolve

100 Another Picture Puzzle

Susan's hands fitting in a missing piece. (1930)

Dissolve

101 Another Picture Puzzle

Susan's hands fitting in a missing piece. (1931)

Dissolve

102 Int. Great Hall — Xanadu — Day — 1932

Close-up of another jigsaw puzzle. Camera pulls back to show Kane and Susan in much the same positions as before, except that they are older.

KANE

One thing I've never been able to understand, Susan. How do you know that you haven't done them before?

Susan shoots him an angry glance. She isn't amused

SUSAN

It makes a whole lot more sense than collecting Venuses.

KANE

You may be right — I sometimes wonder — but you get into the habit —

SUSAN

(*Snapping*) It's not a habit. I do it because I like it.

KANE

I was referring to myself. (*Pauses*) I thought we might have a

picnic tomorrow — Invite everybody to go to the Everglades —

SUSAN

Invite everybody! — Order everybody, you mean, and make them sleep in tents! Who wants to sleep in tents when they have a nice room of their own — with their own bath, where they know where everything is?

Kane has looked at her steadily, not hostilely

KANE

I thought we might invite everybody to go on a picnic tomorrow. Stay at Everglades overnight.

Dissolve

103 *Ext. Xanadu — Road — Day — 1932*

Tight two-shot — Kane and Susan seated in an automobile, silent, glum, staring before them. Camera pulls back revealing that there are twenty cars full of picnickers following them, on their way through the Xanadu estate.

SUSAN

You never give me anything I really care about.

Dissolve Out

Dissolve In

104 *Ext. The Everglades Camp — Night — 1932*

Long shot — of a number of classy tents.

Dissolve

105 *Int. Large Tent — Everglades Camp — Night — 1932*

Two real beds have been set up on each side of the tent. A rather classy dressing table is in the rear, at which Susan is preparing for bed. Kane, in his shirt-sleeves, is in an easy chair, reading. Susan is very sullen.

SUSAN

I'm not going to put up with it.

Kane turns to look at her

SUSAN (*Cont'd*)

I mean it. Oh, I know I always say I mean it, and then I don't — or *you* get me so I don't do what I say I'm going to — but —

KANE

(*Interrupting*) You're in a tent, darling. You're not at home. And I can hear you very well if you just talk in a normal tone of voice.

SUSAN

I'm not going to have my guests insulted, just because you —
(*In a rage*) if people want to bring a drink or two along on a
picnic, that's their business. You've got no right —

KANE

(*Quickly*) I've got more than a right as far as you're concerned,
Susan.

SUSAN

I'm sick and tired of your telling me what I mustn't do! And
what I —

KANE

We can discuss all this some other time, Susan. Right now —

SUSAN

I'll discuss what's on my mind when *I* want to. I'm sick of having
you run my life the way you want it.

KANE

Susan, as far as you're concerned, I've never wanted anything —
I don't want anything now — except what you want.

SUSAN

What *you* want me to want, you mean. What you've decided I
ought to have — what you'd want if you were me. Never what I
want —

KANE

Susan!

SUSAN

You've never given me anything that —

KANE

I really think —

SUSAN

Oh sure, you give me things — that don't mean anything to you

— What's the difference between giving me a bracelet or giving somebody else a hundred thousand dollars for a statue you're going to keep crated up and never look at? It's only money.

KANE

(*He has risen*) Susan, I want you to stop this.

SUSAN

I'm not going to stop it!

KANE

Right now!

SUSAN

(*Screams*) You never gave me anything in your life! You just tried to — to buy me into giving *you* something. You're — it's like you were bribing me!

KANE

Susan!

SUSAN

That's all you ever done — no matter how much it cost you — your time, your money — that's all you've done with everybody. Tried to bribe them!

KANE

Susan!

She looks at him, with no lessening of her passion

KANE (*Cont'd*)

(*Quietly*) Whatever I do — I do — because I love you.

SUSAN

You don't love me! You just want me to love you — sure — I'm Charles Foster Kane. Whatever you want — just name it and it's yours. But you gotta love me!

Without a word, Kane slaps her across the face. He continues to look at her

SUSAN (*Cont'd*)

You'll never get a chance to do that again.

SUSAN

Don't tell me you're sorry.

KANE

I'm not sorry.

Dissolve

106 *Int. Great Hall — Xanadu — Day — 1932*

Kane is at the window looking out. He turns as he hears Raymond enter.

RAYMOND

Mrs. Kane would like to see you, Mr. Kane.

KANE

All right.

Raymond waits as Kane hesitates

KANE (*Cont'd*)

Is Mrs. Kane — (*He can't finish*)

RAYMOND

Marie has been packing her since morning, Mr. Kane.

Kane impetuously walks past him out of the room

107 *Int. Susan's Room — Xanadu — Day — 1932*

Packed suitcases are on the floor. Susan is completely dressed for traveling. Kane bursts into the room.

SUSAN

Tell Arnold I'm ready, Marie. He can get the bags.

MARIE

Yes, Mrs. Kane.

She leaves. Kane closes the door behind her

KANE

Have you gone completely crazy?

Susan looks at him

KANE (*Cont'd*)

Don't you realize that everybody here is going to know about this? That you've packed your bags and ordered the car and —

— And left? Of course they'll hear. I'm not saying good-bye — except to you — but I never imagined that people wouldn't know.

Kane is standing against the door as if physically barring her way

KANE

I won't let you go.

SUSAN

(*Reaches out her hand*) Good-bye, Charlie.

KANE

(*Suddenly*) Don't go, Susan.

Susan just looks at him

KANE (*Cont'd*)

Susan, don't go! Susan, please!

He has lost all pride. Susan stops. She is affected by this

KANE (*Cont'd*)

You mustn't go, Susan. Everything'll be exactly the way you want it. Not the way *I* think you want it — but your way. Please, Susan — Susan!

She is staring at him. She might weaken

KANE (*Cont'd*)

Don't go, Susan! You mustn't go! (*Almost blubbering*) You — you can't do this to me, Susan —

It's as if he had thrown ice water into her face. She freezes

SUSAN

I see — it's *you* that this is being done to! It's not me at all. Not how I feel. Not what it means to me. Not — (*She laughs*) I can't do this to *you!* (*She looks at him*) Oh yes I can.

She walks out, past Kane, who turns to watch her go, like a very tired old man

Dissolve

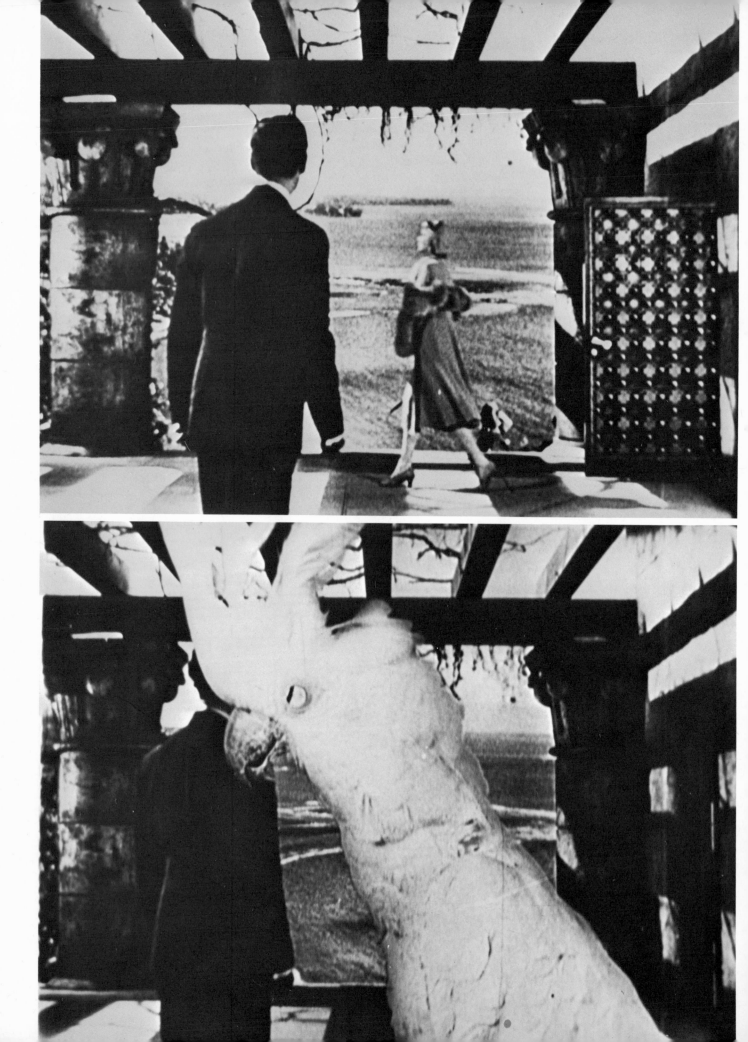

108 *Int. "El Rancho" Cabaret — Night — 1940*

Susan and Thompson at table. There is silence between them for a moment as she accepts a cigarette from Thompson and he lights it for her.

SUSAN

In case you've never heard of how I lost all my money — and it was plenty, believe me —

THOMPSON

The last ten years have been tough on a lot of people —

SUSAN

Aw, they haven't been tough on me. I just lost my money — (*Takes a deep puff*) So you're going down to Xanadu.

THOMPSON

Monday, with some of the boys from the office. Mr. Rawlston wants the whole place photographed carefully — all that art stuff. We run a picture magazine, you know —

SUSAN

Yeah, I know. If you're smart, you'll talk to Raymond — (*Nervously douses out the cigarette*) That's the butler. You can learn a lot from him. He knows where the bodies are buried.

She grabs a glass and holds it tensely in both hands

THOMPSON

You know, all the same I feel kind of sorry for Mr. Kane.

SUSAN

(*Harshly*) Don't you think I do?

She lifts the glass, and as she drains it she notices the dawn light coming through the skylight. She shivers and pulls her coat over her shoulders

SUSAN (*Cont'd*)

Well, what do you know? It's morning already. (*Looks at him*

for a moment) You must come around and tell me the story of your life sometime.

Dissolve Out

Dissolve In

109 Ext. Xanadu — Late Dusk — 1940

The distant castle on the hill, seen through the great iron "K" as in the opening shot of the picture. Several lights are on.

Dissolve

110 Int. Great Hall — Xanadu — Late Dusk — 1940

Camera is in close on Thompson and Raymond — will subsequently reveal surrounding scene.

RAYMOND

Rosebud? I'll tell you about Rosebud — how much is it worth to you? A thousand dollars?

THOMPSON

Okay.

RAYMOND

He was a little gone in the head sometimes, you know.

THOMPSON

No, I didn't.

RAYMOND

He did crazy things sometimes — I've been working for him eleven years now — the last years of his life and I ought to know. Yes, sir, the old man was kind of queer, but I knew how to handle him.

THOMPSON

Need a lot of service?

RAYMOND

Yeah. But I knew how to handle him.

Dissolve Out

Dissolve In

III Int. Corridor and Telegraph Office — Xanadu — Night — 1932

Raymond walking rapidly along corridor. He pushes open a door. At a desk sits a wireless operator. Near him at a telephone switchboard sits a female operator.

RAYMOND

(*Reading*) Mr. Charles Foster Kane announced today that Mrs. Charles Foster Kane has left Xanadu, his Florida home, under the terms of a peaceful and friendly agreement with the intention of filing suit for divorce at an early date. Mrs. Kane said that she does not intend to return to the operatic career which she gave up a few years after her marriage, at Mr. Kane's request. Signed, Charles Foster Kane.

Fred finishes typing and then looks up

RAYMOND (*Cont'd*)

Exclusive for immediate transmission. Urgent priority all Kane Papers.

FRED

Okay.

There is the sound of the buzzer on the switchboard

KATHERINE

Yes . . . yes . . . Mrs. Tinsdall. Very well. (*Turns to Raymond*)

It's the housekeeper.

RAYMOND

Yes?

KATHERINE

She says there's some sort of disturbance up in Miss Alexander's room. She's afraid to go in.

Dissolve Out

Dissolve In

112 Int. Corridor Outside Susan's Bedroom — Xanadu — Night — 1932

The housekeeper, Mrs. Tinsdall, and a couple of maids are near the door but too afraid to be in front of it. From inside can be heard a terrible banging and crashing. Raymond hurries into scene, opens the door, and goes in.

113 Int. Susan's Bedroom — Xanadu — 1932

Kane, in a truly terrible and absolutely silent rage, is literally breaking up the room — yanking pictures, hooks and all off the wall, smashing them to bits — ugly, gaudy pictures — Susie's pictures in Susie's bad taste. Off of tabletops, off of dressing tables, occasional tables, bureaus, he sweeps Susie's whorish accumulation of bric-a-brac.

Raymond stands in the doorway watching him. Kane says nothing. He continues with tremendous speed and surprising strength, still wordlessly, tearing the room to bits. The curtains (too frilly — overly pretty) are pulled off the windows in a single gesture, and from the bookshelves he pulls down double armloads of cheap novels — discovers a half-empty bottle of liquor and dashes it across the room. Finally he stops. Susie's cozy little chamber is an incredible shambles all around him. He stands for a minute breathing heavily, and his eye lights on a hanging whatnot in a corner which had escaped his notice. Prominent on its center shelf is the little glass ball with the snowstorm in it. He yanks it down. Something made of china breaks, but not the glass ball. It bounces on the carpet and rolls to his feet, the snow in a flurry. His eye follows it. He stoops to pick it up — can't make it. Raymond picks it up for him; hands it to him. Kane takes it sheepishly — looks at it — moves painfully out of the room into the corridor.

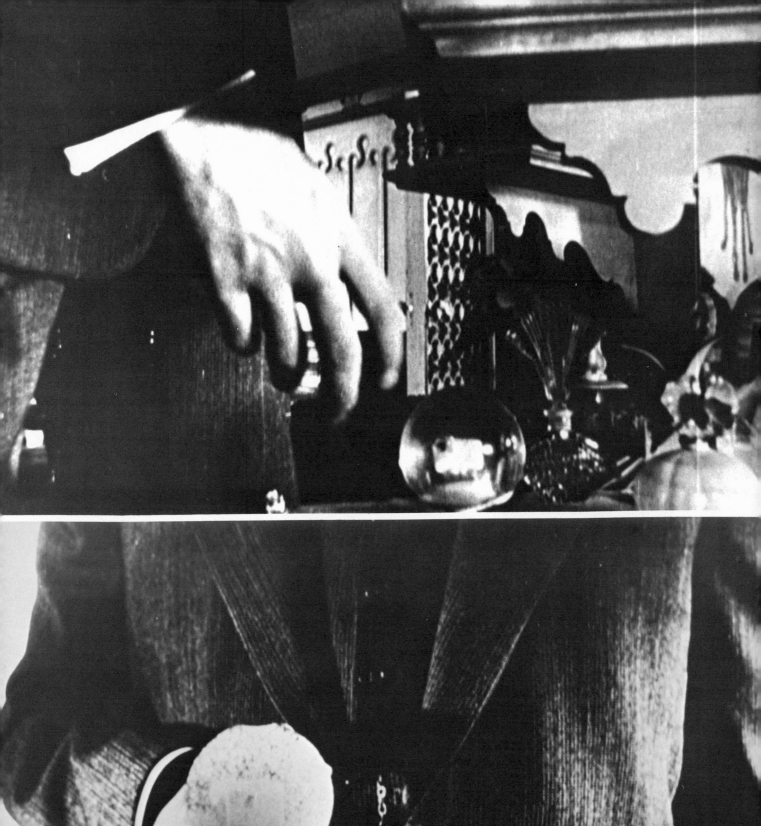

114 Int. Corridor Outside Susan's Bedroom — Xanadu — 1932
Kane comes out of the door. Mrs. Tinsdall has been joined now

by a fairly sizable turnout of servants. They move back away from Kane, staring at him. Raymond is in the doorway behind Kane. Kane still looks at the glass ball.

KANE

(*Without turning*) Close the door, Raymond.

RAYMOND

Yes, sir. (*Closes it*)

KANE

Lock it — and keep it locked.

Raymond locks the door and comes to his side. There is a long pause — servants staring in silence. Kane gives the glass ball a gentle shake and starts another snowstorm

KANE

(*Almost in a trance*) Rosebud.

RAYMOND

What's that, sir?

One of the younger servants giggles and is hushed up. Kane shakes the ball again. Another flurry of snow. He watches the flakes settle — then looks up. Finally, taking in the pack of servants and something of the situation, he puts the glass ball in his coat pocket. He speaks very quietly to Raymond, so quietly it only seems he's talking to himself

KANE

Keep it locked.

He slowly walks off down the corridor, the servants giving way to let him pass, and watching him as he goes. The mirrors which line the hall reflect his image as he moves. He is an old, old man!

Kane turns into a second corridor — sees himself reflected in the mirror — stops. His image is reflected again in the mirror behind him — multiplied again and again and again in long perspectives — Kane looks. We see a thousand Kanes

Dissolve

115 *Int. Great Hall — Xanadu — Night — 1940*

Thompson and Raymond.

RAYMOND

(*Callously*) That's the whole works, right up to date.

THOMPSON

Sentimental fellow, aren't you?

RAYMOND

Yes and no.

THOMPSON

And that's what you know about Rosebud?

RAYMOND

That's more than anybody knows. I tell you, he was a little gone in the head — the last couple of years anyway — but I knew how to handle him. That Rosebud — I heard him say it that other time too. He just said Rosebud, then he dropped that glass ball and it broke on the floor. He didn't say anything after that, so I knew he was dead. He said all kinds of things that didn't mean anything.

THOMPSON

That isn't worth anything.

RAYMOND

You can go on asking questions if you want to.

THOMPSON

(*Coldly*) We're leaving tonight. As soon as they're through photographing the stuff —

Thompson has risen. Raymond gets to his feet

RAYMOND

Allow yourself plenty of time. The train stops at the junction on signal — but they don't like to wait. Not now. I can remember when they'd wait all day . . . if Mr. Kane said so.

Camera has pulled back to show long shot of the great hall, revealing the magnificent tapestries, candelabra, etc., are still there, but now several large packing cases are piled against the walls, some broken open, some shut, and a number of objects, great and small, are piled pell-mell all over the place. Furniture, statues, paintings, bric-a-brac — things of obviously enormous value are standing beside a kitchen stove, an old rocking chair and other junk, among which is also an old sled, the self-same story.

In the center of the hall a photographer and his assistant are busy photographing the sundry objects. In addition there are a girl and two newspapermen — also Thompson and Raymond.

The girl and the second man, who wears a hat, are dancing somewhere in the back of the hall to the music of a phonograph playing "Oh, Mr. Kane!"

116 Int. Great Hall — Xanadu — Night — 1940

The photographer has just photographed a picture, obviously of great value, an Italian primitive. The assistant consults a label on the back of it.

ASSISTANT

No. 9182

The third newspaperman jots this information down

ASSISTANT (*Cont'd*)

Nativity — attributed to Donatello, acquired Florence, 1921, cost: 45,000 lire. Got that?

THIRD NEWSPAPERMAN

Yeh.

PHOTOGRAPHER

All right! Next! Better get that statue over there.

ASSISTANT

Okay.

RAYMOND

What do you think all this is worth, Mr. Thompson?

THOMPSON

Millions — *if anybody wants it.*

RAYMOND

The banks are out of luck, eh?

THOMPSON

Oh, I don't know. They'll clear all right.

ASSISTANT

Venus, fourth century. Acquired 1911. Cost: twenty-three thousand. Got it?

THIRD NEWSPAPERMAN

Okay.

ASSISTANT

(*Patting the statue on the fanny*) That's a lot of money to pay for a dame without a head.

SECOND ASSISTANT

(*Reading a label*) No. 483. One desk from the estate of Mary Kane, Little Salem, Colorado. Value: $6.00. We're supposed to get everything. The junk as well as the art.

THIRD NEWSPAPERMAN

Okay.

A flashlight bulb goes off. Thompson has opened a box and is idly playing with a handful of little pieces of cardboard

THIRD NEWSPAPERMAN (*Cont'd*)

What's that?

RAYMOND

It's a jigsaw puzzle.

THIRD NEWSPAPERMAN

We got a lot of those. There's a Burmese temple and three Spanish ceilings down the hall.

Raymond laughs

PHOTOGRAPHER

Yeh, all in crates.

THIRD NEWSPAPERMAN

There's a part of a Scotch castle over there, but we haven't bothered to unwrap it.

PHOTOGRAPHER

I wonder how they put all those pieces together?

ASSISTANT

(*Reading a label*) Iron stove. Estate of Mary Kane. Value: $2.oo.

PHOTOGRAPHER

Put it over by that statue. It'll make a good setup.

GIRL

(*Calling out*) Who is she anyway?

SECOND NEWSPAPERMAN

Venus. She always is.

THIRD NEWSPAPERMAN

He sure liked to collect things, didn't he?

PHOTOGRAPHER

Anything and everything — he was a regular crow.

THIRD NEWSPAPERMAN

I wonder — You put all this together — the palaces and the paintings and the toys and everything — what would it spell?

Thompson has turned around. He is facing the camera for the first time

THOMPSON

Charles Foster Kane.

PHOTOGRAPHER

Or Rosebud? How about it, Jerry?

THIRD NEWSPAPERMAN

(*To the dancers*) Turn that thing off, will you? It's driving me nuts! — What's Rosebud?

PHOTOGRAPHER

Kane's last words, aren't they, Jerry? (*To the third newspaper-man*) That was Jerry's angle, wasn't it. Did you ever find out what it means?

THOMPSON

No, I didn't.

The music has stopped. The dancers have come over to Thompson

SECOND NEWSPAPERMAN

Say, what did you find out about him anyway?

THOMPSON

Not much.

SECOND NEWSPAPERMAN

Well, what have you been doing?

THOMPSON

Playing with a jigsaw puzzle — I talked to a lot of people who knew him.

GIRL

What do they say?

THOMPSON

Well — it's become a very clear picture. He was the most honest man who ever lived, with a streak of crookedness a yard wide. He was a liberal and a reactionary. He was a loving husband — and both his wives left him. He had a gift for friendship such as few men have — and he broke his oldest friend's heart like you'd throw away a cigarette you were through with. Outside of that —

THIRD NEWSPAPERMAN

Okay, okay.

GIRL

If you could have found out what that Rosebud meant, I bet that would've explained everything.

THOMPSON

No, I don't. Not much anyway. Charles Foster Kane was a man who got everything he wanted, and then lost it. Maybe Rosebud was something he couldn't get or something he lost, but it wouldn't have explained anything. I don't think any word explains a man's life. No — I guess Rosebud is just a piece in a jigsaw puzzle — a missing piece.

He drops the jigsaw pieces back into the box, looking at his watch

THOMPSON (*Cont'd*)

We'd better get along. We'll miss the train.

He picks up his overcoat — it has been resting on a little sled — the little sled young Charles Foster Kane hit Thatcher with at the opening of the picture. Camera doesn't close in on this. It just registers the sled as the newspaper people, picking up their clothes and equipment, move out of the great hall

Dissolve Out

Dissolve In

117 Int. Cellar — Xanadu — Night — 1940

A large furnace, with an open door, dominates the scene. Two laborers, with shovels, are shoveling things into the furnace. Raymond is about ten feet away.

RAYMOND

Throw that junk in, too.

Camera travels to the pile that he has indicated. It is mostly bits of broken packing cases, excelsior, etc. The sled is on top of the pile. As camera comes close, it shows the faded rosebud and, though the letters are faded, unmistakably the word "Rosebud" across it. The laborer drops his shovel, takes the sled in his hand and throws it into the furnace. The flames start to devour it.

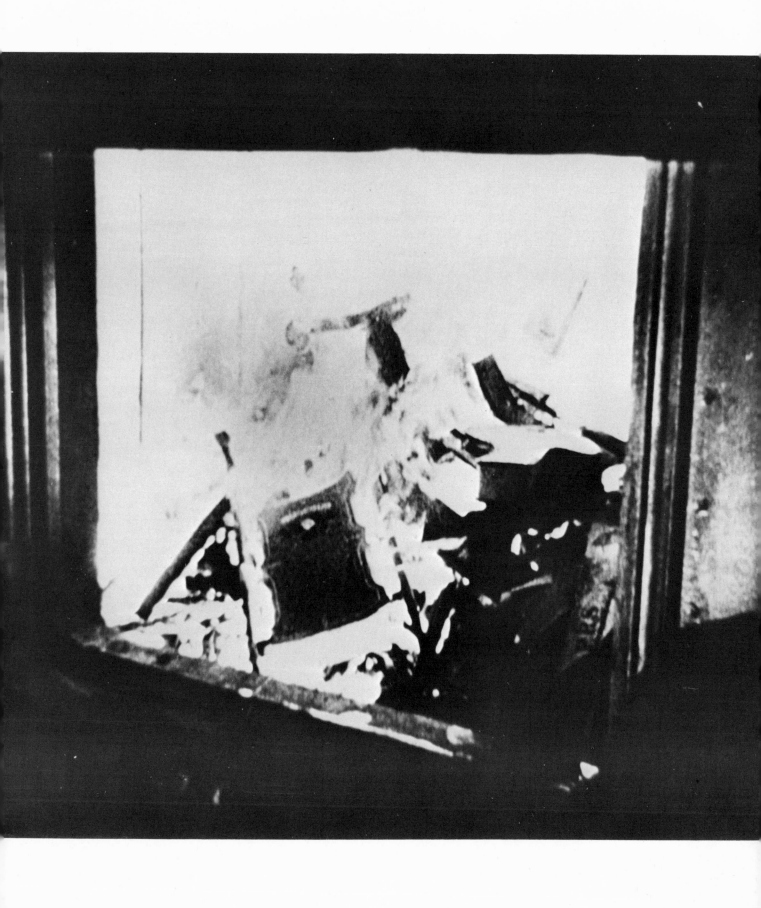

118 Ext. Xanadu — Night — 1940

No lights are to be seen. Smoke is coming from a chimney. Camera reverses the path it took at the beginning of the picture, perhaps omitting some of the stages. It moves finally through the gates, which close behind it. As camera pauses for a moment, the letter "K" is prominent in the moonlight.

Just before we fade out, there comes again into the picture the pattern of barbed wire and cyclone fencing. On the fence is a sign which reads:

PRIVATE — NO TRESPASSING

Fade Out

Notes on the Shooting Script

Prepared by Gary Carey

1. (Shots 1–14, pp. 91–98). The prologue of the script has become somewhat more detailed in the finished film, though the feeling and content are very much the same.

2. (News Digest, pp. 100–121). Nowhere does the finished film vary so greatly from the script as in the news digest. Actually very little of the material has been deleted, but it has been extensively rearranged and some of the dialogue has been rewritten accordingly; the reference to Hearst is deleted.

3. (Shot 16, pp. 122–126). In the film the dialogue has been somewhat abbreviated and one speech overlaps into the next. One of the most striking aspects of the film, the overlapping dialogue, is rarely indicated in the script.

4. (Shot 18, p. 131). In the film, one does not hear Rawlston's voice speaking over the phone.

5. (Insert, p. 136). In the film, the only words of the manuscript which we see are: "Charles Foster Kane — I first encountered Mr. Kane in 1871."

6. (Insert, p. 147). The insert, shot 29, and the insert which follows it are all deleted from the film. In the film, the scene between Kane, Thatcher, and Kane's mother and father ends with the camera holding on the forgotten sled as snow falls on it. Next occurs one of the most famous sequences in the film (although it appears in no version of the script): we see Charles (still a child) opening a Christmas package which contains a sled. Thatcher says, "Merry Christmas, Charles." The camera cuts to a close-up of Charles, who responds, "Merry Christmas," rather sullenly. There follows a very fast cut to (a considerably older) Thatcher as he is saying "and a Happy New Year." Thatcher proceeds to dictate a letter to Kane, reminding him of his responsibilities now that his twenty-first birthday is approaching. Thatcher includes a list of Kane's holdings. There is another cut and we see Thatcher's secretary reading to Thatcher Kane's answer to the New Year letter. In it, he says that the only one of his holdings in which he is interested is the New York "Inquirer."

7. (Shot 30, pp. 148–152). This sequence is expanded in the film. It opens by showing Thatcher reading a series of "Inquirer" headlines, his rage increasing with each example of Kane's yellow journalism. In the ensuing scene as it appears in the film, Leland appears for the first time, entering just after Mr. Bernstein. The film also changes

the object of Thatcher's argument with Kane from the Metropolitan Transfer Company to the Public Transit Company.

8. (Shot 31, p. 152). Preceding this shot in the film, there is a scene between Thatcher, Kane and Mr. Bernstein not found in this version of the script. It is set in 1929. Kane is bankrupt temporarily and he signs over control of his newspapers to Thatcher's corporation. During the scene, Kane passes judgment on himself. He says that had he not been rich, he might have been a really great man. Thatcher asks what he would have liked to have been. Kane answers, "Everything you hate!" The lines from Thatcher's manuscript which open Shot 31 are deleted in the film.

9. (Shot 35, p. 165). In the film the scene ends with Kane's line, "Mr. Carter, you've been most understanding. Good day."

10. (Shot 36, pp. 166–168). The entire scene is eliminated in the finished film.

11. (Shot 38, p. 170). Mike's name is changed to Solly in the film.

12. (Shot 40, p. 174). In the film, Kane is not so coy — he doesn't make the comparison to hens and ostrich eggs.

13. (Shot 41, pp. 175–185). In this scene, dialogue overlaps greatly. It has also, to a certain extent, been rearranged. Leland's worries about Kane's warmongering are reduced to one line in the film and Kane's direct reference to Hearst is also omitted.

14. (Shot 41, pp. 183–185). The character of Georgie couldn't pass the Production Code and was eliminated from the script. The deletion of Georgie necessitated the revision of the entire scene.

15. (Shot 42, pp. 185–187). The entire scene is eliminated from the film because the Production Code did not permit the depiction of a bordello.

16. (Inserts, p. 192). Both inserts are eliminated in the film.

17. (Shot 51, pp. 193–195). Leland's speeches are somewhat shortened and rearranged in the film.

18. (Shot 55, p. 199). This shot is eliminated in the film.

19. (Shot 57, p. 201). The dialogue in the film is as follows:

EMILY

Really, Charles, people will think —

CHARLES

What I tell them to think.

20. (Shot 62, p. 209). Susan sings "Una Voce Poco Fa" from Rossini's *The Barber of Seville*. She sings both in English and Italian. When she finishes, Kane applauds. The applause carries over to Leland being applauded at a political rally. His speech then overlaps into the one which Kane is giving in Shot 63.

21. (Inserts, p. 209). All three inserts are eliminated in the film.

22. (Shot 63, p. 210). This sequence is much more detailed in the finished film. It cuts continually from Kane onstage to shots of Emily and Junior in a box and to Leland and Bernstein sitting in different sections of the auditorium. Kane's speech is completely different. In the film, he is picked up in mid-sentence: ". . . to point out and make public the dishonest, the downright villainy of Boss Jim Gettys's political machine now in complete control of this state. I made no campaign promises because until a few weeks ago I had no hope of being elected. Now, however, there is something more than a hope and Jim Gettys has something less than a chance. Every straw vote, every independent poll shows that I'll be elected. Now I can afford to make some promises. The workingman and the slum child may expect my best work in their interests. The decent, ordinary citizens know that I'll do everything in my power to protect the underprivileged, the underpaid and the underfed. Well, I'd make my promises now if I weren't too busy arranging to keep them. Here's one promise I'll make and Boss Jim Gettys knows I'll keep it. My first official act as governor of this state will be to appoint a special district attorney to arrange for the indictment, prosecution and conviction of Boss Jim Gettys."

At the end of Kane's speech, there is a shot of Jim Gettys (Boss Rogers in the script) watching from someplace high in the auditorium.

23. (Shot 68, pp. 217–224). There is some variation and condensation of the dialogue of the script in the film. The gist, however, remains the same.

24. (Shot 69, pp. 224–225). In the film, there is an additional scene. We see Gettys and Emily Kane outside Susan's house. They bid each other a civilized good-night.

25. (Insert, p. 225). After the insert of the newspaper headline, we see a shot of Leland reading the same headline. He then turns and enters a saloon.

26. (Shot 71, pp. 228–232). The dialogue has been somewhat shortened in the film and some of it overlaps so that there is no feeling of lengthy monologues as one might suspect from reading the script.

27. (Insert, p. 233). In the film, the opera which Susan Alexander sings for her debut is *Salammbô*. There are two operatic versions of the story by Gustave Flaubert, the most famous by Ernest Reyer. Though rarely heard today, Reyer's opera was occasionally heard in America during the 1920's. The aria which Susan sings in the film, however, was actually composed specifically for *Citizen Kane* by Bernard Herrmann.

28. (Shot 75, p. 238, after the sentence: "This is the first time we see murder in Kane's face.") Welles does not convey this in his performance in the film. His face remains a blank.

29. (Shot 76, p. 241). In the film, we see typewriter keys hitting a white page, as Kane finishes Leland's review. The keys spell out, letter by letter, the word "weak."

30. (Shot 82, p. 246). This scene in the film begins with Susan once again singing "Una Voce Poco Fa." She flats a note, her teacher corrects her, works himself into a frenzy

ending with the "Impossible, impossible" which begins the scene in the script. The scene ends with Susan singing again, but with no happier results.

31. (Shot 94, pp. 255-257). In the film, all dialogue is omitted except Kane's final line, "Get Dr. Corey."

32. (Shot 104, p. 265). In the film, this scene of the Everglade camp is much more detailed. It includes a Negro singer crooning a popular ballad. Raymond (the butler) is shown keeping a close eye on the guests' entertainment.

33. (Shot 105, pp. 265–269). The scene in the film omits the argument over Susan's friends' drunkenness. Susan is still harping on what she was saying in the car, that Kane never gives her what she really wants. At one point, the film moves outside to the guests. It returns to Kane and Susan and their argument a few lines before he slaps her. While outside their tent, we hear the singer singing the words, "It can't be love," probably meant as satiric comment on the scene between Kane and Susan.

34. (Shot 111, p. 278). This scene is eliminated in the film.

35. (Shot 112, p. 279). This scene is eliminated in the film. In its place, we see Raymond watching Susan cross the veranda as she leaves Xanadu. This is the first shot of Raymond's flashback, and the cut from Raymond talking to Thompson in this scene is accompanied by a totally unexpected squawk from a cockatoo that a split second later becomes visible on the veranda.

36. (Shot 113, p. 279). At the end of this shot, Kane says, almost indistinctly, "Rosebud."

37. (Shot 114, pp. 284–285). All dialogue is omitted in this sequence in the film.

38. (Shot 116, pp. 288-294). There is some variation in the dialogue in the final film, but the gist is the same. Again, much of it overlaps.

RKO Cutting Continuity of the Orson Welles Production, Citizen Kane

Dated February 21, 1941

(Slightly amended to correct errors in
original transcription)

Running Time: 1 hour, 59 minutes, 16 seconds

LENGTH FT. FRM.	SCENE NO.	
		REEL I — SECTION 1A
19–5	1.	*Fade In* — TITLE #1 — radio broadcasting

AN R.K.O. RADIO PICTURE

Fade Out

12–5	2.	*Fade In* — TITLE #2:

A MERCURY PRODUCTION
by Orson Welles

12–3	3.	TITLE #3:

C I T I Z E N
K A N E

Fade Out

Night Sequence

37–	4.	*Fade In* — EXT. GATE CS — music playing — sign reads: NO **TRESPASSING** Camera pans up over sign up wire fence

Lap Dissolve

9–5	5.	*EXT. GATE CS* — camera panning up over fence — music

Lap Dissolve

12–	6.	*EXT. HOUSE CS* — camera pans up slowly over ornate grillwork design on window

Lap Dissolve

12–	7.	*EXT. GATE MS* — camera pans up over top of gate, showing letter "K" — Xanadu on mountaintop in b.g.

Lap Dissolve

13–2	8.	*EXT. XANADU LS* — castle above in b.g — monkeys in cage at left

Lap Dissolve

12–	9.	*EXT. WATER MS* — camera shooting down — prows of two gondolas in f.g., a wooden wharf in b.g.

Lap Dissolve

19–	10.	*EXT. GROUNDS MLS* — camera shooting past moat to castle in b.g. — statue of animal in f.g. — drawbridge across moat suspended in mid-air

Lap Dissolve

7–5	11.	*EXT. XANADU LS* — camera shooting up past sign at left on golf course in disrepair to castle above in b.g.

Lap Dissolve

11–4	12.	*EXT. XANADU MLS* — camera shooting over water to building and castle in b.g.

Lap Dissolve

LENGTH FT. FRM.	SCENE NO.	
9–	13.	*EXT. CASTLE MLS* — camera shooting up to light in window

Lap Dissolve

| 15–6 | 14. | *EXT. CASTLE MLS* — camera shooting through window — bed inside in b.g. — lights lit — music heard — lights go out |

Lap Dissolve

| 12– | 15. | *INT. ROOM MS* — light comes on softly in b.g., showing covered form on bed |

Lap Dissolve

| 9–3 | 16. | *INT. GLASS GLOBE* — snow falling |

Lap Dissolve

| 3–7 | 17. | *INT. GLASS GLOBE CU* — snow-covered house with snowmen surrounding it — camera moves back, showing Kane's hand holding globe |

| 2–11 | 18. | *CLOSE-UP* of Kane's mouth — lips move |

KANE

Rosebud!

| 5–15 | 19. | *INT. ROOM CU* — Kane's hand holding glass globe — drops it — music — it rolls to b.g. — down steps |

| 1–10 | 20. | *INT. ROOM CU* — glass globe rolling down steps to f.g. — breaks |

| 1–7 | 21. | *INT. ROOM MS* — distorted reflection through broken glass ball — door in b.g. opening — nurse comes in |

| 10–1 | 22. | *INT. ROOM LS* — reflection through broken glass ball — camera shooting through enormous bedroom to door in b.g. — nurse coming in — crosses to right, exits |

| 21–3 | 23. | *INT. ROOM CS* — Kane's body partly on in f.g. — nurse partly on, bending over him — folds his arms on his chest — music — she pulls covers up, leaning over — camera pans up past Kane's face as she covers it up |

Fade Out

Night Sequence

| 17– | 24. | *Fade In — INT. ROOM MS* — shadow of body lying on bed — light shining dimly through window in b.g. |

Fade Out

| 3–6 | 25. | *Drawing of group of flags* — music playing |

ANNOUNCER *(Off)*

News on the march.

Lap Dissolve

| 5–12 | 26. | *Drawing of group of flags* — music playing — TITLE #4: |

NEWS ON THE MARCH

| 5–5 | 27. | TITLE #5: |

OBITUARY
Xanadu's Landlord
NEWS ON THE MARCH

Dusk Sequence

| 16–10 | 28. | *Fade In* — TITLE #6 — pictorial b.g. — camera shooting up to top of castle |

*In Xanadu did Kubla Khan
A stately pleasure dome decree . . .*

b.g. laps into MLS of top of castle — palm waving at right

Lap Dissolve

| 4–8 | 29. | *EXT. CASTLE MLS* — camera shooting up to dome |

Lap Dissolve

| 3–10 | 30. | *EXT. CASTLE MLS* — camera shooting up to carved statue on top of building |

ANNOUNCER *(Off)*

Legendary was . . .

Lap Dissolve

2–8   31.   *EXT. CASTLE MLS* — camera shooting up side of wall

ANNOUNCER *(Off)*

. . . Xanadu where Kubla . . .

Lap Dissolve

3–   32.   *EXT. CASTLE MLS* — camera shooting up to square tower

ANNOUNCER *(Off)*

. . . Khan decreed his stately pleasure dome.

Lap Dissolve

2–13   33.   *EXT. CASTLE LS* — camera shooting up side of wall

ANNOUNCER *(Off)*

Today . . .

Lap Dissolve

Day Sequence

3–7   34.   *EXT. COUNTRY LS* — camera shooting down over trees to palatial estate below

ANNOUNCER *(Off)*

. . . almost as legendary is Florida's Xanadu . . .

Lap Dissolve

3–11   35.   *EXT. COUNTRY LS* — camera shooting down to castle among trees below

ANNOUNCER *(Off)*

. . . world's largest private . . .

Lap Dissolve

4–3   36.   *EXT. VERANDA LS* — people lounging around — others by pool in b.g.

ANNOUNCER *(Off)*

. . . pleasure ground.

3–8   37.   *EXT. COAST LS* — camera shooting along coast

ANNOUNCER *(Off)*

Here, on the deserts of the Gulf Coast . . .

7–   38.   *EXT. COUNTRY LS* — workman working in f.g. — truck passing below — partly built castle above on mountaintop in b.g.

ANNOUNCER *(Off)*

. . . a private mountain was commissioned and successfully built. One hundred thousand trees . . .

1–13   39.   *EXT. BLDG. LS* — camera shooting up scaffold to workmen

ANNOUNCER *(Off)*

. . . twenty thousand tons . . .

1–10   40.   *EXT. BLDG. LS* — camera shooting up partly built wall — man on ledge above, hoisting up timber

ANNOUNCER *(Off)*

. . . of marble are the . . .

2–6   41.   *EXT. TOWER MLS* — camera shooting up — man below at left pulling pulley — another above at right — men in b.g. on roof working

ANNOUNCER *(Off)*

. . . ingredients of Xanadu's mountain.

2–10   42.   *EXT. BLDG. LS* — camera shooting up scaffold to men above at right

Lap Dissolve

5–1   43.   *EXT. GROUNDS MLS* — camera shooting up at statue of man on horse — top of castle seen in b.g.

ANNOUNCER *(Off)*

Contents of Xanadu's palace . . .

Wipe Over Lap Dissolve

2–7   44.   *INT. ROOM MS* — statue of man riding a unicorn, half crated — other crates around it

ANNOUNCER *(Off)*

. . . paintings, pictures, statues . . .

Wipe Over Lap Dissolve

2–9   45.   *EXT. TOWER MLS* — camera shooting up to pointed tower

ANNOUNCER *(Off)*

. . . the very stones of many another palace . . .

Wipe Over Lap Dissolve

2–7   46.   *EXT. BLDG. MLS* — camera shooting up side of carved wall

ANNOUNCER *(Off)*

. . . collection . . .

Wipe Over Lap Dissolve

2–8   47.   *EXT. BLDG. MS* — man leading loaded camel to b.g.

ANNOUNCER *(Off)*

. . . of everything . . .

Wipe Over Lap Dissolve

3–2   48.   *EXT. GROUNDS MS* — man wheeling crate, passing in f.g. — men unloading freight cars at left

ANNOUNCER *(Off)*

. . . so big it can never be . . .

Wipe Over Lap Dissolve

2–5   49.   *EXT. GROUNDS MS* — man wheeling truck to left

ANNOUNCER *(Off)*

. . . catalogued or appraised . . .

Wipe Over Lap Dissolve

5–2   50.   *EXT. DOCK MS* — man waving as load comes down from ship

ANNOUNCER *(Off)*

. . . enough for ten museums . . .

Wipe Over Lap Dissolve

5–2   51.   *EXT. DOCK MLS* — piles of crates around — camera pans to right

ANNOUNCER *(Off)*

. . . the loot of the world.

LENGTH FT. FRM.	SCENE NO.	

Day Sequence

2–9 52. *EXT. STABLES MLS* — four horses in stalls — look to f.g.

ANNOUNCER (*Off*)

Xanadu's . . .

3– 53. *EXT. GROUNDS MLS* — two giraffes, inside cage, lift heads

ANNOUNCER (*Off*)

. . . livestock . . .

3– 54. *EXT. GROUNDS LS* — rare birds flying around in cage

ANNOUNCER (*Off*)

. . . the fowl of the air . . .

3–1 55. *EXT. GROUNDS CS* — large octopus swimming to f.g. in pool

ANNOUNCER (*Off*)

. . . the fish of the sea . . .

2–15 56. *EXT. DOCK MLS* — men below in b.g. — camera following elephant being hoisted down
from ship

ANNOUNCER (*Off*)

. . . the beast of the field and jungle . . .

3– 57. *EXT. SHIP MLS* — camera following donkeys being hoisted up over ship — men and animals
below

ANNOUNCER (*Off*)

. . . two of each . . .

4– 58. *EXT. BLDG. LS* — camera shooting up to top of glass dome — bird flying around inside

ANNOUNCER (*Off*)

. . . the biggest private zoo since Noah.

1–14 59. *EXT. GROUNDS LS* — camera shooting over a formal garden with geometrically designed
topiary shrubs, pools and paths, people walking around on paths

ANNOUNCER (*Off*)

Like . . .

2–7 60. *EXT. WATER MLS* — camera shooting from balcony over railing to building in b.g.

ANNOUNCER (*Off*)

. . . the pharaohs . . .

3–13 61. *EXT. BLDG. MLS* — camera shooting up to top of building — carved work on wall

ANNOUNCER (*Off*)

. . . Xanadu's landlord leaves many stones . . .

2–14 62. *EXT. BLDG. MLS* — camera shooting up to top — carving on walls

ANNOUNCER (*Off*)

. . . to mark his grave.

3–3 63. *EXT. CASTLE MLS* — camera shooting up to domes

ANNOUNCER (*Off*)

Since the Pyramids . . .

3–6 64. *EXT. CASTLE MLS* — camera shooting up carved wall at left — tree at right

ANNOUNCER (*Off*)

. . . Xanadu is the costliest . . .

3–7   65.   *EXT. GROUNDS LS* — camera shooting past a statue of Cupid aiming arrow to top of frame

ANNOUNCER (*Off*)

. . . monument a man has built . . .

4–10   66.   *EXT. GROUNDS LS* — camera shooting over pool — water lilies floating on top — reflection of trees and dome seen in water in b.g.

ANNOUNCER (*Off*)

. . . to himself.

Fade Out

10–   67.   TITLE #7 — music playing

IN XANADU LAST WEEK
WAS HELD 1940'S BIGGEST
STRANGEST FUNERAL.

Day Sequence

24–2   68.   *EXT. CHAPEL MLS* — crowd in f.g. watching pallbearers coming out of entrance in b.g. carrying casket

ANNOUNCER (*Off*)

Here in Xanadu last week, Xanadu's landlord was laid to rest, a potent figure of our century, America's Kubla Khan . . .

12–14   69.   INSERT #1 — *CU* picture of Kane in paper — camera moves back showing headlines

ANNOUNCER (*Off*)

. . . Charles Foster Kane.

Headlines of paper, reading:

New York Daily Inquirer
CHARLES FOSTER KANE DIES
AFTER LIFETIME OF SERVICE
Finds Place in U.S. Hall of Fame
Entire Nation Mourns Great Publisher as Outstanding American

Paper is removed revealing another:

The Daily Chronicle
C. F. KANE DIES AT XANADU ESTATE
EDITOR'S STORMY CAREER COMES TO AN END
Death of Publisher Finds Few Who Will Mourn for Him
(Picture of Kane)

Paper is removed revealing another:

Chicago Globe
DEATH CALLS PUBLISHER CHARLES KANE
POLICIES SWAYED WORLD
Stormy Career Ends for "U.S. Fascist No. 1"
(Picture of Kane)

Paper is removed revealing another:

Minneapolis Record Herald
KANE, SPONSOR OF DEMOCRACY, DIES
Publisher Gave Life to Nation's Service during Long Career

Paper is removed revealing another, partly on:

San Francisco
DEATH FINALLY COMES

14–11   70.   INSERT #2 — paper on top of others — headline reads:

KANE LEADER OF NEWS WORLD
CALLED BY DEATH AT XANADU
Detroit Star
WAS MASTER OF DESTINY
(Picture of Kane)

Paper is removed showing another:

El Paso Journal
END COMES FOR CHARLES FOSTER KANE
Editor Who Instigated "War for Profit" Is Beaten by Death

Paper is removed — camera moves up closer showing foreign paper:

Le Matin
MORT DU GRAND EDITEUR C. F. KANE

Paper is removed showing another:

El Correspondencia
¡EL SR. KANE SE MURIO!

Camera moves closer as paper is removed showing Greek newspaper — this is removed showing Chinese newspaper

16–5   71.   TITLE #8:

> To forty-four million U.S. news-buyers, more newsworthy than the names in his own headlines was Kane himself, greatest newspaper tycoon of this or any other generation.

11–9   72.   *EXT. STREET MLS* — truck passing to left exits, showing old Inquirer Building in b.g. — three colored men standing at left by window — one skates across to right

ANNOUNCER (*Off*)

> Its humble beginnings, in this ramshackle building, a dying daily. Kane's empire, in its glory . . .

15–2   73.   *Picture of map of U.S.* — circles widening out on map

ANNOUNCER (*Off*)

> . . . held dominion over thirty-seven newspapers, two syndicates, a radio network, an empire upon an empire.

2–14   74.   *EXT. BLDG. MLS* — camera shooting across street to Kane grocery store — convertible car passing in f.g.

ANNOUNCER (*Off*)

The first of grocery stores . . .

1–14   75.   *INT. MILL MLS* — huge roll of paper moving up to f.g.

ANNOUNCER (*Off*)

. . . paper mills . . .

Day Sequence

2–7   76.   *EXT. STREET LS* — camera shooting up over trees to row of apartments at right b.g.

ANNOUNCER (*Off*)

. . . apartment buildings . . .

1–13   77.   *EXT. FACTORY LS* — camera shooting over smokestacks of a factory, steam pouring out of them

ANNOUNCER (*Off*)

. . . factories . . .

| LENGTH | SCENE |
| FT. FRM. | NO. |

2–   78.   *EXT. WATER MLS* — man in f.g. — tree crashing into water below in b.g.

ANNOUNCER *(Off)*

. . . forests . . .

3–8   79.   *EXT. WATER MLS* — camera shooting down to liner moving to f.g. below

ANNOUNCER *(Off)*

. . . ocean liners.

Lap Dissolve

3–2   80.   *EXT. COUNTRY LS* — camera shooting to mine buildings on mountainside in b.g. — sign near f.g. reads:

COLORADO LODE MINE CO.

ANNOUNCER *(Off)*

An empire through which for fifty years . . .

2–11   81.   *INT. MINE MS* — ore moving to f.g. in trough

ANNOUNCER *(Off)*

. . . flowed in an . . .

1–15   82.   *INT. MINE MS* — rack vibrating — water pouring over it

ANNOUNCER *(Off)*

. . . unending stream . . .

1–13   83.   *INT. ROOM MCS* — ore bubbling in vats

ANNOUNCER *(Off)*

. . . the wealth of . . .

3–13   84.   *INT. ROOM CS* — piles of bullion stacked up — man rising on at right f.g., putting up another bar

ANNOUNCER *(Off)*

. . . the earth's third richest gold mine.

Wipe Over Lap Dissolve

4–11   85.   *EXT. HIGHWAY LS* — sign in f.g. — town seen in b.g. — sign reading:

COLORADO
STAGE LINE
LITTLE SALEM — 3

ANNOUNCER *(Off)*

Famed in American legend . . .

Wipe Over Lap Dissolve

7–1   86.   *INT. ROOM CU* — picture of Kane Jr. — camera moves back showing framed portrait of mother with him

ANNOUNCER *(Off)*

. . . is the origin of the Kane fortune. How, to boardinghouse-keeper Mary Kane, by a . . .

8–7   87.   *INT. ROOM CS* — picture of Kane's old home — camera moving up closer

ANNOUNCER *(Off)*

. . . defaulting boarder, in 1868, was left the supposedly worthless deed to an abandoned mine shaft . . .

4–8   88.   *INT. MINE CS* — bucket tilting, pouring molten ore into mold

ANNOUNCER (*Off*)

. . . the Colorado Lode.

Fade Out

Day Sequence

6–14   89.   *Fade In — EXT. CAPITOL BUILDING* — camera shooting to building in b.g.

ANNOUNCER (*Off*)

Fifty-seven years later, before a congressional investigation . . .

5–10   90.   *INT. ROOM MCS* — Thatcher and men seated — Thatcher at right, on other side of table

ANNOUNCER (*Off*)

. . . Walter P. Thatcher, grand old man of Wall Street . . .

9–12   91.   *INT. ROOM LS* — men around — Thatcher at end of table in b.g.

ANNOUNCER (*Off*)

. . . for years chief target of Kane Papers' attack on "trusts," recalls a journey he made as a youth.

15–5   92.   *INT. ROOM MCS* — men sitting around — Thatcher in b.g., gesturing, talking — men heard talking indistinctly

THATCHER

My firm had been appointed trustee by Mrs. Kane for a large fortune which she recently acquired. It was her wish that I should take charge of this boy . . . this Charles Foster Kane.

28–3   93.   *INT. ROOM LS* — men around — Johnson in f.g. shouts at Thatcher in b.g. — Thatcher calling to him — man bringing paper to Thatcher

THATCHER

Mr. Johnson . . . Mr. Johnson . . .

JOHNSON

Is it not a fact that on this occasion that boy, Charles Foster Kane, personally attacked you after striking you in the stomach with a sled?
Men laugh — Thatcher picking up paper — men gathering around

THATCHER

Mr. Chairman, I shall read to the committee a prepared statement which I have brought with me, and I shall then refuse to answer any further questions.

23–14   94.   *INT. ROOM MCU* — Thatcher leaning forward, reading from paper — others partly on around him

THATCHER

Mr. Charles Foster Kane, in every essence of his social beliefs and by the dangerous manner in which he has persistently attacked the American traditions of private property, initiative and opportunity for advancement is, in fact, nothing more or less than a Communist.

Wipe Over Lap Dissolve

Day Sequence

5–5   95.   *EXT. SQUARE LS* — camera shooting down to enormous crowd packed in Union Square

ANNOUNCER (*Off*)

That same month in Union Square . . .
Speaker below on platform heard

SPEAKER *(Off)*

The words "Charles . . .

7–4   96. *EXT. SQUARE MLS* — camera shooting over crowd — pans to right — speaker's voice heard reverberating

SPEAKER *(Off)*

. . . Foster Kane" are a menace to every working man in this land.

8–8   97. *EXT. PLATFORM CS* — camera shooting up to speaker talking — loudspeakers around him

SPEAKER

He today is what he always has been and will always be, a Fascist.

4–10   98. *EXT. STREET MS* — crowd around Kane, standing by microphone

ANNOUNCER *(Off)*

And still another opinion . . .

7–1   99. TITLE #9 — music playing

"I AM, HAVE BEEN, AND WILL BE ONLY ONE THING — AN AMERICAN."
Charles Foster Kane

Day Sequence

8–12   100. *EXT. STREET MS* — crowd around Kane applauding — music — Kane smiles, bows — shaking hands with men

Fade Out

9–1   101. TITLE #10:

1895 to 1940
ALL OF THESE YEARS HE COVERED, MANY OF THESE HE WAS.

ANNOUNCER *(Off)*

Kane . . .

4–4   102. *EXT. SQUARE MLS* — soldiers on horseback riding to f.g. — TITLE #11:

1898

ANNOUNCER *(Off)*

. . . urged his country's entry into one war . . .

3–11   103. *EXT. CEMETERY LS* — rows of crosses marking graves — man going to b.g. — TITLE #12:

1919

ANNOUNCER *(Off)*

. . . opposed participation in another.

5–9   104. *EXT. TRAIN MS* — Kane, Teddy Roosevelt and others on platform of train — crowd in b.g. waving — train goes to b.g.

ANNOUNCER *(Off)*

Won the election for one American President at least.

Night Sequence

7–5   105. *EXT. STREET MLS* — crowd carrying banners showing caricatures of Kane

ANNOUNCER *(Off)*

Fought for millions of Americans . . .

3–1   106. *EXT. GROUNDS MLS* — people around fire burning — picture of Kane in b.g.

ANNOUNCER (*Off*)

. . . was hated by as many more.

2–14   107.   *EXT. GROUNDS MS* — man at right watching effigy of Kane burning — music

Wipe Over Lap Dissolve

9–12   108.   *INT. ROOM MS* — machine sending newspapers up above — camera following

ANNOUNCER (*Off*)

For forty years appeared in Kane newsprint no public issue on which Kane Papers took no stand.

Day Sequence

5–3   109.   *EXT. BALCONY CS* — banner in f.g. reading: WE WANT ROOSEVELT — banner moves up revealing Kane standing by Roosevelt and others — laughing, waving.

ANNOUNCER (*Off*)

No public man whom . . .

2–13   110.   *EXT. BLDG. MS* — car in f.g. at curb — Kane and man coming out of entrance of building in b.g.

ANNOUNCER (*Off*)

. . . Kane himself did not support . . .

4–11   111.   *EXT. SQUARE MS* — Kane and officers around him laughing, talking — others on balconies of building above in b.g.

ANNOUNCER (*Off*)

. . . or denounce. Often support . . .

9–1   112.   *EXT. BALCONY MS* — camera shooting up to Kane and Hitler above on balcony — men partly on at right — music

ANNOUNCER (*Off*)

. . . then denounce.

Fade Out

5–   113.   TITLE #13 — music playing

FEW PRIVATE LIVES
WERE MORE PUBLIC.

Day Sequence

6–   114.   *EXT. WHITE HOUSE MS* — Kane and Emily coming forward — both dressed in wedding clothes, Emily carrying a bridal bouquet — people at right and in b.g. following Kane and Emily stop in f.g., laughing

ANNOUNCER (*Off*)

Twice married, twice divorced . . .

9–13   115.   *EXT. LAWN CS* — Kane and Emily in f.g. — crowd around them — Kane kisses Emily on forehead — laughing — kisses her again

ANNOUNCER (*Off*)

. . . first to a President's niece, Emily Norton, who left him in 1916 . . .

5–7   116.   INSERT #3 — article in newspaper, reading:

FAMILY GREETS KANE
AFTER VICTORY SPEECH

(Picture of Kane, holding Junior in his arms, and Emily.
Others around them)

Charles Foster Kane's young son and wife with him outside Madison Square Garden after his windup speech last . . .

ANNOUNCER (*Off*)

. . . died 1918 in a motor accident with their son.

Fade Out

Day Sequence

7–2   117.   *Fade in* — *EXT. TOWN HALL, TRENTON MLS* — newspaper reporters and crowd around — Kane coming out of entrance of building with Susan and group — photographer taking pictures — cop runs up to f.g.

ANNOUNCER (*Off*)

Sixteen years after his first marriage . . .

14–1   118.   *EXT. BLDG. MS* — crowd around Susan and Kane as they try to come forward — photographers taking pictures — Kane striking at people with umbrella

ANNOUNCER (*Off*)

. . . two weeks after his first divorce, Kane married Susan Alexander, singer, at the town hall in Trenton, New Jersey.

Wipe Over Lap Dissolve

2–11   119.   INSERT #4 — *CS* poster

LYRIC THEATRE
On the Stage

SUZAN ALEXANDER
Coming Thursday
(Picture of Susan)

ANNOUNCER (*Off*)

For Wife Two, one- . . .

6–1   120.   INSERT #5 — cover of an opera program

CHICAGO MUNICIPAL
OPERA HOUSE
Presents
SUSAN
ALEXANDER
in
Salammbô
GALA OPENING
(Picture of Susan in costume)

ANNOUNCER (*Off*)

. . . time opera-singing Susan Alexander, Kane built . . .

7–12   121.   *Drawing of Chicago Municipal Opera House*

ANNOUNCER (*Off*)

. . . Chicago's Municipal Opera House. Cost: three million dollars.

12–13   122.   *Iris shot of photograph of Susan, her arm around Kane* — camera moves back, the iris opens out to show others around them on a terrace — Xanadu in b.g.

ANNOUNCER (*Off*)

Conceived for Susan Alexander Kane, half-finished before she divorced him, the still unfinished . . .

Lap Dissolve

7–5   123.   *EXT. COUNTRY LS* — camera shooting over forest to Xanadu on mountaintop in b.g. — music

ANNOUNCER (*Off*)

. . . Xanadu. Cost: No man can say.

END OF REEL 1 — SECTION 1A

LENGTH FT. FRM.	SCENE NO.	

REEL I — SECTION 1B

5–11   1.   TITLE #1 — music playing

IN POLITICS — ALWAYS A BRIDESMAID, NEVER A BRIDE.

Day Sequence

7–10   2.   *EXT. PLATFORM MCS* — Kane making speech

ANNOUNCER (Off)

Kane, molder of mass opinion though he was, in all his life was never . . .

4–10   3.   *EXT. SQUARE LS* — banners flying from building on corner in b.g. — music

ANNOUNCER (Off)

. . . granted elective office by the voters of his country.

3–9   4.   *INT. BLDG. MS* — camera shooting down to paper machines rolling newspapers through

ANNOUNCER (Off)

But Kane Papers were once strong indeed . . .

Wipe Over Lap Dissolve

5–   5.   *INT. ROOM MS* — machinery carrying EXTRA papers upward

ANNOUNCER (Off)

. . . and once the prize seemed almost his.

Wipe Over Lap Dissolve

Night Sequence

8–3   6.   *EXT. STREET MLS* — parade marching to f.g., carrying banners — flares burning

ANNOUNCER (Off)

In 1916, as independent candidate for governor, the best elements of the state behind him . . .

3–6   7.   *INT. ROOM MCS* — people applauding — shaking hands with Kane

ANNOUNCER (Off)

. . . the White House seemingly the next . . .

1–15   8.   *EXT. STREET MLS* — fires burning in b.g. — people moving about

ANNOUNCER (Off)

. . . easy step in a lightning . . .

2–1   9.   *EXT. SKY MLS* — skyrockets exploding

ANNOUNCER (Off)

. . . political career . . .

6–8   10.   *EXT. PLATFORM MCS* — Kane leaning over railing to f.g., shaking hands — music

ANNOUNCER (Off)

. . . then suddenly, less than one . . .

Iris Dissolve

13–   11.   INSERT #1 — music playing — iris shot of headlines in paper, opening out to read:

The Daily Chronicle
CANDIDATE KANE CAUGHT IN
LOVE NEST WITH "SINGER"
THE HIGHLY MORAL MR. KANE AND HIS TAME "SONGBIRD"

<table>
<tr><td>LENGTH
FT. FRM.</td><td>SCENE
NO.</td><td></td></tr>
</table>

Entrapped by Wife as Love Pirate, Kane Refuses to Quit Race
(Pictures of Susan and Kane over apartment house entrance)

ANNOUNCER (Off)

. . . week before election, defeat . . . shameful, ignominious. Defeat that set back for twenty years the cause of reform in the U. S. . . .

6–9   12.   INSERT #2 — heart-shaped framed pictures of Kane and Susan in newspaper

ANNOUNCER (Off)

. . . forever canceled political chances for Charles Foster Kane.

Fade Out

3–8   13.   Fade In — EXT. FACTORY LS — camera shooting through gates to buildings in b.g. — sign on gate reading:

FACTORY CLOSED
NO
TRESPASSING

TITLE #2 superimposed over scene:

1929

1–14   14.   EXT. FENCE MS — sign reading: CLOSED

ANNOUNCER (Off)

Then in the first year . . .

7–6   15.   EXT. BLDG. MS — camera moves up to door, showing gates locked — music — sign reading: CLOSED

ANNOUNCER (Off)

. . . of the Great Depression, a Kane paper closes.

3–8   16.   EXT. WAREHOUSE MS — sign painted on door: CLOSED

ANNOUNCER (Off)

For Kane, in four short years . . .

11–4   17.   CLOSE-UP map showing circles — they diminish, leaving only a few moving

ANNOUNCER (Off)

. . . collapse. Eleven Kane papers merged, more sold, scrapped . . .

Fade Out

7–8   18.   TITLE #3 — music playing

BUT AMERICA STILL READS
KANE NEWSPAPERS AND KANE
HIMSELF WAS ALWAYS NEWS.

Day Sequence

11–1   19.   EXT. BOAT MS — camera shooting down to group of reporters around Kane — men taking pictures — reporter by Kane, talks — title "1935" fades out

REPORTER

. . . Is that correct?

KANE

Don't believe everything you hear on the radio.

60–3   20.   EXT. BOAT CS — reporter at right — Kane facing f.g., smiling, talks into mike

KANE

Read the "Inquirer."
Men heard laughing

REPORTER

How did you find business conditions in Europe?

KANE

How did I find business conditions in Europe, Mr. Bones? With great difficulty.

He laughs heartily — others laughing

REPORTER

Are you glad to be back again, Mr. Kane?

KANE

I'm always glad to be back, young man. I'm an American, always been an American. Anything else? When I was a reporter, we asked them quicker than that. Come on, young fellow.

REPORTER

Well, what do you think of the chances for war in Europe?

KANE

I talked with the responsible leaders of the Great Powers — England, France, Germany and Italy. They are too intelligent to embark upon a project which would mean the end of civilization as we now know it. You can take my word for it, there will be no war.

Flashlight bulbs go off

8–11   21.   *EXT. BLDG. MS* — Kane standing at left with trowel — man standing by cornerstone at right — music — people around — Kane drops dirt from trowel, brushes off coat — man's arm comes on at left, hands him handkerchief.

ANNOUNCER *(Off)*

Kane helped to change the world . . .

14–6   22.   *EXT. BLDG. MS* — Kane and men by cornerstone — Kane taps it, looks around — man removing hook — others working — music

ANNOUNCER *(Off)*

. . . but Kane's world now is history, and the great yellow journalist himself lived to be history, outlived his power to make it.

9–10   23.   *EXT. POOL MS* — Kane sitting on lounge chair by pool, part of statue is seen in right f.g.

ANNOUNCER *(Off)*

Alone in his never finished, already decaying pleasure palace, aloof, seldom visited . . .

7–4   24.   *EXT. GROUNDS MLS* — camera shooting through cross-bars — man in b.g. wheeling Kane forward in wheelchair — music

ANNOUNCER *(Off)*

. . . never photographed, an emperor of newsprint continued to direct . . .

3–10   25.   *EXT. LAWN LS* — man wheeling Kane in wheelchair to f.g. — music

ANNOUNCER *(Off)*

. . . his failing empire. Vainly . . .

5–   26.   *EXT. LAWN CS* — camera following Kane as man pushes him in a wheelchair to right — music

ANNOUNCER *(Off)*

. . . attempted to sway, as he once did, the destinies . . .

9–9   27.   *EXT. LAWN MCS* — man wheeling Kane in wheelchair to f.g. — camera pans down — pans to right following them across road

LENGTH FT. FRM.	SCENE NO.	

ANNOUNCER *(Off)*

. . . of a nation that had ceased to listen to him, ceased to trust him.

Night Sequence

11–4 28. *EXT. STREET LS* — camera shooting across intersection to building — crowd and traffic on streets — neon travel sign, moving across side of building above in b.g., reads:

LATEST NEWS   CHARLES FOSTER KANE IS DEAD

ANNOUNCER *(Off)*

Then, last week, as it must to all men, death came to Charles Foster Kane.

3–6 29. *Fade In* — pictorial title — TITLE #4:

THE END
NEWS ON THE MARCH

ANNOUNCER *(Off)*

News on the march.

2–9 30. *INT. PROJECTION ROOM MS* — end title on screen at left — theater dark — music

1–8 31. *INT. ROOM MS* — light shining from projection machine at right goes out, music stops

2–8 32. *INT. ROOM CS* — camera shooting through window — hand in booth turning off machine

39– 33. *INT. ROOM MS* — men sitting around in dark — light shining from windows above in b.g. — men rise, talking — man in b.g. talks on phone

MAN

That's it.

MAN

Hello.

MAN

Hello.

MAN

Stand by. I'll tell you if we want to run it again.

MAN

Well, how about it, Mr. Rawlston?

RAWLSTON

How do you like it, boys?

MAN

Well, seventy years in a man's life . . .

MAN

That's a lot to try to get into a newsreel.
Thompson at left, turns on light on desk — men smoking — Rawlston walking forward

RAWLSTON

It's a good short, Thompson. All it needs is an angle. All we saw on that screen was Charles Foster Kane is dead. I know that. I read the papers.
Men laugh

MAN

Needs that angle. It isn't enough to tell us what a man did, you've got to tell us who he was.

MAN

Yeh, needs an angle —

22–3   34.   *INT. ROOM MCU* — camera shooting down at Rawlston at left — claps his hands, talks — Thompson at right — man sitting in b.g.

RAWLSTON

Certainly. Wait a minute, wait a minute. What were Kane's last words? Do you remember, boys?

Rawlston goes to b.g. — men talking indistinctly

RAWLSTON

What were the last words he said on earth? Maybe he told us all about himself on his deathbed.

MAN

Yeh, and maybe he didn't.

MAN

Yes, all we saw on that screen was a big American.
Rawlston exits left f.g.

MAN

One of the biggest.

35–4   35.   *INT. ROOM MS* — Thompson and man in f.g. — Rawlston going to b.g. — talking, turning before screen

RAWLSTON

Yes, but how did he differ from Ford, Hearst — for that matter — or John Doe? Yes, sure —

MAN

I tell you, Thompson, a man's dying words —

MAN

What were they?

MAN

You don't read the papers.
Men all laugh — talk indistinctly

MAN

When Charles Foster Kane died, he said but just one word —

MAN

Yeh, Rosebud.

MAN

That's all he says, Rosebud?

MAN

Tough guy, huh.

MAN

Yes, just one word.

MAN

But who is she?

MAN

What was it?
Rawlston steps forward

RAWLSTON

Here is a man who could have been President, who was as loved and hated and as talked about as any man in our time . . .

10–8   36.   *INT. ROOM MCU* — Rawlston talking, Thompson at left

RAWLSTON

. . . but when he comes to die, he's got something on his mind called Rosebud. Now what does that mean?

MAN *(Off)*

Maybe it was a horse he bet on once.

MAN *(Off)*

Yeh, and didn't come in.
Rawlston moves quickly to left

RAWLSTON

All right . . .
He exits

9–3   37.   *INT. ROOM MLS* — Rawlston crossing to right, talking — Thompson on table — others sitting around in darkness

RAWLSTON

. . . but where was the race?

MAN

Rosebud.

RAWLSTON

Thompson!

THOMPSON

Yes, sir.

RAWLSTON

Hold this picture up a week, two weeks if you have to.

17–7   38.   *INT. ROOM MCS* — Rawlston at right f.g., Thompson on table at left — lights shining down from booth in b.g. — Thompson talks indistinctly — Rawlston waving, shouts

RAWLSTON

Find out about Rosebud, get in touch with everybody that ever knew him, or knew him well — that manager of his, ah . . . Bernstein — his second wife. She's still living.

MAN

Susan Alexander Kane.

15–8   39.   *INT. ROOM MLS* — group around — Rawlston at right — man in b.g. talks

MAN

She's running a nightclub in Atlantic City.

MAN

Yeh, that's right.
Rawlston moves around to Thompson

RAWLSTON

See them all. Get in touch with everybody that ever worked for him — whoever loved him — whoever . . . hated his guts. I don't mean . . .

15–11   40.   *INT. ROOM MCU* — Rawlston talking — Thompson left f.g., back to camera

RAWLSTON

. . . going through the city directory, of course.
Men laugh

THOMPSON

I'll get on it right away, Mr. Rawlston.
Rawlston smiles, punches Thompson on arm

RAWLSTON

Good. Rosebud dead or alive. It will probably turn out to be a very simple thing.

Night Sequence

37–5   41.   *EXT. BLDG. CU* — billboard picture of Susan suddenly illuminated by lightning, music and thunder heard — rain pouring down picture — lightning flashes — camera moves up to top of building — rain pouring down — neon sign flashing on building

"EL RANCHO"
Floor Show
SUSAN ALEXANDER KANE
Twice Nightly

Camera moves through sign to skylight below — rain pouring down, thunder heard, lightning flashing — Susan seen below at table

Lap Dissolve

122–   42.   *INT. CAFE MLS* — camera shooting down to Susan at left, at table — music playing — camera moves up to her — headwaiter comes on at right — Thompson coming on at right — Susan bows head on her arms on table — coughing — two men look at her, waiter talks

HEADWAITER

Miss Alexander, this is Mr. Thompson . . . Miss Alexander.
She raises head — talks huskily

SUSAN

I want another drink, John.

HEADWAITER

Right away. Will you have something, Mr. Thompson?

THOMPSON

I'll have a highball, please.
Thompson goes to table, sits down — camera moving up close to them — she looks up angrily

SUSAN

Who told you you could sit down?

THOMPSON

I thought maybe we could have a talk together.

SUSAN

Well, think again. Can't you people leave me alone? I'm minding my own business, you mind yours.

THOMPSON

If I could just have a little talk with you, Miss Alexander.

SUSAN

Get out of here!
She shouts at him

SUSAN

Get out!
He rises — she puts hand to head

THOMPSON

I'm sorry.

SUSAN

Get out.

THOMPSON

Maybe some other time —

SUSAN

Get out!
Storm heard — camera pans up, showing Thompson in f.g. — headwaiter facing him, nods to b.g. — music — camera pans — they go to b.g. — stop by another waiter

HEADWAITER

Gino, get her another highball. She just won't talk to nobody, Mr. Thompson.

THOMPSON

Okay.
Thompson goes up steps to right, exits — telephone heard — two waiters looking to f.g. — dialing heard

GINO

Another double?

HEADWAITER

Yeh.

103–15   43.   *INT. CAFE MLS* — camera shooting down through booth to café in b.g. — Thompson in f.g. talking on phone — two waiters in b.g. — Susan sitting at table left b.g. — headwaiter on hand — Gino exits right — John comes to booth

THOMPSON

Hello, I want New York City. Courtland 7-9970. This is Atlantic City 4-6827. All right.
Coins heard dropping in phone

THOMPSON

Hey, she's —

HEADWAITER

Yeh, she'll snap out of it. Why, until he died, she's just as soon talk about Mr. Kane as anybody.
Thompson talks on phone

THOMPSON

Hello.

HEADWAITER

Sooner.

THOMPSON

This is Thompson. Let me talk to the Chief, will you?

Thompson closes door on headwaiter — Gino coming on left b.g. with drink — goes to Susan — she drinks — waiter exits

THOMPSON

Hello, Mr. Rawlston. She won't talk. The second Mrs. Kane — about Rosebud or anything else. I'm calling from Atlantic City. Then tomorrow I'm going over to Philadelphia to the Thatcher Library, to see that private diary of his. Yeh, they're expecting me. Then I've got an appointment in New York with Kane's general manager, what's his name, ah, Bernstein. Then I'm coming back here. Yeh, I'll see everybody, if they are still alive. Good-bye, Mr. Rawlston.

He hangs up phone, opens door, talks to headwaiter

THOMPSON

Hey —

HEADWAITER

John.

THOMPSON

John, you just might be able to help me.

HEADWAITER

Yes, sir.

THOMPSON

When she used to talk about Mr. Kane, did she ever say anything about Rosebud?

HEADWAITER

Rosebud?

Thompson tips John

HEADWAITER

Thank you, Mr. Thompson, thanks. As a matter of fact, just the other day, when the papers were full of it, I asked her. She never heard of Rosebud.

Fade Out

Day Sequence

53–10   44.   *Fade In — INT. LIBRARY MS — camera shooting up to statue of Thatcher above — music playing — camera pans down to engraving on base — camera moving back:* WALTER PARKS THATCHER

BERTHA *(Off)*

The directors of the Thatcher Memorial Library have asked me . . .

Camera moving back shows Thompson standing in f.g. — Bertha sitting at desk, holding phone, talking — echoes heard

BERTHA

. . . to remind you again, Mr. Thompson . . .

THOMPSON

Yes.

BERTHA

. . . of the conditions under which you may inspect certain portions of Mr. Thatcher's unpublished memoirs.

THOMPSON

I remember them.

BERTHA

Yes, Jennings, I'll bring him right in.
She puts phone down

THOMPSON

All I want is one —

BERTHA

Under no circumstances are direct quotations from his manuscript to be used by you.

THOMPSON

That's all right. I'm just looking for one . . .

BERTHA

You may come with me.
She rises, goes to b.g. — he follows

Lap Dissolve

62–7   45.   *INT. HALL MS* — Bertha opening huge vault door — Thompson coming on in f.g., follows her through into vaults — light shining down on long table — guard coming forward from great distance with book — camera moving in to vault — Bertha talks

BERTHA

Jennings . . .
He puts book down at end of table

BERTHA

Thank you, Jennings.
He tips hat, goes to b.g.

BERTHA

Mr. Thompson, you will be required to leave this room at four-thirty promptly. You will confine yourself, it is our understanding, to the chapter in Mr. Thatcher's manuscript regarding Mr. Kane.
She comes forward

THOMPSON

That's all I'm interested in.
She turns, looks at him

THOMPSON

Thank you.
He goes to chair, turns as she talks — guard in b.g., closing vault door

BERTHA

Pages eighty-three to one-forty-two.
Door heard slamming — Bertha moves to right f.g., closes door, exits — door closing before camera — music

Lap Dissolve

11–   46.   *INT. VAULT MCS* — Thompson at table, back to camera — light shining down on table from above — guard seen dimly in b.g. — music — camera moves up over Thompson's shoulder toward book

Lap Dissolve

3–3   47.   INSERT #3 — music playing — handwriting on page reads:

Charles Foster Kane

20–9   48.   INSERT #4 — rather old-fashioned handwriting on paper reads:

I first encountered Mr. Kane in 1871 . . .

Lap Dissolve

LENGTH FT. FRM.	SCENE NO.	
8–6	49.	*EXT. COUNTRY LS* — snow falling — music — Kane Jr. on sled above in b.g. — rides down toward left, rises — throws snowball to f.g.
3–13	50.	*EXT. HOUSE MS* — music — sign above porch, reading:

MRS. KANE'S
BOARDINGHOUSE

Snow falling — wind heard — snowball hits sign — music stops

END OF REEL 1 — SECTION 1B

REEL 2 — SECTION 2A

Day Sequence

158–10   1.   *INT. ROOM MLS* — window in f.g. — Charles outside in b.g., playing in snow, yelling indistinctly — throwing snowball

CHARLES

Come on, boys . . .
Camera moves back — mother comes on at left f.g., calls

MOTHER

Be careful, Charles.

THATCHER (*Off*)

Mrs. Kane —

MOTHER

Pull your muffler around your neck, Charles.
Camera moves back, showing Thatcher standing at right of window

THATCHER

Mrs. Kane, I think we'll have to tell him now.

MOTHER

I'll sign those papers now, Mr. Thatcher.

She comes to f.g., following camera into a second room. Father coming on, following with Thatcher

FATHER

You people seem to forget that I'm the boy's father.

MOTHER

It's going to be done exactly the way I've told Mr. Thatcher.

She sits down at table in f.g. — Thatcher sits down by her, showing her papers — throughout, Kane is visible through window, playing in snow

FATHER

There ain't nothin' wrong with Colorado. I don't see why we can't raise our son just 'cause we came into some money. If I want to, I can go to court. A father has the right to. A boarder that beats his bill and leaves worthless stock behind, that property is just as much my property as anybody's, now that it's valuable, and if Fred Graves had any idea all this was going to happen, he'd have made out those certificates in both our names.

THATCHER

However, they were made out in Mrs. Kane's name.

FATHER

He owed the money for the board to both of us.

THATCHER

The bank's decision in all matters concerning —

FATHER

I don't hold with signing my boy away to any bank as guardeen just because —

MOTHER

I want you to stop all this nonsense, Jim.

FATHER

— we're a little uneducated —
Father arguing as Thatcher reads document

THATCHER

The bank's decision in all matters concerning his education, his places of residence, and similar subjects, is to be final.

FATHER

The idea of a bank being the guardeen . . .
Charles can be seen playing in the snow through the window in the b.g.

MOTHER

I want you to stop all this nonsense, Jim.

THATCHER

We will assume full management of the Colorado Lode of which, I repeat, Mrs. Kane, you are the sole owner.

MOTHER

Where do I sign, Mr. Thatcher?

THATCHER

Right here, Mrs. Kane.
Mother signs document — father coming to her

FATHER

Mary, I'm askin' you for the last time. Anybody'd think I hadn't been a good husband or a father —

THATCHER

The sum of fifty thousand dollars a year is to be paid to you and Mr. Kane as long as you both live, and thereafter to the survivor —

FATHER

Well, let's hope it's all for the best.

MOTHER

It is.
Father goes to b.g., mumbling — mother rises — Kane can be heard shouting outside. The words, however, are indistinct

FATHER

Don't know why I have to sign my own boy away to a bank.

MOTHER

Go on, Mr. Thatcher.
Father closes window in b.g. — mother goes to b.g.

THATCHER

Everything else, the principal as well as all monies earned, is to be administered by the bank in trust for your son, Charles Foster Kane, until he reaches his twenty-fifth birthday, at which time . . .

172–1   2.   *INT. ROOM CU* — mother at window, staring to f.g. — two men in b.g. — Thatcher talking

THATCHER

. . . he is to come into complete possession.
Mother calls to f.g.

MOTHER

Charles!
Music plays

MOTHER

Go on, Mr. Thatcher.
Thatcher steps forward

THATCHER

Well, it's almost five, Mrs. Kane. Don't you think I'd better meet the boy?

MOTHER

I've got his trunk all packed. I've had it packed for a week, now.
She turns, goes to left b.g. with Thatcher, talking as they exit — father follows — camera moving away from window, pans across outside of house, moving back slightly to pick up Thatcher, mother and father as they exit from house

THATCHER *(Off)*

I've arranged for a tutor to meet us in Chicago. I'd have brought him along with me . . .
Mother and two men come out of house — it is snowing — she calls to f.g.

MOTHER

Charles.

CHARLES *(Off)*

Lookee, Mom.

MOTHER

You better come inside, son.
Three come to f.g. — camera moving back, showing Charles with sled by snowman

THATCHER

Well, well, well, that's quite a snowman.

CHARLES

I took the pipe out of his mouth —

THATCHER

Did you make it all by yourself, my lad?

CHARLES

If it keeps on snowing, maybe I'll make some teeth and whiskers.

LENGTH   SCENE
FT. FRM.   NO.

Mother comes to them — camera moving close — father in b.g.

MOTHER

This is Mr. Thatcher, Charles.

CHARLES

Hello.

THATCHER

How do you do, Charles.

FATHER

He comes from the East.

CHARLES

Hi.

FATHER

Hello, Charlie.
Charles goes to father — comes back as mother talks

MOTHER

Charles.

CHARLES

Yes, Mommy.

MOTHER

Mr. Thatcher is going to take you on a trip with him tonight. You'll be leaving on Number Ten.

FATHER

That's the train with all the lights on it.

CHARLES

You goin', Mom?

THATCHER

Oh, no. Your mother won't be going right away, Charles, but she'll . . .

CHARLES

Where'm I going?

FATHER

You're going to see Chicago and New York, and Washington, maybe. Ain't he, Mr. Thatcher?

THATCHER

He certainly is. I wish I were a little boy going on a trip like that for the first time.

CHARLES

Why aren't you comin' with us, Mom?

MOTHER

We have to stay here, Charles.

FATHER

You're gonna live with Mr. Thatcher from now on, Charlie. You're gonna be rich. Your Ma figures — well — that is — me and her decided this ain't the place for you to grow up in. You'll probably be the richest man in America someday, and you ought to get an education.

MOTHER

You won't be lonely, Charles.

THATCHER

Lonely. Of course not. Why, we're going to have some fine times together. Really we are, Charles. Now can we shake hands? Oh, come, come, come. I'm not as frightening as all that, am I? Now, what do you say . . . what do you say? Let's shake —
Charles lunges at Thatcher with sled — all talking at once

FATHER

Charlie!

MOTHER

Why, Charles . . .

THATCHER

Why, you almost hurt me, Charles.

FATHER

Charlie!

THATCHER

Sleds aren't to hit people with. Sleds are to sleigh with.
Charles pushes Thatcher down in snow — father goes to him — mother runs after Charles to b.g. — he runs back to f.g., falls down — mother picks him up — father helping Thatcher up — camera moving up to them

FATHER

What's the matter with the boy.

CHARLES

Mom, mom!

MOTHER

Charles, we've got to get you ready. Jim —

FATHER

I'm sorry, Mr. Thatcher. What that kid needs is a good thrashing.

MOTHER

That's what you think, is it, Jim?

FATHER

Yes.

MOTHER

That's why . . .

10–15   3.   *EXT. HOUSE CU* — mother holding Charles — snow falling — music playing — she talks

MOTHER

. . . he's going to be brought up where you can't get at him.
Camera moves down to Charles's face as he stares up to left

Lap Dissolve

18– 4. *EXT. HOUSE MS* — sled in snow — snow falling — train whistle heard — music playing

Lap Dissolve

Night Sequence

14– 5. *INT. ROOM CU* — string being torn from a package — paper torn off, showing a sled — camera moves back to show Charles holding and looking at the sled — Christmas tree fills b.g.

THATCHER *(Off)*

Well, Charles . . .
Camera pans up, showing Thatcher looking down

THATCHER

. . . Merry Christmas.

2–13 6. *INT. ROOM CS* — camera shooting down — two servants in b.g. — Charles rising up with sled, talks — music

CHARLES

Merry Christmas.

44– 7. *INT. ROOM CU* — Thatcher by window, looking around to right f.g., talks

THATCHER

And a Happy New Year.
Camera moves back as he comes to f.g. — dictating to man sitting at desk writing

THATCHER

In closing, may I again remind you that your twenty-first birthday, which is now approaching, marks your complete independence from the firm of Thatcher and Company, as well as the assumption by you of the full responsibility for the world's sixth largest private fortune. Have you got that?

SECRETARY

The world's sixth largest private fortune.

THATCHER

Yes.
He sits down at desk — camera moves up close

THATCHER

Charles, I don't think you quite realize the full importance of the position you are to occupy in the world, and I am therefore sending for your consideration a complete list of your holdings, extensively cross-indexed . . .

40–9 8. *INT. OFFICE CS* — man's hands holding letter

SECRETARY *(Off)*

Dear Mr. Thatcher . . .
Camera moves back, showing Thatcher sitting on other side of desk — man by him — secretary in f.g. exits

SECRETARY *(Off)*

It's from Mr. Kane.

THATCHER

Go on.

SECRETARY *(Off)*

Sorry, but I'm not interested in gold mines, oil wells, shipping or real estate . . .
Thatcher puts on glasses, snatches letter — camera moving up close to him

THATCHER

Not interested?

SECRETARY *(Off)*

One item —

THATCHER

Not int—
He reads

THATCHER

One item in your list intrigues me, the New York "Inquirer," a little newspaper I understand we acquired in a foreclosure proceeding. Please don't sell it. I am coming back to America to take charge. I think it would be fun to run a newspaper.
He takes off glasses, putting letter down

THATCHER

I think it would be fun to run a newspaper!

Lap Dissolve

Night Sequence

45-   9.   *TRANSITION* — music playing

INT. TRAIN MCS — camera moving along aisle, showing passengers seated, reading "Inquirer" newspapers — camera stops on Thatcher in f.g., talking

THATCHER

Traction Trust exposed.

Lap Dissolve

Day Sequence

INT. ROOM CS — Thatcher standing before mirror holding newspaper, lowers it, talking

THATCHER

Traction Trust bleeds public white.

INT. ROOM CU — Thatcher partly on, right f.g., holding newspaper, reading

THATCHER

Traction Trust smashed by "Inquirer."
He goes to door in b.g., closes it, leans against it angrily

Lap Dissolve

INT. ROOM CU — Thatcher's hands holding newspaper — reading

THATCHER

Landlords refuse to clear slums.
He rises before camera, throws paper down, turns to f.g.

Lap Dissolve

INT. ROOM CU — Thatcher holding paper up before camera, turns it, talking

THATCHER

"Inquirer" wins slum fight.

Lap Dissolve

Hands holding newspaper — Thatcher partly on, seated, reading headline — he lowers paper as man is heard yelling indistinctly — he glares out window to f.g.

Lap Dissolve

INT. ROOM CU — Thatcher sitting at table, looking at paper propped up before him — he reads

THATCHER

Copper robbers indicted.
He throws napkin down

Lap Dissolve

Day Sequence

217–12   10.   *INT. ROOM MCU* — Thatcher holding paper, reading headline

THATCHER

Galleons of Spain off Jersey coast.
He throws paper down, showing Kane sitting below on other side of desk, drinking from cup — people in office in b.g. working

THATCHER

Is that really your idea of how to run a newspaper?
Kane smiles, puts cup down — Bernstein coming on at left — comes to Kane

KANE

I don't know how to run a newspaper, Mr. Thatcher. I just try everything I can think of.

THATCHER

Charles, you know perfectly well there's not the slightest proof that this . . .
Leland comes to desk — all talking at once

KANE

Hello, Mr. Bernstein.

THATCHER

. . . that this armada is off the Jersey coast.

BERNSTEIN

Excuse me, Mr. Kane.

KANE

Can you prove it isn't?

BERNSTEIN

This just came in.

KANE

Mr. Bernstein, I'd like you to meet Mr. Thatcher.

LELAND

I'll just borrow a cigar.

BERNSTEIN

How do you do, Mr. Thatcher?

KANE

Mr. Leland.

LELAND

Hello.

KANE

Mr. Thatcher, my ex-guardian.

BERNSTEIN

From Cuba ...

KANE

We have no secrets from our readers, Mr. Bernstein. Mr. Thatcher is one of our most devoted readers. He knows what's wrong with every copy of the "Inquirer" since I took over. Read the cable.
Bernstein reads message to Kane — Kane lighting pipe

BERNSTEIN

Girls delightful in Cuba stop. Could send you prose poems about scenery but don't feel right spending your money stop. There is no war in Cuba. Signed Wheeler. Any answer?

KANE

Yes. Dear Wheeler, you provide the prose poems, I'll provide the war.

BERNSTEIN

That's fine, Mr. Kane.

KANE

Yes, I rather like it myself. Send it right away.

BERNSTEIN

Right away.
Leland and Bernstein go to b.g., exit — Thatcher goes around to Kane

THATCHER

I came to see you about this campaign of yours. The "Inquirer's" campaign against the Public Transit Company.
Thatcher sits down by Kane — camera moves slowly up to them as they argue

KANE

Mr. Thatcher, do you know anything we can use against them?

THATCHER

You're still a college boy, aren't you?

KANE

Oh, now, Mr. Thatcher, I was expelled from college, a lot of colleges, you remember? I remember.

THATCHER

Charles, I think I should remind you of a fact you seem to have forgotten.

KANE

Yes.

THATCHER

You are yourself one of the largest individual stockholders in the Public Transit Company.

KANE

The trouble is, you don't realize you're talking to two people. As Charles Foster Kane, who owns eighty-two thousand, three hundred and sixty-four shares of Public Transit Preferred — you see, I do have a general idea of my holdings — I sympathize with you. Charles Foster Kane is a scoundrel, his paper should be run out of town, a committee should be formed to boycott him. You may, if you can form such a committee, put me down for a contribution of one thousand dollars —

THATCHER

My time is too valuable for me to waste on such nonsense.
Kane leans toward Thatcher

KANE

On the other hand I am also the publisher of the "Inquirer." As such, it is my duty — I'll let you in on a secret — it is also my pleasure — to see to it that the decent, hard-working people of this community aren't robbed blind by a pack of money-mad pirates just because . . .
Thatcher leaps up — Kane leaping up

KANE

. . . they haven't anybody to look after their interests.
Thatcher goes to b.g. angrily — takes wraps from rack — Kane going to him, helps him on with coat

KANE

I'll let you in on another little secret, Mr. Thatcher. I think I'm the man to do it. You see, I have money and property. If I don't look after the interests of the underprivileged, maybe somebody else will — maybe somebody without any money or property.

THATCHER

Yes, yes, yes.

KANE

And that would be too bad.

THATCHER

Well, I happened to see your financial statement today, Charles.

KANE

Oh, did you?

THATCHER

Tell me, honestly, my boy, don't you think it's rather unwise to continue this philan-thropic enterprise . . . this "Inquirer" that is costing you a million dollars a year?

KANE

You're right, Mr. Thatcher. I did lose a million dollars last year. I expect to lose a million dollars this year. I expect to lose a million dollars next year. You know, Mr. Thatcher at the rate of a million dollars a year . . .

10–2   11.   *INT. ROOM CU* — Kane talking to Thatcher partly on, right f.g.

KANE

. . . I'll have to close this place in sixty years.

Lap Dissolve

Kane smiling — music heard

12–5   12.   INSERT #1 — paper passing camera — music — handwriting on it reads:

In the winter of 1929 . . .

Lap Dissolve

Day Sequence

210–7   13.   *INT. ROOM MCU* — Bernstein in f.g., before camera, reading document

BERNSTEIN

With respect to the said newspapers, the said Charles Foster Kane hereby relinquishes all control thereof, and of the syndicates pertaining thereto . . .
He lowers paper, showing Thatcher seated in b.g.

BERNSTEIN

. . . and any and all other newspaper, press and publishing properties of any kind whatsoever, and agrees to abandon all claim thereto . . .
He lowers paper

KANE *(Off)*

Which means we're bust all right.
Kane comes on in b.g. — going to b.g.

BERNSTEIN

Well, out of cash.

THATCHER

Charles.

KANE

I've read it, Mr. Thatcher, just let me sign it and go home.

THATCHER

You're too old to call me Mr. Thatcher, Charles.

KANE

You're too old to be called anything else. You were always too old.
He comes back to f.g.

BERNSTEIN

In consideration thereof, Thatcher and Company agrees to pay to Charles Foster Kane, as long as he lives, the sum of —

KANE

My allowance.

THATCHER

You will continue to maintain over your newspapers a large measure of control — ah, measure of control — and we shall seek your advice. This depression is temporary. There's always the chance that you'll die richer than I will.

KANE

It's a cinch I'll die richer than I was born.
He sits down at desk, signs paper

BERNSTEIN

We never lost as much as we made.

THATCHER

Yes, but your methods. You know, Charles, you never made a single investment. You always used money to —

KANE

To buy things.
He mumbles as he writes

KANE

To buy things. My mother should have chosen a less reliable banker.
He pushes papers away, leans back

KANE

Well, I always gagged on that silver spoon. You know, Mr. Bernstein, if I hadn't been very rich, I might have been a really great man.

THATCHER

Don't you think you are?

KANE

I think I did pretty well under the circumstances.

THATCHER

What would you like to have been?

KANE

Everything you hate.

Lap Dissolve

6–9   14.   *INT. ROOM CS* — camera shooting down at Thompson sitting at table in vault — he flips the pages of Thatcher's manuscript

END OF REEL 2 — SECTION 2A

REEL 2 — SECTION 2B

Day Sequence

42–   1.   *INT. ROOM MS* — Thompson sitting on other end of desk in b.g. — closing book disgusted — guard behind him

THOMPSON

Oh.
Guard steps up to him

GUARD

I beg your pardon, sir?

THOMPSON

What?

GUARD

What did you say?
Door in b.g. opens — Bertha comes in

BERTHA

It's four-thirty. Isn't it, Jennings?

GUARD

Yes'm . . . ma'am.
Thompson rises — camera pans up, showing picture of Thatcher on wall in b.g.

BERTHA

You have enjoyed a very rare privilege, young man. Did you find what you were looking for?

THOMPSON

No.
Guard looks up, takes off hat — Thompson steps toward others

THOMPSON

You're not Rosebud, are you?

BERTHA

What?

THOMPSON

Rosebud, and your name is Jennings, isn't it?

GUARD

Yes, sir, I've —

THOMPSON

Good-bye, everybody. Thanks for the use of the hall.
He goes out doorway in b.g. — music plays

Lap Dissolve

Late Afternoon Sequence

245–0 2. *INT. ROOM MS* — Thompson sitting at right of desk — Bernstein on other side of desk, left b.g., sitting in a chair with a very high back, talking — picture of Kane on wall in b.g. — camera moves up slowly

BERNSTEIN

Who's a busy man, me? I'm chairman of the board. I got nothing but time. What do you want to know?

THOMPSON

Well, Mr. Bernstein, we thought maybe — if we could find out what he meant by his last words — as he was dying —

BERNSTEIN

That Rosebud, huh? Maybe . . . some girl? There were a lot of them back in the early days and —

THOMPSON

It's hardly likely, Mr. Bernstein, that Mr. Kane could have met some girl casually and then, fifty years later, on his deathbed `. . .`

BERNSTEIN

Well, you're pretty young, Mr. — er — Mr. Thompson. A fellow will remember a lot of things you wouldn't think he'd remember.
Camera moves past Thompson to Bernstein as he leans on desk

BERNSTEIN

You take me. One day, back in 1896, I was crossing over to Jersey on the ferry, and as we pulled out, there was another ferry pulling in, and on it there was a girl waiting to get off. A white dress she had on. She was carrying a white parasol. I only saw her for

one second. She didn't see me at all, but I'll bet a month hasn't gone by since, that I haven't thought of that girl. Who else have you been to see?
Bernstein picks up cigarette — Thompson leans on in f.g., lighting it

THOMPSON

Well, I went down to Atlantic City —

BERNSTEIN

Susie?
Thompson exits

BERNSTEIN

Thank you. I called her myself the day after he died. I thought maybe somebody ought to. She couldn't even come to the phone.

THOMPSON *(Off)*

I'm going down to see her again in a couple of days. About Rosebud, Mr. Bernstein, if you'd just talk about anything connected with Mr. Kane that you can remember — after all, you were with him from the beginning.

BERNSTEIN

From before the beginning, young fellow. And now it's after the end. Have you tried to see anybody except Susie?

THOMPSON *(Off)*

I haven't seen anybody else, but I've been through that stuff of Walter Thatcher's. That journal of his —
Bernstein rises — camera pans, showing Thompson sitting in f.g. — Bernstein goes to window in b.g. — rain falling outside

BERNSTEIN

Thatcher — that man was the biggest darn fool I ever met.

THOMPSON

He made an awful lot of money.

BERNSTEIN

Well, it's no trick to make a lot of money, if all you want . . .
He looks at ticker tape

BERNSTEIN

. . . is to make a lot of money.
He crosses to left — camera pans, showing Kane's picture

BERNSTEIN

You take Mr. Kane. It wasn't money he wanted.
Bernstein crosses to right b.g. — sits down — Thompson sitting right f.g.

BERNSTEIN

Thatcher never did figure him out. Sometimes, even, I couldn't. You know who you ought to see? Mr. Leland. He was Mr. Kane's closest friend. They went to school together.

THOMPSON

Harvard, wasn't it?

BERNSTEIN

Oh, Harvard, Yale, Princeton, Cornell, Switzerland. He was thrown out of a lot of colleges. Mr. Leland never had a nickel. One of those old families where the father is worth ten million, then one day he shoots himself and it turns out there's nothing but debts. He was with Mr. Kane and me the first day Mr. Kane took over the "Inquirer."

Lap Dissolve

Day Sequence

46–   3.   *EXT. BLDG. MS* — camera panning down Inquirer Building — music playing — camera pans down to hansom cab in f.g. — Leland and Kane seated in it — Kane takes pipe from mouth, talks

KANE

Take a look at it, Jedediah. It's going to look a lot different one of these days. Come on.
They rise, exit left — cab moves away, showing two men running up steps into building — horses come on at right with wagon — driver on seat — Bernstein on furniture on wagon — driver talks — music stops

DRIVER

There ain't no bedrooms in this joint. That's a newspaper building.

BERNSTEIN

You're getting paid, mister, for opinions, or for hauling?

DRIVER

Ugh.

Lap Dissolve

Day Sequence

19–   4.   *INT. OFFICE CS* — Leland and Kane in f.g. — open doors — look into office in b.g.

KANE

Jedediah.

LELAND

After you, Mr. Kane.
They go through office to b.g. — Leland going around post

82–15   5.   *INT. OFFICE MLS* — Kane at right f.g., looking around — Leland in b.g. — camera moves back through office — the two stop by man at desk — Kane takes off hat, talks

KANE

Excuse me, sir, but I —
Man motions — Carter comes on at left, ringing bell — people rise up from desks — Carter comes down to f.g., smiling

CARTER

Welcome, Mr. Kane.
Camera follows Carter to b.g. to two men — Carter takes Leland's hand — men around

CARTER

Welcome. Welcome to the "Inquirer," Mr. Kane.

LELAND

Oh, this —

CARTER

I am Herbert Carter, the editor in chief.

KANE

Thank you, Mr. Carter. This is Mr. Leland —

CARTER

How do you do, Mr. Leland.

KANE

Our new dramatic critic. I hope I haven't made a mistake, Jedediah, have I? It is dramatic critic you want to be?

LELAND

You know that's right.

KANE

Are they standing for me?

CARTER

You — oh, Mr. Kane.

KANE

That's right. Yes. Sit down, gentlemen.

CARTER

Standing?

KANE

How do you do?

CARTER

How do you do. Oh, I thought it would be a nice little gesture.

KANE

Ask them to sit down, will you, please, Mr. Carter.

CARTER

The new publisher. You may resume your duties, gentlemen.
Men sit down — camera moves up closer to the three

KANE

Thank you.

CARTER

I didn't know your plans . . .

KANE

I don't know my plans myself.

CARTER

. . . so I was unable to make any preparations.

KANE

As a matter of fact, I haven't got any plans.

CARTER

No?

KANE

Except to get out a newspaper.
They turn to b.g. as terrific crash is heard

7–15   6.   *INT. OFFICE MS* — Bernstein on floor — furniture falling around him — noises heard — he grins

BERNSTEIN

Oops.

KANE *(Off)*

Mr. Bern— . . .

80–15   7.   *INT. OFFICE MLS* — Bernstein on floor in f.g. — furniture around him — three in b.g. looking at him — men at desks — Kane talking

KANE

. . . —stein.
Bernstein rises — goes to group

BERNSTEIN

Yes, Mr. Kane.

KANE

Mr. Bernstein, would you come here a moment, please.

BERNSTEIN

Yes, Mr. Kane.
Three cross to left — Carter trying to talk — Bernstein walks toward them

KANE

Mr. Carter, this is Mr. Bernstein.

BERNSTEIN

How do you do?

LELAND

Mr. Bernstein.

KANE

Mr. Bernstein is my general manager.

CARTER

General m-m-m . . .
Kane exits right — Carter turns, takes Bernstein's hand, shaking it

BERNSTEIN

How do you do, Mr. Carter.

KANE *(Off)*

Mr. Carter —

CARTER

Yes? How do you do?

KANE *(Off)*

Mr. Carter —

345

CARTER

Yes, Mr. Bernstine.
Carter crossing to left, going to Kane — others exit

BERNSTEIN *(Off)*

Stene.

CARTER

Kane.

They go to door at left — music plays — Carter trying to talk as expressmen come on, passing into office with furniture — Bernstein goes in

KANE

Mr. Carter — is this your office, Mr. Carter?
Kane moves to left of door — Leland coming on, goes inside office

CARTER

My . . . my little private sanctum is at your disposal, but I —

EXPRESSMAN

Excuse me.

CARTER

But I don't think I understand.

BERNSTEIN

Excuse me.

KANE

Mr. Carter, I'm going to live right here in your office as long as I have to.

LELAND

Mr. Carter . . .

CARTER

Live here?

LELAND

Mr. Carter . . .

CARTER

Yes?

LELAND

Excuse me.

CARTER

But a morning newspaper, Mr. Kane — after all . . .
Expressman comes out, pushing past Carter

EXPRESSMAN

Excuse me.
Bernstein and Leland come out, pushing past Carter

CARTER

. . . we're practically closed . . . closed for twelve hours . . . a day . . . twelve hours . . .

KANE

Mr. Carter, that's one of the things that's going to have to be changed. The news goes on for twenty-four hours a day.
Carter sputtering — three men come on with furniture, pushing Carter around as they go through doorway

CARTER

Twenty-fo—

EXPRESSMAN

Excuse me.

KANE

That's right, Mr. Carter.

LELAND

Excuse me.

BERNSTEIN

Excuse me.

CARTER

Mr. Kane, it's impossible . . .

Lap Dissolve

Late Afternoon Sequence

90—   8.   *INT. OFFICE MS* — Leland crossing to right with cartoon — camera pans to right — Kane and Carter at desk — dishes in front of Kane — Leland showing Kane a crudely drawn cartoon, talking

LELAND

I've drawn that cartoon . . .

KANE

But here's what I mean.

CARTER

Mr. Kane.

LELAND

I'm no good as a cartoonist.

KANE

You certainly aren't.

LELAND

Look at that.

KANE

You're the drama critic, Leland. Here's a front-page story in the "Chronicle."

LELAND

You still eating?

Leland sits down in f.g. — Kane is serving himself food from one of the dishes in front of him

KANE

I'm still hungry. Now look, Mr. Carter, here's a front-page story in the "Chronicle," about a Mrs. Harry Silverstone in Brooklyn who's missing. Now, she's probably murdered. Here's a picture of her in the "Chronicle." Why isn't there something like it in the "Inquirer"?

Camera pans — Kane yelling — general confusion

CARTER

Because we're running a newspaper, Mr. Kane, not a scandal sheet.

KANE

Joseph!

Waiter comes on — Carter sputtering — Bernstein sitting at right

MAN

Yes, sir.

KANE

I'm absolutely starving to death.

LELAND

We'll go over to Rector's later and get something decent.

CARTER

Excuse me, Mr. Bernstine.

BERNSTEIN

That's all right.
Kane showing paper to Carter

KANE

Look, Mr. Carter, here is a three-column headline in the "Chronicle." Why hasn't the "Inquirer" got a three-column headline?

CARTER

The news wasn't big enough.

KANE

Mr. Carter, if the headline is big enough, it makes the news big enough.

BERNSTEIN

That's right, Mr. Kane.

KANE

The murder of this Mrs. Harry Silverstone . . .
Carter walks around raving — camera pans showing Leland at left f.g.

CARTER

There's no proof that the woman was murdered, or even that she's dead.

KANE

It says that she's missing. The neighbors are getting suspicious.

CARTER

It's not our function to report the gossip of housewives. If we were interested in that kind of thing, Mr. Kane, we could fill the paper twice over daily.

KANE

Mr. Carter . . .

8–9   9.   *INT. ROOM CS* — camera shooting up past Kane, sitting at right f.g., to Carter, coming from b.g. — Leland sitting at left

KANE

. . . that's the kind of thing we are going to be interested in from now on. Mr. Carter . . .

11–8   10.   *INT. ROOM CS* — Kane sitting, looking up to left, talking

KANE

. . . I want you to take your best man up to see Mr. Silverstone in Brooklyn. Have him tell Mr. Silverstone if he doesn't produce his wife, Mrs. Silverstone, at once, the "Inquirer" will have him arrested.

2–11   11.   *INT. ROOM CU* — camera shooting up to Carter, sputtering

KANE *(Off)*

Have him tell Mr. Silverstone he's a . . .

5–11   12.   *INT. OFFICE MCS* — Kane right b.g., behind desk — Leland at left — Carter sputtering

KANE

. . . detective from the . . . er . . .

LELAND

Central Office.

KANE

The Central Office.

4–8   13.   *INT. OFFICE CU* — Carter staring to f.g.

KANE *(Off)*

If Mr. Silverstone gets suspicious and asks to see your man's badge . . .

8–12   14.   *INT. OFFICE CU* — Kane looking up to left f.g., talking

KANE

. . . your man is to get indignant and call Mr. Silverstone an anarchist.

2–1   15.   *INT. OFFICE CU* — Bernstein leaning over to left, looks to f.g. as he hears Leland laughing

KANE *(Off)*

Loudly, so the neighbors . . .

5–4   16.   *INT. OFFICE MCS* — Kane rising, talking — Carter sputtering — Leland seated at left, smiling

KANE

. . . can hear.

CARTER

Really —

KANE

You ready for dinner, Jedediah?

LELAND

Anytime.

CARTER

Mr. Kane.

KANE

Yes, Mr. Carter?

CARTER

I can't see that the function . . .

2–11   17.   *INT. ROOM CU* — Bernstein looking around to right f.g., smiling — Carter and Kane heard talking indistinctly

CARTER *(Off)*

. . . of a respectable newspaper . . .

KANE *(Off)*

You've been most understanding.

10–   18.   *INT. OFFICE MCS* — three at desk — Carter sputtering — Kane talks

KANE

Thank you so much, Mr. Carter, good-bye.
Carter glares at other two, turns

CARTER

Good-bye.
Music starts to play

Lap Dissolve

Dawn Sequence

13–9   19.   *EXT. BLDG. MS* — Carter on steps, putting on hat — music — camera moves back — boy at left yelling, waving paper

BOY

Paper, paper. Read all about it in the early morning "Chronicle." Read all about the mystery of the lady that vanished in Brooklyn. Read all about it in the early morning paper.

8–8   20.   *EXT. STREET LS* — camera shooting across street to Inquirer Building — Carter crossing to right — boy waving, shouting indistinctly

Lap Dissolve

15–9   21.   *EXT. WINDOW MS* — Leland leaning out window — Kane by him, holding paper against window glass, writing — camera moves up to them

Lap Dissolve

171–5   22.   *INT. OFFICE MS* — Bernstein sitting at right f.g. — Leland turning from window in b.g. — Kane writing on paper held against glass — music

LELAND

We'll be on the street soon, Charlie, another ten minutes.

BERNSTEIN

Three hours and fifty minutes late, but we did it.
Kane turns, smiling

KANE

Tired?

LELAND

A tough day.

KANE

A wasted day.

BERNSTEIN

Wasted?

LELAND

Charlie.

BERNSTEIN

You only made the paper over four times tonight, that's all.

KANE

I've changed the front page a little, Mr. Bernstein. That's not enough, no. There's something I've got to get into this paper besides pictures and print. I've got to make the New York "Inquirer" as important to New York as the gas in that light.
He turns out gas

LELAND

What're you going to do, Charlie?

KANE

My Declaration of Principles. Don't smile, Jedediah.
Kane comes to f.g. with paper, puts it on table

KANE

I've got it all written, the declaration.

BERNSTEIN

You don't wanta make any promises, Mr. Kane, you don't wanta keep.

KANE

These'll be kept. I'll provide the people of this city with a daily paper that will tell all the news honestly. I will also provide them —
Leland comes to two in f.g.

LELAND

That's the second sentence you've started with "I."

KANE

People are going to know who's responsible, and they're going to get the truth in the "Inquirer," quickly and simply and entertainingly. And no special interests are going to be allowed to interfere with that truth.
Leland sits down at left — Kane picking up paper

KANE

I will also provide them with a fighting and tireless champion of their rights as citizens and as human beings.
Kane puts paper down and signs it

LELAND

May I have that, Charlie?

KANE

I'm going to print it.
He rises, yells

KANE

Solly!

MAN *(Off)*

Oh, Solly.
Solly comes on at right — Kane handing him paper — camera pans — Bernstein exits

SOLLY

Yes, Mr. Kane.

KANE

Here's an editorial, Solly. I want you to run it in a box on the front page.

SOLLY

This morning's front page, Mr. Kane?

KANE

That's right, Solly. That means we'll have to remake again, doesn't it, Solly?

SOLLY

Yes.

KANE

Better go down and tell them.

SOLLY

All right.

LELAND

Solly, when you're through with that, I'd like to have it back.
Solly exits — camera pans, showing Bernstein seated at right f.g.

LELAND

I'd like to keep that particular piece of paper myself. I have a hunch it might turn out to be something pretty important, a document . . .

BERNSTEIN

Sure.

LELAND

. . . like the Declaration of Independence, or the Constitution . . .

4–9   23.   *INT. ROOM CU* — Leland smiling, talking

LELAND

. . . and my first report card at school.

END OF REEL 2 — SECTION 2B

REEL 3 — SECTION 3A

Day Sequence

6–14   1.   *INT. ROOM CU* — Kane smiling, collar undone, blinks eyes, nodding — music plays

Lap Dissolve

52–   2.   TRANSITION — music playing

Article in "Inquirer," reading:

MY DECLARATION OF PRINCIPLES

I. I will provide the people of this city with a daily newspaper that will tell all the news honestly.

II. I will also provide them with a fighting and tireless champion of their rights as citizens and as human beings.

(Signed) *Charles Foster Kane* (signature)

CHARLES FOSTER KANE

THE PUBLISHER

Camera moves back, showing enormous bundles of stacked papers

Lap Dissolve

EXT. WINDOW MS — Kane, Bernstein and Leland leaning out window — sign on glass superimposed over scene

"INQUIRER"

CIRCULATION

26,000

Lap Dissolve

EXT. "CHRONICLE" WINDOW MS — Kane, Bernstein and Leland are reflected in it — on the window is painted:

"CHRONICLE"

CIRCULATION

495,000

KANE

I know you're tired, gentlemen, but I brought you here for a reason. I think this little pilgrimage will do us good.

LELAND

The "Chronicle's" a good newspaper.

KANE

The "Chronicle's" a good idea for a newspaper. Notice the circulation.

BERNSTEIN

Four hundred ninety-five thousand.

KANE

Uh-huh.

BERNSTEIN

But, Mr. Kane, look who's . . .

12–10   3.   *INT. "CHRONICLE" WINDOW* — picture of the "Chronicle's" staff — camera moves into CU of picture

BERNSTEIN *(Off)*

. . . working for the "Chronicle." With them fellas, it's no trick to get circulation.

KANE *(Off)*

You're right, Mr. Bernstein.

BERNSTEIN *(Off)*

You know how long it took the "Chronicle" to get that staff together? Twenty years.

KANE *(Off)*

Twenty years . . . well . . .
Camera moves in closer to picture of men

Lap Dissolve

43–   4.   *INT. ROOM MS* — same group of men seated, as before, posing

KANE *(Off)*

Six years ago I looked at a picture of the world's greatest newspapermen.
Kane comes on at left — camera moving back — photographer at right with camera

KANE

I felt like a kid in front of a candy store. Well, tonight, six years later, I got my candy, all of it.
Crowd heard laughing — Kane crossing — photographer takes picture with flashlight — men rising

KANE

Welcome, gentlemen, to the "Inquirer."

PHOTOGRAPHER

That's all.

KANE

Make up an extra copy and mail it to the "Chronicle." It will make you all happy to learn that our circulation this morning was the greatest in New York, six hundred and eighty-four thousand.
All laugh — camera moves back — they follow Kane to f.g.

5–14   5.   *INT. BANQUET ROOM LS* — camera shooting down over long table — crowd of men seated, applaud — Bernstein at end of table, rising, talks

BERNSTEIN

Six hundred eighty-four thousand one hundred and thirty-two.

2–7   6.   *INT. ROOM CS* — group at table — Kane laughing, talks — men applaud

KANE

Right.

6–7   7.   *INT. ROOM LS* — men seated at long table — Bernstein sitting down in f.g. — men laughing, talking — Kane at far end in b.g. talks

KANE

Having thus welcomed you, I hope you'll forgive my rudeness in taking leave of you.

4–5   8.   *INT. ROOM CS* — two seated, whispering — their caricatures carved in ice behind them

KANE *(Off)*

I'm going abroad next week for a vacation.

5–1   9.   *INT. ROOM LS* — men sitting at long table — Kane in b.g. talking, walking forward

KANE

I have promised my doctor for some time now that I would leave when I could.

16–14 10. *INT. ROOM MS* — group at end of table — Bernstein in b.g. — Kane coming on right f.g., talking

KANE

I now realize I can.
Men laugh — Bernstein rises

BERNSTEIN

Say, Mr. Kane, so long as you're promising, there's a lot of pictures and statues in Europe you ain't bought yet.
Men laugh

KANE

You can't blame me, Mr. Bernstein.

7–12   11.   *INT. ROOM LS* — Bernstein in f.g. at end of table — men seated, laughing — Kane standing left b.g., talking

KANE

They've been making statues for two thousand years, and I've only been buying for five.

8–8   12.   *INT. ROOM CS* — Kane right f.g. — men at table laughing — Bernstein in b.g., leaning on table, talking

BERNSTEIN

Promise me, Mr. Kane.

KANE

I promise you, Mr. Bernstein.

BERNSTEIN

Thank you.
Bernstein sits down

KANE

Mr. Bernstein.

BERNSTEIN

Yes?

4–2   13.   *INT. ROOM LS* — men at table — Bernstein in f.g. — Kane standing at left near b.g., talking

KANE

You don't expect me to keep any of those promises, do you?

3–2   14.   *INT. ROOM CS* — two seated — Bernstein shakes head — crowd heard laughing, applauding

8–3   15.   *INT. ROOM LS* — men laughing, applauding — Kane standing at left, talking — waiters lined up at left

KANE

And now, gentlemen, your complete attention, if you please.

3–   16.   *INT. ROOM CU* — Kane puts fingers in mouth, whistles

65–5   17.   *INT. ROOM LS* — men at table at right — Kane turning to left — waiters going to table — music starts to play — lights come on — band coming on in b.g. playing "Hot Time in the Old Town Tonight" — Kane yells

KANE

Well, gentlemen, are we going to declare war on Spain, or are we not?

LELAND

What?
Band marches around — Kane goes to b.g. — men laughing, talking indistinctly — Kane in b.g. whistles again, waves — band exits — chorus girls march on — men rising, yell, applaud — Kane following leader to f.g.

MEN

Oh, mama, here they come.
Shoot me while I'm happy.
Kane yells — girls dancing

KANE

I said are we going to declare war on Spain, or are we not?

LELAND

The "Inquirer" already has.

KANE

You long-faced, overdressed anarchist.

LELAND

I'm not overdressed.

KANE

You are, too. Mr. Bernstein, look at his necktie.

MEN

Let's have the song about Charlie.
Mr. Kane . . .

18–14   18.   *INT. ROOM MLS* — girls at left — men stepping up onto table yelling — Kane turning to right

MEN

Let's have the song about Charlie.
Let's hear Mr. Kane.
Is there a song about you, Mr. Kane?
Kane crossing to right — camera following — men in f.g. — Kane shouts above noise — girls looking around

KANE

You buy a bag of peanuts in this town, and you get a song written about you.
Men pull him down onto seat — girls lean over, putting hats on men

5–11   19.   *INT. ROOM MS* — girls before camera move back, showing Kane and men — all laughing, yelling — music heard: "Oh, Mr. Kane!"

4–12   20.   *INT. ROOM MLS* — camera shooting over Kane and men in f.g. — chorus girls lined up in b.g. — Bennet coming from b.g. — much confusion — music

2–14   21.   *INT. ROOM MCS* — Kane and men sitting in f.g., talking indistinctly — others in b.g. — music

MAN

I've seen that feller, he's good.

KANE

Yes.

3–4   22.   *INT. ROOM LS* — Kane and men sitting in f.g. — Bennet and girls in b.g. — music — Bennet talks

BENNET

Good evening, Mr. Kane.

4–15   23.   *INT. ROOM MCS* — men around Kane — others in b.g. — all laughing — singing and music heard

BENNET *(Off)*

There is a man —

GIRLS *(Off)*

There is a man —

BENNET *(Off)*

A certain man —

GIRLS *(Off)*

A certain man —

43–3   24.   *INT. ROOM MLS* — group in f.g. — Bennet and girls in b.g., singing — music

BENNET

And for the poor you may be sure
That he'll do all he can.
Who is this one —

GIRLS

Who is this one —

BENNET

This fav'rite son —

GIRLS

This fav'rite son —

BENNET

Just by his action
Has the Traction magnates on the run.
Who loves to smoke —

GIRLS

Who loves to smoke.

BENNET

Enjoys a joke —

GIRLS

Ha-ha-ha-ha.

GIRL

Ha.

BENNET

Who wouldn't get a bit upset
If he were really broke
With wealth and fame —

GIRLS

With wealth and fame —

BENNET

He's still the same —

GIRLS

He's still the same.

BENNET AND OTHERS

I'll bet you five you're not alive
If you don't know his name.
They crowd up to Kane — pull him with them — much confusion, indistinct talking as they push Kane to b.g.

1–11   25.   *INT. ROOM MLS* — group sitting on either side of table — Bennet leans on at right f.g., singing — music

BENNET

What is his name —

1–9   26.   *INT. ROOM CS* — Leland sitting right f.g. — Bernstein at end of table, sings — music

BERNSTEIN

What is his name . . .

1–7   27.   *INT. ROOM CS* — girls lean to f.g., singing — Kane in b.g., laughing — music

GIRLS

It's Charlie Kane.

9–11   28.   *INT. ROOM CU* — Leland in f.g. — Bernstein behind him, sings — Leland joining in — crowd heard singing

BOTH

It's Mister Kane.

CROWD

He doesn't like that Mister
He likes good old Charlie Kane.

5–7   29.   *INT. ROOM LS* — girls dancing — music — Kane joining in — men in b.g., waving, cheering — harmonizing

4–4   30.   *INT. ROOM CU* — Leland and Bernstein in f.g., yelling — crowd heard

2–8   31.   *INT. ROOM CS* — colored band playing — fat man in f.g., laughing

3–13   32.   *INT. ROOM MLS* — men at table yelling — much confusion

5–1   33.   *INT. ROOM MS* — girls and Kane dancing — music

6–15   34.   *INT. ROOM CU* — Leland in f.g., blinking — Bernstein at left behind him, talks — music and yelling heard

BERNSTEIN

Isn't it wonderful? Such a party.

LELAND

Yes.

BERNSTEIN

What's the matter?

4–15   35.   *INT. ROOM MS* — girls dancing around with Kane — Bennet sings off-screen

BENNET *(Off)*

Who says a miss —

CROWD

Who says a miss —

BENNET *(Off)*

Was made to kiss —

LENGTH FT. FRM.	SCENE NO.	

CROWD

Was made to kiss —

3–14   36.   *INT. ROOM MLS* — Kane dancing with girls — singing heard — Kane yelling — music

CROWD

And when he meets one always tries —

14–13   37.   *INT. ROOM MCS* — Kane dancing with girl in f.g. — others around — singing heard — Kane joining in, singing

KANE AND CROWD

To do exactly this.
Who buys the food, who buys the food
Who buys the drinks, who buys the drinks
Who thinks that dough was made to spend
And acts the way he thinks.
Now is it Joe —
Kane kisses girl — she pushes him off-scene to left

CROWD

No, no, no, no.

1–15   38.   *INT. ROOM CU* — Leland in f.g. — Bernstein behind him singing — others heard

CROWD

No, no, no, no.

20–11   39.   *INT. ROOM CS* — Bernstein partly on, right f.g. — Leland sitting at table at left, talks — girls and Kane dancing in b.g. — others heard singing — Kane throwing coat around

CROWD

I'll bet you ten you aren't men
If you don't really know —

LELAND

Bernstein, these men who are now with the "Inquirer," who were with the "Chronicle" until yesterday . . .
Kane yelling at Leland, throwing coat to him — girls dancing — men heard yelling

KANE

Jedediah, catch.

MEN

Oh, Mama, please give me that.
What?
The blonde?
No, the brunette.
Where did you learn that, Charlie?

LELAND

Bernstein . . .

5–8   40.   *INT. ROOM MCU* — Leland, left f.g., talking to Bernstein — reflection in window in b.g. of Kane dancing with girls — much confusion — music

LELAND

Bernstein, these men who were with the "Chronicle" . . .

12–7   41.   *INT. ROOM MCU* — Bernstein right f.g. — Leland at left, trying to make himself heard above noise — music — Kane and girls dancing in b.g.

LELAND

. . . weren't they just as devoted to the "Chronicle" policy as they are now to our policies?
Girls backing away, leaving Kane alone

BERNSTEIN

Sure, they're just like anybody else.

12–13   42.   *INT. ROOM MCU* — Bernstein talking to Leland at left f.g. — reflection in window in b.g. of Kane looking around

BERNSTEIN

They got work to do, they do it. Only they happen to be the best men in the business.
Yelling and cheering heard — two look off to left — reflection in window of Kane dancing with girls

3–9   43.   *INT. ROOM MCS* — Kane and girls dancing — yelling and music heard — girls going into pin-wheel routine.

3–3   44.   *INT. ROOM MLS* — girls and Kane dancing around post in pinwheel routine — yelling and music heard

7–5   45.   *INT. ROOM CS* — Leland talking to Bernstein — Kane and girls dancing in b.g. — Kane yelling — crowd heard — music

LELAND

Do we stand for the same things the "Chronicle" stands for, Bernstein?

12–6   46.   *INT. ROOM MCU* — Bernstein yells to Leland at left f.g. — music and noise heard — reflection in glass of Kane dancing with girls

BERNSTEIN

Certainly not. Listen, Mr. Kane, he'll have them changed to his kind of newspapermen in a week.

9–7   47.   *INT. ROOM CS* — Leland yelling at Bernstein above noise — Kane and girls dancing in b.g., singing indistinctly

LELAND

There's always the chance that they'll change Mr. Kane . . . without his knowing it.

5–6   48.   *INT. ROOM MCS* — girls posing as they finish dancing — yelling — Kane in back center — music
Lap Dissolve

Night Sequence

16–8   49.   *INT. OFFICE MCS* — Bernstein rushing through doorway, looks to f.g., yelling — camera follows him to right, passing statues

BERNSTEIN

Mr. Leland, Mr. Leland . . . I got a cable from Mr. Kane . . . Mr. Lel—
He stops by glass partition — Leland, on other side, raises head, grunts — Bernstein waving paper

BERNSTEIN

Mr. Leland.

LELAND

Hmm?

BERNSTEIN

Mr. Leland, I got a cable here from Mr. Kane.

LELAND

What?

BERNSTEIN

From Paris, France.

LELAND

What?

BERNSTEIN

From Paris, France.

20–11   50. *INT. OFFICE LS* — Leland yelling through window to Bernstein in b.g. — office filled with statues

LELAND

Oh, come on in.

Leland picks up crate, comes to f.g., singing indistinctly — Bernstein rushing through doorway in b.g., yelling

LELAND *(Singing)*

Who by his actions has the Traction magnates on the run . . .
He rises

BERNSTEIN

Oh, Mr. Leland, it's a good thing he promised not to send back any more statues.

LELAND

Bern—

62–   51. *INT. OFFICE CU* — Leland left f.g., talking — Bernstein at right

LELAND

—stein . . .
Bernstein grunts, hands Leland paper

BERNSTEIN

Look, he wants to buy the world's biggest diamond. Mr. Leland, why didn't you go to Europe with him? He wanted you to.

LELAND

Oh, I wanted Charlie to have fun, and with me along . . . Bernstein, am I a stuffed shirt? Am I a horse-faced hypocrite? Am I a New England schoolmarm?

BERNSTEIN

Yes. If you thought I'd answer you very different from what Mr. Kane tells you, well, I wouldn't.

LELAND

World's biggest diamond. I didn't know Charlie was collecting diamonds.

BERNSTEIN

He ain't. He's collecting somebody that's collecting diamonds. Anyway, he ain't only collecting statues.

They smile at each other

Lap Dissolve

Day Sequence

13–   52. *INT. OFFICE CS* — Bernstein partly on, left f.g., looking at loving cup on table — Leland and employees behind cup — Bernstein talking

BERNSTEIN

Welcome home, Mr. Kane, from four hundred sixty-seven employees of the New York "Inquirer."

BOY *(Off)*

Here he comes.
They jump up, hurry to b.g. — Bernstein picking up cup — music plays

73–4   53.   *INT. OFFICE MS* — men rushing on in f.g., going to b.g. — Kane coming on — music — men crowd around Kane as he rushes forward — camera moving back — he takes Leland's hand — all talking at once

KANE

Hello, everybody.

MEN

Hello, Mr. Kane. Welcome, Mr. Kane.

KANE

Hello, Mr. Bernstein.

BERNSTEIN

Hello, Mr. Kane.

KANE

Hello, Jed.
They come forward — camera moving back — general excitement

LELAND

You got a moustache.

KANE

I know.

LELAND

It looks awful.

KANE

It does not look awful. Have we got a society editor?

TOWNSEND

Right here, Mr. Kane.

LELAND

Miss Townsend is the society editor.
Kane goes to Miss Townsend

BERNSTEIN

Miss Townsend, Mr. Charles Foster Kane.
Kane hands paper to Miss Townsend, embarrassed — takes paper away, then hands it back again

KANE

Miss Townsend, I've been away so long, I don't know your routine. I . . . I got a little social announcement. I wish you wouldn't treat this any differently than you would any other social announcement.

BERNSTEIN

Mr. Kane, Mr. Kane . . . on behalf of all the employees of the "Inquirer" —

KANE

Mr. Bernstein, thank you very much everybody . . . I'm sorry, I can't accept it now. Good-bye.
He starts to b.g. — rushes back to Bernstein, grabs cup, runs to b.g. with it

BERNSTEIN

Say, he was in an awful hurry.
All turn to f.g.

BOY *(Off)*

Hey . . .

3–3   54.   *INT. WINDOW MLS* — boy at left by open window — Emily seen seated in barouche below -- boy talking

BOY

Hey, everybody, lookee out here.

22–4   55.   *INT. OFFICE MCS* — Leland holding onto Townsend's arm — pulls her to f.g., talking — men following

LELAND

Let's go to the window.
Two stop in f.g. — Townsend talking excitedly — stops Bernstein as he passes

TOWNSEND

Mr. Leland, Mr. Bernstein —

BERNSTEIN

Yes, Miss Townsend?
She reads paper

TOWNSEND

This — this announcement — Mr. and Mrs. Thomas Monroe Norton announce the engagement of their daughter, Emily Monroe Norton, to Mr. Charles Foster Kane.

BERNSTEIN

Huh?

LELAND

Come on.
They rush to right f.g. — nearly exit

END OF REEL 3 — SECTION 3A

REEL 3 — SECTION 3B

Day Sequence

3–7   1.   *EXT. BLDG. MS* — camera shooting up to windows of building — four men look out, look down to f.g.

8–4   2.   *INT. OFFICE MLS* — Townsend and two men looking out window at Emily in barouche below — Kane by it, handing cup to footman — girl talks — music plays
Kane below, waves up to three

TOWNSEND

Emily Monroe Norton, she's the niece of the President of the United States

7–8   3.   *EXT. WINDOW CS* — camera shooting up to Bernstein and Leland, looking down to f.g. — Bernstein talks

BERNSTEIN

President's niece, huh. Before he's through, she'll be a President's wife.

3–15   4.   *INT. OFFICE MLS* — three looking out window at Emily and Kane below — Kane sits down heavily in barouche as driver drives to right — men laugh — music

4–2   5.   *EXT. BLDG. MS* — camera shooting to group at windows laughing — music

5–11   6.   *EXT. BLDG. LS* — camera shooting along front of Inquirer Building — sign on building — men up at windows, waving — horse heard — music

Lap Dissolve

Night Sequence

135–10   7.   *INT. OFFICE MS* — Bernstein sitting on other side of desk talking to Thompson at right, near f.g.

BERNSTEIN

The way things turned out, I don't need to tell you. Miss Emily Norton was no Rosebud.

THOMPSON

It didn't end very well, did it?

BERNSTEIN

It ended. Then there was Susie. That ended too.
Bernstein rises, goes to fireplace at left — camera following

BERNSTEIN

You know, Mr. Thompson, I was thinking. This Rosebud you're trying to find out about . . .
Camera moves back — Thompson coming on

THOMPSON

Yes?

BERNSTEIN

Maybe that was something he lost. Mr. Kane was a man who lost almost everything he had. You ought to talk to Mr. Jed Leland. Of course, he and Mr. Kane didn't exactly see eye to eye. You take the Spanish-American War. I guess Mr. Leland was right. That was Mr. Kane's war. We didn't really have anything to fight about. But do you think if it hadn't been for that war of Mr. Kane's we'd have the Panama Canal? I wish I knew where Mr. Leland was. A lot of the time now they don't tell me these things. Maybe even he's dead.

THOMPSON

In case you'd like to know, Mr. Bernstein, he's at the Huntington Memorial Hospital on 180th Street.

BERNSTEIN

You don't say. I had no idea . . .

THOMPSON

Nothing particular the matter with him, they tell me, just —

BERNSTEIN

Just old age. It's the only disease, Mr. Thompson, that you don't look forward to being cured of.

Lap Dissolve

Day Sequence

15–   8.   *EXT. BLDG. MLS* — camera shooting past Thompson's face as he looks at hospital building — camera pans to roof of building, showing a bridge above it

Lap Dissolve

212–   9.   *EXT. HOSPITAL ROOF CS* — Thompson sitting right f.g. — Leland sitting at left, wearing glasses and visor, talking — others in b.g. — music — camera moving up closer to Leland

LELAND

I can remember absolutely everything, young man. That's my curse. That's one of the greatest curses ever inflicted on the human race, memory. I was his oldest friend, and as far as I was concerned, he behaved like a swine. Not that Charles was ever brutal. He just did brutal things. Maybe I wasn't his friend, but if I wasn't, he never had one.
He leans forward, taking off glasses

LELAND

Maybe I was what you nowadays call a stooge, hmm?

THOMPSON *(Off)*

Mr. Leland, you were about to say something about Rosebud . . .

LELAND

You don't happen to have a good cigar, do you? I've got a young physician here who thinks I'm going to give up smoking.

THOMPSON *(Off)*

No, I'm afraid I haven't. Sorry.
Leland leans back, laughing

LELAND

A good cigar? Oh, oh, I changed the subject, didn't I? Dear, dear, what a disagreeable old man I have become. You're a reporter and you want to know what I think about Charlie Kane. Well, I suppose he had some private sort of greatness. But he kept it to himself. He never gave himself away. He never gave anything away. He just left you a tip. Hmm? He had a generous mind. I don't suppose anybody ever had so many opinions. But he never believed in anything except Charlie Kane. He never had a conviction except Charlie Kane in his life. I suppose he died without one. That must have been pretty unpleasant. Of course, a lot of us check out without having any special convictions about death. But we do know what we're leaving. We do believe in something.
He leans forward

LELAND

You're absolutely sure you haven't got a cigar?

THOMPSON *(Off)*

Sorry, Mr. Leland.

LELAND

Oh, never mind, never mind.

THOMPSON *(Off)*

Mr. Leland.

LELAND

Huh?

THOMPSON *(Off)*

What do you know about Rosebud?

LELAND

Rosebud? Oh, oh, his dying words, Rosebud, yeh. I saw that in the "Inquirer." Well,

I've never believed anything I saw in the "Inquirer." Anything else? I can tell you about Emily. I went to dancing school with Emily. I was very graceful. Oh, we were talking about the first Mrs. Kane . . .

THOMPSON *(Off)*

What was she like?

LELAND

She was like all the girls I knew in dancing school. Very nice girls, very nice. Emily was a little nicer. Well, after the first couple of months she and Charlie didn't see much of each other except at breakfast. It was a marriage just like any other marriage.
The background of the Kane breakfast room fades in behind Leland, the two images are held in juxtaposition for a moment, then the image of Leland dissolves out

Lap Dissolve

Day Sequence

43–   10.   *INT. ROOM MLS* — Emily by table in b.g. — Kane, in evening clothes, coming on at right b.g. with plates — goes to her, towel over his arm — kisses her on forehead — putting dishes down, sits down at left as they talk — music

EMILY

Charles!

KANE

You're beautiful.

EMILY

I can't be.

KANE

Yes, you are. You're very, very beautiful.
Camera moves up closer to them

EMILY

I've never been to six parties in one night before. I've never been up this late.

KANE

It's just a matter of habit.

EMILY

What do you suppose the servants will think?

KANE

They'll think we enjoyed ourselves.

EMILY

Dearest.

KANE

Didn't we?

EMILY

I don't see why you have to go straight off to the newspaper.

KANE

You never should have married a newspaperman. They're worse than sailors. I absolutely adore you.

4–15   11.   *INT. ROOM MCU* — Emily talks — music

EMILY

Oh, Charles, even newspapermen have to sleep.

5–11   12.   *INT. ROOM MCU* — Kane, looking to right f.g., talks — music

KANE

I'll call up Bernstein and have him put off my appointments till noon.

2–8   13.   *INT. ROOM MCU* — Emily smiling — music

1–12   14.   *INT. ROOM MCU* — Kane looking to right f.g., talks — music

KANE

What time is it?

4–8   15.   *INT. ROOM MCU* — Emily seated, talks — music

EMILY

I don't know. It's late.

8–11   16.   *INT. ROOM MCU* — Kane smiling, talks — music

KANE

It's early.
Camera swings to right

Swing Dissolve

Day Sequence

5–6   17.   *INT. ROOM CS* — camera swinging, stops on Emily seated by flowers — music

EMILY

Charles, do you know how long you kept me waiting last night when . . .

4–   18.   *INT. ROOM CS* — Kane sitting on other side of flowers, looking to f.g. — music

EMILY *(Off)*

. . . you went to the newspaper for ten minutes?

5–1   19.   *INT. ROOM CS* — Emily looking over flowers to f.g., talking — music

EMILY

What do you do on a newspaper in the middle of the night?

KANE *(Off)*

Emily . . .

10–8   20.   *INT. ROOM CS* — Kane on other side of flowers, putting out match, talking — music

KANE

. . . my dear, your only corespondent is the "Inquirer."
Camera swings to right

EMILY *(Off)*

Sometimes I think I'd . . .

Swing Dissolve

2–7   21.   *INT. ROOM MCU* — camera swinging, stops on Emily seated at table, talking —

EMILY

. . . prefer a rival of flesh and blood.

KANE *(Off)*

Ah, Emily . . .

2–11   22.   *INT. ROOM CS* — Kane sitting on other side of flowers, frowning, talking — music

KANE

. . . I don't spend that much time on the newspaper.

5–12   23.   *INT. ROOM CS* — Emily looking over flowers to f.g. — music — she frowns, talking

EMILY

It isn't just the time. It's what you print, attacking . . .

2–11   24.   *INT. ROOM CS* — Kane on other side of flowers — music

EMILY *(Off)*

. . . the President.

KANE

You mean Uncle John.

4–15   25.   *INT. ROOM CS* — Emily looking over flowers to f.g., talking — music

EMILY

I mean the President of the United States.

KANE *(Off)*

He's still Uncle John . . .

6–12   26.   *INT. ROOM CS* — Kane talking — music

KANE

. . . and he's still a well-meaning fathead.

EMILY *(Off)*

Charles.

KANE

Who's letting a pack of high-pressure crooks run his administration.

6–3   27.   *INT. ROOM CS* — Emily looking over flowers to f.g., talks — music

KANE *(Off)*

This whole oil scandal —

EMILY

He happens to be the President, Charles, not you.

7–4   28.   *INT. ROOM CS* — Kane looking to f.g., talks — music

KANE

That's a mistake that will be corrected one of these days.
Camera swings to right

LENGTH FT. FRM.	SCENE NO.	

EMILY (*Off*)

Your Mr. Bernstein . . .

Swing Dissolve

8–11   29.   *INT. ROOM CS* — camera shooting on Emily talking — music

EMILY

. . . sent Junior the most incredible atrocity yesterday, Charles. I simply can't have it . . .

9–8   30.   *INT. ROOM CS* — Kane at table, cutting meat — puts knife and fork down — music

EMILY (*Off*)

. . . in the nursery.
He frowns

KANE

Mr. Bernstein is apt to pay a visit to the nursery now and then.

2–9   31.   *INT. ROOM CS* — Emily talks — music

EMILY

Does he have to?

6–2   32.   *INT. ROOM CS* — Kane frowns, talks — music

KANE

Yes.
Camera swings to right

EMILY (*Off*)

Really, Charles . . .

Swing Dissolve

1–6   33.   *INT. ROOM CS* — camera stops on Emily at table — she talks

EMILY

. . . people will think —

7–12   34.   *INT. ROOM CS* — Kane holding cup, frowning, talks

KANE

What I tell them to think.
Camera swings to right

Swing Dissolve

6–5   35.   *INT. ROOM CS* — camera stops on Emily seated, holding paper, looking to f.g. — looks at paper

17–   36.   *INT. ROOM CS* — Kane sitting at table — paper open before him — he glances to f.g., looks at paper — camera moves back from table, showing Emily sitting at right end of table
Leland in wheelchair fades in left f.g. over the scene of the breakfast room; the two images are held in juxtaposition for a second before the breakfast scene fades out

Lap Dissolve

95–   37.   *EXT. ROOF CS* — Leland sitting at left, nodding — Thompson partly on, right f.g., talking — people in b.g.

THOMPSON

Wasn't he ever in love with her?

LELAND

He married for love. Love . . . that's why he did everything. That's why he went into politics. It seems we weren't enough. He wanted all the voters to love him, too. All he really wanted out of life was love. That's Charlie's story. How he lost it. You see, he just didn't have any to give. Oh, he loved Charlie Kane, of course. Yeh. Very dearly. And his mother, I guess he always loved her.

THOMPSON

How about his second wife?

LELAND

Susan Alexander? You know what Charlie called her? The day after he'd met her, he told me about her. He said she was a cross-section of the American public. I guess he couldn't help it. She must have had something for him. That first night, according to Charlie, all she had was a toothache.

Lap Dissolve

Night Sequence

122–   38.   *EXT. STREET MS* — camera shooting down at cobblestone street, all wet — horse heard — camera pans up, showing Susan coming from drugstore in b.g. — wagon crosses in f.g., exits — camera moving up to sidewalk — Susan putting medicine in her mouth, smiles — picking up her skirts — she laughs — camera pans to right, showing Kane standing by post, mud spattered all over him — he takes his handkerchief out, looks around as Susan comes on at left, going down walk to b.g., giggling at him — stops — he talks

KANE (Severely)

What are you laughing at, young lady?

SUSAN

Ow.
She winces — turns to b.g.

KANE

What is the matter with you, young lady?

SUSAN

Soothache.

KANE

What?

SUSAN

Toothache.
He goes to her — camera moving up closer — Susan laughing

KANE

Toothache. Oh, oh, you mean you've got a toothache. What's funny about that?

SUSAN

You're funny, mister. You've got dirt on your face.

KANE

Not dirt — it's mud.

SUSAN

Do you want some hot water? I live right here.

KANE

What's that, young lady?

SUSAN

I said if you want some hot water, I could get you some . . . hot water.

KANE

All right, thank you very much.
They go up steps into building — exit

Lap Dissolve

Night Sequence

42–5   39.   *INT. ROOM MLS* — Susan in b.g. by dresser, groaning — Kane coming on at right, wiping face on towel, talking — camera shooting through hall door into room

SUSAN

Ow! . . . Ow!

KANE

Do I look any better now?

SUSAN

This medicine doesn't do a bit of good.

KANE

What you need is to take your mind off it.
Kane walks to door, closes it — camera holds on closed door

SUSAN *(Off)*

Hey.

Camera moves in towards door — it is opened — Kane and Susan are seen in the open doorway

SUSAN

Excuse me, but my landlady prefers me to keep this door open when I have a gentleman caller.

KANE

All right.

SUSAN

Ow.

KANE

You have got a toothache, haven't you?
She exits — her reflection seen in mirror in b.g. as she sits down

SUSAN

I really have.

KANE

Hey — why don't you try laughing at me again?

SUSAN

What?
Kane goes to b.g. — turns

KANE

I'm still pretty funny.

37I

SUSAN

I know . . .

12–4   40.   *INT. ROOM CS* — reflection of Susan seen in mirror — Kane partly on, standing at left — Susan talks

SUSAN

. . . but you don't want me to laugh at you.

KANE

I don't want your tooth to hurt, either. Look at me. See that?

SUSAN

What are you doing?

4–15   41.   *INT. ROOM MCU* — Kane wiggling ears — turns head as he talks

KANE

I'm wiggling both my ears at the same time.

7–12   42.   *INT. ROOM CS* — reflection in mirror of Susan seated, laughing up at Kane partly on at left

KANE

That's it, smile.
She giggles

END OF REEL 3 — SECTION 3B

REEL 4 — SECTION 4A

Night Sequence

11–3   1.   *INT. ROOM CU* — Kane looking to f.g., smiling, talking

KANE

It took me two solid years at the best boys' school in the world to learn that trick. The fellow who taught me is now president of Venezuela.

8–13   2.   *INT. ROOM CS* — reflection in mirror of Susan laughing up at Kane, partly on beside her — he laughs, talks

KANE

That's it.

Lap Dissolve

7–   3.   *INT. ROOM CS* — reflection on walls of hands making shadow of rooster — Susan and Kane heard laughing, talking

SUSAN *(Off)*

Is it a giraffe?

KANE *(Off)*

No, not a giraffe.

79–9   4.   *INT. ROOM CS* — Susan and Kane laughing — Kane making shadowgraphs with hands

SUSAN

Oh, I bet it's —

KANE

What?

SUSAN

Well, then it's an elephant.

KANE

It's supposed to be a rooster.

SUSAN

A rooster!
Camera moves up to them slowly — Kane smoking pipe

SUSAN

Gee, you know an awful lot of tricks. You're not a professional magician, are you?

KANE

No, I'm not a magician.

SUSAN

I was just joking.

KANE

You really don't know who I am?

SUSAN

You told me your name, Mr. Kane, but I'm awfully ignorant. I guess you caught on to that. You know, I bet I've heard your name a million times.

KANE

But you really like me, though, even though you don't know who I am?

SUSAN

Oh, I surely do. You've been wonderful. Gee, without you I don't know what I would have done. Here I was with a toothache, and I don't know many people.

KANE

I know too many people. I guess we're both lonely. You want to know what I was going to do tonight, before I ruined my best Sunday clothes?

SUSAN

I bet they're not your best Sunday clothes. You've probably got a lot of clothes.

KANE

No, I was just joking.

3–9   5.   *INT. ROOM CU* — Susan smiling

KANE *(Off)*

I was on my . . .

7–8   6.   *INT. ROOM CU* — Kane smiling, talking — music heard

KANE

. . . way to the Western Manhattan Warehouse, in search of my youth.

6–10   7.   *INT. ROOM CU* — Susan listening — music

KANE *(Off)*

You see, my mother died, a long time ago.

15–5   8.   *INT. ROOM CU* — Kane looking to f.g., talking — music

KANE

Well, her things were put in storage out West. There wasn't any other place to put them. I thought I'd send for them now. Tonight I was going to take a look at them. A sort of sentimental journey.

3–7   9.   *INT. ROOM CU* — Susan looking to f.g. — music

5–13   10.   *INT. ROOM CU* — Kane looking to f.g., talks — music

KANE

I run a couple of newspapers. What do you do?

52–3   11.   *INT. ROOM CS* — two facing each other — Susan talks — music

SUSAN

Me?

KANE

Hmm. How old did you say you were?

SUSAN

Oh, I didn't say.

KANE

I didn't think you did. If you had, I wouldn't have asked you again, because I'd have remembered. How old?

SUSAN

Pretty old.

KANE

How old?

SUSAN

Twenty-two in August.

KANE

That's a ripe old age. What do you do?

SUSAN

Oh, I work at Seligman's. I'm in charge of the sheet music.

KANE

Is that what you want to do?

SUSAN

No, I wanted to be a singer, I guess. That is, I didn't. My mother did.

KANE

What happened to the singing?

SUSAN

Well, Mother always thought — she always talked about grand opera for me. Imagine! Anyway, my voice isn't that kind. It's just — well, you know what mothers are like.

8–12   12.   *INT. ROOM CU* — Kane nods, talks

KANE

Yes. You got a piano?

6–14   13.   *INT. ROOM CU* — Susan nods, talks

SUSAN

A piano? Yes, there's one in the parlor.

7–4   14.   *INT. ROOM CU* — Kane looking to f.g., talks

KANE

Would you sing for me?

SUSAN *(Off)*

Oh, you wouldn't want to hear me sing.

KANE

Yes, I would.

9–6   15.   *INT. ROOM CU* — Susan talks, hesitatingly

SUSAN

Well, I —

KANE *(Off)*

Don't tell me your toothache is still bothering you?

SUSAN

Oh, no, it's all gone.

10–12   16.   *INT. ROOM CU* — Kane smiling, talks

KANE

All right. Let's go to the parlor.

Lap Dissolve

Night Sequence

34–   17.   *INT. ROOM MS* — Susan sitting at piano playing, singing — Kane sitting behind her at right, listening

SUSAN

Yes, Lindor shall be mine
I have sworn it for weal or woe
Yes, Lindor . . .

Lap Dissolve

28–   18.   *INT. ROOM MLS* — Susan at piano at left, singing — Kane at right b.g., listening

SUSAN

Lo giu-rai la vince-ro . . .
*(Translation: I have sworn it, for weal or woe . . .)**
As she finishes, Kane applauds*

Lap Dissolve

Night Sequence

24–3   19.   *EXT. STREET MLS* — people with banners and placards — Leland standing on back seat on open car, talking to crowd around him — people applauding

*The direct translation is: *I have sworn it, I will conquer.*

LELAND

There is only one man who can rid the politics of this state of the evil domination of Boss Jim Gettys.

MAN

Hooray.

PEOPLE

Shhhh.
Camera moves over crowd up to Leland

LELAND

I am speaking of Charles Foster Kane, the fighting liberal, the friend of the working-man, the next governor of this state, who entered upon this campaign . . .

17–2   20.   *INT. GARDEN CU* — banner with picture of Kane — his name above it

KANE *(Off)*

. . . with one purpose only . . .
Camera pans down, showing Kane in Madison Square Garden — officials behind him, listening

KANE

. . . to point out and make public the dishonesty, the downright villainy of Boss Jim Gettys's political machine . . .

9–3   21.   *INT. GARDEN LS* — camera moving over crowd facing Kane and officials onstage in b.g. — Kane talking

KANE

. . . now in complete control of the government of this state.

32–   22.   *INT. STAGE MLS* — Kane standing, talking — officials seated in b.g. — camera moving up closer to Kane

KANE

I made no campaign promises because until a few weeks ago I had no hope of being elected.
Crowd laughing, applauding

KANE

Now, however, I have something more than a hope.
Crowd applauding — laughing — camera moving up

KANE

And Jim Gettys . . . and Jim Gettys has something less than a chance.
Terrific applause heard

7–9   23.   *INT. GARDEN CS* — boy and Emily in box — she motions, he sits down by her — applause heard

KANE *(Off)*

Every straw vote, every inde—

7–4   24.   *INT. GARDEN MLS* — camera shooting up to Kane at left, talking — men in b.g.

KANE

—pendent poll shows that I will be elected.
Terrific applause and cheering heard

12–5   25.   *INT. GARDEN CS* — Kane in b.g. — men in b.g. applauding — crowd heard — Kane shouts over noise

KANE

Very well, now I can afford to make some promises.

3–3   26.   *INT. GARDEN CS* — boy waving to f.g. — Emily at right — applause heard

| 6–11 | 27. | *INT. GARDEN CS* — Kane looking to left — men in b.g. applauding — terrific applause heard — Kane waves to left, shouts — cheering stops |

KANE

The workingman . . .

| 10–5 | 28. | *INT. GARDEN MCU* — camera shooting up past Leland, sitting at left — others around |

KANE *(Off)*

. . . the workingman and the slum child may expect my best efforts in their interests.

| 16–5 | 29. | *INT. GARDEN CS* — Kane talking — others in b.g., moving to right f.g. |

KANE

The decent, ordinary citizens know I'll do everything in my power to protect the under-privileged, the underpaid, and the underfed.

| 5–1 | 30. | *INT. GARDEN CS* — Bernstein and group looking down to right — applaud |
| 8–8 | 31. | *INT. GARDEN CS* — two at railing — Junior at left, talks — crowd heard |

JUNIOR

Mother, is Pop governor yet?

EMILY

Not yet, Junior.

| 15–15 | 32. | *INT. GARDEN CS* — Kane in f.g. at desk — people in b.g. applauding — Kane looks around, talks |

KANE

Well, I'd make my promises now if I weren't too busy arranging to keep them.
Terrific applause and cheering heard

| 5–3 | 33. | *INT. ROOM CS* — camera shooting up to Leland in crowd, applauding, laughing — crowd cheering, laughing |
| 34–13 | 34. | *INT. GARDEN MLS* — camera shooting down to Kane below, talking — men behind him applauding — crowd heard |

KANE

But here's one promise I'll make, and Boss Jim Gettys knows I'll keep it.
Camera moves down to Kane

KANE

My first official act as governor of this state will be to appoint a special district attorney to arrange for the indictment, prosecution and conviction of Boss Jim W. Gettys.
Men leap up, applauding — crowd heard

| 12–15 | 35. | *INT. GARDEN LS* — Gettys looking down at Kane and crowd below — terrific roar from crowd heard — music starts to play — Gettys puts on hat, exits right f.g. |
| 24–9 | 36. | *INT. GARDEN MS* — men around Kane on platform, talking — crowd heard — music — they come down steps to f.g. — flashlight pictures taken — people talking indistinctly |

Lap Dissolve

Night Sequence

| 23–4 | 37. | *INT. GARDEN MS* — crowd following Kane to f.g. — camera moving back — general confusion — indistinct talking heard |

HILLMAN

If the election were held today, you'd be in by a hundred thousand votes.

POLITICIAN

Gettys isn't even pretending.

Junior comes on — Kane picking him up

JUNIOR

Hello, Pop.

POLITICIAN

He isn't just scared any more, he's sick.

KANE

Hello, son, how are you?
He talks to men

KANE

I think it's beginning to dawn on Jim Gettys that I mean what I say. Did you like your old man's speech?

JUNIOR

I was in a box, Daddy.
Emily comes on at right

COP

Mrs. Kane —

JUNIOR

I could hear every word.

KANE

Wonderful. Hello, Emily.

PHOTOGRAPHER

Hold it.

3–13   38.   *EXT. ENTRANCE MLS* — camera shooting down to crowd around Kane and Emily — flashlights going off — crowd talking

MEN

Great speech, Mr. Kane, great.
Wonderful speech, Mr. Kane . . .

11–1   39.   *EXT. SQUARE MCS* — crowd around Kane and family — people all talking — Kane putting boy down — Emily kissing boy

MAN

. . . wonderful.

EMILY

Officer, will you get us a taxi?

COP

Yes, Mrs. Kane.

EMILY

Good night, darling.

JUNIOR

Good night, Mother.
Man takes Junior to right

LENGTH FT. FRM.	SCENE NO.	

COP

Taxi for Mr. Kane.

KANE

Hey, where's Junior going?

EMILY

I'm sending Junior home in the car, Charles, with Oliver.

2–8   40.   *EXT. CAB CU* — boy looking out to f.g., waves as cab moves to right — crowd heard

JUNIOR

Good night, Father.

4–6   41.   *EXT. SQUARE* CS — Kane and Emily in f.g. — crowd around — Kane waves, calls — general confusion

KANE

Good night, son.

5–12   42.   *EXT. SQUARE LS* — camera shooting down — crowd below — much yelling and indistinct talking — Kane and Emily in crowd — cab coming on from right b.g., stops at right

END OF REEL 4 — SECTION 4A

REEL 4 — SECTION 4B

Night Sequence

5–12   1.   *EXT. STREET CS* — Kane and Emily in f.g. — men around them — general talking and confusion — Emily comes to right f.g., exits — Kane talking

KANE

Emily.
He comes to right f.g.

4–13   2.   *EXT. STREET MS* — crowd around — Emily getting into cab — officer pushing people away — Kane going to cab — crowd noise

13–7   3.   *INT. CAB CU* — Emily partly on, right f.g. — Kane looking in door, talks — crowd heard

KANE

Why did you send Junior home in the car? What are you doing in a taxi?

EMILY

There's a call I want you to make with me, Charles.

KANE

It can wait.

EMILY

No, it can't.

KANE

What's this all about, Emily?

11–5   4.   *EXT. CAB MCU* — Kane partly on, left f.g. — Emily inside cab, holding up envelope — talking — crowd heard

EMILY

It may not be about anything at all. I intend to find out.

LENGTH FT. FRM.	SCENE NO.	

KANE

Where are you going?

EMILY

I'm going to 185 West 74th . . .

| 8– | 5. | *INT. CAB CU* — Emily partly on, right f.g., talking — Kane looking in doorway |

EMILY

. . . Street. If you wish, you may come with me.

| 4–9 | 6. | *EXT. CAB MCU* — Kane partly on, left f.g. — Emily inside cab, looking at him |
| 5–10 | 7. | *INT. CAB CU* — Emily partly on, right f.g. — Kane staring in at her, talks |

KANE

I'll come with you.

Lap Dissolve

Night Sequence

| 29– | 8. | *EXT. ENTRANCE MS* — Kane and Emily by door — bell heard ringing as Kane pushes it — camera moves up close — Kane talks |

KANE

I had no idea you had this flair for melodrama, Emily.
Shadow comes on inside — maid opens door

MAID

Come right in, Mr. Kane.
Maid steps back — Emily goes inside, Kane follows — maid closing door

Lap Dissolve

| 42– | 9. | *INT. HALL MLS* — camera shooting up to top landing of stairs — door in b.g. above opens — Susan, coming out, talks as Kane and Emily come on upstairs in f.g. |

SUSAN

Charlie . . .
They glance up at her — go up to right — camera follows them up to door

SUSAN

Charlie . . . Charlie, he forced me to send your wife that letter. I didn't want to. He's been saying the most terrible —
Gettys comes on in doorway

GETTYS

Good evening, Mrs. Kane. I don't suppose anybody would introduce me.

| 36–4 | 10. | *INT. HALL CS* — Emily right f.g. — Kane by her — Gettys in doorway talking — Susan by him |

GETTYS

I'm Jim Gettys.

EMILY

Yes?
He steps back — she goes into room

GETTYS

I made Miss — Miss Alexander send you that note, Mrs. Kane. She didn't want to at first.

KANE

Where are you going?

EMILY

I'm going to 185 West 74th . . .

| 8– | 5. | *INT. CAB CU* — Emily partly on, right f.g., talking — Kane looking in doorway |

EMILY

. . . Street. If you wish, you may come with me.

| 4–9 | 6. | *EXT. CAB MCU* — Kane partly on, left f.g. — Emily inside cab, looking at him |
| 5–10 | 7. | *INT. CAB CU* — Emily partly on, right f.g. — Kane staring in at her, talks |

KANE

I'll come with you.

Lap Dissolve

Night Sequence

| 29– | 8. | *EXT. ENTRANCE MS* — Kane and Emily by door — bell heard ringing as Kane pushes it — camera moves up close — Kane talks |

KANE

I had no idea you had this flair for melodrama, Emily.
Shadow comes on inside — maid opens door

MAID

Come right in, Mr. Kane.
Maid steps back — Emily goes inside, Kane follows — maid closing door

Lap Dissolve

| 42– | 9. | *INT. HALL MLS* — camera shooting up to top landing of stairs — door in b.g. above opens — Susan, coming out, talks as Kane and Emily come on upstairs in f.g. |

SUSAN

Charlie . . .
They glance up at her — go up to right — camera follows them up to door

SUSAN

Charlie . . . Charlie, he forced me to send your wife that letter. I didn't want to. He's been saying the most terrible —
Gettys comes on in doorway

GETTYS

Good evening, Mrs. Kane. I don't suppose anybody would introduce me.

| 36–4 | 10. | *INT. HALL CS* — Emily right f.g. — Kane by her — Gettys in doorway talking — Susan by him |

GETTYS

I'm Jim Gettys.

EMILY

Yes?
He steps back — she goes into room

GETTYS

I made Miss — Miss Alexander send you that note, Mrs. Kane. She didn't want to at first.

380

SUSAN

I —

GETTYS

But she did it.

SUSAN

Charlie, the things he said — he threatened to —
Kane steps through doorway to Gettys angrily

KANE

Gettys . . .
Camera moves up to two men — Susan exits — Emily inside room

KANE

. . . I don't think I will postpone doing something about you until I'm elected. To start with, I think I'll break your neck.

GETTYS

Maybe you can do it, and maybe you can't, Mr. Kane.
Gettys goes inside, exits — Kane starts in, stops

EMILY

Charles.

175–11   11.   *INT. ROOM CS* — Emily at right — Kane at left, turning to her as she talks

EMILY

Your breaking this man's neck would scarcely explain this note.
She glances down at note, reads

EMILY

Serious consequences for Mr. Kane, for yourself and for your son.
Susan comes on through doorway at left

SUSAN

He just wanted to get her to come here and —

EMILY

What does this note mean, Miss —

SUSAN

I'm Susan Alexander. I know what you're thinking, but —

EMILY

What does this note mean, Miss Alexander?
Kane turns to b.g. — Emily turns around to right

GETTYS *(Off)*

She don't know, Mrs. Kane.
Camera pans, showing Gettys in b.g. — Kane going to him

GETTYS

She just sent it because I made her see it wouldn't be smart for her not to send it.

KANE

In case you don't know, Emily, this gentleman —

GETTYS

I'm not a gentleman. Your husband is only trying to be funny, calling me one. I don't even know what a gentleman is. You see, my idea of a gentleman *(laughs shortly)* —
Gettys comes to Emily

GETTYS

Well, Mr. Kane, if I owned a newspaper and if I didn't like the way somebody was doing things, some politician, say — I'd fight him with everything I had, only I wouldn't show him in a convict suit with stripes, so his children could see the picture in the paper, or his mother.

KANE

You're a cheap, crooked grafter, and your concern for your children and your mother —

GETTYS

We're talking now about what you are. Mrs. Kane, I'm fighting for my life, not just my political life, my life.
Susan comes to them

SUSAN

Charlie, he said unless you withdrew your name, he'd tell everybody —

GETTYS

That's what I said.

EMILY

You mean —

GETTYS

Here's the chance I'm willing to give him. It's more of a chance than he'd give me. Unless Mr. Kane makes up his mind by tomorrow that he's so sick he has to go away for a year or two, Monday morning every paper in this state, except his, will carry the story I'm going to give them.

EMILY

What story?

GETTYS

The story about him and Miss Alexander, Mrs. Kane.
Susan comes to them

SUSAN

There isn't any story. It's —

GETTYS

Shut up.

SUSAN

Mr. Kane is just —

GETTYS

We've got evidence that would look bad in the headlines.
He turns to Kane

GETTYS

Do you want me to give you the evidence, Mr. Kane?
He turns to Emily

GETTYS

I'd rather Mr. Kane withdrew without having to get the story published. Not that I care about him, but I'd be better off that way.

SUSAN

What about —

GETTYS

So would you, Mrs. Kane.

SUSAN

What about me? Charlie, he said my name'd be dragged through the mud. That everywhere I went from now —

EMILY

There seems to me to be only one decision you can make, Charles. I'd say that it's been made for you.

KANE

You can't tell me the voters of this state —

EMILY

I'm not interested in the voters of this state right now.

35–9   12.   *INT. ROOM MS* — camera shooting past Kane, partly on right f.g. — Gettys and two women in b.g. — Emily talking

EMILY

I am interested in our son.

SUSAN

Charlie, if they publish this story, it will be all in —

EMILY

They won't. Good night, Mr. Gettys.
She turns, starts out doorway, looks back at Kane

EMILY

Are you coming, Charles?

KANE

No.

7–5   13.   *INT. ROOM CS* — camera shooting up — Gettys and Susan in f.g. — Kane walking slowly to them, stops, talks

KANE

I'm staying here.

3–7   14.   *INT. ROOM CS* — camera shooting up between Gettys and Kane in f.g. — Emily in doorway in b.g., staring

5–7   15.   *INT. ROOM CS* — two standing on either side — Kane facing f.g., talks

KANE

I can fight this all alone.

EMILY *(Off)*

Charles . . .

8–   16.   *INT. ROOM MCS* — Gettys, left f.g. — Emily facing f.g., talks

EMILY

. . . if you don't listen to reason, it may be too late.

30–5   17.   *INT. ROOM CS* — camera shooting up to Kane, standing between Susan and Gettys — he talks

KANE

Too late for what? For you and this public thief to take the love of the people of this state away from me?

SUSAN

Charlie, you got other things to think about. Your little boy, you don't want him to read about you in the papers.

KANE

There's only one person in the world to decide what I'm going to do, and that's me.

69–2   18.   *INT. ROOM CS* — camera shooting between Kane and Gettys to Emily in b.g., staring — Emily talks

EMILY

You decided what you were going to do, Charles, some time ago.
She turns out doorway into hall, exits

GETTYS

You're making a bigger fool of yourself than I thought you would, Mr. Kane.

KANE

I've got nothing to talk to you about.

GETTYS

You're licked. Why don't you —

KANE

Get out. If you want to see me, have the warden write me a letter.

GETTYS

If it was anybody else, I'd say what's going to happen to you would be a lesson to you. Only you're going to need more than one lesson. And you're going to get more than one lesson.

KANE

Don't worry about me, Gettys.
*Gettys puts on hat, goes out doorway into hall, exits — Kane goes to door, shouting —
Susan right f.g.*

KANE

Don't worry about me. I'm Charles Foster Kane. I'm no cheap, crooked politician . . .
He exits out doorway, yelling

KANE

. . . trying to save himself . . .

7–4   19.   *INT. HALL LS* — camera shooting down through hall — Kane rushing down above at right, yelling — Gettys below, going down steps

KANE

. . . from the consequences of his crimes.
He runs to railing, looks down — Gettys goes down

KANE

Gettys!

3–6   20.   *INT. HALL CU* — Gettys coming down to f.g., smiling slightly — exits left f.g. — Kane leaning over banister in b.g., shouting

KANE

I'm going to send you to . . .

1–12   21.   *INT. HALL CU* — Kane shouting to f.g.

KANE

. . . Sing Sing.

3–   22.   *INT. HALL MLS* — Kane above in b.g., shouting — Susan running on at left above

KANE

Sing Sing, Gettys.

36–10   23.   *EXT. ENTRANCE MCS* — Emily at right, by door — Gettys coming out, closing door

KANE (*Off*)

Sing Sing . . .
Gettys closes door, takes off hat

GETTYS

Have you a car, Mrs. Kane?

EMILY

Yes, thank you.

GETTYS

Good night.

EMILY

Good night.
Emily exits right f.g. — music plays — Gettys comes to left f.g., exits — camera moves back

Lap Dissolve

Night Sequence

6–5   24.   INSERT #1 — article in paper — picture of entrance of building — camera moves back, showing pictures of Susan and Kane — newsboys heard yelling indistinctly — music — headlines reading:

The Daily Chronicle
CANDIDATE KANE CAUGHT IN
LOVE NEST WITH "SINGER"
THE HIGHLY MORAL MR. KANE AND HIS TAME "SONGBIRD"

Entrapped by Wife
as Love Pirate, Kane
Refuses to Quit Race

BOY (*Off*)

Extra, extra — read all about it — extra, extra.

26–11   25.   *EXT. BLDG. CU* — Leland looking to f.g. — music stops

BOY (*Off*)

Paper?

LENGTH FT. FRM.	SCENE NO.	

LELAND

No, thanks.

Leland turns away — turns to b.g., goes into saloon — men inside — he goes to bar — doors swinging shut

Lap Dissolve

Night Sequence

25–13   26.   *INT. ROOM CU* — type on table — camera moves back, showing type set — newspaper proof sheet reading:

KANE ELECTED

BERNSTEIN *(Off)*

With a million majority already against him . . .

Camera moving back, showing Bernstein holding paper — puts it down — men at left, others around

BERNSTEIN

. . . and the church counties still to be heard from, I'm afraid we got no choice.

FOREMAN

This one?

Man points to paper at right — man pulls paper up, showing headline

CHARLES FOSTER KANE DEFEATED
FRAUD AT POLLS!

Bernstein nods

BERNSTEIN

That one.

Lap Dissolve

Dawn Sequence

31–12   27.   *EXT. STREET CS* — Leland's feet crossing, passing paper lying in cobblestone street — headline reads: FRAUD AT POLLS — music plays — camera moves back, showing street cleaner working — Leland stops by wagon, looks around, goes to entrance of headquarters in b.g. — goes up steps, exits

Lap Dissolve

137–8   28.   *INT. ROOM MS* — camera shooting up to men putting on coats — Bernstein talks

BERNSTEIN

Well, good night, again.

Men cross to left f.g., exit — Bernstein putting on coat — Kane comes out doorway at left

BERNSTEIN

Is there anything I can —

KANE

No, thanks, Mr. Bernstein, you better go home and get some sleep.

BERNSTEIN

You, too. Good night, Mr. Kane.

KANE

Good night, Mr. Bernstein.

Bernstein comes to left f.g., exits — Kane crosses to right, camera following — he goes to b.g. — door in b.g. opens — Leland comes in, staggering — comes to Kane

KANE

Hello, Jedediah.

LELAND

I'm drunk.
Kane turns to f.g.

KANE

Well, if you've got drunk to talk to me about Miss Alexander, don't bother. I'm not interested.
He goes around post, goes to b.g. — Leland turns, watching

KANE

I've set back the sacred cause of reform, is that it? All right, if that's the way they want it, the people have made their choice. It's obvious the people prefer Jim Gettys to me.

145–9   29.   *INT. OFFICE MLS* — camera shooting past Kane, partly on, left f.g., to Leland in b.g. — Leland talks

LELAND

You talk about the people as though you owned them. As though they belong to you. As long as I can remember, you've talked about giving the people their rights as if you could make them a present of liberty, as a reward for services rendered.

KANE

Jed.

LELAND

You remember the workingman?

KANE

I'll get drunk, too, Jedediah, if it'll do any good.

LELAND

It won't do any good.
Kane goes to Leland

LELAND

Besides you never get drunk. You used to write an awful lot about the workingman —

KANE

Aw, go on home.

LELAND

He's turning into something called organized labor. You're not going to like that one little bit when you find out it means your workingman expects something as his right and not your gift. Charlie, when your precious underprivileged really get together — oh, boy, that's going to add up to something bigger than your privilege, and then I don't know what you'll do. Sail away to a desert island, probably, and lord it over the monkeys.

KANE

I wouldn't worry about it too much, Jed. There'll probably be a few of them there to let me know when I do something wrong.

LELAND

You may not always be so lucky.

KANE

You're not very drunk.

LELAND

Drunk — what do you care?
Kane comes back to left f.g. — camera following him to left

LELAND *(Off)*

You don't care about anything except you. You just want to persuade people that you love them so much that they ought to love you back.
Kane stops at table, looks to right

LELAND *(Off)*

Only you want love on your own terms.

END OF REEL 4 — SECTION 4B

REEL 5 — SECTION 5A

Day Sequence

104–11   1.   *INT. OFFICE MLS* — Kane partly on, right f.g. — camera shooting up — Leland in b.g., moving forward, talks

LELAND

It's something to be played your way, according to your rules.
He comes to Kane — camera tilting up

LELAND

Charlie, I want you to let me work on the Chicago paper.

KANE

What?

LELAND

Well, you said yourself you were looking for someone to do dramatic crimitism . . . criticism . . . I am drunk.
Kane laughs

LELAND

I want to go to Chicago.

KANE

You're too valuable here.

LELAND

Well, Charlie, then there's nothing to do but to ask you to accept my . . .

KANE

All right, you can go to Chicago.

LELAND

Thank you.

KANE

I guess I'd better try to get drunk anyway.
He picks up glass and bottle, pours drink

KANE

But I warn you, Jedediah, you're not going to like it in Chicago. The wind comes howling in off the lake, and gosh only knows if they've ever heard of lobster Newburg.

LELAND

Will Saturday after next be all right.

KANE

Anytime you say.

LELAND

Thank you.
Two stare at each other — Kane holds up glass

KANE

A toast, Jedediah, to love on my terms. Those are the only terms anybody ever knows, his own.
He drinks

62–   2.   INSERT #1 — sign going away from camera — music heard

KANE MARRIES SINGER

Scene superimposed over sign, showing Kane and Susan coming down steps — crowd around — much confusion — Kane smashing around with umbrella

MAN

Here he comes.
Sign fading out

PHOTOGRAPHER

Hey, Mr. Kane, I'm from the "Inquirer."

KANE

Huh? All right, fire away, boys. I used to be a reporter myself.

REPORTER

How about a statement, Mr. Kane?

ANOTHER

Give us something to print.
Crowd laughing — camera moves back — Kane with arm around Susan, coming forward to car — confusion

ANOTHER

On the level, Mr. Kane, are you through with politics?
Kane talks to reporter partly on, right f.g.

KANE

What's that, young man?

REPORTER

Are you through with politics?

KANE

Am I through with politics. I would say vice versa. We're going to be a great opera star.

REPORTER

Are you going to sing at the Metropolitan, Mrs. Kane?

ANOTHER

Are yuh?

KANE

We certainly are.

SUSAN

Charlie said if I didn't, he'd build me an opera house.

KANE

That won't be necessary.
Car goes to left with them — camera pans

Lap Dissolve

Night Sequence

5–5   3.   INSERT #2 — music playing — sign reading:

KANE BUILDS
OPERA HOUSE

Lap Dissolve

37–15   4.   *INT. STAGE ROOM CU* — Susan with mouth open, singing aria — tears in eyes — she turns as director comes on at right, raving, waving hands

MATISTI

No, no, no, no, no, no.
He talks indistinctly as camera moves back — hands at left putting plumed cap on Susan's head — much yelling and confusion — camera pans up to spotlight, blinking — music — camera pans back down to Susan with people around her, adjusting her costume — Matisti raving indistinctly, others wringing their hands — more people coming on — camera moving back — general confusion

8₃–11   5.   *INT. STAGE LS* — Susan in center, others around her — stagehands moving around with equipment — general excitement — music playing loudly — people rushing around — man waves, calls

MAN

Places everybody . . . onstage, everybody. Places, please.
Helpers rush offstage — spotlight rises, exits — Susan posing — curtain goes up, showing stage — Susan sings

SUSAN

Ah, cruel . . .
Camera moves upward — Susan and others exit — camera moving up over top of set

SUSAN *(Off)*

Tu m'as trop entendu . . .
Camera moving up to top of set — Susan heard singing indistinctly — camera stops on two men up on catwalk looking down — one puts fingers to nose, holding his nose

Lap Dissolve

26–   6.   *INT. OFFICE MS* — shadow of Kane comes on outside, comes into room, moves slowly to f.g., listening

BERNSTEIN *(Off)*

Mr. Leland is writing it from the dramatic angle?

EDITOR *(Off)*

Yes.

EDITOR *(Off)*

And we've covered it from the news end.

EDITOR *(Off)*

Naturally.

BERNSTEIN *(Off)*

And the social. How about the music notice? You got that in?

EDITOR *(Off)*

Oh, yes, it's already made up.

124–12   7.   *INT. OFFICE LS* — Bernstein and men talking — Kane by doors in b.g.

EDITOR

Our Mr. Mervin wrote a swell review.

BERNSTEIN

Enthusiastic?

MERVIN

Yes, sir.

EDITOR

Naturally.

KANE

Mr. Bernstein —
Group turning — men talking as Kane comes to them

MERVIN

Mr. Kane.

BERNSTEIN

Hello, Mr. Kane.

KANE

Gentlemen.

EDITOR

Mr. Kane, this is a surprise.

EDDIE

Hello, Mr. Kane, everything has been done exactly to your instructions.

KANE

Got a nice plant here.

EDITOR

We've got two spreads of pictures.

KANE

Fine. The music notice on the front page?

MERVIN

Yes, Mr. Kane.

EDITOR

But there's still one notice to come. The dramatic.

KANE

The dramatic notice. Mr. Bernstein, that's Mr. Leland, isn't it?

BERNSTEIN

Yes, Mr. Kane, we're waiting for it.

KANE

Where is he?

MERVIN

Right in there, Mr. Kane.
*Kane crosses to right — camera swings around — others exit — he goes down through
office to b.g. — two men working in b.g.*

BERNSTEIN *(Off)*

Mr. Kane —
Kane continues to b.g. — Bernstein coming on in f.g.

BERNSTEIN

Mr. Kane —
Kane goes into office in b.g., exits — Bernstein turns — man coming partly on at left f.g.

BERNSTEIN

Mr. Leland and Mr. Kane, they haven't spoken together for years.
Another man comes on

EDDIE

You don't suppose —

BERNSTEIN

There's nothing to suppose. Excuse me.
Bernstein hurries into office in b.g.

16–8	8.	*INT. ROOM CS* — camera shooting up over desk — Leland asleep, head on typewriter in f.g., bottle and glass by him — Bernstein coming in doorway in b.g., stops, comes to desk, shakes Leland — looks up worried
8–9	9.	*INT. OFFICE MCS* — Bernstein right f.g., behind Leland, asleep on desk — Kane in b.g. on other side — Bernstein turns, exits
10–10	10.	*INT. OFFICE CS* — camera shooting over desk — Leland asleep on typewriter in f.g. — Bernstein turning by door in b.g., talking — coming back to f.g.

BERNSTEIN

He ain't been drinking before, Mr. Kane. Never. We would have heard.

KANE *(Off)*

What does it say there?

6–2 11. *INT. OFFICE MCS* — Bernstein at right f.g. behind Leland, lying on typewriter — Kane standing on other side of desk, talks

KANE

The notice — what's he written?
Bernstein looks around

35–3 12. *INT. OFFICE CS* — Leland asleep on typewriter at right — Bernstein by him, looks at paper in typewriter, talks

BERNSTEIN

"Miss Susan Alexander, a pretty but hopelessly incompetent amateur . . .
He reads hesitatingly

BERNSTEIN

". . . last night opened the new Chicago Opera House in a performance of" — I still can't pronounce that name, Mr. Kane —

34–13 13. *INT. OFFICE MCS* — Bernstein leaning over, looking at paper in typewriter — Leland with head on it — Kane standing on other side

BERNSTEIN

"Her singing, happily, is no concern of this department. Of her acting, it is absolutely impossible to —"

KANE

Go on.

BERNSTEIN

That's all there is.
Kane reaches toward typewriter

5–5 14. *INT. OFFICE CS* — Leland asleep on typewriter — Bernstein standing at left — Kane's hand coming on in f.g., rips paper from typewriter, exits

19–7 15. *INT. OFFICE MCS* — Leland asleep on typewriter — Bernstein at right near f.g., leaning over — Kane on other side of desk, laughing — talks

KANE

Of her acting it is absolutely impossible to say anything except that in the opinion of this reviewer it represents a new low. Have you got that, Mr. Bernstein?

3–6 16. *INT. OFFICE CS* — Leland asleep on typewriter — Bernstein looking to f.g.

KANE *(Off)*

In the opinion of this reviewer —

BERNSTEIN

I didn't see that.

2–11 17. *INT. OFFICE MCS* — Bernstein at right of Leland — Kane standing in b.g., talking

KANE

It isn't here, Mr. Bernstein, I'm dictating it.

5–5 18. *INT. OFFICE CS* — Leland on typewriter — Bernstein at left, talks

BERNSTEIN

But Mr. Kane, I —

LENGTH FT. FRM.	SCENE NO.	

KANE *(Off)*

Get me a typewriter.

7–13   19.   *INT. OFFICE MCS* — Bernstein at right of Leland, asleep on typewriter — Kane in b.g., talking, smiling

KANE

I'm going to finish Mr. Leland's notice.

Lap Dissolve

5–4   20.   INSERT #3 — keys hitting paper in typewriter — spelling word W E A K

Lap Dissolve

66–   21.   *INT. OFFICE CS* — Leland with head on typewriter — sits up, blinking — bottle and glass by him — he looks around, puts cigar to mouth, looks to f.g. — Bernstein comes on left f.g. with match, lights cigar

LELAND

Hello, Bernstein. Hello.

BERNSTEIN

Hello, Mr. Leland.
Leland chuckles, looking around

LELAND

Where's my notice, Bernstein? I've got to finish my notice.

BERNSTEIN

Mr. Kane is finishing it for you.

LELAND

Charlie?
They look at door in b.g. — Leland rising

LELAND

Charlie — Charlie — out there?
Leland goes to door in b.g. — Bernstein leans back, exits

LELAND

Huh, I guess he's fixing it up.

40–3   22.   *INT. OFFICE CS* — camera shooting up to Leland, turning to f.g., talking

LELAND

I knew I'd never get that through.
Bernstein comes on at left

BERNSTEIN

Mr. Kane is finishing your review just the way you started it. He's writing a bad notice like you wanted it to be. I guess that'll show you.

Leland turns, goes through doorway into room in b.g.

58–5   23.   *INT. OFFICE LS* — Kane partly on, right f.g., typing — Leland coming from office in far b.g. — comes to f.g. — Bernstein in doorway in b.g. — Leland stops by railing at right — Kane glances up, talks

KANE

Hello, Jedediah.

LELAND

Hello, Charlie, I didn't know we were speaking.

KANE

Sure we're speaking, Jedediah. You're fired.
He swings carriage back, types — Leland staring at him

END OF REEL 5 — SECTION 5A

REEL 5 — SECTION 5B

Night Sequence

21–10   1.   *INT. ROOM CU* — Leland's face before camera — he turns to right b.g. — typewriter heard — music playing — he goes to b.g.

Lap Dissolve

195–   2.   *EXT. ROOF CS* (the images held in juxtaposition for a second) — Leland sitting at left, below camera — scene of editorial room at right, showing Kane sitting, typewriting — Bernstein in doorway in far b.g., watching

THOMPSON *(Off)*

Everybody knows that story, Mr. Leland, but why did he do it?
Scene of Kane in office fades out — light shining down on Leland

THOMPSON *(Off)*

How could a man write a notice like that when —
Leland smiles

LELAND

You just don't know Charlie. He thought that by finishing that notice he could show me he was an honest man. He was always trying to prove something. That whole thing about Susie being an opera singer, that was trying to prove something.
He leans forward, laughing — camera moves back slightly, showing Thompson partly on below at right f.g.

LELAND

You know what the headline was the day before the election? Candidate Kane found in love nest with quote singer unquote. He was going to take the quotes off the singer.
He calls to b.g.

LELAND

Hey, nurse!
He talks to Thompson

LELAND

Five years ago he wrote from that place down in the South, what's it called? Shangri-La? El Dorado? Sloppy Joe's? What's the name of that place? All right, Xanadu. I knew what it was all the time. You caught on, didn't you? I guess maybe I'm not as hard to see through as I think. Well, I never even answered his letter. Maybe I should have. I guess he was pretty lonely down there in that coliseum all those years. He hadn't finished it when she left him. He never finished it. He never finished anything, except my notice. Of course, he built the joint for her.

THOMPSON

That must have been love.
Nurse comes on in b.g. — comes toward them, stops

LELAND

Oh, I don't know. He was disappointed in the world, so he built one of his own, an absolute monarchy. It was something bigger than an opera house, anyway.
He turns, calls — another nurse coming to f.g.

395

LELAND

Nurse.

NURSE

Yes, Mr. Leland.

LELAND

Oh, I'm coming.
He leans toward Thompson

LELAND

Listen, young feller, there's one thing you can do for me.

THOMPSON

Sure.

LELAND

Stop at the cigar store on your way out, will you, and get me a couple of good cigars.

THOMPSON

I'll be glad to.

LELAND

Thank you.
Leland rises — camera pans — Thompson rising at left f.g.

LELAND

One is enough. You know, when I was a young man, there was an impression around that nurses were pretty. Well, it was no truer then than it is today.

NURSE

I'll take your arm, Mr. Leland.

LELAND

All right, all right. You won't forget about those cigars, will you?

THOMPSON

I won't.

LELAND

And have them wrapped up to look like toothpaste, or something, or they'll stop them at the desk. You know that young doctor I was telling you about — well, he's got an idea he wants to keep me alive.
Nurses take Leland by arm, take him to b.g. — music playing

Lap Dissolve

Day Sequence

25–7   3.   *EXT. BLDG. CU* — picture of Susan — camera pans upward, showing sign over building

"EL RANCHO"

Susan Alexander Kane
Camera moves up to sign, passes through it to skylight on top of building

Lap Dissolve

103–8   4.   *INT. ROOM MCS* — Thompson sitting at right f.g., talks to Susan sitting at table, drinking — music

THOMPSON

I'd rather you'd just talk. Anything that comes into your mind about yourself and Mr. Kane.

Susan puts glass down, simpering

SUSAN

You wouldn't want to hear a lot of what comes into my mind about myself and Mr. Charlie Kane. You know, maybe I shouldn't have ever sung for Charlie the first time I met him, but I did an awful lot of singing after that. To start with, I sang for teachers at a hundred bucks an hour. The teachers got that. I —

THOMPSON

What did you get?

SUSAN

I didn't get a thing except music lessons. That's all there was in it.

THOMPSON

He married you, didn't he?

SUSAN

He didn't mention anything about marriage until after it was all over, and until it got in the papers about it, and he lost the election, and that Norton woman divorced him. He was really interested in my voice. Why do you suppose he bought that opera house for? I didn't want it. I didn't want a thing. It was his idea. Everything was his idea, except my leaving him.

Lap Dissolve

Day Sequence

220–6   5.   *INT. ROOM LS* — camera shooting down — Susan at right f.g., singing — pianist and Matisti sitting at piano

SUSAN

Una voce poco fa
Qui nel cor mi ri-suo-nò
Il mio cor . . .
Matisti rises, singing — camera moving around piano closer to them

MATISTI

Il mio cor — don't forget — Ta-ta-ta, ta-ta-ta, ta-ta-ta, ta-ta-ta. Now, don't get nervous. Don't get nervous, please. Let's come back. Da capo—
Pianist plays — Matisti gestures, talks — Kane coming in doorway in b.g.

MATISTI

Look at me, Mrs. Kane — darling —
She sings — he talks in time with music

MATISTI

Now, get the voice out of the throat. Place the tone right in the mask — mmmmmm . . .

SUSAN *(Singing)*

Una voce poco fa
Qui nel cor mi ri-suo-nò
Il mio cor fe-ri-to è già . . .

MATISTI

Diaphram-a . . .

SUSAN *(Singing)*

E Lindoro fu che il piagò
Sì, Lindo —
Susan stops, breaking on high note — he gestures wildly, sings

MATISTI

La-la-la-la — you're out of pitch. La-la-la — Some people can sing. Some can't. Impossible. Impossible.
All look to b.g. as Kane in b.g. shouts at Matisti — coming toward them

KANE

It is not your job to give your opinion of Mrs. Kane's talents. You're supposed to train her voice, Signor Matisti.

MATISTI

Mr. Kane —

KANE

Nothing more. Please sit down and continue with the lessons.

MATISTI

But Mr. Kane —

KANE

Please.
Kane stopping by them

MATISTI

But I will be the laughing stock of the musical world. The people will think —

KANE

People will think. You're concerned with what people will think, Signor Matisti? I may be able to enlighten you a bit. I'm something of an authority about what people will think. The newspapers for example. I run several newspapers between here and San Francisco. It's all right, darling, Signor Matisti is going to listen to reason. Aren't you, signor?

MATISTI

How can I persuade you, Mr. Kane.

KANE

You can't.
Matisti turns, mumbling, sits down by pianist — pianist plays — Susan sings

SUSAN

Il mio cor fe-ri-to è già
E Lindoro fu che il piagò
Sì, Lindo —
She looks down, ending on false note — others look down

KANE

It's all right, darling, go ahead.
She sings — Kane smiling, talking to Matisti

SUSAN

Sì, Lindo-ro mio sa-rà
Lo giu-ra-i —

KANE

I thought you'd see it my way.

SUSAN

. . . la vin-ce-rò
E Lindo-ro mio sa-rà
Lo giu-ra-i, la vin-ce-rò

Lap Dissolve

Night Sequence

18–   6.   *INT. STAGE CU* — Susan singing, pained expression

SUSAN

Ah, cruel —
Matisti comes on at right, gesturing wildly

MATISTI

No, no, no, no, no.

PROMPTER

I should say not.
Others gathering around

MATISTI

You must wait for the chord.

PROMPTER

Wait for the chord.

MAID

Miss Alexander —

WOMAN

Please —
Man putting plumed hat on Susan — camera pans up to work light above — orchestra heard

MATISTI *(Singing)*

One . . . ah, cruel . . . one . . . ah, cruel . . .
One . . . ah, cruel . . .

46–1   7.   *INT. STAGE LS* — Susan posing — lights come on — curtain rises in b.g. — footlights appear — Susan begins to sing (NOTE: Words of song and translation given at end of this reel. Song running through scenes 8 to 30, inclusive)

7–   8.   *INT. THEATER CU* — Kane looking to f.g. — singing heard

7–11   9.   *INT. THEATER MLS* — camera shooting past man's head in f.g. to Susan on stage in b.g., singing — people behind her

7–13   10.   *INT. THEATER CS* — Leland looking at program — others partly on behind him — singing heard

10–11   11.   *INT. STAGE LS* — Susan by footlights, singing — lights seen in theater in b.g.

12–   12.   *INT. STAGE CS* — Susan's legs appear at right strutting to left past footlights, exits — Matisti and prompter in prompter's box in b.g. — singing heard

3–3   13.   *INT. THEATER CU* — Matisti closes one eye, listening — singing heard

11–6   14.   *INT. THEATER MCS* — Bernstein and men in box — others in b.g. — singing heard

Lap Dissolve

6–10   15.   *INT. STAGE MS* — Susan seated on furs, surrounded by members of the cast, singing

8–6   16.   *INT. THEATER CU* — man and Matisti looking to f.g. — Matisti motions, nodding — makes signs — singing heard

7–1   17.   *INT. THEATER MCU* — Bernstein and man in f.g. — he nods — others in b.g. — singing heard

7–9   18.   *INT. THEATER CS* — Leland tearing up program — others in b.g. — singing heard

7–11   19.   *INT. THEATER LS* — camera shooting past Kane, sitting partly on, right f.g. — Susan onstage in b.g., singing — cast around her

8–7   20.   *INT. THEATER CU* — Kane looking to f.g. — glances to right — singing heard — laughter and indistinct talking heard

WOMAN'S VOICE

Perfectly dreadful . . .

11–4   21.   *INT. STAGE CU* — Susan singing — music heard

7–15   22.   *INT. THEATER CU* — Kane looks forward grimly — singing, laughter and music heard

9–9   23.   *INT. THEATER MCU* — Matisti behind lights, motions, hand to mouth — man at left by him — singing heard

6–13   24.   *INT. THEATER CS* — Leland sitting with torn program, blows on it — others behind — music and singing heard

8–7   25.   *INT. THEATER MCU* — two behind lights — Matisti turning, waving arms, biting fingers — singing heard

4–6   26.   *INT. THEATER CS* — Susan gesturing dramatically, singing — others in b.g.

9–7   27.   *INT. THEATER MCU* — two behind lights — Matisti jumping up and down — whispers to man by him — singing and music heard

5–1   28.   *INT. THEATER CU* — Susan finishes singing, raising her arms above her head in a grand gesture — music

3–14   29.   *INT. THEATER CU* — Kane looking to f.g. — singing heard — Susan holding note — music

3–13   30.   *INT. THEATER LS* — camera shooting past Kane partly on, left f.g., watching Susan and cast in b.g. onstage — Susan stops singing, sinks down dramatically — music

7–1   31.   *INT. THEATER CS* — Leland waving torn program — others behind him, applaud slightly

4–14   32.   *INT. THEATER MCS* — Bernstein and men in box applauding — light applause heard — people rising in b.g.

(Words of song — and translation — sung through scenes 8 to 30 inclusive)

Ah! Cruel, tu m'as trop entendu!
Les Dieux m'en sont témoins,
Ces Dieux qui dans mon flanc
Ont allumés le feu fatal à tout mon sang.

Dites-moi comment que j'expie! Ce péché si fort
Toujours m'emplit.
Je ne peux pas résister encore.
Oh, Dieux, arrachez-moi.
Ces feux fatals allument ma mort.

Voilà mon coeur, voilà mon coeur
C'est là que ta main doit frapper
Voilà mon coeur, frappe
Prête-moi ton épée, frappe.

Ah, cruel man, you have heard me all too long!
The gods are my witnesses,
Those gods who in my sides
Have lit the fatal fire which runs through my blood.

Tell me how to atone! This great sin
Always engulfs me.
I can stand it no longer.
Oh, gods, pull me away.
These fatal fires light my death.

Here is my heart, here is my heart
Here is where your hand must strike
Here is my heart, strike
Lend me your sword, strike.

END OF REEL 5 — SECTION 5B

REEL 6 — SECTION 6A

Night Sequence

11–13   1.   *INT. THEATER CU* — Kane seated in box, looking grimly to f.g. — applause heard — camera moves back, showing others in box applauding

3–4   2.   *INT. THEATER MLS* — camera shooting past Kane, partly on at left f.g., looking down at stage — flowers below — light applause heard

10–12   3.   *INT. THEATER CU* — Kane looking to f.g. — light applause heard — he glances around slightly, applauds

3–7   4.   *INT. THEATER MLS* — camera shooting down to flowers onstage — Susan comes out from behind curtains, right b.g. — applause heard

4–10   5.   *INT. THEATER CU* — Kane applauding loudly — others heard applauding

5–8   6.   *INT. THEATER MLS* — camera shooting down to Susan onstage — flowers around — others move up

3–7   7.   *INT. THEATER CU* — Kane rising, applauding — camera tilts up, following him

4–12   8.   *INT. THEATER MLS* — camera shooting down to Susan — flowers around — she backs away to right b.g. with rose, exits behind curtains — light applause heard

17–   9.   *INT. THEATER CU* — camera shooting up to Kane, now applauding alone — house lights come on — he stops applauding abruptly — looks around

Lap Dissolve

Day Sequence

2–14   10.   INSERT #1 — article in newspaper —

STAGE VIEWS
by
JED LELAND
(Picture of Leland)

SUSAN *(Off)*

Stop telling me he's your friend.

5–11   11.   INSERT #2 — article in newspaper — shadow on paper at right — headline reads:

APPLAUSE LAVISHED ON SUSAN ALEXANDER FOR RENDITION

SUSAN *(Off)*

A friend don't write that kind of review.
Hand turns paper violently

SUSAN *(Off)*

All these other . . .

3–9   12.   *INT. ROOM MCU* — camera shooting down at Susan, raving

SUSAN

. . . papers panning me, I could expect that . . .

4–15   13.   *INT. ROOM MCU* — Kane sitting in chair, holding paper — pipe in mouth, frowning

SUSAN *(Off)*

. . . but for the "Inquirer" to run a thing like that . . .
Knocking heard

SUSAN *(Off)*

. . . spoiling my . . .

8–8   14.   *INT. ROOM LS* — Kane seated at left f.g., folding paper — Susan sitting on floor at right b.g., raving — papers on floor around her — knocking heard

SUSAN

. . . whole debut . . .
She looks to b.g., yells

SUSAN

Come in.
Kane rises

KANE

I'll get it.
He goes to b.g. — Susan raving

SUSAN

Friend! Not the kind of friends I know . . .

3–9   15.   *INT. ROOM MS* — Susan sitting on floor, raving — papers around her

SUSAN

. . . but, of course, I'm not high-class like you . . .

7–2   16.   *INT. ROOM MS* — Kane going to door in b.g. — knocking heard

SUSAN *(Off)*

. . . and I never went to any swell schools . . .
He turns by door

KANE

That'll be enough, Susan.
He opens door — boy comes in with message — Kane takes it

KANE

Yes?

BOY

From Mr. Leland, sir.

KANE

Leland?

1–15   17.   *INT. ROOM MCS* — Susan sitting on floor, talks angrily — papers around her

SUSAN

Jed Leland.

BOY *(Off)*

He wanted me to . . .

10–1   18.   *INT. ROOM MLS* — Susan sitting on floor at right f.g. — Kane and boy at doorway in b.g. — boy talking

BOY

. . . make sure you got this personally.

KANE

Thanks.

BOY

Yes, sir.
Boy goes out, exits — Kane closing door — comes to f.g.

SUSAN

Is that something from him?
She exits as camera pans to left, following Kane to left f.g.

2–10   19.   *INT. ROOM MCU* — Susan sitting on floor, screams

SUSAN

Charlie —

9–   20.   *INT. ROOM MCS* — Kane coming to left f.g., opening envelope — camera shooting up from floor, follows him to the left f.g. — he stops before fireplace, opening up letter

SUSAN *(Off)*

As for you, you ought to have your head examined. Sending him a letter telling . . .

5–5   21.   *INT. ROOM MCU* — Susan talking angrily

SUSAN

. . . him he's fired with a twenty-five thousand dollar check in it.

24–10   22.   *INT. ROOM CS* — camera shooting up from floor to Kane taking paper from envelope

SUSAN *(Off)*

What kind of firing do you call that?
Kane takes pieces of check from envelope, scattering them on floor

SUSAN *(Off)*

You did send him a check for twenty-five thousand dollars, didn't you?
He looks down, crumpling envelope, drops it

KANE

Yes, I sent him a check for twenty-five thousand dollars.
He opens other paper, looks at it

6–2   23.   *INT. ROOM MLS* — camera shooting down past Kane, standing partly on, left f.g., to Susan sitting on floor in b.g. — papers around her — Kane's hand opening up his Declaration — Susan talks

SUSAN

What's that?

2–15   24.   *INT. ROOM CS* — camera shooting up to Kane, looking at paper — he talks quietly

KANE

A Declaration of Principles.

1–2   25.   *INT. ROOM MS* — Susan sitting on floor, looking up to f.g., talks

SUSAN

What?

1–8   26.   *INT. ROOM MCS* — camera shooting up at Kane, looking at paper — he looks down to f.g.

KANE

Hmm?

SUSAN *(Off)*

What . . .

1– 27. *INT. ROOM MCU* — Susan talking

SUSAN

. . . is it?

10–13 28. *INT. ROOM MCU* — camera shooting up to Kane, looking down to right f.g. — he looks at paper, talks

KANE

An antique.

13–10 29. *INT. ROOM MCU* — Susan shouting angrily

SUSAN

You're awful funny, aren't you? Well, I can tell you one thing you're not going to keep on being funny about, and that's my singing. I'm through.

8–5 30. *INT. ROOM MCS* — camera shooting up to Kane, standing before fireplace, looking at paper — he tears it up

SUSAN *(Off)*

I never wanted to do it in the first place.
Kane talks quietly

KANE

You'll continue with your singing, Susan.

4–11 31. *INT. ROOM MCU* — camera shooting up to Kane as he talks, tearing up paper

KANE

I don't propose to have myself made ridiculous.

5–8 32. *INT. ROOM MLS* — camera shooting down past Kane, partly on, left f.g., tearing up paper, to Susan sitting in b.g among papers — she rises, talking

SUSAN

You don't propose to have yourself made ridiculous!

7–6 33. *INT. ROOM CU* — Susan looking to f.g., screaming

SUSAN

What about me? I'm the one that's got to do the singing. I'm the one that gets the razzberries.

6–2 34. *INT. ROOM MCU* — camera shooting up to Kane as he tears up paper

SUSAN *(Off)*

Oh, why don't you let me alone?
He throws papers down, takes pipe from mouth, yells

KANE

My reasons satisfy me, Susan.

9–8 35. *INT. ROOM MCS* — camera shooting up at Kane, standing at left before fireplace, stuffing hands in pocket, talking

KANE

You seem unable to understand them.

LENGTH	SCENE
FT. FRM.	NO.

He comes forward, looking down to f.g., angrily

KANE

I will not tell them to you again.

6–10   36.   *INT. ROOM CU* — Susan staring up to left f.g. — shadow of Kane covers her face — her eyes shining, terrified

KANE *(Off)*

You'll continue your singing.

10–6   37.   *INT. ROOM MCU* — Kane partly on at left f.g. — his shadow covering Susan, kneeling at right, terrified — she sinks back to right, staring up at him

Lap Dissolve

61–10   38.   TRANSITION — Susan heard singing — other voices singing with her

Headline of Washington "Inquirer": WASHINGTON OVATION FOR SUSAN ALEXANDER — BRILLIANT DIVA ESTABLISHED AS OPERATIC STAR — scene of audience and spotlight superimposed over it

Lap Dissolve

Front page of newspaper: SUSAN ALEXANDER OPENS SAN FRANCISCO OPERA SEASON — Susan at right in costume, moving around

Lap Dissolve

Heading of San Francisco "Inquirer" — series of superimposed shots showing audience — spotlight — newspaper — Matisti in box; making signs — Susan onstage, arms upraised; singing

Lap Dissolve

Heading of St. Louis "Inquirer": ST. LOUIS DEBUT SCHEDULED FOR SUSAN ALEXANDER — series of superimposed shots showing audience — spotlight — Susan onstage — newspaper — prompter — Susan picking up flowers — lights flashing

Lap Dissolve

Heading of Detroit "Inquirer": DETROIT HAS "SELL-OUT" FOR SUSAN ALEXANDER — series of scenes superimposed showing newspaper — audience — prompter — flashlight — Susan singing

Lap Dissolve

Heading of New York "Inquirer": NEW YORK IN FUROR FOR SUSAN ALEXANDER — series of superimposed scenes showing audience — Susan — flashlight — Susan Kane — Susan — prompter — flashlight — Susan Kane — flashlight — Susan's voice dying out as transition. Kleig light suddenly shuts off

Fade Out

Night Sequence

80–   39.   *Fade In* — *INT. BEDROOM MLS* — camera shooting over bed to door in b.g. — knocking heard — Susan's head in f.g. by tray — Susan heard wheezing — pounding head — door in b.g. flies open, Kane and man rush in, stop — come to Susan — Kane kneels by bed, turns her head around — turns, talking

KANE

Get Dr. Corey.
Man goes to b.g., exits into hall

Lap Dissolve

59–11   40.   *INT. ROOM CU* — satchel before camera, hand closing it — removes it, showing Susan in bed — nurse on other side, kneeling by her

DOCTOR *(Off)*

She'll be perfectly all right in a day or two, Mr. Kane.
Nurse rises, showing Kane sitting at table behind her — nurse goes to b.g. — Susan wheezing — Kane holding bottle, talks — doctor coming on at right to him — nurse turning in b.g.

KANE

I can't imagine how Mrs. Kane came to make such a foolish mistake. The sedative

405

Dr. Wagner gave her was in a somewhat larger bottle. I guess the strain of preparing for the new opera has excited and confused her.

DOCTOR

Yes, I'm sure that's it.
He goes to nurse in b.g.

KANE

No objection to my staying here with her, is there?

DOCTOR

No, not at all. I'd like the nurse to be here, too. Good-bye, Mr. Kane.
He goes out doorway in b.g., exits — Kane looking at bottle

Lap Dissolve

10–5   41.   *INT. ROOM CS* — Kane seated, looking down to left f.g., grimly

Lap Dissolve

15–   42.   *INT. ROOM LS* — Susan in bed at left center — Kane sitting in b.g. by bed — lights shining in windows in b.g.

Lap Dissolve

61–11   43.   *INT. ROOM CU* — Susan's head on pillow, perspiration on face — she turns to f.g. weakly, opening eyes — Kane leans on in f.g. — she talks — music heard (hurdy-gurdy)

SUSAN

Charlie — I couldn't make you see how I felt, Charlie, but I couldn't go through with that thing again. You don't know what it means to feel that the whole audience doesn't want you.

KANE

That's when you got to fight them.

24–3   44.   *INT. ROOM MCU* — Susan partly on in f.g. — Kane leaning over her from b.g., grimly — talks, smiles

KANE

All right, you won't have to fight them any more. It's their loss.

10   45.   *INT. ROOM CU* — Kane partly on in f.g. — Susan on pillow, looking up, smiles weakly

Fade Out

Night Sequence

12–7   46.   *Fade In* — *EXT. XANADU LS* — camera shooting up mountain — lights lit — castle above — music playing

Lap Dissolve

5–   47.   *EXT. CASTLE MLS* — camera shooting up to castle on mountaintop — music heard

Lap Dissolve

3–7   48.   *INT. ROOM CU* — Susan on at a table, doing a jigsaw puzzle

KANE (*Off*)

What are you doing?
Camera moves back — Susan looks around to f.g. sullenly

4–6   49.   *INT. ROOM LS* — Kane coming through archway in b.g. — talks — music

SUSAN

Jigsaw puzzles.

12–3   50.   *INT. ROOM CS* — Susan sitting at left, puzzle before her — she leans on table, looking to f.g., talks

SUSAN

Charlie, what time is it?

144–   51.   *INT. ROOM LS* — Kane walking forward, talks — echoes heard — camera following him to right
— music

KANE

Eleven-thirty.

SUSAN *(Off)*

In New York.

KANE

Huh?

SUSAN *(Off)*

I said what time is it in New York.

KANE

Eleven-thirty.

SUSAN *(Off)*

At night?

KANE

Um-hmm.
He stops by enormous fireplace — Susan sitting at right near f.g. by table and puzzle

KANE

The bulldog's just gone to press.

SUSAN

Well, hurray for the bulldog.
He stops by her, picks up piece of puzzle

SUSAN

Gee, eleven-thirty. The shows're just getting out. People are going to nightclubs and
restaurants. Of course, we're different because we live in a palace.

KANE

You always said you wanted to live in a palace.

SUSAN

A person could go crazy in this dump. Nobody to talk to, nobody to have any fun with.

KANE

Susan —

SUSAN

Forty-nine thousand acres of nothing but scenery and statues. I'm lonesome.

KANE

Till just yesterday we've had no less than fifty of your friends at any one time. I think
if you'll look carefully in the west wing, Susan, you'll probably find a dozen vacationists still in residence.

SUSAN

You make a joke out of everything.
He goes to fireplace in b.g.

SUSAN

Charlie, I want to go to New York. I'm tired of being a hostess. I wanta have fun. Please, Charlie. Charles, please!

KANE

Our home is here, Susan. I don't care to visit New York.

Lap Dissolve

Night Sequence

29–5   52.   TRANSITION — music playing

Int. Room CS — Susan's hands fitting pieces of puzzle —

Lap Dissolve

Int. Room CU — Susan's hands putting last pieces into center of puzzle

Lap Dissolve

Int. Room CS — camera shooting down at Susan's hands putting pieces into puzzle

Lap Dissolve

Int. Room CU — Susan's hands fitting pieces into puzzle

Lap Dissolve

Int. Room CU — Susan's hands at left, fitting pieces into puzzle

Lap Dissolve

Int. Room CS — Susan's hands at right, fitting pieces into puzzle

Lap Dissolve

14–6   53.   *INT. HALL LS* — Kane coming down grand staircase from above — music — he comes down to right f.g. — camera pans — he stops, looks at Susan on floor before fireplace in far b.g., working puzzle — he talks, his voice sounds very hollow and distant, as if in an echo chamber

KANE

What are you doing?

4–6   54.   *INT. HALL MS* — Susan sitting on floor, puzzle before her — she looks to f.g. sullenly

10–2   55.   *INT. HALL MLS* — Kane looking at Susan before fireplace in b.g. — he steps down to right, talks

KANE

Oh.

He exits right, talking

KANE *(Off)*

One thing I can never understand, Susan, how do you know you haven't done them before?

6–   56.   *INT. HALL MCS* — Susan sitting on floor — puzzle before her — she looks off to left, talking bitterly

SUSAN

It makes a whole lot more sense than collecting statues.

END OF REEL 6 — SECTION 6A

REEL 6 — SECTION 6B

Night Sequence

13–1   1.   *INT. HALL LS* — Susan sitting in f.g. — Kane walking in b.g. — stops by chair, talks, sitting down

KANE

You may be right. I sometimes wonder, but you get into the habit.

5–4   2.   *INT. HALL MCS* — Susan sitting on floor, working puzzle, talks

SUSAN

It's not a habit. I do it because I like it.

LENGTH FT. FRM.	SCENE NO.	
6–12	3.	*INT. HALL LS* — Susan partly on, left f.g. — Kane seated in b.g., talks

KANE

I thought we might have a picnic tomorrow, Susan.

SUSAN

Huh?

KANE

I thought we might have a picnic tomorrow . . .

| 19–15 | 4. | *INT. HALL MCS* — Susan looks up to f.g. |

KANE *(Off)*

Invite everybody to spend the night at the Everglades.
She throws pieces of puzzle down

SUSAN

Invite everybody! Order everybody, you mean, and make them sleep in tents. Who wants to sleep in tents when they've got a nice room of their own, with their own bath, where they know where everything is?

| 10– | 5. | *INT. HALL LS* — Kane talks to Susan, sitting on floor before fireplace in b.g. |

KANE

I thought we might have a picnic tomorrow, Susan.

Lap Dissolve

Day Sequence

| 11– | 6. | *INT. CAR MCU* — Susan and Kane riding in back seat — cars seen following through window in b.g. — music — Susan talks |

SUSAN

You never give me anything I really care about.
Kane glances at her

Lap Dissolve

| 10– | 7. | *EXT. BEACH LS* — line of cars going to b.g. — music |

Lap Dissolve

| 46–6 | 8. | *EXT. CAMP CU* — colored man singing — music |

SINGER

It can't be love . . .
He turns, goes to b.g., singing — camera moving back, showing couples dancing

SINGER

For there is no true love
I know I've played at the game
Like a moth in a blue flame
Lost in the end just the same . . .
Camera follows Raymond walking slowly across to left — people before tent — singing heard — man passes cook at barbecue pit — camera moves up to pit

SINGER *(Off)*

All these years
My heart's been floatin' 'round
In a puddle of tears, hmm.
I wonder what it is . . .

Lap Dissolve

5–4   9.   *INT. TENT MLS* — Susan sitting at right f.g., back to camera, talking — Kane seated in chair in b.g. — singing heard very indistinctly

SUSAN

Oh, sure, you give me things, but that don't mean anything to you.

15–3   10.   *INT. TENT CU* — Kane slouched down in chair, talks — singing heard very indistinctly

KANE

You're in a tent, darling, we're not at home. I can hear you very well if you speak in a normal tone of voice.

SUSAN (Off)

What's the difference between giving . . .

4–14   11.   *INT. TENT CU* — Susan talking loudly — singing heard indistinctly

SUSAN

. . . me a bracelet or giving somebody else a hundred thousand dollars . . .

7–7   12.   *INT. TENT CU* — Kane slouched down in chair

SUSAN (Off)

. . . for a statue you're going to keep crated up and never even look at?
Kane glances down, lips moving slightly

SUSAN (Off)

It's just money. It doesn't mean anything.

3–5   13.   *INT. TENT CU* — Susan talking — singing heard indistinctly

SUSAN

You never really gave me anything that really belonged to . . .

5–2   14.   *INT. TENT CU* — Kane moving lips — singing heard indistinctly

SUSAN (Off)

. . . you, that you care about.
Kane talks quietly

KANE

Susan, I want you to stop this.

SUSAN (Off)

I'm not going . . .

8–   15.   *INT. TENT CU* — Susan shouting hysterically — singing heard indistinctly

SUSAN

. . . to stop it.

KANE (Off)

Right now.

SUSAN

You never gave me anything in your life. You just tried to buy me into giving . . .

4–7   16.   *INT. TENT CU* — Kane sitting up in chair — singing heard indistinctly

SUSAN *(Off)*

. . . you something.
Kane rises

KANE

Susan!
He glares down to f.g. angrily

2–7   17.   *INT. TENT CU* — Susan looking up to left f.g., terrified — music — indistinct singing heard

12–2   18.   *EXT. CAMP MS* — colored man singing — musicians playing — people in b.g. keeping time to music

SINGER

It can't be love . . .

4–8   19.   *INT. TENT CS* — Susan sitting before camera — Kane standing, looking down at her — indistinct singing heard — music

6–   20.   *INT. TENT CU* — Susan staring up to left f.g. — singing heard indistinctly

5–7   21.   *INT. TENT CS* — Susan before camera — indistinct singing heard — Kane standing, looking menacingly down at her, talks

KANE

Whatever I do, I do because I love you.

11–1   22.   *INT. TENT CU* — Susan looking up to left f.g., talks — indistinct singing heard

SUSAN

You don't love me. You want me to love you. Sure, I'm Charles Foster Kane.

4–1   23.   *INT. TENT CS* — Susan seated before camera — Kane looking down at her — indistinct singing heard — Susan talking

SUSAN

Whatever you want, just name it and it's yours.

3–13   24.   *INT. TENT CU* — Susan looking up to left f.g., talking — music

SUSAN

But you gotta love me.
Kane's hand slaps her — she cringes back

5–3   25.   *INT. TENT CS* — Susan in f.g., cringing — Kane standing, looking down at her — music and laughter heard

4–5   26.   *INT. TENT CU* — Susan looking up to left, talks

SUSAN

Don't tell me you're sorry.

7–10   27.   *INT. TENT CS* — Susan in f.g., back to camera — Kane standing, looking down at her, talks

KANE

I'm not sorry.

5–6   28.   *INT. TENT CU* — Susan looking up to left f.g., sullenly — laughter and indistinct talking heard

Lap Dissolve

Day Sequence

33–10   29.   *INT. HALL MCS* — Raymond crossing past stained glass windows to right b.g. — camera pans to right — he goes to b.g. — Kane coming down steps in b.g., passes him to f.g. — Raymond following him to f.g., talking

RAYMOND

Mr. Kane, Mrs. Kane would like to see you, sir.
They stop in f.g.

RAYMOND

Marie has been packing her since morning.
Kane exits right f.g.

Lap Dissolve

17–   30.   *INT. HALL CU* — Kane in f.g., opening door, showing Susan and maid in room in b.g. — Susan talks

SUSAN

Tell Arnold I'm ready, Marie. Tell him he can get the bags.

MARIE

Yes, madame.
Maid hurries to f.g., exits right f.g. — Kane going into room, talks, swinging door shut

KANE

Have you gone completely crazy?

50–4   31.   *INT. ROOM MS* — camera shooting up past open bag to Kane, coming to left f.g. — stops — talking

KANE

Don't you know that our guests, everyone here, will know about this?
He crosses to left — camera pans with him to Susan — doll in f.g. before camera

KANE

You've packed your bags, you've sent for the car.

SUSAN

And left you? Of course they'll hear. I'm not saying good-bye, except to you, but I never imagined that people wouldn't know.

KANE

I won't let you go.
Susan crosses to right — camera pans — he stops by her, pulling her close to him

SUSAN

Good-bye, Charlie.
She pushes him away — exits right — he calls

KANE

Susan!

3–3   32.   *INT. ROOM MLS* — camera shooting past open bag in f.g., to Susan going to door in b.g. — she stops, looks around

45–7   33.   *INT. ROOM MLS* — Susan partly on, right f.g., looking at Kane in b.g. — he comes forward, stops, talks

KANE

Please don't go. Please, Susan.
He comes closer to her

KANE

From now on, everything will be exactly the way you want it to be, not the way I think you want it, but your way. Susan —

2–10   34.   *INT. ROOM MCU* — Kane partly on, left f.g. — Susan at left by door, smiling slightly

15–9   35.   *INT. ROOM MCU* — Susan partly on, right f.g. — Kane facing her, talking

KANE

You mustn't go. You can't do this to me.

28–7   36.   *INT. ROOM MCU* — Kane partly on, left f.g. — Susan by door, staring — talks

SUSAN

I see, it's you that this is being done to. It's not me at all. Not what it means to me. I can't do this to you. Oh, yes, I can.

2–1   37.   *INT. ROOM MCU* — Susan partly on, right f.g. — Kane facing her, stares

10–4   38.   *INT. ROOM MCU* — Kane partly on, left f.g. — Susan by door — turns, opens it, goes out, exits — Kane pulls door open, watching Susan go through hall to b.g.

4–   39.   *INT. ROOM MCU* — Kane in doorway, staring to f.g.

9–10   40.   *INT. ROOM MCU* — Kane partly on, left f.g. — Susan going through hall in b.g. — opens door, goes out

Lap Dissolve

Dawn Sequence

74–6   41.   *INT. ROOM CS* — two sitting at table — Thompson in f.g., lighting Susan's cigarette — camera moves back from them slightly — Susan talks

SUSAN

In case you never knew it, I lost all my money and it was plenty, believe me.

THOMPSON

The last ten years have been tough on a lot of people.

SUSAN

Aw, they haven't been tough on me. I just lost all my money. So you're going down to Xanadu?

THOMPSON

Yes, Monday with some of the boys from the office. Mr. Rawlston wants the whole place photographed, all that art stuff. We run a picture magazine, you know.

SUSAN

Yes, I know. Look, if you're smart, you'll get in touch with Raymond. He's the butler. You'll learn a lot from him. He knows where all the bodies are buried.

THOMPSON

You know, all the same I feel kind of sorry for Mr. Kane.
She looks at him, surprised

SUSAN

Don't you think I do?
She drains glass, stares up, pulling coat collar around herself

SUSAN

Oh, what do you know, it's morning already.
Camera moves back and up from them — light shining — music playing

SUSAN

Come around and tell me the story of your life sometime.

Lap Dissolve

6–   42.   *EXT. ROOF MS* — camera moving back from skylight — moves back through sign on roof — music

Lap Dissolve

5–   43.   *EXT. GATE CU* — letter "K" atop the gate at Xanadu

Lap Dissolve

Late Afternoon Sequence

34–   44.   INT. ROOM CU — Raymond lighting cigarette, talks

RAYMOND

Rosebud?

Camera moves back slowly, showing Thompson partly on, right f.g.

RAYMOND

I'll tell you about Rosebud, Mr. Thompson. How much is it worth to you, a thousand dollars?
Raymond steps down to left — camera pans, following him — he stops on grand staircase, looks up to f.g.

THOMPSON (Off)

Okay.

Thompson comes on at right f.g., stepping down by Raymond — Raymond turns

RAYMOND

Well, I'll tell you, Mr. Thompson . . .

43–10   45.   INT. HALL MLS — two men above on steps — they come down to f.g. — Raymond talking

RAYMOND

He acted kind of funny sometimes, you know.

THOMPSON

No, I didn't.

RAYMOND

Yes, he did crazy things sometimes.
They stop on steps in f.g.

RAYMOND

I've been working for him eleven years now, in charge of the whole place, so I ought to know.
Raymond steps down to left — Thompson follows — camera following

RAYMOND

Rosebud.

THOMPSON

Yes.
Camera follows Raymond down to crypt at left — he puts out cigarette — Thompson coming on in f.g., going to him

RAYMOND

Well, like I tell you, the old man acted kind of funny sometimes, but I knew how to handle him.

THOMPSON

Need a lot of service?

RAYMOND

Yeh, but I knew how to handle him. Like that time his wife left him.

Lap Dissolve

Day Sequence

11–10   46.   EXT. VERANDA MS — cockatoo in f.g., Raymond in b.g. — cockatoo shrieks and flies away —

LENGTH FT. FRM.	SCENE NO.	

Susan comes out of doorway at right, crosses to left, exits — Raymond watches, begins to cross to doorway in b.g.

6–5   47. *INT. HALL LS* — camera shooting through hall, showing Kane in doorway in far b.g.— Raymond comes on left f.g., stops

11–4   48. *INT. HALL MCU* — Kane staring to f.g., turns slowly

35–9   49. *INT. ROOM CS* — camera shooting up at Kane turning — staggers toward b.g. — looks around — looks at open bag on bed, closes it — picks it up

27–12   50. *INT. ROOM MS* — Kane slams bag across to right — picks up another, throws it to right — goes to bed, picks up another bag, throws it down — tears bedspread from bed — tearing down canopy

28–9   51. *INT. ROOM MCS* — Kane tearing canopy from bed — turns, goes to b.g., knocking things from table — turns table over — slams things around — staggers wildly to f.g.

11–14   52. *INT. ROOM MLS* — Kane staggering wildly to f.g. — camera shooting up from floor — follows him to left f.g. — he pulls furniture from wall — goes to b.g.

66–12   53. *INT. ROOM MCS* — Kane staggering on at right, pulls books from case at left — throws vase — throws furniture — staggers to right b.g., pulling mirror from wall — staggers around — comes to right f.g. — camera moves back — he knocks things about — picks up crystal ball, goes slowly to b.g., stumbling, looking at ball

END OF REEL 6 — SECTION 6B

REEL 7

Day Sequence

17–4   1. *INT. ROOM CU* — Kane's hand holding glass globe — snow swirling around inside — Kane heard whispering

KANE (*Off*)

Rosebud.

Camera pans up to Kane's face as he stares down, tears in eyes

7–6   2. *INT. ROOM MLS* — Raymond coming slowly to f.g. — servants and guests crowded together in b.g. — Raymond stops in f.g.

46–15   3. *INT. ROOM CU* — Kane staring up to f.g., tears in eyes — music playing — he moves slowly to f.g. — camera follows him through doorway — bedroom behind him wrecked — he comes through doorway stiffly, passing Raymond — camera moves back, showing people around — Kane turns, goes to left, ignoring people — camera pans — he exits left b.g. — reflection of Kane seen in mirror as he crosses in b.g.

31–9   4. *INT. ROOM LS* — Kane moving slowly to f.g., dazed — group in hall in b.g. watching — music — camera pans to right as Kane comes to right f.g. — camera showing numerous reflections in mirrors as Kane passes to right — he passes camera, exits right — music stops

Lap Dissolve

Late Afternoon Sequence

61–9   5. *INT. ROOM CS* — Thompson partly on, right f.g. — Raymond facing him — leaning on corner of crypt — Thompson talks

THOMPSON

I see, and that's what you know about Rosebud.

RAYMOND

Yeh. I heard him say it that other time, too. He just said "Rosebud," then he dropped the glass ball and it broke on the floor. He didn't say anything after that, and I knew he was dead. He said all kinds of things that didn't mean anything.

THOMPSON

Sentimental fellow, aren't you?

RAYMOND

Umm, yes and no.

THOMPSON

Well, that isn't worth a thousand dollars.
Thompson crosses to left — camera pans — he starts down stairs — Raymond turns, talks

RAYMOND

You can keep on asking questions if you want to.
Thompson turns

THOMPSON

We're leaving tonight as soon as they're through taking pictures.
He goes downstairs to left b.g. — camera pans — photographer below

29–6   6.   *INT. HALL LS* — photographer in f.g. taking picture — Thompson coming down steps behind him — Raymond, up on steps above in b.g., calls down

RAYMOND

Allow yourself plenty of time.
Camera moving back through hall — Raymond following Thompson down

RAYMOND

The train stops at the junction on signal, but they don't like to wait.
Camera moving back, showing general activity of photographers, newspaper people — and others around — checking Kane's collection

GIRL

Number 9182.

RAYMOND

I can remember when they'd wait all day if Mr. Kane said so.

GIRL

Nativity . . .
Camera moving back past girl, partly on, with camera, left f.g., taking picture

BOY

Nativity . . .

MAN

Another picture.

BOY

Attributed Donatello, acquired Florence, 1921.

THOMPSON

Let's get going.

GIRL

I got it.

MAN

No good.

MAN

All right. Next. Take a picture of that.

GIRL

Okay.

ASSISTANT

Venus, fourth century, acquired 1911. Cost: twenty-three thousand.

ASSISTANT

Got it?

BOY *(Off)*

Hey!

6–2   7.   *INT. HALL LS* — camera shooting down to hall full of boxes, crates and statues — people around, looking up to camera

BOY *(Off)*

Can we come down?

ASSISTANT

Yeh, come on.

6–8   8.   *INT. HALL LS* — camera shooting up past Thompson's face, partly on, left f.g. — over packing cases, statues, etc., up to balcony — boy above waves, calls

BOY

Okay.

RAYMOND *(Off)*

How much do you think this is all worth . . .

51–   9.   *INT. HALL CU* — Raymond standing by packing case, looking up to left, talking — Thompson's silhouette on box in b.g.

RAYMOND

. . . Mr. Thompson?

THOMPSON

Millions . . .
They cross to left, passing men working

THOMPSON

. . . if anybody wants it.

RAYMOND

Well, at least he brought all this stuff to America.

SANTORO

What's that?

EDDIE

Another *Venus*.

BILL

Twenty-five thousand bucks. That's a lot of money to pay for a dame without a head.

DICK

Twenty-five thousand dollars.
Two come around to left f.g., passing men checking items

THOMPSON

Millions.

RAYMOND

The banks are out of luck, huh?

THOMPSON

Oh, I don't know. They'll clear all right.

O'CONNELL

He never threw anything away.
*Camera pans around to left, showing Walter reading inscription on loving cup —
Thompson and Raymond exit right — girl coming forward*

WALTER

"Welcome home, Mr. Kane, from 467 employees of the New York 'Inquirer.'"
Girl stops by stove — others around

HARRIET

One stove from the estate of Mary Kane, Little Salem, Colorado, value $2.00.

ALLAN

We're supposed to get everything, the junk as well as the art.

44–6   10.   *INT. HALL MLS* — men moving around — packing cases and statues in b.g. — one man crossing
to left, talks

WALTER

He sure liked to collect things, didn't he?
*Camera pans to left — men crossing — Thompson and Raymond come to left f.g. —
camera moving back, passing girl*

THOMPSON

Anything and everything.

RAYMOND

A regular crow, huh?
Girl follows two to f.g. — man following her

LOUISE

Hey, look, a jigsaw puzzle.

O'CONNELL

We got a lot of those.

WALTER

There's a Burmese temple and three Spanish ceilings down the hall.

KATHERINE

Yeh, all in crates.

HEUTNER

There's a part of a Scotch castle over there, but we haven't bothered to unwrap it yet. *Camera moving back as Thompson comes around to f.g., picking up coat — men and girls following*

WILSON

I wonder. You put all this stuff together, the palaces and the paintings and the toys and everything, what would it spell?
Thompson turns in f.g.

THOMPSON

Charles Foster Kane.

ALLAN

Or Rosebud. How about it, Jerry?
All laugh

KATHERINE

What's Rosebud?

92–11   11.   *INT. HALL CS* — Thompson in f.g. — group facing him — Raymond talks

RAYMOND

That's what he said when he died.
Camera moves back, showing others around

EDDIE

Did you ever find out what it means?

THOMPSON

No, I didn't.

WALTER

What did you find out about him, Jerry?

THOMPSON

Not much, really.
Thompson drops pieces of jigsaw puzzle into box — girl holding box — he takes box from her, comes to f.g., camera moving back

THOMPSON

We'd better get started.

WALTER

What have you been doing all this time?

THOMPSON

Playing with a jigsaw puzzle.

LOUISE

If you could have found out what Rosebud meant, I bet that would've explained everything.

THOMPSON

No, I don't think so. No. Mr. Kane was a man who got everything he wanted, and then lost it. Maybe Rosebud was something he couldn't get or something he lost. Anyway,

it wouldn't have explained anything. I don't think any word can explain a man's life. No, I guess Rosebud is just a piece in a jigsaw puzzle, a missing piece.
Thompson puts on coat — group following him toward f.g. below

THOMPSON
Well, come on, everybody, we'll miss the train.

Lap Dissolve

9–10   12.   *INT. HALL LS* — camera shooting down, showing hall packed with statues, boxes, etc. — Thompson and others coming to left f.g. — music playing

Lap Dissolve

Night Sequence

11–   13.   *INT. CELLAR LS* — camera shooting down over crates, statues and boxes, etc.

Lap Dissolve

76–9   14.   *INT. CELLAR LS* — camera shooting down over crates, etc. — it moves slowly over collection to b.g. — music — camera moving over iron bed — moves closer to belongings of Kane's mother — man comes on in b.g. — picks up sled — turns, exits

22–   15.   *INT. CELLAR MLS* — men throwing articles into furnace — Raymond in b.g., gesturing — talks — man coming on in f.g. with sled

RAYMOND
Throw that junk in, too.
Man goes to furnace — camera follows him — he turns, exits — camera moves up to furnace door, showing sled burning — lettering on it reads "Rosebud" . . .

Lap Dissolve

36–   16.   *INT. FURNACE CU* — sled burning — lettering on it reading "Rosebud" — letters burning off — camera moving up closer

Lap Dissolve

70–   17.   *EXT. MOUNTAIN MLS* — camera shooting up side of castle — smoke pouring out of chimney — camera moves up, following smoke — camera pans down to part of entrance gate — sign on it reading: NO TRESPASSING

Lap Dissolve

EXT. MOUNTAIN LS — castle above at right b.g. — part of entrance gate left f.g. — TITLE #1 fades in:

THE END

Fade Out

14–7   18.   *Fade In* — TITLE #2 — *music playing*

Most of the principal actors in CITIZEN KANE are new to motion pictures. The Mercury Theatre is proud to introduce them.

Fade Out

93–6   19.   *Fade In* — *EXT. HOSPITAL ROOF MCU* — Leland sitting, smiling — takes off sun visor, talking

LELAND
I guess I was what you nowadays call a stooge, huh.

TITLE #3:

JOSEPH COTTEN

Lap Dissolve

INT. ROOM MCU — Thompson partly on, right f.g. — Susan on other side of table at left, talking

SUSAN
Everything was his idea, except my leaving him.

TITLE #4:

DOROTHY COMINGORE

Lap Dissolve

LENGTH   SCENE
FT. FRM.   NO.

INT. ROOM CU — mother talking — Thatcher and father in b.g.

MOTHER

I've got his trunk all packed. I've had it packed for a week now.

TITLE #5:

AGNES MOOREHEAD

Lap Dissolve

INT. ROOM MCU — Emily looking over flowers to f.g., talks

EMILY

Sometimes I think I'd prefer a rival of flesh and blood.

TITLE #6:

RUTH WARRICK

Lap Dissolve

INT. ROOM MCU — Kane right f.g., back to camera — Gettys at left, talks

GETTYS

Only you're going to need more than one lesson. And you're going to get more than one lesson.

TITLE #7:

RAY COLLINS

Lap Dissolve

INT. ROOM CU — Carter looking off, sputtering

TITLE #8:

ERSKINE SANFORD

Lap Dissolve

INT. ROOM MCS — Thompson right f.g. — Bernstein at left — sitting on other side of desk, talking

BERNSTEIN

Who's a busy man, me? I'm chairman of the board. I got nothing but time. What do you want to know?

TITLE #9:

EVERETT SLOANE

THOMPSON

Well, Mr. Bernstein, we thought maybe — if we could find out what he meant by his last words — as he was dying . . .

TITLE #10:

WILLIAM ALLAND

Lap Dissolve

INT. HALL CS — Thompson partly on, right f.g. Raymond before him — Thompson talks

THOMPSON

Sentimental fellow, aren't you?

RAYMOND

Umm, yes and no.

TITLE #11:

PAUL STEWART

Lap Dissolve

INT. OFFICE MCU — Thatcher seated, reading newspaper

THATCHER

I think it would be fun to run a newspaper.
He looks around disgusted — music playing

THATCHER

I think it would be fun to run a newspaper.

TITLE #12:

GEORGE COULOURIS

Fade Out

80–15   20.   *Fade In* — TITLE #13 — music playing

And

Matisti . . . . .FORTUNIO BONANOVA
The headwaiter . . . . .GUS SCHILLING
Mr. Rawlston . . . . .PHILIP VAN ZANDT
Miss Anderson . . . . .GEORGIA BACKUS
Kane's father . . . . .HARRY SHANNON
Kane III . . . . .SONNY BUPP
Kane, age 8 . . . . .BUDDY SWAN
Kane . . . . .ORSON WELLES

Lap Dissolve

TITLE #14:

Music Composed and Conducted by
BERNARD HERRMANN

Special Effects by . . . . .VERNON L. WALKER, A.S.C.
Art Director . . . . .VAN NEST POLGLASE
   Associate . . . . .PERRY FERGUSON
Editing . . . . .ROBERT WISE
Recording . . . . { BAILEY FESLER
                                          { JAMES G. STEWART
Costumes . . . . .EDWARD STEVENSON

Distributed by R.K.O. Radio Pictures, Inc.

This picture made under the   Approved
  jurisdiction of I.A.T.S.E.   MPPDA
  Affiliated with American   Certificate
  Federation of Labor.   No. 6555

R C A
SOUND   SYSTEM

Copyright MCMXLI R.K.O. Radio Pictures, Inc.
All Rights Reserved

Lap Dissolve

TITLE #15:

Original Screenplay
HERMAN J. MANKIEWICZ
ORSON WELLES

Lap Dissolve

LENGTH	SCENE
FT. FRM.	NO.

TITLE #16:

ORSON WELLES
Direction — Production

GREGG TOLAND, A.S.C.
Photography

Fade Out

6–4   21.   *Fade In* — TITLE #17 — music playing

R.K.O.
RADIO
PICTURES
REG. U.S. PAT. OFF.

Fade Out

Appendix

The Credits of
Herman J. Mankiewicz

The Road to Mandalay. MGM, 1926.

    Director, Tod Browning. Story, Tod Browning and Herman J. Mankiewicz. Script, Elliott Clawson. With Lon Chaney, Lois Moran, Owen Moore, Henry B. Walthall, Sojin.

Stranded in Paris. Paramount. 1926.

    Director, Arthur Rosson. From the play *Jennie's Escape* by Hans Bachwitz and Fritz Jakobstetter. Adaptation, Herman J. Mankiewicz and John McDermott. Script, Ethel Doherty and Louise Long. With Bebe Daniels, James Hall, Ford Sterling.

Fashions for Women. Paramount, 1927.

    Director, Dorothy Arzner. From the play *The Girl of the Hour* by Gladys B. Unger, from the French story by Paul Armont and Leopold Marchand. Adaptation, Herman J. Mankiewicz and Jules Furthman. Script, Percy Heath. With Esther Ralston, Raymond Hatton, Einar Hanson.

The City Gone Wild. Paramount, 1927.

    Director, James Cruze. Script, Charles and Jules Furthman. Titles, Herman J. Mankiewicz. With Thomas Meighan, Marietta Millner, Louise Brooks.

Figures Don't Lie. Paramount, 1927.

    Director, Edward Sutherland. Script, Ethel Doherty and Louise Long. Titles, Herman J. Mankiewicz. With Esther Ralston, Richard Arlen, Ford Sterling.

The Gay Defender. Paramount, 1927.

    Director, Gregory La Cava. Original story, Ray Harris and Sam Mintz. Script, Kenneth Raisback. Titles, George Marion, Jr. and Herman J. Mankiewicz. With Richard Dix, Thelma Todd.

A Gentleman of Paris. Paramount, 1927.

    Director, Harry D'Arrast. From *Bellamy the Magnificent* by Ray Horniman. Adaptation, Benjamin Glazer. Script, Chandler Sprague. Titles, Herman J. Mankiewicz. With Adolphe Menjou, Shirley O'Hare, Arlette Marchal.

Honeymoon Hate. Paramount, 1927.

    Director, Luther Reed. From an original story by Alice M. Williamson. Adaptation, Doris Anderson. Script, Ethel Doherty. Titles, George Marion, Jr. and Herman J. Mankiewicz. With Florence Vidor, Tullio Carminati, William Austin.

The Spotlight. Paramount, 1927.

    Director, Frank Tuttle. From the story *Footlights* by Rita Weidman. Script, Hope Loring. Titles, Herman J. Mankiewicz. With Esther Ralston, Neil Hamilton.

Two Flaming Youths. Paramount, 1927.

    Director, John Waters. Script, Percy Heath and Donald Davis. Titles, Herman J. Mankiewicz. With W. C. Fields, Chester Conklin.

Avalanche. Paramount, 1928.

> Director, Otto Brower. From a story by Zane Grey. Script, Herman J. Mankiewicz, J. W. Rubin, and Sam Mintz. Titles, Herman J. Mankiewicz. With Jack Holt, Doris Hill, Olga Baclanova, John Darrow.

Abie's Irish Rose. Paramount, 1928.

> Director, Victor Fleming. From the play by Anne Nichols. Script, Jules Furthman. Titles, Herman J. Mankiewicz and Julian Johnson. With Jean Hersholt, Charles Rogers, Nancy Carroll.

The Barker. 1st National, 1928.

> Director George Fitzmaurice. Script, Benjamin Glazer. Titles, Herman J. Mankiewicz. Dialogue, Joseph Jackson. With Milton Sills, Betty Compson, Dorothy Mackaill, Douglas Fairbanks, Jr.

The Big Killing. Paramount, 1928.

> Director, F. Richard Jones. Script, Grover Jones and Gilbert Pratt. Titles, Herman J. Mankiewicz. With Wallace Beery, Raymond Hatton, Mary Brian.

Drag Net. Paramount, 1928.

> Director, Josef von Sternberg. Script, Charles and Jules Furthman. Titles, Herman J. Mankiewicz. With George Bancroft, William Powell, Evelyn Brent, Leslie Fenton.

Gentlemen Prefer Blondes. Paramount, 1928.

> Director, Mal St. Clair. From the novel by Anita Loos. Script, Anita Loos and John Emerson. Titles, Anita Loos and Herman J. Mankiewicz. With Ruth Taylor, Alice White, Margaret Seddon, Holmes Herbert.

His Tiger Lady. Paramount, 1928.

> Director, Hobart Henley. From the play *Super of the Gaiety* by Alfred Savoir. Script, Ernest Vajda. Titles, Herman J. Mankiewicz. With Adolphe Menjou, Evelyn Brent, Rose Dione, Emile Chautard.

The Last Command. Paramount, 1928.

> Director, Josef von Sternberg. Script, John F. Goodrich. Titles, Herman J. Mankiewicz. With Emil Jannings, Evelyn Brent, William Powell.

Love and Learn. Paramount, 1928.

> Director, Frank Tuttle. Script, Louise Long. Titles, Herman J. Mankiewicz. With Esther Ralston, Lane Chandler, Hedda Hopper.

The Magnificent Flirt. Paramount, 1928.

> Director, Harry D'Arrast. Script, Harry D'Arrast and Jean de Limur. Titles, Herman J. Mankiewicz. With Florence Vidor, Albert Conti, Loretta Young, Ned Sparks.

Mating Call. Paramount, 1928.

> Director, James Cruze. From a novel by Rex Beach. Script, Walter Wood. Titles, Herman J. Mankiewicz. With Thomas Meighan, Evelyn Brent, Renee Adoree.

Night of Mystery. Paramount, 1928.

> Director, Lothar Mendes. From the play *Captain Ferreol* by Victorien Sardou. Script, Ernest Vajda. Titles, Herman J. Mankiewicz. With Adolphe Menjou, Nora Lane, Evelyn Brent, William Collier, Jr.

Something Always Happens. Paramount, 1928.

> Director, Frank Tuttle. Script, Florence Ryerson. Titles, Herman J. Mankiewicz. With Esther Ralston, Neil Hamilton, Sojin, Roscoe Karns.

Take Me Home. Paramount, 1928.

> Director, Marshall Neilan. Script, Ethel Doherty. Titles, Herman J. Mankiewicz. With Bebe Daniels, Neil Hamilton, Lilyan Tashman, Joe E. Brown.

Three Week Ends. Paramount, 1928.

Director, Clarence Badger. Script, Louise Long, Percy Heath, Sam Mintz. Titles, Paul Perez and Herman J. Mankiewicz. With Clara Bow, Neil Hamilton, Harrison Ford, Julia Swayne Gordon.

The Water Hole. Paramount, 1928.

Director, F. Richard Jones. From the story by Zane Grey. Titles, Herman J. Mankiewicz. With Nancy Carroll, Jack Holt.

What a Night! Paramount, 1928.

Director, Edward Sutherland. From an original story by Grover Jones and Lloyd Corrigan. Screenplay, Louise Long. Titles, Herman J. Mankiewicz. With Bebe Daniels and Neil Hamilton.

The Canary Murder Case. Paramount, 1929.

Director, Mal St. Clair. From the novel by S. S. Van Dine. Script, Florence Ryerson and Albert S. LeVino. Dialogue, S. S. Van Dine. Titles, Herman J. Mankiewicz. With William Powell, Louise Brooks, James Hall, Jean Arthur.

The Dummy. Paramount, 1929.

Director, Robert Milton. From the play by Harvey J. O'Higgins and Harriet Ford. Script and dialogue, Herman J. Mankiewicz. With Ruth Chatterton, Mickey Bennett, Fredric March, ZaSu Pitts, Jack Oakie.

The Love Doctor. Paramount, 1929.

Director, Melville Brown. From the play *The Boomerang* by Winchell Smith and Victor Mapes. Script, Guy Bolton and J. Walter Ruben. Dialogue, Guy Bolton. Titles, Herman J. Mankiewicz. With Richard Dix, June Collyer.

The Man I Love. Paramount, 1929.

Director, William Wellman. Original story and dialogue, Herman J. Mankiewicz. Script, Percy Heath. With Richard Arlen, Mary Brian, Howard Green, Pat O'Malley, Olga Baclanova.

Marquis Preferred. Paramount, 1929.

Director, Frank Tuttle. From a novel by Frederick Arnold Kammer. Script, Ernest Vajda and Ethel Doherty. Titles, Herman J. Mankiewicz. With Adolphe Menjou, Nora Lane, Chester Conklin, Mischa Auer.

Men Are Like That. Paramount, 1929.

Director, Frank Tuttle. From the play *The Show-Off* by George Kelly. Script, Herman J. Mankiewicz and Marion Dix. Dialogue, Herman J. Mankiewicz. With Hal Skelly, Doris Hill, Charles Sellon, Helene Chadwick.

Mighty. Paramount, 1929.

Director, John Cromwell. From an original story by Robert N. Lee. Script, Grover Jones, William Slavens McNutt, Nellie Revelle. Dialogue, Grover Jones and William Slavens McNutt. Titles, Herman J. Mankiewicz. With George Bancroft, Esther Ralston, Raymond Hatton, Warner Oland.

Thunderbolt. Paramount, 1929.

Director, Josef von Sternberg. From an original story by Charles and Jules Furthman. Script, Jules Furthman. Dialogue, Herman J. Mankiewicz. Titles, Joseph L. Mankiewicz. With George Bancroft, Fay Wray, Richard Arlen, Tully Marshall.

Honey. Paramount, 1930.

Director, Wesley Ruggles. From the novel and play *Come Out of the Kitchen* by Alice Duer Miller and A. E. Thomas. Script and dialogue, Herman J. Mankiewicz. Music and lyrics, W. Franke Harling and Sam Coslow. With Nancy Carroll, Stanley Smith, Skeets Gallagher, Lillian Roth, Jobyna Howland, Mitzi Green, ZaSu Pitts.

Ladies Love Brutes. Paramount, 1930.

Director, Rowland V. Lee. From the play *Pardon My Glove* by Zoë Akins. Script and dialogue, Waldemar Young and Herman J. Mankiewicz. With George Bancroft, Mary Astor, Fredric March.

Laughter. Paramount, 1930.

Director, Harry D'Arrast. Script, Harry D'Arrast and Douglas Doty. Dialogue, Donald Ogden Stewart. Producer, Herman J. Mankiewicz. With Nancy Carroll, Fredric March, Frank Morgan, Glenn Anders, Diane Ellis.

Love Among the Millionaires. Paramount, 1930.

Director, Frank Tuttle. From an original story by Keene Thompson. Script, Grover Jones and William Conselman. Dialogue, Herman J. Mankiewicz. With Clara Bow, Stanley Smith, Skeets Gallagher, Stuart Erwin, Mitzi Green.

The Royal Family of Broadway. Paramount, 1930.

Directors, George Cukor and Cyril Gardner. Based on the play *The Royal Family* by Edna Ferber and George S. Kaufman. Script, Herman J. Mankiewicz and Gertrude Purcell. With Ina Claire, Fredric March, Henrietta Crosman.

True to the Navy. Paramount, 1930.

Director, Frank Tuttle. Script, Keene Thompson and Doris Anderson. Dialogue, Herman J. Mankiewicz. With Clara Bow, Harry Green, Fredric March, Sam Hardy.

The Vagabond King. Paramount, 1930.

Director, Ludwig Berger. From the play *If I Were King* by Justin Huntly McCarthy, and the operetta *The Vagabond King* by William H. Post, Brian Hooker and Rudolph Friml. Screen adaptation and additional dialogue, Herman J. Mankiewicz. With Dennis King, Jeanette MacDonald, O. P. Heggie, Lillian Roth, Warner Oland.

Ladies' Man. Paramount, 1931.

Director, Lothar Mendes. From an original story by Rupert Hughes. Script and dialogue, Herman J. Mankiewicz. With William Powell, Kay Francis, Carole Lombard, Gilbert Emery.

Man of the World. Paramount, 1931.

Director, Richard Wallace. Original story and script, Herman J. Mankiewicz. With William Powell, Carole Lombard, Wynne Gibson, Guy Kibbee, Lawrence Gray.

Monkey Business. Paramount, 1931.

Director, Norman McLeod. Associate Producer, Herman J. Mankiewicz. Original story and script, S. J. Perelman and Will B. Johnstone. Additional dialogue, Arthur Sheekman. With the Marx Brothers, Thelma Todd, Tom Kennedy.

Dancers in the Dark. Paramount, 1932.

Director, David Burton. From the play *The Jazz King* by James Ashmore Creelman. Adaptation, Brian Marlow and Howard Emmett Rogers. Screenplay, Herman J. Mankiewicz. With Miriam Hopkins, Jack Oakie, William Collier, Jr., Eugene Pallette, Lyda Roberti.

Girl Crazy. RKO, 1932.

Director, William A. Seiter. From the musical comedy by John McGowan and Guy Bolton. Music and lyrics, George and Ira Gershwin. Script, Herman J. Mankiewicz and Tim Whelan. Dialogue, Tim Whelan, Herman J. Mankiewicz, Edward Welch and Walter DeLeon. With Bert Wheeler, Robert Woolsey, Eddie Quillan, Mitzi Green, Kitty Kelly, Arline Judge.

Horse Feathers. Paramount, 1932.

Director, Norman McLeod. Script, Bert Kalmar, Harry Ruby, S. J. Perelman and Will B. Johnstone. Music and lyrics, Bert Kalmar and Harry Ruby. Associate producer, Herman J. Mankiewicz. With the Marx Brothers, Thelma Todd, David Landau, Nat Pendleton.

The Lost Squadron. RKO, 1932.

Director, George Archainbaud. Script, Wallace Smith Original story, Dick Grace. Dialogue, Wallace Smith and Herman J. Mankiewicz. With Richard Dix, Mary Astor, Erich von Stroheim, Joel McCrea, Dorothy Jordan, Hugh Herbert.

Million Dollar Legs. Paramount, 1932.

Director, Edward Cline. Script, Joseph L. Mankiewicz. Producer, Herman J. Mankiewicz. With Jack Oakie, W. C. Fields, Lyda Roberti, Andy Clyde, Susan Fleming, Ben Turpin, George Barbier, Hugh Herbert, Dickie Moore, Billy Gilbert, Teddy Hart, Hank Mann.

Another Language. MGM, 1933.

Director, Edward H. Griffith. From the play by Rose Franken. Script, Herman J. Mankiewicz and Gertrude Purcell. Dialogue, Herman J. Mankiewicz and Donald Ogden Stewart. With Helen Hayes, Robert Montgomery, Louise Closser Hale, John Beal, Henry Travers, Margaret Hamilton.

Dinner at Eight. MGM, 1933.

Director, George Cukor. From the play by Edna Ferber and George S. Kaufman. Screenplay, Frances Marion and Herman J. Mankiewicz. Additional dialogue, Donald Ogden Stewart. With Marie Dressler, John Barrymore, Wallace Beery, Jean Harlow, Lionel Barrymore, Lee Tracy, Billie Burke.

Meet the Baron. MGM, 1933.

Director, Walter Lang. Original story, Herman J. Mankiewicz and Norman Krasna. Script, Allen Rivkin and P. J. Wolfson. Dialogue, Arthur Kober and William K. Wells. With Jack Pearl, Jimmy Durante, ZaSu Pitts, Ted Healy, Edna May Oliver.

The Show-Off. MGM, 1934.

Director, Charles F. Reisner. From the play by George Kelly. Script, Herman J. Mankiewicz. With Spencer Tracy, Madge Evans, Lois Wilson, Grant Mitchell.

Stamboul Quest. MGM, 1934.

Director, Sam Wood. Original story, Leo Mirinski. Script, Herman J. Mankiewicz. With Myrna Loy, George Brent, C. Henry Gordon, Lionel Atwill, Mischa Auer.

After Office Hours. MGM, 1935.

Director, Robert Z. Leonard. Original story, Laurence Stallings and Dale Van Every. Script, Herman J. Mankiewicz. With Constance Bennett, Clark Gable, Stuart Erwin, Billie Burke, Harvey Stephens.

Escapade. MGM, 1935.

Director, Robert Z. Leonard. From the German film *Maskerade* by Walter Reisch. Script, Herman J. Mankiewicz. With William Powell, Luise Rainer, Frank Morgan, Virginia Bruce, Reginald Owen, Mady Christians, Laura Hope Crews.

It's in the Air. MGM, 1935.

Director, Charles F. Reisner. Script, Byron Morgan and Lew Lipton. With Jack Benny, Una Merkel, Ted Healy, Nat Pendleton, Mary Carlisle. (Mankiewicz is not on the screen credits but he is listed in the records of the Screen Writers Guild.)

John Meade's Woman. Paramount, 1937.

Director, Richard Wallace. Original story, John Bright and Robert Trasker. Script, Vincent Lawrence and Herman J. Mankiewicz. With Edward Arnold, Francine Larrimore, Gail Patrick, George Bancroft, John Trent, Aileen Pringle, Sidney Blackmer.

My Dear Miss Aldrich. MGM, 1937.

Director, George B. Seitz. Original story and script, Herman J. Mankiewicz. With Edna May Oliver, Maureen O'Sullivan, Walter Pidgeon.

The Emperor's Candlesticks. MGM, 1937.

Director, George Fitzmaurice. From a novel by Baroness Orczy. Script, Monckton Hoffe and Harold Goldman. With William Powell, Luise Rainer, Robert Young, Maureen O'Sullivan, Frank Morgan. (Mankiewicz is not on the screen credits but he is listed in the records of the Screen Writers Guild.)

It's a Wonderful World. MGM, 1939.

Director, W. S. Van Dyke II. Original story, Ben Hecht and Herman J. Mankiewicz. Script, Ben Hecht. With Claudette Colbert, James Stewart, Guy Kibbee, Nat Pendleton.

Keeping Company. MGM, 1941.

Director, S. Sylvan Simon. Original story, Herman J. Mankiewicz. Script, Harry Ruskin, James H. Hill and Adrian Scott. With Frank Morgan, Ann Rutherford, John Shelton, Irene Rich, Gene Lockhart, Virginia Weidler.

Citizen Kane. RKO, 1941.

The Wild Man of Borneo. MGM, 1941.

Director, Robert B. Sinclair. Based on the play by Marc Connelly and Herman J. Mankiewicz. Script, Waldo Salt and John McClain. Producer, Joseph L. Mankiewicz. With Frank Morgan, Mary Howard, Billie Burke, Donald Meek, Marjorie Main, Bonita Granville.

Rise and Shine. 20th Century-Fox, 1941.

Director, Allan Dwan. Based on the book *My Life and Hard Times* by James Thurber. Script, Herman J. Mankiewicz. With Jack Oakie, Linda Darnell, George Murphy, Walter Brennan.

Pride of the Yankees. RKO, 1942.

Director, Sam Wood. Original story, Paul Gallico. Script, Jo Swerling and Herman J. Mankiewicz. With Gary Cooper, Teresa Wright, Babe Ruth, Walter Brennan, Dan Duryea.

Stand by for Action. MGM, 1942.

Director, Robert Z. Leonard. Suggested by the story *A Cargo of Innocence* by Laurence Kirk. Original story, Captain Harvey Haislip and R. C. Sherriff. Script, George Bruce, John L. Balderston and Herman J. Mankiewicz. With Robert Taylor, Brian Donlevy, Charles Laughton, Walter Brennan, Marilyn Maxwell.

This Time for Keeps. MGM, 1942.

Director, Charles F. Reisner. Based upon characters created by Herman J. Mankiewicz (in *Keeping Company*). Script by Muriel Roy Boulton, Rian James and Harry Ruskin. With Ann Rutherford, Robert Sterling, Guy Kibbee, Irene Rich, Virginia Weidler.

The Good Fellows. Paramount, 1943.

Director, Jo Graham. Based on the play by George S. Kaufman and Herman J. Mankiewicz. Script, Hugh Wedlock, Jr. and Howard Snyder. With Helen Walker, James Brown, Cecil Kellaway.

Christmas Holiday. Universal, 1944.

Director, Robert Siodmak. From the novel by W. Somerset Maugham. Script, Herman J. Mankiewicz. With Deanna Durbin, Gene Kelly, Richard Whorf, Gladys George.

The Enchanted Cottage. RKO, 1945.

Director, John Cromwell. From the play by Sir Arthur Wing Pinero. Script, De Witt Bodeen and Herman J. Mankiewicz. With Dorothy McGuire, Robert Young, Herbert Marshall, Mildred Natwick, Spring Byington, Hillary Brooke.

The Spanish Main. RKO, 1945.

Director, Frank Borzage. Original story, Aeneas MacKenzie. Script, George Worthing Yates and Herman J. Mankiewicz. With Paul Henreid, Maureen O'Hara, Walter Slezak, Binnie Barnes.

A Woman's Secret. RKO, 1949.

Director, Nicholas Ray. Based on the novel *Mortgage on Life* by Vicki Baum. Script, Herman J. Mankiewicz. Producer, Herman J. Mankiewicz. With Maureen O'Hara, Melvyn Douglas, Gloria Grahame, Bill Williams, Victor Jory.

The Pride of St. Louis. 20th Century-Fox, 1952.

Director, Harmon Jones. From an original story by Guy Trosper. Script, Herman J. Mankiewicz. With Dan Dailey, Joanne Dru, Richard Crenna.

This list is composed of the titles that I could locate on which Herman J. Mankiewicz received credit; there are undoubtedly others, but this list gives some indication of the course of his career. Hollywood credits should not be interpreted as accurate guides to who did what on any given film, and they are ludicrously inaccurate for writers under studio contract in the period beginning in the mid-thirties when the studios assigned teams in relays. So many writers worked on a project that often the writers who were assigned to a script in its early stages never did find out whether their work was discarded or used, or (as sometimes happened) inserted into a different project; a full set of screen credits would have exposed the movies that resulted to ridicule. From talks with Mankiewicz's agents and with screenwriters who worked with him, and from publicity releases in the trade press (the releases often list those who are at work on a property at an early stage), it would appear that he probably worked on over a hundred titles without credit. The screenwriter Frank Davis says that once when he was assigned to take over a script Mank had been working on, he felt bad about it and apologized to him. Mank said, "Frank, that's great. You write me out of it, and then you find somebody to write you out." Davis says, "I got him out of it all right, but I was stuck."

Screenwriters — and this hasn't changed — often spend more time working on scripts that are locked away than on those that are filmed. In Herman Mankiewicz's case, the unrealized projects ranged from a political film that he tried to set up in 1933 — *The Mad Dog of Europe* — which ran into (highly publicized) troubles with Will Hays, who feared the loss of European markets if Hollywood antagonized Hitler, to typical forties assignments — such as his job in 1947 of trying to convert *Alice Adams* into a musical.

At the end of his life, Mankiewicz said that of all the movies he had worked on, his favorite was *Laughter*.

P. K.

Index
to Raising Kane